# HIT

and

How Jon Peters
and Peter Guber
Took Sony
for a Ride
in Hollywood

# RUN

NANCY GRIFFIN

and

KIM MASTERS

A TOUCHSTONE BOOK
Published by Simon & Schuster

 TOUCHSTONE
Rockefeller Center
1230 Avenue of the Americas
New York, NY 10020

First Touchstone Edition 1997
TOUCHSTONE and colophon are
registered trademarks of Simon & Schuster Inc.
Designed by Edith Fowler
Photo research by Natalie Goldstein
Manufactured in the United States of America

10  9  8  7  6  5  4  3  2  1

The Library of Congress has cataloged the Simon & Schuster
edition as follows:
Griffin, Nancy.
    Hit and run : how Jon Peters and Peter Guber
took Sony for a ride in Hollywood /
Nancy Griffin and Kim Masters.
        p.  cm.
    Includes bibliographical references and index.
    1. Peters, Jon.   2. Guber, Peter.
3.  Motion picture producers and directors—
United States—Biography.   4.  Guber-Peters
Company.   5. Columbia Pictures.   I. Masters,
Kim.   II. Title.
PN1998.3.P46G75  1996
791.43' 0232' 0973—dc20
[B]          96-13102   CIP
ISBN 0-684-80931-1
        0-684-83266-6 (Pbk)

# Contents

CONTENTS

# PROLOGUE

*"If God didn't want them sheared, He would not have made them sheep."*
*The Magnificent Seven*

WALTER YETNIKOFF, freshly out of drug rehab, found himself at the epicenter of a multi-billion-dollar deal.

It was September 1989, and the head of the Sony Corporation's successful music division was playing a pivotal role in the Japanese electronics giant's acquisition of a major Hollywood studio. For Yetnikoff, who expected to run the combined entertainment empire, the purchase would represent the realization of a long-cherished dream. But there was a hang-up. If the deal were to "make," in the industry parlance, Sony needed managers to put in charge of the new studio. Under pressure to fill the vacancy, Yetnikoff had an idea: He would call his old friends, film producers Peter Guber and Jon Peters.

A few days after Yetnikoff contacted Guber and Peters, Sony confirmed a swirl of rumors that it was buying Columbia Pictures Entertainment. The cost, $3.4 billion plus $1.6 billion in debt, was considered high for an entertainment company that had been faltering.

The news of the acquisition was not welcomed in the United States. There was an outcry over the sale of a venerated and uniquely American institution to a foreign acquirer. Sony, seen as something of a brash upstart at home, was viewed by many in the United States as part of a rich and invincible army of invaders snapping up American properties, from Rockefeller Center in the East to the rolling resorts of Hawaii. The fact that Sony was willing to meet a rich price only inflamed American anxiety.

Sony expressed its regret over American reaction to the deal. But it wasn't concerned about the criticism that it had paid too much. The company had been mocked for overspending when it bought CBS Records in 1987, and the music division had flourished under Yetnikoff's leadership despite his substance-abuse problems. Having made one successful foray into the entertainment world, Sony had every reason to think it could win again in the movie business.

Sony was hardly the first to fall into the Hollywood trap. The movie business has long attracted an array of hopeful outsiders, from insurance companies to purveyors of soft drinks. Many have learned the hard way that Hollywood is a world apart—a risky business where the uninitated are routinely shorn. It is a fantasy factory where the insiders are often more skilled at creating illusions about themselves than they are at spinning magic for the big screen.

On paper, Guber and Peters looked like genuine movie moguls. They were high-profile producers who had just made *Batman,* the largest-grossing film of all time, for Warner Bros. Their names were on such hits as *Rain Man* and *The Color Purple.* But the real players knew that Guber and Peters were hardly hands-on filmmakers. When Steven Spielberg made *The Color Purple,* he had a provision in his contract explicitly barring them from the set. Guber and Peters had visited the set of *Rain Man* only once, while the production chores were handled by director Barry Levinson's associate, Mark Johnson. When the picture won the Academy Award, Guber and Peters got to neither collect nor keep the Oscar. They happily took credit for the film and had themselves photographed jubilantly brandishing a statuette. But they had to borrow it from writer Barry Morrow, who had won for best screenplay.

Guber and Peters may have seemed an impressive pair, but their greatest gift was for promotion—especially self-promotion. What was lacking was any credential or experience that would qualify them to run a major studio. Peters, perennially known as Barbra Streisand's former hairdresser, had never worked as a studio executive. He was a seventh-grade dropout and a reform-school ruffian. Many said he could barely read, and he certainly had never quite learned to control his violent temper. The ponytailed Guber at least had a law degree and he had done a stint as an executive at Columbia in the seventies—

until he was fired. He subsequently ran a fledgling production company financed by PolyGram. In short order, PolyGram lost $100 million and pulled out of the movie business.

The two men were hardly untalented; they had an eye for material and a genius for packaging and selling their projects. But in an industry where avarice is not uncommon, Guber and Peters distinguished themselves for greed. They were grabbers who snatched up material, credit, and money, leaving a swath of dazed victims in their wake. Their first loyalty was always to themselves. It was an ethic that Japanese executives—coming from a tradition of teamwork and long-term commitments to their firms—could hardly be expected to grasp.

Hollywood's surprise at Sony's hiring of Guber and Peters turned to stunned disbelief when the industry learned how much Sony had agreed to pay for their services. Warner boss Terry Semel said Guber confided that he wanted to "make more money than anyone in the history of the motion picture industry" and now he had come close. Aside from buying Guber and Peters's money-losing production company for $200 million—about 40 percent more than its market value—Sony gave the two a rich compensation package that included $2.75 million each in annual salary (excluding hefty annual bonuses), a $50 million bonus pool, and a stake in any increase in the studio's value over the ensuing five years.

As soon as the ink on the deal was dry, Warner slapped Sony with a billion-dollar lawsuit. Guber and Peters had just signed a generous contract with that studio, but Sony had failed to review the agreement when it negotiated with them. Forced into a settlement worth as much as $800 million, Sony found that the expense of hiring Guber and Peters had gone up dramatically. And many in the movie business suspected that Sony's nightmare was only beginning.

If Guber and Peters regretted that Sony had to cough up so much to hire them, they didn't show it by exercising restraint. They spent big from the start, setting off a round of inflation that is still taking a toll on the movie business today. Guber and Peters were about to take Sony on the wildest and most profligate ride that Hollywood had ever seen. For five years, Sony executives in Tokyo and New York would stand by while the studio lost billions and became a symbol for the worst kind of excess in an industry that is hardly known for moderation.

There were box-office bombs, lavish renovations, and extravagant parties against a backdrop of corporate intrigue, expensive firings, and even a call-girl scandal. The ill-advised pairing of a Japanese corporation with a couple of Hollywood's cleverest rogues would culminate, as one insider delicately put it, in "the most public screwing in the history of the business."

# 1

# SON OF COCHISE

"Jon Peters was raised by wolves. That's why, when people complain about him—it's like having a wolf in your house. It's not his fault. He's a wild thing."

ANDREW SMITH
*screenwriter*

On the sunny afternoon of September 16, 1955, ten-year-old John Peters was playing in the street near his family's ranch house at 13215 Bloomfield Street in Sherman Oaks, a San Fernando Valley suburb of Los Angeles. As a Studebaker pulled into the driveway, the boy waved to his father, who was returning home from his job as the owner of the S&J Cafe, a blue-collar joint in Hollywood.

A few minutes later John was alarmed when neighbors came running into his house. He rushed inside to see his father slumped in an armchair, sweating and breathing heavily. John would always remember the look on Jack Peters's face, the way his father had smiled at him before he died of heart failure.

That night, John's mother didn't want to remain in the house, so she and her son went to stay with a relative who lived nearby. After he was supposed to be asleep, John climbed out the window and went home. "I sat alone there, hoping my father would come back," he says. When he realized that would never happen, he adds, "I was devastated. It was like my world kind of ended."

Struggling to cope with his loss, John became so angry and rebellious that neither his mother nor his teachers could control him. He grew still more unmanageable when his mother married a man he hated a couple of years after his father's death. At the age of thirteen, John appeared to be headed for a life of crime when his mother pushed him out of the house to fend for himself.

The hallmarks of Peters's turbulent career were forged in this early family wreckage: a need to succeed and acquire great wealth; an unpredictable temperament, veering wildly between violent rages and boyish vulnerability; the compulsion to win, and then reject, the love of women. Peters would create a mythology that revolved around his early loss and his endless quest to replace his father.

He dropped the "h" from his first name and reinvented himself as Jon Peters, the wild-man producer destined to make mega-hit movies and millions of dollars, but also doomed to be known perennially as Barbra Streisand's ex–hairdresser and lover. He located a surrogate father in his partner of eleven years, Peter Guber, who possessed the education, sophistication, and self-control that he lacked—and who ultimately would abandon him, as his own father had done.

Jack Peters was an uneducated man who did his own cooking at his truck-stop restaurant on Santa Monica Boulevard and Highland Avenue in Hollywood. Strong and darkly handsome, he was 75 percent Cherokee Indian by birth, a pleasant man whose temper occasionally ran hot. When Jack married Helen Pagano, he joined a clan of hairdressers of Neapolitan descent; his bride's three brothers, Alfred, Eugene, and Adolph, owned Pagano's, a thriving salon on Wilshire Boulevard in Beverly Hills. Helen had a daughter Patricia by a previous marriage that had ended in divorce.

Having suffered a gunshot wound in the groin as a World War I marine, Jack was told he would not father children; he and Helen were startled when she became pregnant. John Pagano Peters was born on June 2, 1945, in St. Joseph's Hospital in Burbank, near the Disney Studios.

"My father gave me an enormous amount of love," says Jon, "and he made me a warrior. I learned to fight, to defend myself. I was Cochise's son." Although he suffered from rheumatic heart disease, Jack Peters took his son on camping trips and taught him how to shoot and use knives in the wilderness. On weekends they went horseback riding in Griffith Park. Jon loved to gaze at the wild animals that were kept in the park and used in Hollywood films—giraffes, elephants, lions.

One day in Griffith Park, a casting director for *The Ten Commandments* approached Jack Peters and his son to ask if Jon wanted to appear in a film. Multitudes of people with dark hair and complexions were needed to cross the Red Sea. Jon was chosen to ride a donkey and lead a goat by a rope. The scene took many days to film on a Paramount soundstage, with director Cecil B. DeMille hovering on a crane and bellowing to the crowds below. Jon was so excited that he refused to wash off his makeup when he went home at night.

(When he got into show business himself, Peters embellished a good story. "I rode a donkey into the Red Sea," he said in a press release. "I saw DeMille with a whip and boots and a hat. There must have been 5,000 extras, and there was this incredible man directing traffic. The image stayed with me.")

Small, dark, and wiry, Jon was naturally athletic and excelled at gymnastics at the Dixie Canyon Elementary School. He dominated the neighborhood boys, even the bigger ones. "Jon was always the leader," says Silvio Pensanti, Jon's admiring younger cousin. Silvio attended Catholic school and remembers that while he was always worrying about going to Hell, Jon never seemed scared of anything. The local bullies left Silvio alone because they knew that Jon would come after them. "Nobody messed with Jon Peters, ever," he recalls. "Because the harder you hit him, the madder he got. That's part of his success today. You want to take Jon on? You and what army? I'm dead serious —this man has no fear."

After Jack Peters died, Helen learned to drive and commuted to Beverly Hills every day to work as the cashier at Pagano's. When she married Aldo Bairo, Jon resented his new stepfather from the start, and the Bloomfield Street house was filled with the sound of their screaming battles. Jon told friends that his stepfather beat him. He ran away from home several times.

After grammar school Jon enrolled in Van Nuys Junior High School, where he was such a disciplinary problem that he was placed in a special class. "Obviously I'm an intelligent person," he later told an interviewer, "but I found myself in the retarded class in school because I'm an emotional guy." He hung around with a motorcycle gang and was picked up by the police and put on probation after stealing a car. He was eventually expelled and his family enrolled him in the Sherwood Oaks private school. Meanwhile, Jon's clashes with his stepfather got

13

worse and Helen came reluctantly to the conclusion that her husband and her son could not live under the same roof. Something would have to give.

While his school and home life were a shambles, Jon's cockiness served him well in extracurricular matters. Obsessed with Elvis—he once entered an Elvis look-alike contest—he wore tight pants and a jelly roll hairdo. "This guy, at ten and eleven, was dating," Silvio says. "Heavy duty, I mean going out on dates. Jon was a good-looking, fast-talking kid. Women loved him. He was doing good with seventeen-, maybe eighteen-year-old girls."

One of Silvio's great pleasures was to hang out at Jon's house when he was getting ready for a date. "It was my favorite thing to do, sit in the bathroom, sit on the tub, and he'd be just like the Fonz. 'How do I look, Sil?' He'd get in his mother's car and go." Obviously he was years away even from possession of a learner's permit. "Did Jon need a driver's license?" Silvio asks. "Think about it."

Jon never suspected a ruse the day his mother said she was going to meet him at school for lunch. She showed up with police officers who handcuffed him and took him downtown to Juvenile Hall; Helen had told the police that she could no longer control her son. Jon was stripped and sprayed for lice, then sent to the David Gonzales juvenile detention camp in Malibu. For a year he labored on a Youth Authority roadwork gang in the Santa Monica Mountains by day, and was chained to his bed at night. His one pleasure was the boxing program; he sparred with his fellow delinquents on Sundays. And he considered his mother's ambush a betrayal for which he did not forgive her until she was stricken with stomach cancer years later. They made peace before she died in 1988.

Jon was released from detention camp after his mother told authorities that she would keep him off the streets by sending him to the Comer and Duran Beauty School in Hollywood. "The first time I walked in, there was nothin' but beautiful girls there," he said later. "I thought, 'What a great way to make a living.' " Jon had found his niche. He was fourteen.

But there was still so much strife at home that within a year Helen felt she again had to separate her husband and her son. She made arrangements for Jon to fly to Manhattan to stay with two male family friends.

"I'm going to the Big Apple," Jon informed Silvio. Helen

and the two boys drove to the airport in her '53 Pontiac, and she put her son on a plane with $120 in his pocket. Silvio cried and clung to the chain-link fence at the airfield as he watched Jon walk away.

When Jon arrived at the home of Helen's friends, he discovered that they were gay; fearful that they might molest him, he slipped out a window one night. That was the beginning of his life on the streets. He took a room in a YMCA on 57th Street and briefly held a job at an all-night Manhattan salon in the Great Northern Hotel, where he dyed prostitutes' pubic hair to match their poodles. Then he took off again, seeking his fortune in the City of Brotherly Love.

A CURVY, PETITE seventeen-year-old with short blond hair and dark eyes, Marie Zampitella was roaming the floor of the Manhattan auditorium, checking out the hairdressers. A student at Little Flower Catholic High School in Philadelphia, Marie had ridden the bus to New York City that morning with her nineteen-year-old girlfriend, Madge. On this Saturday in September 1961, hundreds of beauticians had turned out for an annual trade show where stylists from around the country demonstrated the latest haircuts and beauty companies hawked their products.

Half Italian and half Polish, Marie lived with her grandmother in Port Richmond, a working-class suburb of Philadelphia. She wanted to be a beautician. For her first trip to the big city she had borrowed an outfit from her sister-in-law: a navy blue miniskirt with a belt that cinched her tiny waist, black high heels and black stockings.

As the two girls wandered, they noticed a dark young man staring at them. He approached and introduced himself as Jon Peters. He claimed to be eighteen, said he cut hair at the Gary Elliot salon on Walnut Street in Philadelphia, and drove a white convertible Corvette. In fact, Jon was sixteen and he was not allowed to cut hair at Gary Elliot's, but merely to assist the stylists. But Marie was impressed. "He knew what to say, how to carry himself," she recalls. When two of his acquaintances came by, Jon introduced Marie as his girlfriend. "Why did you say that? It's a lie," Marie scolded after they left.

"It's not a lie," said Jon, "because you're *going* to be my girlfriend."

As Jon walked the two girls around the floor, he told them

15

about his dream of becoming a famous hairdresser. "See this guy?" he said, gesturing toward a well-known stylist named Monti Rock, who was demonstrating a new cut on a model. "I definitely am better than he is. Someday I'm going to be on this stage, and it's going to be a bigger stage."

As the time drew near for the girls to catch their bus home, Jon said he would be happy to drive them if his Corvette weren't in the repair shop. He ducked into a phone booth, saying he would check whether the car could be picked up. "Would you believe it's not ready?" he said, emerging. Marie recalls, "Then he looks at me with puppy eyes and says, 'Let me ask you something. Do you think you could lend me $2.50?' " He didn't have the bus fare back to Philadelphia.

When they arrived in Philly, Jon wanted to show Marie where he lived, in an attic room above Elliot's salon. "There was this old mattress on the floor—no sheets or anything," she remembers. "I was shocked. No refrigerator. There were playmate calendars on the walls." As Marie stared at the calendars, Jon explained, "I have to surround myself with *something*. It gets lonely."

The courtship lasted seven months. His behavior was exemplary. He rode the trolley cars to her grandmother's house, ate the gnocchi Marie cooked for him, and spoke respectfully to her relatives. Occasionally he spent his meager paycheck to take her for a steak dinner. He told her what to wear and styled her hair. "I was this little doll he could dress up," she recalls.

As a sixteen-year-old pretending to be an eighteen-year-old licensed hairdresser, Jon auditioned for his first job cutting hair at the salon in the venerable Nan Duskins department store. Marie's friend Madge posed as his model. He cut her platinum blond hair into a simple, elegant bob, then "caramelized" the color to add depth and texture. Hired by Nan Duskins on the spot, Jon was soon cutting the hair of Philadelphia heiresses. Marie came in and was treated to her first professional pedicure. "Get used to it," he told her.

Teenagers in love, Jon and Marie's romance mingled innocence and ambition. Marie loved Jon's sweet, needy side, but was distressed by his black moods and violent outbursts. "Anyone who knows him knows that he's a good-hearted person," she says. "And he's tougher than nails. . . . I was infatuated with the guy who wanted to be tough, but I didn't want him to be too tough." When her brother Salvatore got a job as a stevedore on the Philadelphia docks, she remembers, Jon liked to hang around, observing the ways of organized crime and its brutal characters.

One day when they went to the movies, a guy in the audience said something that ticked Jon off. Jon pulled off his shoes and put all of his change into one of his socks as a makeshift weapon. He backed down after Marie pleaded with him.

Then there were the fibs. While Jon was still insisting that he was eighteen, Marie suspected otherwise. "I wasn't trusting his little stories, and I said, 'I don't care how old you are, just tell me the truth.' " At first he protested, "I'm eighteen!" But as she kept pressing him, he admitted, "Well, I'm seventeen. . . ." Then finally, sheepishly: "Sixteen." His deceptions, Jon explained, were a matter of survival. "Sometimes in life you have to tell a fib," Marie remembers him saying. "I could never have gotten you to like me, and I would never have gotten my job if I told the truth."

"I don't know if you should marry him," Marie's mother told her doubtfully. "He tells a lot of lies." But Marie begged: "Oh please, Mom, he's going to make me happy and show me a completely new lifestyle." Finally, Marie and Jon convinced her family to allow her to move with him to California and get married.

With both the bride and groom underage, parental consent papers were required when John Pagano Peters wed Henrietta Regina Cecelia Zampitella—also called "Marie"—at the Los Angeles County Courthouse in downtown L.A. on an April day in 1962. Jon was not yet seventeen.

The newlyweds moved in briefly with Helen and Aldo, until one night Aldo, after a few drinks, suggested that Jon take his "whore bride" and leave the house. Jon pounced on him and gave him a black eye. When Helen tried to separate them, she broke her leg. Jon and Marie moved into their first apartment, though they couldn't afford any furniture.

While he worked on completing requirements for a beautician's license back at the Comer and Duran School, Jon worked nights as a bouncer and valet at the Peppermint Stick Lounge, where Chubby Checker and the Rivingtons played. Before long he was doing Chubby's mother's hair, and singer Dee Dee Sharp's. He peppered the entertainers with questions about how their business worked, taking it all in.

17

Although small for a bouncer, Jon made up for his size when he detonated. Marie began working as a waitress at the Peppermint Stick but had to quit after Jon punched out a customer who addressed her, "Hi, cutie." From then on she'd just hang out when he worked and watch him park cars—hoping no one would cross him.

The first time he took it, Jon flunked his test for his beautician's license. He had brought Marie as a model and was demonstrating a manicure when she shrieked at him for cutting a cuticle too close. "We had a big fight and the guy failed me," Jon says. He returned with a different model and passed.

After acquiring his license, Jon worked at a little salon near a main drag in the San Fernando Valley. He and Marie started a business dyeing and styling wigs. Jon made a blond, blunt-cut wig for Jayne Mansfield, who posed with him for a promotional photograph, her famous chest overflowing her tight dress.

Jon was itching to snare a rich clientele, as he had done in Philadelphia. He talked his way into the hottest salon in the Valley, Bill White's on Ventura Boulevard. Jon's goal was to be a millionaire by the time he was twenty-one. With talent and sheer chutzpah, he swiftly became the busiest stylist at Bill White's shop, "doing" as many as thirty-five heads a day. He wore tight black pants and a white shirt and danced around the chairs, checking himself out in the mirror. He got extra work styling hair for B-movies and fan-magazine spreads on starlets. "He knew he had hands of gold," says Marie.

One night Jon treated Marie to a special evening at the Cocoanut Grove, where the couple heard Barbra Streisand sing. As he watched the star on stage, Marie remembers, he whispered, "I will do her hair. She will be the next person in my life."

As a street kid who always learned by watching and imitating, Peters found a new role model. Gene Shacove owned and operated his own salon on Wilshire Boulevard and Beverly Drive in Beverly Hills. Shacove was hip and handsome, a stud with a blow dryer, the real-life model for Warren Beatty's character in *Shampoo.* (Later, in embellishing his own legend, Peters would lead interviewers to believe that he, not Shacove, had been the inspiration for *Shampoo.* "That was me," he told *Women's Wear Daily* in 1978, "making love to a lot of women, but too afraid to communicate with any of them.")

18

Being "the fun guy in hair," as Shacove called himself, meant driving Corvettes and throwing parties attended by fabulous young women. When Jon and Marie were invited to Shacove's soirées, Jon saw exactly what he wanted. "There were models, actresses—Jon was infatuated," Marie says. "He was a young boy and he thought I was beautiful, but he was changing." One day when a Playboy bunny came to Bill White's to have Jon do her hair, Marie realized that life as she knew it was over. "I thought, 'Oh my God, he's doing these kinds of girls? How long can this last?' I could see the look in his eye."

Jon began acquiring the hobbies and toys he coveted as his income allowed. He bought himself a black Corvette and a 35-foot two-deck cabin cruiser, which he barely knew how to operate. He spent a lot of time hanging out at the car races. "Everything always had to be dangerous and exciting," says Marie. "He would drive too fast. I'd ask him to slow down and he'd drive faster."

Before long, Marie's fears that Jon would grow restless in the marriage were borne out. He started to court other women— first a model, and eventually an actress who would open up new worlds to him. Early in 1967, after five years of marriage, Jon and Marie divorced. "I'll always love you and I'll always care for you," Jon told Marie, "but I need to go on and do the big things that I can't do if I'm married."

Although hurt and angry over their split, Marie eventually forgave Jon, as have many other women who have loved him since. Before they split, Jon gave her a powder blue Corvette, which she found waiting in the garage one afternoon covered with blankets. She figured it was his way of apologizing.

"I'll tell you one thing," she says today of her marriage to Jon. "My hair always looked great."

# 2

## THE CINDERELLA STORY

"WHEN I MET JON, I was appearing in *The Happiest Millionaire* —a perfect Jon Peters story," says Lesley Ann Warren. "It was Walt Disney's last movie before he died. I was eighteen, just."

A lovely ingenue with large expressive eyes, a singer and a dancer, Warren was the ideal leading actress for a Disney family musical. She was a nice Jewish girl from New York who had appeared in several New York theater productions and shone in a 1965 CBS production of *Cinderella*. This was her feature film debut.

With the success of the musical riding on her shoulders, the pressure on Lesley Ann during filming of *The Happiest Millionaire* on Disney's Burbank soundstages was intense, especially for a naive eighteen-year-old far from home and family. One day on the set her nerves got the better of her and she fainted. The movie's musical director, Jack Elliott, called his wife Bobbi and asked if he could bring Lesley Ann to their home for the weekend where they could care for her.

That Sunday night in September 1966, the Elliotts planned to attend the Emmy Awards. Bobbi asked Jon Peters, her friend and hairdresser since he was eighteen, to come to the house and style her hair for the black-tie event.

Lesley Ann was sitting in the Elliotts' living room that afternoon when "this guy whirled into the room, overwhelming in his energy, and charming and funny and playful and seductive," she says. Bobbi recalls: "Jon was very taken with the Hollywood business, and he met Miss Lesley and—I mean, she was really quite something, quite a beautiful young girl, and terribly vulnerable. And here was this dashing guy." When the Elliotts left for the Emmies, Jon stayed behind to keep Lesley Ann company.

"He pursued me relentlessly," Lesley Ann says. "I was very, very timid and shy—I had just been transplanted from New York, and I didn't even know how to drive. He would show up at my apartment on Doheny at seven in the morning with coffee and orange juice and danishes and announce that he was going to drive me to the set. In those days the dressing rooms on the Disney lot were like little homes, and at the end of the day twenty boxes would fly into the room, and Jon would follow. He'd bring me hats, dresses. I was very sheltered. I was a good girl, and this was the wildest behavior I had ever seen."

Lesley Ann didn't know it at the time, but she was being treated to the Jon Peters come-on. The pattern was always the same: He set his sights on his object of desire and overpowered her with sheer energy and conviction. Women have been irresistibly drawn to Peters's unusual combination of macho protectiveness and an almost feminine empathy and vulnerability. Producer Polly Platt, who has known Peters for twenty years, says: "Somehow in his childhood his survival must have depended on the love of women—and did he ever learn how to get it."

As he pursued Lesley Ann, Peters demonstrated another trait that has repeated itself in his key relationships: He connects with people who have what he lacks. Self-conscious about his lack of formal education, he has allied himself with others who have learned things from books. He supplies the street smarts and chutzpah; they supply knowledge and discernment.

"Jon attaches himself to what we might call intellectual, refined, powerful people," Platt observes. "He recognizes where the holes are in himself and wants to patch them up."

Lesley Ann was like a princess to Jon. Since she was dating someone else (and Jon was not yet divorced), he became her indispensable platonic friend. He cut her hair short like Twiggy's while she was filming *The Happiest Millionaire,* making Disney apoplectic. Before she went out on a date he would arrive at her West Hollywood studio apartment with its twin beds, do her hair, and help her put together an outfit to wear before her boyfriend picked her up. He coached her for interviews and drove her to her auditions; he told her that when he sat in the car waiting for her, he prayed to God to take his business away and give Lesley Ann the job. He oversaw her finances, making investments and ensuring that her contracts were favorable.

"He took over my business management—he took over my life, basically," says Warren. "It was fabulous because I had been getting a raw deal. I was very naive and I had never been motivated by money."

Sometimes when she came home from the set exhausted, he'd sleep in the other twin bed, talking to her soothingly, listening to her troubles. He never made sexual advances.

Then one day Lesley Ann's boyfriend became violent with her. She called Peters on the phone, crying hysterically. "Jon found him and took care of it," she says. "He got almost zenlike in his rage. He is really protective—that's one of his greatest assets. He said, 'Give me his name, tell me where he works.' He scared the shit out of him, and the guy never came back. I never heard from him again." Lesley Ann never knew exactly what Jon had done to eliminate her boyfriend from the scene. But from then on, "we were together all the time."

Jon was gentle with her and their sexual relationship developed slowly. He took her to an expensive hotel in Laguna Beach for a weekend. When they got up to their room, he became amorous, they undressed—and she panicked. He was sweet and understanding and drove her back to Los Angeles. A few months later, they did make love. One day, when they were out for a drive in his black Jaguar, he asked her to marry him.

Before the wedding, Jon flew to New York without Lesley Ann to meet her parents. He told Margot and William Warren that he was half-Jewish, hoping they would like him. In May 1967, with Jon's divorce final, he and Lesley Ann invited a few close friends to their secret wedding in Las Vegas.

The wedding took place in a penthouse suite of the Sands Hotel, presided over by the mayor of Las Vegas. Jon wore a white suit and dressed his bride in a mini appliquéd with big lace flowers. They had matching haircuts. After the Las Vegas wedding, the couple was married again in a religious service in New York. Peters, who always proclaimed his affinity for Jewish people, eagerly participated in the traditional ceremony.

Jon bought his bride a big, two-story house on Sutton Street in Sherman Oaks south of Ventura Boulevard, the poshest section of the Valley. He threw in a couple of German shepherds, too. "It was all very grand gestures," says Lesley Ann. "His way of doing things was to surprise me with really big things, like cars and houses and dogs."

One day Jon and Lesley Ann, who was six months pregnant at the time, were strolling on Robertson Boulevard after shopping at Charles Buccieri's antique store. A car drove by, and a man in the passenger seat rolled down his window and yelled "Cinderella sucks!" at the actress. Incensed, Peters chased the car, caught up with it, and yanked the heckler out of the car. "I was going to beat him up for insulting my wife," recalls Peters.

"Wait!" protested the man as Peters prepared to throttle him. "I'm in acting class with Lesley Ann, I'm a friend. I was joking. I'm Jack." It was Jon's first encounter with Jack Nicholson, who soon began showing up at the salon for trims.

Jon's primal, controlling instincts were in full force when his son Christopher was born on September 23, 1968. With his wife in labor in the passenger seat, Jon raced down the freeway shoulder to Cedars Sinai Hospital. Warren recalls, "When we got to the hospital, he somehow got hold of a doctor's cap and gown and gloves and pretended he was a doctor. He was giving orders to the nurses—it was amazing—yelling at people and taking over the delivery room."

JUST FOUR MONTHS before his son was born, Jon Peters had opened his own salon on Ventura Boulevard in Encino. His new partner was Paul Cantor, an established hairdresser with a clientele in the San Fernando Valley. Although he was twenty-three, Jon was now telling people that he was younger—enabling him to claim, further weaving his own myth, that he was a millionaire at twenty-one.

Peters and Cantor had invested just $2,000 apiece of their own money in the joint venture; they financed the salon's $85,000 renovation with a bank loan procured against the signature of their investor, a beauty supply man named Lou Goldbaum. "That was an astronomical amount of money at the time," recalls Cantor. "Looking back on it, it was insanity."

"Peters and Cantor" was more than a salon—it quickly became known as a happening place. With his own patch of turf, Jon unleashed the full force of his personality, decorating the shop in bright yellow and green pop-art patterns. He stayed on top of the trends, making research trips to Europe. He favored short, sleek bobs and geometric cuts. Another of his specialties was a bad-girl look, seductively mussed, achieved by precise cutting in layers. "He made you look like you'd just been rompin' around in the sack," says his cousin Silvio.

"The women both adored him and were afraid of him," says Lesley Ann Warren. "I mean, Jon would *tell* you how to do your hair. He would dance in front of the mirror. The pull was his sexuality."

He played on a woman's insecurities: While a client might be timid about how she ought to look, *he* never was. "One of Jon's greatest talents was that he had the guts to go with what people might be afraid to do—but would turn them on," Cantor says. If a client balked at how Jon wanted to cut her hair, he would throw her out. Irate husbands whose wives came home in tears were always calling the shop to complain.

He had begun attracting some celebrity clients, such as *I Dream of Jeannie*'s Barbara Eden. But he was no "hairdresser to the stars," because he never catered to their egos. His ego was easily as big as theirs, and *he* wanted to be the star. "You know something? Your hair looks terrible," he reportedly told gossip columnist Rona Barrett at a dinner party, then proceeded to tell her how he would fix it. She became a client, along with dozens of other women who responded to Jon's outrageous blend of flattery and insult.

Peters's lifelong pattern of abusing, reconciling with, and then abusing people again emerged. "Jon has a Jekyll and Hyde personality," says Allen Edwards, who was one of the rising hairdressers at Peters and Cantor. "[For me,] if someone is a friend, he is a friend, and you are nice to him. I'd go out to a car race in Ontario with Jon, and the next day he'd come in and yell and scream at me. I couldn't take that."

But Edwards—who later opened his own chain of top salons —was mesmerized. "He was so wild, and his mood swings were so strong," he says. "Jon has a very violent side, which sort of excited me. There is a sleepy violent side to me, and I got to live vicariously. It was a man-to-man, primitive sort of thing."

The Peters and Cantor salon was like Jon's gladiatorial theater, with client-spectators in robes watching the action. One very busy Saturday, Jon startled Edwards by picking him up suddenly from behind. Edwards became angry, grabbed Jon by the crotch, and the two got tangled up and fell onto the floor, tussling as clients gaped. Another time a pizza deliveryman said something Jon didn't like and Jon threatened him. The guy left and came back with a knife; Peters tossed him outdoors and beat the daylights out of him. On still another occasion,

Jon fired a makeup artist, who hired a thug to get revenge. A big bruiser showed up at the salon after hours—and Jon reportedly put him in the hospital.

"Jon appeared small until he got mad," notes Cantor. "What's that animal that blows up? He became huge when he got angry."

"You do not want to fight this guy, period," says Silvio. "Shoot yourself in the leg and have the ambulance come get you, 'cause I guarantee you'll be better off. It used to scare the shit out of me. Jon's fights lasted about four seconds. Boom! Boom! Boom! The guy's down—it's over."

Eventually Peters and Cantor owned four successful salons in the Valley. Jon also purchased a wig factory in Hong Kong and two beauty supply companies. "Jon was hellbent on making money hand over fist," says Warren. The couple advanced relentlessly. In 1968 they moved into a house in Beverly Hills; a year and a half later they bought a beach house in the exclusive Malibu Colony.

Jon enhanced his reputation as a rising star by staging extravagant hair shows for the trade. For one spectacle at the Ambassador Hotel in downtown Los Angeles, two thousand hairdressers watched an unlikely futuristic vision concocted by Peters: A pair of nearly nude male and female models, wearing skullcaps, cavorted down the runway to deafening rock music.

In 1971, Lesley Ann was rehearsing the lead role of Polly Peachum in a Los Angeles Actors Studio production of *The Threepenny Opera*. When the show's financing fell through, Jon invested $10,000 of his own money and took up the producing reins for the first time outside of a hair salon. "Lesley Ann was so good, Jon wanted her to be seen," the show's director, Lee Grant, recalls. "I remember Jon said, 'She's sitting there on the curb like a little girl with her ballet shoes over her shoulder and she needs somewhere to go.' "

Grant was in charge of the actors and staging, but Peters got involved in the lighting and sets and publicity. The show turned out to be "a marvelous disaster," says Grant, though Warren got good reviews.

From that moment on, Jon set his sights on a career in show business. "It's an exciting life, and he got it real quickly that this was ultimately where he wanted to go," says Warren.

That transition would have to wait for a couple of years.

Conquering Beverly Hills—as a hairdresser—was the crucial next step for Jon, a symbol that he had catapulted himself out of the smoggy, suburban Valley and into the epicenter of glamour. He and Cantor bought into a salon at 301 North Rodeo Drive owned by Alfred, Eugene, and Adolph Pagano— the uncles who had given up on Jon when he was a juvenile delinquent. This time, though, there was no more "Peters and Cantor." Jon Peters was a name brand now. When the Beverly Hills shop opened in 1973, it was simply "The Jon Peters Salon."

The hippie days were over and Jon wanted an elegant look to signal his rise in status. He hired his old friend Bobbi Elliott to turn the Beverly Hills space into an airy retreat with top-of-the-line French country fabrics, wicker furniture, and plants. Elliott scoured Los Angeles for antiques and found a Victorian couch with a curved back for $700 which she covered in leopard-skin velvet for Jon's private cutting room.

By this time, Peters was making $100 an hour, working mornings in the Valley and afternoons in Beverly Hills. He cut the hair of many household names, including Jack Nicholson and Warren Beatty. He would take two assistants with him to Beatty's suite at the Beverly Wilshire Hotel, and keep the star entertained as he cut by goading the assistants to reveal their latest sexual exploits.

Appointments at the salon were scheduled so tightly that clients waited hours to see him. "He was totally outrageous," remembers Sandy Gallin, who later became Michael Jackson's manager. "He would work on three or four people at one time. I would come in and he would always stop what he was doing and say, 'Look at how angry this one is!' I saw him throw a woman out one day. It was a big show."

When the *Los Angeles Times* ran a big spread on the design of The Jon Peters Salon, Bobbi Elliott recalls being stung that Peters took all the credit for the work she had done. "It broke my heart at the time," she says. "Now, it doesn't mean I wouldn't give him a hug and a kiss if I saw him. But I learned a lesson from him—not to trust him."

26   LESLEY ANN would also learn to distrust Jon. The marriage started to show signs of strain as the women's movement swept the country and she began reading Germaine Greer. She

wanted to assert her independence, while Jon still expected her to cook and serve him at home—even when she was working. "I joined consciousness-raising groups and started marching. That changed our relationship," she says.

Although Peters denies that he ever abused Warren, one close friend of theirs says she knew Lesley Ann was physically intimidated by her husband. Asked if she feared Peters, Warren quickly answers, "I'm not willing to talk about any of that." But she admits "he had a tremendous quick temper—I think Jon will always have access to his temper. You know, he is volatile and he's fiery and he's explosive." She adds, "We fought like cats and dogs. We were just at each other's throats."

The relationship burned itself out. Jon had begun to stray, seducing celebrity clients, including starlets Susanne Benton and Leigh Taylor-Young. He didn't want to be married to Lesley Ann but apparently he didn't want to relinquish control either. In June 1974—after they were officially separated—she successfully sought a restraining order from the Santa Monica court that prohibited Jon from "annoying, harassing, molesting and making disparaging, derogatory comments" in front of their child.

As if to explain why she was willing to endure his destructive rages, she continues, "The thing that always kept my heart open to Jon was his little-boy stuff. He's like a kid . . . and from one minute to the next, he could change to his sweet side."

"I was very sad that it didn't work out, for both of their sakes," says Bobbi Elliott, who had introduced them. "Jon saw other vistas. . . . In a way I think maybe he used her as a stepping stone."

## 3

# THE DIVA
# AND THE HAIRDRESSER

Jon Peters sees his life as a kind of dream ladder, an ascending succession of fantasies that he transforms into reality. His belief in his own will is so strong that he literally thinks that wishing will make it so: that if he declares something to be true, it will come to pass. He had used this method to attract celebrity clients to his salon. "He would put in the paper that he had done so-and-so's hair," says Lesley Ann Warren, "and then he would meet them and they'd fall in love with him, and he *would* do their hair."

For years, Jon had been bragging that he cut Barbra Streisand's hair. One day in 1973 a young woman who worked for Streisand came into his new shop on Rodeo Drive. "Look," he told her. "You tell Miss Streisand that I, Jon Peters, will go anywhere, anytime, for free to do her hair. Because I think she's phenomenally talented. And honestly, I took credit for doing her hair for so long in Encino, now that I'm in Beverly Hills I want to do something nice to pay her back."

That summer, Peters was in Paris styling hair for the fashion collections—and carrying on an affair with actress Jacqueline Bisset—when he received a phone call. Streisand wanted to see him—though the superstar was not responding to his message. Scheduled to begin filming a new comedy, *For Pete's Sake*, in a month, Streisand was looking for someone to style her wigs. She had asked the film's director, Peter Yates, to find out who was responsible for a short haircut she had admired on a woman she met. Yates made inquiries and informed her that the stylist was Jon Peters.

What happened that August afternoon in 1973 when Peters pulled his red Ferrari through the imposing gates of Streisand's Carolwood Drive home in Beverly Hills has become Hollywood legend—largely thanks to Jon, who has repeated the story many times in interviews. He was wearing tight bell-bottom trousers, Indian jewelry, and an earring. Streisand kept him waiting half an hour. Impatient, Peters was on his way out the door when he heard a girlish, breathy voice behind him. "Hi," she said. "I'm sorry I kept you waiting. Can you come upstairs?"

Peters was astounded at how petite and feminine, how sexy Streisand was, so unlike the dowdy characters she had played in her films. Following her up the stairs, he exclaimed, "My God!"

"What are you looking at?" she demanded.

"I'm looking at your butt," he replied. "You've got a great ass."

Streisand hired Peters as her hair and wardrobe consultant on *For Pete's Sake*. When the picture began shooting in September, he was flown to Manhattan and put up in the Plaza Hotel. Still married to Warren, he and Streisand began an affair.

Director Yates was thrilled with the hairdresser's influence on his star. Peters made her a flattering, short wig and encouraged her to wear close-fitting jeans and jerseys. "She was going through a phase where she wanted to wear muumuus," says Yates. "And I found Jon extremely helpful because he helped persuade Barbra that she in fact could look marvelous in jeans and tighter clothes."

For all her talents and tough exterior, Streisand was a shy, extremely vulnerable woman, riddled with self-doubt and terrified of going out in public and being mobbed by fans. Her relentless perfectionism and indecision led to constant clashes with her collaborators. A long way from having the confidence she would eventually develop to direct films, she instead exasperated her directors by bombarding them with her ideas. She saw herself as a brave and determined soldier, fighting for artistry and excellence. Peters, with machismo to spare, was more than willing to do battle for her—with his fists, if he thought it necessary.

Streisand and Peters bonded over the loss of their fathers. Streisand's father, a Brooklyn high school English teacher, had died when Barbra was fifteen months old; like Jon, she had

29

endured an unloving stepfather. Together, they would try to heal their psychological scars and nurture their inner children through therapy and dabbling in the self-improvement philosophies that blow through Southern California as regularly as the Santa Ana winds. Jon talked incessantly of the benefits of therapy, and Streisand began seeing his and Lesley Ann's psychiatrist. Streisand said at the time that Jon was helping her find "my own truth. Jon started me in this direction, and we both go to a therapist who is a genius. He has helped me assert my own authority."

When she was growing up in Brooklyn, Streisand had believed that she was allergic to fresh air. In Hollywood, she had been closeted in stuffy recording studios. But Peters would build her a fortress retreat where they could play in the fields, creating the pastoral childhood neither of them had had.

By Christmas, Peters, now separated from Lesley Ann, was carrying on a very public affair with Streisand. They decided to move in together. On Valentine's Day, 1974, Peters and Streisand went property hunting (though Streisand would keep her home in Beverly Hills). Under Streisand's name, they purchased a bucolic eight-acre spread with a stream running through it at 5750 Ramirez Canyon Road in Malibu. A mundane three-bedroom stucco house with aluminum sliding doors stood on the property. In the next few years Streisand would buy adjoining parcels of land until the estate, which they called "the Ranch," encompassed twenty-four acres.

The couple embarked on a massive renovation, decorating, and landscaping project. "Nothing like it has ever been tried on the kind of scale we're attempting," Jon bragged. His taste was monumental and rustic, hers thrift-shop chic. In the main house, called the Barn, Peters hired carpenters to cover the interior with "aged" wood and install stained leaded-glass windows. Streisand hung her collection of antique hats and boas and fans and handbags everywhere. There were Tiffany lamps and old linens, hanging ivy and ferns and philodendrons. The effect was one of counterculture abundance.

When guests came, they were invited to collapse onto a fur-covered mattress piled with pillows in front of the great stone fireplace. A joint was passed around, and the house was illuminated by candlelight, which Streisand deemed flattering.

Except for Barbra's English garden and some flower beds,

the outdoors was Jon's domain. He planted two thousand trees. "See this mountain?" Peters asked a friend who dropped by, pointing at a substantial hill rising up out of Ramirez Gorge. "I want the sunrise here in the morning, so I'm going to move the mountain over here." He pointed in another direction. The friend thought he was joking until her next visit, when she noticed that the hill had in fact been moved a dozen feet.

Peters and Streisand had an eight-foot metal fence built around the property, along with TV scanners and electronic gates. The high security was not a function of star paranoia: Jon installed it after a menacing stalker repeatedly trespassed on their property, gaining access from a creek bed. Jon went out looking for the man, found him prowling the grounds, and leveled him with a left hook. The local sheriff apprehended the stalker and put him on a plane back to the Midwest.

While the pet lion cub which prowled the Ranch didn't attack anyone, the guard dogs did their job too well. Photographer Francesco Scavullo, who shot the advertising campaign for *A Star Is Born*, once drove all the way out to Malibu only to get a nasty bite from a Doberman named Red. Scavullo didn't take the couple to court, but Muriel Harris, a business acquaintance who was invited for a meeting in January 1977, sued for negligence after a Doberman attacked her. The case was settled out of court.

Peters may have created a Garden of Eden but his relationship with his Eve was anything but peaceful. The couple fought so much while renovating the Barn that they temporarily lived in separate houses. Ultimately there were five completely renovated dwellings in the compound—the smallest was 3,500 square feet—each in a different style. Barbra's house was a Deco showpiece, in shades of burgundy and gray; every piece of her wardrobe in its closets was coordinated with the color scheme.

People around Streisand and Peters sometimes witnessed disconcertingly fierce domestic battles followed by the billing and cooing of reconciliation. Jon said they fought like wild animals; during one of their fights, he remembered, "Barbra sat on my chest and spat at me. I spat back." This was a prelude to sex; the newly liberated Streisand even boasted to *Playboy* about her assertiveness in bed.

Jon remembers satisfying Barbra's sexual curiosity as well as her physical desires. One day, when the two were soaking in the hot tub at the Ranch, Streisand confided that she had never seen an uncircumcised penis. Jon could not oblige her, but he knew that an old friend who was working for the couple as a driver and gofer could. He called the man over and had him drop his trousers while Streisand inspected his organ closely.

Usually, however, people who observed Jon and Barbra's mating rituals felt like voyeurs. "I remember an overspilling of this passion that I was watching the two of them experience," recalls songwriter Paul Williams, who collaborated with Streisand at the Ranch. "It was a strange kind of feeling of being an outsider when you were with them."

"They were like teenagers in love," says Andrew Smith, another collaborator who wrote the screenplay for *The Main Event*. "It wasn't like two Hollywood giants being in love. We all felt like their mommy and daddy: We were like the older people, and they were these kids who were having this affair. And that made it funny to watch."

Jon sought refuge from the intensity of his relationship with Barbra by engaging in macho pursuits with his neighbor and new friend, Geraldo Rivera. Rivera, then a reporter on ABC's *Good Morning America,* moved with his wife, Sherry, to a property next door to the Ranch in 1976.

"Jon came over one Saturday with his son Christopher," says Rivera, recalling his first encounter with Peters. "We lived in a glass house, and Sherry and I were engaged in an intimate act. Now, most people would have gone away. But Jon stood there and said, 'Come on! Come on! We're neighbors, we've gotta meet!' He sort of stood there cheering us on. That set the tone for our relationship."

Jon and Geraldo shared a passion for motorcycles. When Rivera bought a Kawasaki 900, Jon bought the 1,000 model, "because he had to have 100 cc's more." Wearing only bikini bathing briefs, barefoot and helmetless, the two men would tear through Malibu's winding canyon roads at breakneck speeds, on at least one occasion narrowly avoiding flying off a cliff.

Streisand and Peters were eager to work together, but before they could start, Streisand had to fulfill a commitment to do one last picture for her mentor, *Funny Girl* producer Ray Stark. Jon did not approve of her reprising her role as Ray Stark's mother-in-law, comedienne Fanny Brice. He feared it would only cement her matronly image. Nevertheless, Streisand went before the *Funny Lady* cameras in April 1974.

On the set, relations were often tense between director Herb Ross and Streisand. A frequent visitor, Jon watched intently while keeping close tabs on leading man James Caan, as well as Streisand's old *Funny Girl* flame Omar Sharif, who also appeared in the film.

One day Peters bought Streisand a diamond-and-sapphire butterfly brooch. He often said that she reminded him of a butterfly, and had had one depicted in stained glass and installed in their Malibu ranch bedroom. He decided that they would name their first joint show business venture, a record album, *ButterFly*.

Streisand exercised her contractual right to total creative control by pressuring her record label, Columbia, to hire Peters as her producer, even though his musical experience consisted of wiggling his hips like Elvis in front of the mirror as a kid. She and Jon selected an eclectic mix of material, ranging from David Bowie's "Life on Mars" to Bob Marley's "Guava Jelly" and Buck Owens's "Crying Time." This was a bold departure from the classic Streisand, encased in a Bob Mackie gown, belting out Broadway show tunes. Now she was crooning lyrics like "Rub it on my belly like guava jelly."

After months of recording sessions Columbia felt the tracks Streisand had laid down were lackluster. Columbia Records executive Charles Koppelman brought in recording engineer Al Schmitt to rescue the project. But Streisand and Peters rejected his advice, and when *ButterFly* was released in October 1974, the reviews were withering. Bowie's opinion of Barbra's version of "Life on Mars" was blunt. "Sorry, Barb," he told *Playboy*, "but it was atrocious." (The album made it to #13 on the *Billboard* chart and eventually went gold in spite of the reviews.)

The album's cover image, which came to Jon as he was riding in his car, foreshadowed his career-long taste in high-concept marketing: a housefly sitting on a stick of butter. He explained that the butter represented the sweetness of Streisand's talent, while the pesky fly stood for all the perils of stardom that threatened to sully her.

*ButterFly* resulted in a barrage of bad publicity for Jon, who

33

was labeled a no-talent Svengali. "There was too much about music I didn't understand," Peters acknowledged later. "I could have learned it, mind you." Streisand later admitted that *ButterFly* was the least favorite of all her albums.

Within a year of their meeting, Jon was unofficially acting as Streisand's manager and pressuring her to drop her manager and good friend of fifteen years, Marty Ehrlichman. When Ehrlichman finally stepped aside in 1978, he had little affection for Peters. "My thoughts on what he does and how he does it, well, they're not for publication," he said later.

Peters also alienated other members of Streisand's trusted inner circle, including her best friend Cis Corman, and songwriters Alan and Marilyn Bergman. All of them would tiptoe around him during the years he and Streisand were together, from 1973 to 1979. In Peters's view they were dull and stodgy, they were not rock 'n' roll, and he considered them a bad influence on her. "Jon dismissed them all as being old and untalented, which wasn't fair," says Warner Bros. music executive Gary Le Mel.

The widespread view that Jon had "an absolute iron grip on Barbra," as columnist Robin Adams Sloan speculated, was too simplistic. He encouraged Streisand to take more control of her own career, to defy convention. His response to being told, "That's not the way it's done," was to break the rules. He shook things up, and even if he couldn't always set them right, he blasted Streisand out of her narrow artistic rut.

"Barbra Streisand tends to bring out worship in people: She's a national treasure, and you don't screw around with her music," says Andrew Smith. "And Jon, to his credit, was not intimidated by that. . . . He offered her a certain power and aggressiveness that she didn't have, and a sense of getting things done."

"He would calm her down, pull her back like a horse," says Lee Solters, Streisand's press agent for fifteen years. "He knew when and how to talk to her. . . . His input was very, very important. It wasn't self-serving; it was for her own good."

"He was the best thing that ever happened to her," adds producer Polly Platt. "If it hadn't been for him, she wouldn't have grown an inch. The woman I knew on *What's Up, Doc?* was brilliant, frightened, and racked with insecurity. If you told me she was going to direct a movie, I wouldn't have believed it."

34

# 4

# A STAR IS BORN

"You've got a nice ass," says Kris Kristofferson to Streisand when his character meets hers in *A Star Is Born*—thus immortalizing Jon Peters's line upon meeting Barbra. *A Star Is Born* was Jon and Barbra's $6 million home movie, an unapologetic, narcissistic celebration of their volatile romance.

In April 1974, while Streisand was working on *Funny Lady* and recording *ButterFly*, Peters had gotten his hands on a script called *Rainbow Road*, written by Joan Didion and John Gregory Dunne. He immediately seized on it as an opportunity for Streisand to portray a hip, sexy character and explore his favorite milieu, the world of rock 'n' roll.

*Rainbow Road* was a reworking of the classic melodrama *A Star Is Born*, originally filmed in 1937 with Fredric March and Janet Gaynor. The story follows a self-destructive aging star, John Norman Howard, through his love affair with rising young actress Esther Hoffman, and tracks his downward spiral and her simultaneous ascent. A semi-musical version was made in 1954 starring James Mason and Judy Garland. Dunne and Didion had set the story against a rock backdrop, envisioning Carly Simon and James Taylor in the leading roles.

Jon quickly learned that *Rainbow Road*, which was owned by Warner Bros., had already been turned down by Simon and Taylor—and by Streisand, who had told her agent Sue Mengers that she was not interested in remaking an old movie. She gave Jon the same response. "I called her up and said, 'I got this great thing,'" Jon remembers. "She said, 'Schmuck, it's been made three times.'" But Jon persuaded Streisand to reconsider, setting in motion a chain of events that is replayed in Hollywood whenever a superstar shows even a flicker of interest in a project. In such situations, agents and executives conduct negotiations with the urgency of diplomats deciding the fate of nations. Anyone tied to the movie, even those who originated it, can be swept away at the star's whim. Meanwhile a studio, eager to secure the big-name talent that could mean long lines at the box office, agrees to enormous concessions.

When Warner Bros. caught wind of a possible Barbra Streisand musical, the studio's projections indicated that all she'd have to do would be show up and warble a few songs and *Rainbow Road* would rake in $50 million. So intent was Warner on nailing down this Streisand picture that her agents were able to extract every deal point the star demanded over months of arduous negotiations.

Warner studio head John Calley, an old flame of Barbra's, swallowed extra hard over Streisand's first requirement: She was in only if Jon Peters was named the producer; she would be executive producer. John Foreman, who had worked on producing the film for a year, was swiftly shoved aside with the consolation prize of an executive producer credit. In July 1974, columnist Joyce Haber reported that Barbra Streisand would star in *Rainbow Road* and that Peters would produce the film. The same day, Lesley Ann Peters filed for divorce.

"THE WORLD IS WAITING to see Barbra's and my story," Jon boasted to *New Times* magazine's Marie Brenner. *A Star Is Born* is stuffed full of the most intimate, as well as the most prosaic, details of the couple's love affair. Much of Streisand's hippie wardrobe in the film came from her own closet, for which she gave herself a screen credit. Jon and Barbra had their own furniture trucked in to dress the set and ordered the scenic designers to reproduce the stained-glass butterfly in their bedroom.

Jon promised that the movie would deliver "a beautiful, sensual Barbra, the Barbra I have experienced." He coiffed her with a headful of frizzy curls, which Streisand ordered cinematographer Robert Surtees to film with a halo of backlighting. Esther is sexually aggressive with John, disrobing in love scenes before he does. Streisand cavorts in hot pants, which she insisted on wearing—with Peters's blessing—despite the objections of production designer Polly Platt. When exercising her right to final cut on the film, the star included numerous shots of her derriere.

36

*A Star Is Born* was Jon Peters's proving ground, and he knew that it would make or break him in Hollywood. If the movie failed, his detractors would be delighted—and blame him for having led Streisand astray. In the ways he exercised his new power and imposed his taste on the film, *A Star Is Born* is the prototypical Jon Peters project. It was one of the most famously tumultuous productions in Hollywood history, punctuated by Peters periodically threatening to punch out various people. On several occasions he got into shoving matches with collaborators. With a protracted and tortuous preproduction, the film did not go before the cameras until early 1976. By the time Peters and Streisand were done, they had gone through no fewer than fourteen screenwriters, three directors, and four musical collaborators.

One of Peters's first moves as a rookie producer was to upgrade the decor in Streisand's Barwood Films offices. He produced *A Star Is Born* through Barwood and the First Artists Company, a partnership to which Streisand belonged that distributed its movies through Warner and occupied bungalows on the Burbank lot. Maintaining that a stimulating work environment fosters creativity, Jon installed a huge stereo system and played rock music constantly. Assistants found it hard to concentrate with Springsteen blaring. He cruised antique stores for rugs and furniture. "There were these mirrors all around," says producer Laura Ziskin, then an assistant who watched, amazed, as Jon contemplated his own image all day. "He'd be talking on the phone and performing for himself," she says.

While the *Star* script was being revised by a string of writers in 1975, Peters was still cutting hair two mornings a week. In the afternoons he'd spin over to Warner Bros. in his Ferrari or his black Mercedes convertible, on the console of which he would place a bud vase with a single rose in it. He dressed in tight pants and shirts with big collars, sometimes adding a vest. He kept his hair and beard perfectly trimmed.

As *Star* moved toward production, Jon made his career transition. Peters and Cantor sold the beauty salons to Allen Edwards in 1976. The deal gave Edwards the right to use the Jon Peters name, which effectively precluded Peters from returning to hairdressing should he fail in the movie business. He deliberately closed that door behind him. But when he gathered two hundred employees from all his salons at the Rodeo Drive

37

shop to tell them he was retiring his scissors to devote his full attention to making *A Star Is Born,* he wept.

Suddenly elevated to the status of sole producer on a major Hollywood motion picture, Peters was terrified of making a fool of himself. Sensitive to people's perception of him as a gigolo, he masked his fear with a disorienting mixture of bullying and self-deprecating humor. "It was his first movie," says Polly Platt, "and he made lots of hairdressing jokes. He made fun of himself, dissipating your ability to make the nasty crack. In other words, he was very clever, and I believe that even now when he makes those kinds of remarks, it diffuses your ability to put him down."

For a producer with no experience, Jon had remarkable success in convincing Warner to approve his creative decisions. He spent plenty of the studio's money for his big ideas, prevailing upon John Calley and production executive Frank Wells with his enthusiasm and bullheadedness. He won approval to record all the music on *A Star is Born* live, which had never been done before in a big film and posed formidable technical challenges. And he persuaded the studio to let him stage a live concert featuring Streisand and Kristofferson for a crowd of fifty-five thousand at Sun Devil Stadium in Tempe, Arizona.

Jon turned his inexperience into a virtue by dreaming up schemes that anyone else would have considered impractical—and refusing to back off unless he was absolutely convinced they couldn't be done. He encouraged others to do the same. "Jon will never give you one of those, 'Oh, you want to do *that,*' " Platt explains. "You can feel free to express your artistic ideas, some of which you might be frightened to say to more of an intellectual, to someone of 'good taste.' Jon is not afraid of any idea."

He spent what was necessary to bring in the best talent, including veteran music producer Phil Ramone as the film's music director, and Jules Fisher, lighting designer for the Rolling Stones. "He's a powerhouse," says Ramone. "He knew what he wanted and he wasn't going to give in. He said, 'What do you need?' "

While Peters's daring style was exhilarating to some, he was less effective in the areas that require sustained, methodical effort—notably screenwriting. Not only did he have a brief attention span but he was barely literate. Writers found it irk-

38

some, even ridiculous, to be given notes by him. "Jon had no idea how to read scripts," says Jane Jenkins, then working as his assistant. "I used to do synopses of rewrites to explain the changes with each new version."

By now, Dunne and Didion were off the project. Shortly after Streisand committed to it, they had been invited to the Malibu ranch for script discussions. Their seven-year-old daughter Quintana came along, and frolicked with Barbra's son Jason. "I wasn't crazy about their playing in the cage with the pet lion cub," Dunne wrote in *Esquire* magazine, "but I figured what the hell, this was Hollywood."

The conversation was cordial, Dunne noted, but Streisand had worried him with her talk about "my film" and "my project." She asked for "more schmalz" and she wanted her character to have more prominence. "Barbra and Jon saw the picture as being about their own somewhat turbulent love affair," wrote Dunne. "It began to look like a long summer." The screenwriters had worked hard to lend the story as much rock-'n'-roll grit as they could and didn't want to sacrifice that to "schmalz." Dunne and Didion happily negotiated their release from the picture with a $125,000 fee and 10 percent of the net profit, which would amount to a windfall.

*A Star Is Born* became a rapidly revolving door as a succession of writers was brought in to synthesize Jon and Barbra's ever-evolving vision. Jon hired his friend Jonathan Axelrod to rework the script but told people *he* was doing the rewrite. When Axelrod's agent objected, Peters fired Axelrod. Jay Presson Allen, Buck Henry, and Alvin Sargent all took passes at the screenplay and quickly departed.

Jon's biggest concern was that the John Norman character shouldn't do anything wimpy in the story. "He's a man I identify with greatly," he admitted, explaining that the story of *A Star Is Born* "touches on the facts of my life, the street fighter and overachiever. The macho thing is very much me. I fought for what I believed in and I wasn't above using violence."

One plot point that particularly upset Peters, and which he was determined to change, was John's suicide. It was a key component of the story and every previous version had ended with John dying by his own hand. But Peters could not tolerate such weakness in his alter ego; he insisted that John's death should be ambiguous, possibly an accident. (He would personally climb onto a crane to direct the sequence of John's Ferrari coming over a hill before it crashed and burst into flames.)

As the line between reality and film fiction became increasingly blurred, Jon inevitably fancied himself as a leading man for his lady love. When Kristofferson initially turned down the project because Streisand wouldn't allow his name to appear with hers above the title, Peters pounced. Why shouldn't *he* play John Norman? Streisand agreed it was a great idea.

With dread in their hearts, Warner executives asked the key question: Can he sing? Jerry Schatzberg, the director then attached to the film, drove to the Ranch to discuss the matter. At the meeting Jon attempted a rendition of "Don't Be Cruel," accompanied by Streisand. All the hip-wiggling in the world couldn't disguise the fact that he couldn't sing a note. Although he halfheartedly suggested that he lip-synch to a dubbed soundtrack, he and Barbra dropped the notion.

"I was off-key the whole time," Jon says, recalling the effort. "I figured, fuck it, I'll try anything. She's the biggest star in the world! Whatever sticks, I'll do."

When Jon told Frank Wells that he had given up the idea of taking the starring role, the Warner executive was overjoyed. "He gave me a kiss and said, 'Thank God! Thank God!' " Jon remembers.

But Warner's nail-biting didn't end there. When Schatzberg fled the project, Jon announced that he would take over as director of *A Star Is Born.* "It's a story I felt only I could tell," he explained. He dismissed his complete lack of filmmaking experience. "Directing is a thing I've done my whole life!" he insisted. "It's getting people to do what I want them to do!"

As a first-time director, he said, he would surround himself with crack talent—the best editor, director of photography. He boasted to journalist Brenner that he had hired esteemed editor Dede Allen to cut *A Star Is Born,* although he hadn't actually made her an offer. Allen turned him down, suggesting he might hire her twenty-four-year-old assistant.

But Streisand ultimately had misgivings about working with her lover behind the camera. A series of A-list directors was approached—Bob Fosse, Hal Ashby, Sidney Lumet, and Robert Altman—but none would touch the project. At last Streisand and Peters hired Frank Pierson, the writer of *Dog Day Afternoon, Cool Hand Luke,* and *Cat Ballou,* who had previously directed only one small picture, *The Looking Glass War.*

Given Streisand's need to control, and in light of her later directing achievements, it seems odd that at this juncture she didn't just decide to direct *Star* herself. But she told Pierson that she didn't want to bruise Jon's ego. "I couldn't just take over as director from Jon, could I?" she said. "But I couldn't let Jon direct. Can you imagine Jon Peters directing?"

Meanwhile, the search for a leading man continued. Streisand and Peters invited Marlon Brando to the Ranch, with an eye to asking him to co-star; they thought that perhaps they could excise the songs and make *A Star Is Born* into a drama. "He was cute!" Jon told Pierson. "The son of a bitch, he wanted to fuck Barbra—I was ready to kill him! I take him off, and I kiss him!" Warner would surely have been horrified by the prospect of a *Star* without music, but nothing came of the meeting.

Next, Jon and Barbra flew to Las Vegas to try to lure Elvis into the project. The King, then in his corpulent downward spiral, was playing the Hilton. They took in his show and went backstage afterwards. Elvis sat on the floor and said to Streisand, "You know, you're the only one that ever intimidated me. I came to your show and I came back to see you, and you never looked me in the face. All you did was paint your nails."

"Elvis, you can't come with the whole entourage," Peters told Presley, "and you have to be able to work one-on-one with Barbra." He engaged in some negotiations with Presley's manager, Colonel Tom Parker, but Presley turned the offer down. So it was back to Kristofferson, with an offer of billing above the title this time. He accepted.

ON FEBRUARY 2, 1976, with a budget of $6 million and a sixty-day shooting schedule, the cameras rolled. Peters scored a crucial early triumph: Warner had agreed to his unusual notion of recording the music live after executives at the studio saw some footage. On the first shooting day, Streisand performed "Queen Bee" in a suburban Los Angeles club, decorated like an Arizona bar. "We screened it at Warner Bros. and the thing worked," recalls Ramone. "And most of the people who were skeptics were astounded that Barbra really came off the way one would want her to, free to sing and react to the people and not having to lip-synch."

Having cleared that hurdle, the film plunged into two months of chaos. Peters and Streisand locked horns with director Pierson, who was driven to the brink by the star's indecision

41

and micro-managing. Streisand had little understanding of the logistics of filmmaking; she was obsessed mostly by whether the gauzy backlighting she ordered was flattering her cheekbones and whether Pierson was shooting enough close-ups of her. If she didn't like the footage, she would scream, "This is shit! God, what are we going to do? I told you not to do that! Why did you do it? It's wrong!"

For Jon, *A Star Is Born* was like walking on a balance beam in the middle of a hurricane—and often he helped cause the turbulent weather. "Jon really hated Frank," says Jane Jenkins. At the same time his relationship with Streisand was as stormy as ever; if they weren't fighting he was holding her hand, cajoling her through her dramatic scenes and live performances.

As the show's producer, Jon was supposed to have an overview of the picture and keep it moving within its budget. He was determined to show Warner and Hollywood that he was a capable leader. After all, he had his future after Barbra to think about. "It wasn't all Barbra, Barbra, Barbra," says Platt. "He really understood that the whole film had to be good, whereas most boyfriends attend to the Barbra Streisand industry."

Jon's brainstorms ranged from clever to delusional. His idea of staging a live concert in front of fifty-five thousand fans was inspired, Pierson acknowledged. But the director balked at Jon's notion of paying Evel Knievel $25,000 to stand in for Kristofferson with a colossal stunt, riding a motorcycle off the stage and into the audience, then ramping up back onto the stage, scattering the instruments and equipment.

"There were a lot of valid contributions," says Pierson about Peters on *Star*, "and there were a lot that I fouled off into the left-field seats. . . . We fought like hell, as everybody knows." Pierson says that Peters's wild ideas helped to focus his own thinking. "You may not like what he's talking about or wants to do, and that stimulates you to come up with a better idea. He sure ain't boring."

Kristofferson posed a special challenge to Peters. Here was a magnetic star who was supposed to be playing *him*. The singer-songwriter, a former Rhodes Scholar, had appeared in *Cisco Pike, Blume in Love,* and *Alice Doesn't Live Here Anymore,* but 42 hadn't quite broken through to movie stardom. The *Star* shoot was extremely uncomfortable for Kristofferson, who was caught in the middle of the fighting with Pierson and buffeted between the two sides. Barbra's leading man took to fortifying himself with tequila and beer chasers, usually starting before lunch.

With his musical roots in folk and country, Kristofferson was terrified about looking like an idiot while trying to play a rock star. He was backed up by his own band in the film, but some rock musicians had been brought in as well. When rehearsals began, recalls *Star* composer Paul Williams, "all of a sudden Kris is up on stage singing with these guys, and experiencing what he described as 'a deep sense of impending shame.' "

Jon began complaining that the singer was not adequately embodying his vision of a rock-'n'-roll icon, and provoked Kristofferson into heated exchanges and shoving matches on the set. The friction was at its worst when Streisand and Kristofferson shot a love scene in a bathtub surrounded by lit candles.

Kristofferson had earned a reputation in Hollywood as a superlative lover; he had romanced Janis Joplin and Carly Simon, among others. Streisand didn't dare tell Peters that she, too, had once had an affair with her co-star. The day before the bathtub scene, Peters took Kristofferson aside and tried to lay down some guidelines. "Kris, please, this is my lady," he implored. "We're engaged. I love her. Do it with a bathing suit—don't go in there naked. I don't want your dick floating around in the tub with her leg right there."

At Streisand's insistence, Jon stayed clear of the set the next day. Kristofferson hesitated not a minute before slipping into the tub buck naked. Pierson, knowing Peters might turn up on the set at any moment and punch his leading man's lights out, sent for a pair of flesh-colored shorts and ordered Kristofferson to put them on. Streisand took off the top of her bathing suit and sank into the bubbles. Nothing untoward took place under the water, but when they finished the scene, Jon appeared and flew into a rage. He and Streisand had a ferocious fight that ended with him chasing her around the Warner lot until she found a ride home in another car.

Jon denied that he ever hit Barbra but acknowledged that they had some wild tussles that included plenty of wrestling and clawing. He had punched a hole through the kitchen wall at the Ranch and also broken several lamps.

Once, when he and Streisand were driving to a meeting with Warner executives at the Burbank lot to discuss setting up *A*

43

*Star Is Born,* they got into a heated quarrel. With his left hand on the wheel, Jon had reached over and grabbed her, ripping her blouse off. Barbra swung a leg up and pressed a stiletto heel into his neck as Jon sped down the Hollywood Freeway, struggling to maintain control of the car.

"Their relationship was pretty volatile and intense," says Jane Jenkins, Jon's assistant. "There would be bursts of conflict. She would be a needy little girl where she would need a big strong man to protect her. Then there were times when he would decimate her. I heard him scream at Barbra once in a way that I would have run a hundred miles. I remember her calling back an hour later with this little-girl voice and saying, 'Is Jon there?' And I wanted to say, 'Don't talk to him!' "

While *Star* was filming at Warner, Platt and Streisand were walking one day at lunch hour among the soundstages, talking about a scene to be shot that afternoon on a recording studio set. Jon was working out elsewhere on the lot in an exercise room, pumping up with weights. "Come into my trailer and we'll have lunch," Streisand said to Platt.

Streisand served Platt a steak and potato that had been intended for Jon's lunch, then sat down herself to a plate of ravioli. Peters entered the trailer after his workout, saw Platt eating his steak, and exploded. He threw a glass of ice water at Streisand's plate, spraying ravioli on her white silk blouse and into her hair. Peters stormed out of the trailer and Streisand calmly began cleaning up the mess. The production schedule was set back a couple of hours while the star's wardrobe, hair, and makeup were repaired. "What he did," Platt recalls, "was so full of abandon and irresponsibility that you knew you were dealing with a man who would go over the edge and do almost anything."

And yet he was the only person who could have coaxed the paralytically stage-shy Streisand into singing before a crowd of fifty-five thousand, as he did at the Sun Devil concert. Marty Ehrlichman, still the star's manager at the time, objected to the live venue; he thought Streisand was too old and middle-of-the-road to perform before a huge crowd of young rockers. Neither had Warner been keen on the risk and expense of trying to film thousands of unruly extras. Calley and Wells had suggested that the filmmakers use footage from Woodstock to simulate the concert ambience. But Jon was adamant.

Three weeks before the designated date, the concert was not

44

yet organized. Peters called in legendary promoter Bill Graham and paid him an exorbitant fee to pull the concert together in three days. Graham lined up Santana and Peter Frampton, and allotted four hours for filming scenes of Streisand and Kristofferson singing. Tickets went on sale for $3.50; the production would make money on the event.

The day before the concert, Warner publicists invited 150 members of the press to the stadium for lunch and a press conference with Streisand, Kristofferson, and Peters. The journalists, who had heard that sparks were flying on the set, were disappointed by the canned, upbeat remarks they were fed by the principals. Then they got lucky: During a rehearsal, Streisand and Kristofferson lit into each other, not realizing that their mikes were open.

"Listen to me when I talk to you, goddamnit!" screamed Streisand.

"Fuck off," retorted Kristofferson. "I'll be goddamned if I listen to anything more from you."

Jon jumped in. "You owe my lady an apology," he yelled. He and Kristofferson didn't come to blows, but vowed to catch up with each other when the film was finished.

"If I need any shit from you," Kristofferson told Peters in his parting riposte, "I'll squeeze your head!"

The next day dawned hot. As the sun drew higher the assembled fans drank beer, smoked pot, and cheered for Frampton and Santana. But everything that could go wrong did: The set decoration was botched, there were electrical glitches, the number-one camera on a boom failed, and no one could hear directions because of the roar of the crowd. The audience turned hostile when it was left without entertainment for hours as Pierson and the crew struggled to set up shots. Watching the crowd grow restless, Graham screamed, "Don't you know what you're doing? They're going to kill us!"

Backstage Peters soothed Streisand, telling her that the crowd was going to love her. When the star finally took the stage, she sang "People"—not for the film, but to placate the audience. To everyone's astonishment, her magic worked. The angry rockers leapt to their feet in a standing ovation.

THE PRODUCTION wrapped in April 1976, on time and within budget. Six weeks later, as Pierson's contract required, he screened his cut of *A Star Is Born* for Streisand and Peters.

When the lights went up, Streisand huddled with her inner circle, including Cis Corman, Marilyn and Alan Bergman, and her assistant Joan Ashby, until five in the morning. At last the superstar could seize control. "She couldn't wait until [Pierson] finished his six weeks," editor Peter Zinner recalls.

The next day, Zinner and a team of editors adjourned to a $500,000 state-of-the-art editing facility that Streisand had installed in the pool house at the Malibu ranch. All summer they toiled under her instructions, working fourteen-hour days to accommodate her changing whims. She had her Polish cook make wonderful meals so they never had to leave the property.

As Streisand worked seven days a week—*A Star Is Born* was scheduled to open a week before Christmas—Jon turned his attention to selling the film. Marketing was the area where his bold sensibility truly broke new ground. He pushed First Artists and Warner to coordinate a range of marketing tie-ins that have since become common practice in the industry, including a novelization, a TV special on the making of *Star*, and a Barbara Walters interview, the first of her television specials. And Jon spearheaded the film's steamy ad campaign featuring a Scavullo photograph of Streisand and co-star Kristofferson in a semi-nude *Gone With the Wind* embrace.

At that time Terry Semel was head of Warner distribution, presiding over a team of marketing executives that included Sid Ganis, Joe Hyams, and Rob Friedman. Jon and Barbra befriended Semel, inviting him and his wife Jane to parties at the ranch. It was the beginning of a long and mutually beneficial relationship between the two men.

The greenhorn producer refused to accept conventional marketing strategies. "Jon was very involved in the marketing campaign," one Warner source recalls. "He was never a detail man, always a style man—a cheerleader and motivator. He was very enthusiastic, very naive. He wanted to push the envelope at every corner. The thing he hated most was hearing, 'We don't do it that way.' It was like a red flag to a bull."

Close to the movie's opening, First Artists hired a new marketing executive named Frank Merino. While Jon was away on a brief vacation, the company's music chief, Gary Le Mel, was ordered to move out of his office, which adjoined Jon's, so Merino could take it over. "I don't think that's a good idea," Le Mel said, thinking that Jon would be none too pleased to

46

find his territory invaded by a newcomer. Nevertheless, Le Mel relocated to an office above the studio tailor shop nearby.

"The following Monday I'm in the tailor shop and I hear an ambulance siren, and I just knew that something had happened with this guy," says Le Mel.

Something had. In a meeting in Jon's office, Merino had expounded on how he felt the *Star* soundtrack album and other marketing elements were being mishandled. "I'm going to save this project," Merino declared.

"Who the fuck are you?" Peters yelled. "We've been killing ourselves on this movie for two years!"

"I suddenly realized these guys were going to come to blows," remembers Laura Ziskin, who was present. "They both stood up, and [Frank] grabbed Jon by the shirt, and Jon punched him. I said, 'Let go of his shirt!' The guy wouldn't let go."

With a left hook and a right cross, Peters sent Merino flying ten feet across the room, literally leaving the executive's empty loafers on the rug in front of him. "He hit me! He hit me! You saw him!" Merino shouted as he staggered to his feet, his eye swelling.

"When I heard the siren and ran down and saw the guy being wheeled out on a gurney, his head was like this," says Le Mel, holding one hand inches away from his face.

Adds Ziskin, "After the guy left, Jon said, 'You have to tell them he hit me first.' "

Merino had called the cops and Jon fled to Semel's office, where he hid from the authorities under his friend's desk. Semel talked to the officers before Jon emerged and explained that he had acted in self-defense. Merino quit. No charges were filed.

WHEN *A STAR IS BORN* opened the critics were scathing. Most of them didn't buy Streisand as a rock diva and pummeled the film for its preposterous story line, soft-focus lighting, and abundant close-ups of Streisand's face and backside. "The sinking feeling one gets from the picture relates largely to her," wrote *The New Yorker*'s Pauline Kael. "One is never really comfortable with her, because even when she's singing she isn't fully involved in the music; she's trying to manage our responses."

*The Village Voice* quipped, "A bore is starred."

Rex Reed was less polite: "If there's anything worse than the noise and stench that rises from the album, it's the movie itself. It's an unsalvageable disaster. This is why Hollywood is in the toilet . . . I blame a studio for giving $5.5 million to an actress and her boyfriend to finance their own ego trip."

But it hardly mattered. *A Star Is Born* remains the biggest hit of the star's film career, having grossed more than $90 million at the box office. The soundtrack album sold 8 million units and held the number-one *Billboard* slot for six weeks. Jon and Barbra jointly netted an estimated $15 million on the film.

Although *Star* was passed over in the major Academy Award categories, Streisand and Williams won the best song Oscar for "Evergreen." When they also won a Grammy, Williams stepped up to the microphone and said, "I want to thank Barbra for a beautiful melody and Dr. Jack Walstader for the Valium that got me through the experience." The film also won three Golden Globes. *A Star Is Born* reaffirmed Streisand's power and established Jon Peters as a contender in Hollywood.

On an overseas promotional tour, Jon and Barbra made stops in London, Rome, Sydney, and Tokyo. In Japan, they attended a cocktail party where Streisand was introduced to a small, pleasant white-haired man who told her he was a devoted fan. It was Akio Morita, one of the founders of the Sony Corporation.

# 5

## ON HIS OWN

"Heeeyyy, sweetie, how ya doin'?"

When Peters worked the phones in the early days of his career, he wooed business callers and friends with his street camaraderie. Screenwriter Andrew Smith says, "When he picks up the phone it's like some guy from the neighborhood, you know, it's 'Hey, sweetie, how ya doooo-in'?' That's how he talks. There's a sweetness to him. He's always doing that 'heeeey,' and he's pinching and kissing."

Jon Peters was delighted to join Hollywood's long parade of self-made, uneducated businessmen. Jack Warner, Harry Cohn, and Louis B. Mayer were tough, profane tycoons who habitually intimidated adversaries. Jon would become one of the last of this breed of colorful characters in an industry where corporate conformity and discipline—paper-thin, perhaps—would take hold in the eighties.

But back in the mid- to late seventies when Jon had his first success, Hollywood still felt like the Wild West. Unfettered by the codes of behavior that maintained civility in other industries, Jon prospered as he did as he pleased. He quickly sized up the movie business as a place that would adapt to his style. "He's a cowboy and a gunslinger and an outlaw," says producer Howard Rosenman.

Peters's heroes were Walt Disney; MCA chairman Lew Wasserman; and, later, the man who built Warner into a multi-billion-dollar global conglomerate, Steve Ross. From the start he envisioned himself as a rich, successful purveyor of entertainment; what hooked him were the high stakes and the possibility of windfall profits rather than a love of filmmaking. "I'm into being like a mogul, a big tycoon," he said. "I'm looking to build an entertainment empire."

Even before *A Star Is Born* started filming in early 1976, Peters had hustled more deals for himself. The executives who handed opportunities to an unproven producer may have had more interest in cozying up to Streisand than anything else, but Peters was perfectly willing to take advantage of them.

In June 1975, he had signed a three-picture deal with Columbia Pictures president David Begelman, which included *Eyes,* a thriller set in the New York fashion world. He had pitched the idea to a Columbia executive named Roz Heller, a hairdressing client since his Encino days and Hollywood's first female studio vice president.

Peters submitted *Eyes* in the form of a ten-page treatment written by a recent graduate of USC Film School, John Carpenter. When Heller showed the treatment to Peter Guber, then the studio's head of production, he turned it down.

"Is Barbra going to do this?" Guber asked.

"No," Heller replied.

"Forget it," Guber retorted. "Jon Peters is a hairdresser. He's not a producer."

Eventually, Heller and Jon had gone over Guber's head to his boss, Begelman.

When he was asked later if he had misgivings about hiring Streisand's hairdresser–boy-toy to make movies, Begelman was testy. "Don't give me any of that ——," he snarled to a *New York* magazine reporter. "I'm running a business, not a gossip shop." He told *People,* "A person's sex life or hangups are none of my business. Peters happens to be a persistent young man with ideas, and this business is always looking for enterprising young men."

Peters founded his own company, the Jon Peters Organization (JPO) in 1977, and *Eyes,* retitled *Eyes of Laura Mars,* became his first solo production. He was eager to establish a base of operations independent of Streisand, from which he could either collaborate with her or work alone.

JPO took over a ground-floor suite in the back of a producers' building near the Hollywood Way gate of the Burbank lot, then co-owned by Warner and Columbia Pictures. The offices in front of Jon's were occupied by Peter Guber and his FilmWorks Company. (Guber—the executive who had declined to give Jon a movie deal at Columbia—had since been pushed out of his studio job. He had just produced his first hit, a sultry underwater thriller called *The Deep*.)

Jon transformed his new home in a lush Deco style. The reception area, papered with the same palm-frond wallpaper as the Beverly Hills Hotel, reminded visitors of a beauty salon. The color scheme was claret and gray, with velvet couches and smoked-glass lamps. His own office was furnished with antiques, and the wall facing his desk was completely mirrored, as usual, to allow him to keep an eye on himself.

With his goal of building an empire in mind, Jon ventured into several areas of show business. He became the agent of his friend Geraldo Rivera, who recalls that when he told his then-agent Jerry Weintraub that the former hairdresser was usurping his role, Weintraub took it badly. "The rap on Jon twenty years ago was that he was a gigolo," says Rivera.

At the time, ABC boss Roone Arledge was telling Rivera that he wanted him to give up his job as a reporter on *Good Morning America* and help him launch a new magazine show named *20/20*. As Rivera's representative, Jon requested a meeting with Arledge. "Roone, ABC lawyer Irwin Weiner, and Jon and I went to lunch at Alfredo's, a very dignified restaurant on Central Park South," says Rivera. "Three of us were wearing coats and ties, but Jon was dressed very casually—I think they had to lend him a jacket."

Over lunch the men engaged in pleasant chitchat, with Arledge outlining his dreams for ABC. "Suddenly Jon slams both hands down on the table, making the water glasses jump," says Rivera. "He said, 'I can't stand this any longer. Are you gonna pay him a million bucks, or what?!' The whole restaurant looked at us. I couldn't believe it—it was a big scene. And the result was that I became the first network nonanchor to get paid $1 million. So Jon's tactics, however unorthodox, worked."

Peters also continued to exploit his opportunities in the music world. The *Star* soundtrack had been immensely profitable for CBS—Streisand's most successful record to date—and it had boosted sales of her catalogue. When her contract expired in 1977, Jon negotiated a new five-year deal with CBS Records boss Walter Yetnikoff that was the richest package ever awarded a recording artist.

51

"He really knew how to nail a deal point," says Michael Meltzer, who then worked as Peters's story editor and observed the negotiations closely. "He'd be on the phone with lawyers. . . . It wasn't over his head. People said he couldn't read, but he was very good at putting together the salient points of an economic business deal."

As Streisand's manager, Peters took a 15 percent cut of her earnings. In the next couple of years he would rake in an estimated $20 million as he pushed her aggressively into recording more commercial material. He reinvented her as a disco diva by insisting she record the theme song for *The Main Event,* a movie they made together in 1978. He also teamed her with Donna Summer for their hit duet "No More Tears (Enough Is Enough)." Peters flew to Florida with Yetnikoff to make a deal with Bee Gees singer-songwriter Barry Gibb that yielded collaborations with Streisand on their platinum album *Guilty,* which overtook sales of the *Star* soundtrack.

Jon used his Streisand leverage to cut a deal for himself with CBS, too. Walter Yetnikoff was one of the few human beings on the planet who could surpass Jon in profanity and outrageous behavior. They were on the phone constantly, trading gossip and jokes in their street patois, boasting about their exploits with women. In January 1977, Yetnikoff handed Peters a fat deal to scout, develop, and produce new musical talent on his own label. Jon made much of his interest in music but this deal turned out to be little more than rock-'n'-roll fantasy; he envisioned himself discovering the next Led Zeppelin or Bruce Springsteen, but he was too consumed by his film projects to devote much time or energy to his music scouting. He had his assistants solicit demo tapes and he went out to clubs to catch new acts when he could. He signed a rock group called Michalski and Oosterveen and produced their album, but it went nowhere.

Still, Jon knew how to salvage something from his effort. He had Michalski and Oosterveen record a song, "Fire," for the soundtrack of *Eyes of Laura Mars.* Although the album was thin and lackluster, it had a single by Barbra Streisand—"Prisoner." He had discovered a savvy marketing tactic: mix songs recorded by stars with others by weaker artists to boost soundtrack revenues. For *Eyes of Laura Mars,* Streisand's willingness to record a song for a film in which she didn't star had made the difference.

□

*EYES OF LAURA MARS* was a thriller about a clairvoyant Manhattan fashion photographer, played by Faye Dunaway, who takes kinky pictures and has premonitions about a series of murders. It co-starred Tommy Lee Jones and featured titillating visuals and a slick production design that couldn't make up for a weak story line and a silly ending. As *Eyes* producer, Peters clashed with Dunaway and went through five screenwriters and two directors.

Even though it was a treatment by the recent USC grad John Carpenter that had secured Peters the *Eyes* deal, Jon claimed in *Variety* that he had written the treatment himself. Carpenter wrote four drafts of the screenplay, all of which left Peters dissatisfied. He wanted more eroticism and glamour. Finally, he fired Carpenter—who went on to make a name for himself as a horror film director. Carpenter described his experience working with the producer as one he would not want to repeat. "Jon can't take any criticism of any kind because of his massive insecurity," Carpenter told a reporter. "He was brutally critical if he didn't agree with me, but he couldn't take it if I'd come back and say an idea of his wasn't going to work."

"I'm not a producer who comes up with a concept and lets somebody make it their way whether I agree or not," Jon retorted. "I have definite ideas—and it's my money. I'd rather get it done my way than be loved."

In subsequent rewrites by Joan Tewkesbury, Mart Crowley, David Zelag Goodman, and Julian Barry, Dunaway's character was made more provocative, walking on the dark side with her sadomaschostic photographs. The screenplay was not finished when shooting began in the fall of 1977.

Roman Polanski was Jon's dream director for *Eyes*—but he was in exile in France. (Polanski had fled the country to avoid sentencing after pleading guilty to unlawful intercourse with a minor.) Peters hired and fired Michael Miller before settling on Irvin Kershner, who had directed Streisand in *Up the Sandbox*. Dunaway, who had just won an Academy Award for her brilliant portrayal of a ruthless television executive in *Network*, wasn't Jon's first choice either, but Streisand had turned him down, saying that she hated thrillers.

Dunaway was 40 pounds overweight when she was cast and still heavy as principal photography approached. A former Columbia executive recalls asking then–studio chief Dan

53

Melnick, "What are you, paying her by the pound?" In one of her first scenes Dunaway was scheduled to wear a Theoni V. Aldredge ball gown with ruffles at the neck. "They locked her up for the last few weeks to lose weight," says the same source.

Meanwhile, Peters concerned himself with the film's hip, New York fashion world look. He was closely involved in recruiting the top models who appear in the film, Lisa Taylor and Darlanne Fluegel. He personally streaked Dunaway's hair and chose an old industrial building on the Hudson River as the location for the photographer's lush studio. He commissioned Helmut Newton, then the reigning prince of whips-and-leather photography, to provide *Eyes* with images to stand in for the protagonist's work.

As shooting began, Dunaway, high-strung in the best of times, was even more insecure than usual. She wasn't looking her sleekest and was in the process of breaking up with her husband, Peter Wolf. She battled with Jon over the unfinished screenplay—she found herself inventing much of her own dialogue—and later spoke of "the agony of writing as you go."

While Jon called Kershner a "genius" in interviews, privately he told his staff that he felt the movie's direction was weak. Nevertheless, he threw himself into the marketing campaign, which cost Columbia $7 million—as much as the film's budget. For months before *Eyes of Laura Mars* opened in August 1978, there were billboards plastered with an arresting graphic of Dunaway's eyes. Streisand's "Prisoner" single was also released early, with ads proclaiming "The Eyes of Laura Mars, the Voice of Barbra Streisand."

Though *Eyes* was destined to be a disappointment at the box office, grossing only $20 million, Jon and Dunaway sheathed the knives and plugged the movie like professionals. "He has great instincts," Dunaway said, "and he's totally unafraid to admit he's wrong."

"It was a volatile, highly emotional set," Peters admitted. "Fortunately, my nineteen years in the beauty shop served me well. I am used to dealing with temperament." After praising Dunaway, he added, "My only concern now is that after all the problems on my first two pictures people will begin to think I must be some kind of crazy person."

54

□

IN THE FALL OF 1978, Streisand still owed First Artists the final film of a three-picture contract. Streisand, Peters, and Sue Mengers stayed up nights reading scripts, trying to find a suitable project. The screenplay for *The Main Event* had been kicking around Hollywood for several years: a screwball comedy about a female perfume manufacturer who goes broke and decides to manage her last remaining asset, a washed-up prizefighter. Peters and Mengers decided *The Main Event* should be Barbra's next film. Knowing Streisand would dismiss it as a dumb comedy and resist it, they plotted to convince her.

Mengers threw a dinner party at her mansion at which Peters and Streisand were to meet producer Howard Rosenman, who had developed the script with Renee Missel. Mengers advised Rosenman to wear his hippest clothes (he chose a Ralph Lauren tweed jacket and white painter's pants) and to appeal to Streisand's serious side when pitching his film. As Gore Vidal, Paul Newman, Paul Schrader, and other guests chatted, Mengers steered Rosenman to Peters and Streisand.

Rosenman plugged *The Main Event,* but then Marshall Brickman, who had declined Rosenman's invitation to rewrite the script, told Barbra, "It's a piece of shit."

But Jon was undeterred. "He said, 'Oh, we're going to make this movie,' " Rosenman remembers. " 'It's going to be about me and Barbra.' And I kept hitting the *Swept Away* theme, saying, 'It's about a woman who has ownership of the man. . . . Capitalism and communism and Marxism—appealing to this feminist Hegelian side of her.' "

Streisand reluctantly came on board, appropriating, as usual, producer responsibilities for herself and Peters. Rosenman and Missel were relegated to executive producer credits and Rosenman had to fight for their compensation, practicing a form of Hollywood brinkmanship unusual for an unestablished talent. Rosenman's lawyer, Norman Garey, negotiated a $400,000 fee and five net points on their behalf.

But at a meeting to cement the deal, Peters informed Garey that Rosenman and Missel's fee and deal points were being halved. Garey called Rosenman and delivered the bad news. Rosenman went ballistic, and instructed Garey to "tell Mr. Jon Peters to take this phone, put it in some grease and shove it up his asshole."

Jon grabbed the phone. "You fucking cocksucker!" he bel-

55

lowed. "You are nothing, and I have given you a Barbra Streisand movie. What are you, out of your fucking mind?"

"Let me tell you something," screamed Rosenman. "You graduated from the Valley school of hair design, and I graduated summa cum laude! I have an education!"

In his fury, Rosenman told Peters that he was upping the ante: He demanded another $100,000 and an additional two and a half deal points for himself and Missel. Furthermore, if he didn't get a check for $50,000 by the close of that business day, he would take his project and go home. Rosenman says he felt confident that Jon and Barbra would capitulate because he knew that Streisand's production company had already shelled out $1 million to secure Ryan O'Neal as her co-star.

The $50,000 check arrived before evening. The biggest female star in Hollywood had caved in to a young, unproven producer with a fearsome temper—and the nerve to risk everything. Perhaps Streisand and Peters had given in because it had been difficult to get O'Neal to commit to *The Main Event.* O'Neal and Streisand had carried on an affair while making *What's Up, Doc?,* and he reportedly still carried a torch for her. She wanted him, too—but only as a co-star. Recognizing the leverage he had, O'Neal had insisted on a little ritual before he signed to do *The Main Event.*

"I will only do this movie if you will cut my hair," he told Peters. A messenger was sent to Jon's house to retrieve his gold scissors in their black case. O'Neal showed up at the JPO office and was ushered out onto the patio. The actor took his shirt off, and a humbled Peters gave him a trim.

Critics maligned *The Main Event,* but that didn't stop it from being a solid hit when it opened in late June 1979, pulling in $54 million at the box office. That summer, discogoers heard Streisand belting "Extra, extra, I'm in love . . ." on the 12-inch dance track made for clubs—a track that Peters virtually coerced her to record.

Streisand never liked *The Main Event* or its soundtrack, and told Jon that she would not be making any more dumb comedies in the future.

56   IN FEBRUARY 1978, five top executives from United Artists dramatically resigned. At the time UA was a thriving film financing and distribution company, having racked up such recent Oscar-

winning hits as *One Flew Over the Cuckoo's Nest* and *Rocky*. But the company had been acquired by Transamerica, one of many corporations that would wade into the Hollywood waters only to find itself out of its depth.

The United Artists executives—Arthur Krim, Robert Benjamin, Eric Pleskow, Mike Medavoy, and William Bernstein—launched Orion, a joint venture with Warner Bros. Eager to get their mini-studio up and running, the partners began signing up talent. John Travolta, Jon Voight, Burt Reynolds, and Peter Sellers all signed non-exclusive deals to make films.

On April 4, 1978, Jon Peters signed an exclusive three-year pact to make pictures for Orion. Short of cash, Jon asked his agent, Jeff Berg of International Creative Management, if he would accept a slightly used red Jeep in lieu of his fee for negotiating the deal. Berg, seeking to build a relationship with this up-and-comer, accepted.

The deal had evolved from Peters and Streisand's growing friendship with Mike Medavoy and his wife, Marcia. The mutual advantages of their association were obvious. Medavoy wanted to rope Streisand into the Orion family and Peters's deal was designed to include at least one Streisand picture. And Orion fervently hoped Peters would develop other properties—prefererably commercial musicals—in which Streisand would star.

For Peters, the Orion deal meant he could continue the working relationship he had developed with the Warner Bros. marketing team during the launch of *A Star Is Born*. And he felt he could pick up some tricks of the trade from Medavoy, a former agent who was not strong on script development but who cultivated good talent relationships. "Mike was one of the few people Jon would listen to," remembers Hillary Ripps, Jon's personal assistant at the time. "Jon sometimes felt he knew it all, but he wasn't stupid. He knew he could learn from Medavoy."

In 1979 Peters acquired a new key employee with a Medavoy connection: He lured Mark Canton, formerly an executive assistant to Medavoy at United Artists, away from a job as a junior executive at MGM. Peters had met Canton when the two collaborated on developing a remake of the old MGM drama *The Women*, in which Streisand would co-star with Faye Dunaway; the film was never made.

An ingratiating thirty-year-old whose father had been a well-known Hollywood publicist, Canton was ambitious to run a studio one day. At the age of eight he had staged Academy Award ceremonies in which his younger brother Neil would pretend to hand him an Oscar and Mark would make an acceptance speech.

Jon could see that Canton was both eager to please and easily dominated. When he invited Canton to the Ranch for lunch and offered him a vice president's job with emphasis on developing material, Canton hesitated. He would have to take a pay cut. But he knew he needed production experience, and he accepted.

At his new job at JPO, Canton was easily overwhelmed. If Pleskow or Medavoy or agents such as Mike Ovitz called, he became tremulous with anxiety. "Afterwards there would be five minutes of 'How do you think I did?' " says a co-worker.

Jon's first Orion release, *Die Laughing,* was a witless comedy starring seventies teen heartthrob Robby Benson. Benson was co-producer, and he also wrote and sang five songs for the film. Banking that Benson's good looks would lure young fans, Jon bought into the production and assigned Canton to oversee the San Francisco shoot as associate producer. Benson proved to have little comic and even less musical talent, and the result was what *Los Angeles* magazine called "a sour little rat pellet of a film." Released in March 1980, *Die Laughing* died at the box office overnight.

But Jon would redeem himself in a matter of months. That summer, after just over two years of existence, Orion sorely needed a hit. The company had released a number of prestige films that had not performed well at the box office, including *The Great Santini* and *A Little Romance.* Orion's only cash cow had been Blake Edwards's *10,* the sex farce starring Dudley Moore and Bo Derek. (The film's success surprised the Orion executives, who had agreed to make it only as a way of getting the director's next film, *The Ferret.*)

Peters came to the rescue with a sophomoric mainstream comedy, *Caddyshack.* A loose, goofy *Animal House* on the links, *Caddyshack* featured Michael O'Keefe surrounded by a wacky clutch of comedic talent, including Rodney Dangerfield, Chevy Chase, and Bill Murray. It was writer Harold Ramis's first time out as a director. Ramis co-wrote the script with Brian Doyle-

Murray and the late, troubled Doug Kenney, who had a serious cocaine habit.

*Caddyshack*'s blazing young talents enjoyed working in a spontaneous—and occasionally drug-induced—state. Dangerfield's vulgar, Borscht Belt style provided a counterpoint to the young hipsters surrounding him. The shoot was like a $6 million, eleven-week cruise with a shipload of unruly teenage boys. The cast and crew took over a motel in Fort Lauderdale, Florida, near the Rolling Hills golf course and clubhouse, which served as the film's fictitious country club. Debauchery reigned every night.

Peters, understanding that the best way to manage this lawless bunch was to leave them alone, visited the set only a few times. "Jon's number-one contribution to the project—and I'm willing to bet this is on any project—is incredible enthusiasm and a belief that he's on the right team, that whoever he's got is a genius," Ramis says. "And that anything can be done. He helped me believe that. I really borrowed confidence from him."

The first test screenings made it clear that *Caddyshack* needed extensive post-production work. A gopher that torments the groundskeeper played by Bill Murray had become a star in his own right and Jon was determined to enhance the rodent's presence with special effects. He convinced Orion, although it was seriously strapped for cash, to cough up an additional $500,000 to allow him to hire more editors and special-effects wizard John Dykstra. With gopher puppets and opticals, Dykstra created scenes of the gopher underground, added lighting effects, and blew up the golf course when Murray's character resorts to dynamite to remedy the gopher infestation.

For the *Caddyshack* poster Peters was not pleased with the Norman Rockwellian sketches the studio came up with, which he thought were boring. He made his feelings known to the Warner Bros. marketing team. "I want to see the gopher! I want to see the gopher!" Jon insisted.

Ramis, Chase, and Murray had appropriated Peters's office as their hangout during the film. "Why don't you guys design a poster?" Jon suggested as the deadline loomed. He gave them copies of the one-sheet sketches, a still of the gopher, scissors, and glue, creating a little playground. They fell upon the floor like kids, giggling and cutting and pasting.

"I said, 'What if we take the four guys and put them in the golf holes?' " Ramis recalls. " 'And take this gopher that's way out of scale and have it hovering over the back of the country club—you know, like a monster?' "

When they were finished, Jon took their creation to Medavoy's office. "Look, here's the poster," he said, holding it triumphantly aloft. The final one-sheet was essentially what Ramis and his rogue collaborators designed in fifteen minutes on the floor of Jon's office.

After *Caddyshack* premiered at Radio City in July 1980, good news rolled in: It was another critic-proof hit. David Denby of *New York,* one of the kinder critics, called the film "a perfectly amiable mess." *Caddyshack* was Orion's saving grace, pulling in $45 million.

# 6

## A SURVIVOR IS BORN

IT WAS THE FINAL WEEK of summer camp, 1954, and twelve-year-old Peter Guber badly wanted to win the badminton tournament. A talkative boy of medium build with dark, curly hair, Peter was an overnighter at Camp Brunonia for Boys, a posh, predominantly Jewish camp in Maine.

Nestled in piney woods on a lake, Brunonia was in most ways a pleasant place for a boy from the Boston suburbs to pass a steamy August. But for Peter, there was one problem: He felt he had never emerged from the shadows of his older brothers Charlie and Mike, who were outstanding Brunonians, excelling at athletics. He was tired of being seen as a little squirt.

"Peter, from the time he was a very little boy, was in extreme competition with his brothers," recalls Jerry Isenberg, a Hollywood television producer and hometown friend of Peter's, and his campmate at Brunonia. "Charlie and Mike Guber were seven and ten years older than Peter. They were big people around the camp, and Peter was just the kid."

As it turned out, the badminton court would not be the arena in which Peter prevailed. "I did beat Peter in the finals of the tournament," says Isenberg. "I don't think he was so happy. He gets frustrated with himself . . . he was very competitive, even then." The aggressiveness and will to win that Guber displayed early in life, adds Isenberg, were qualities that would later help him profit spectacularly as a Hollywood mogul. "It's the same person. . . . It's almost like he's a perfect animal designed for this business."

HOWARD PETER GUBER was born on March 1, 1942, in Richardson House, Boston, Massachusetts. His birth certificate lists his

61

father Samuel's occupation as metal broker; Sam Guber owned a successful junk business in Somerville, a short commute from his home in the leafy town of Newton, the "garden suburb" of Boston. When Samuel married the former Ruth Anshen in 1929, his bride's father—a contractor—built the couple a house at 407 Ward Street. They raised their three sons in this two-story, neo-Tudor home, the very picture of cozy middle-class comfort.

"Peter was a very popular kid, very outgoing," recalls Deborah Gilman, who lived with her husband Saul across Ward Street, and who watched the Guber boys grow up. Her son Roger remembers being invited as a young boy by Peter into the Guber kitchen, where Peter recommended that he read *Gulliver's Travels*. Peter's childhood acquaintances invariably describe him as bright, fidgety, and loquacious. "He had terrific energy, talked very fast," says Isenberg. "He was a very smart, very wired kid."

The Gubers were a close family with a strong work ethic, respected in the community. The three brothers walked a few blocks up gently sloping Ward Street and took a left onto Fellsmere to attend the John Ward Elementary School. When they were older, they took the bus to sprawling Newton North High School, "home of the Tigers," known for its powerhouse football teams and high academic standards. Peter learned to play a fierce tennis game at the Pine Brook Country Club, where the Gubers spent their leisure hours.

In the fall of 1960 Peter enrolled in Syracuse University in upstate New York. A huge campus of thirteen thousand students four hours north of New York City, Syracuse had earned a reputation as a rah-rah football and party school. It also attracted arty types such as underground musician Lou Reed and future film director Peter Hyams (*The Presidio*), both of whom were on campus at the same time as Guber.

In college Peter set his life course on a conventional path, enrolling in a pre-law curriculum. Ambitious and hardworking, he cut a straight figure in his Weejuns and chinos and bulky sweaters. When he took a girl out on a date, he preferred an evening of bowling to going to the movies. He drove a stick-shift Corvair, a source of great pride.

Peter stayed in top physical shape by playing intramural football. "He was sort of a madman on the field," recalls a fraternity brother. "He wasn't graceful or talented, but he was powerful."

He was rushed by Zeta Beta Tau (ZBT), nicknamed "Zillions Billions Trillions" because it had so many wealthy members. The fraternity needed smart, presentable pledges and Peter Guber filled the bill. He was good-looking and friendly, although some found him pushy. In certain circles, he was the butt of jokes. He had an annoying habit of putting his face too close to people when he talked to them. "We called him Peter Guber Peter Guber," recalls classmate Neil Bief. "He always said everything twice."

Another classmate remembers Peter as fretful about his future and constantly measuring himself against others. "I couldn't get Peter out of my room at three o'clock in the morning," he says. "We'd be kind of talking and talking and I'd be doing my art projects, color and design projects. And he'd be hanging over my shoulder, saying over and over, 'God, I wish I could be creative, I wanna be creative, I gotta be creative, but I can't! I can't! I've gotta be a lawyer!' He kept repeating it; it was a constant theme, he'd bring it up all the time. It's the main thing I remember about him, this big hole he had inside himself."

A female Syracuse acquaintance recalls Guber telling her that he wanted to get both a law degree and a medical degree. When she asked him why, he replied, "If doctors make a lot of money and lawyers make a lot of money, imagine what you'd make if you were both!"

His likely-to-succeed drive enhanced Guber's attractiveness to the girls at Iota Alpha Pi (IAP), the sister sorority to ZBT, known for counting the campus's wealthiest and prettiest Jewish girls among its members. As a freshman, Lynda Gellis, the daughter of Brooklyn kosher meats magnate Isaac Gellis, was already the self-styled queen of IAP. Cute and petite, she had a teased red flip hairdo and heavy Brooklyn accent. An education major, she was far more socially than intellectually ambitious. Regarded as a "catch" because of her family's fortune, she was expected to marry well. Lynda began dating Peter Guber, then a sophomore, a young man on a fast track to a prosperous future.

"They were perfect for each other," recalls one of her sorority sisters, who observed their courtship. "I can remember the beginning of civil rights stirrings at Syracuse, and Lynda was not an activist. Peter's first interest was Peter and Lynda's first interest was Lynda. I don't think Lynda really had a career in mind. It was the old thing—you go to college and get your m-r-s degree. That was the mentality."

After spending his junior year abroad on Syracuse's Florence campus, Peter become more seriously involved with Lynda as a senior. That summer they worked as counselors at Camp Tagola in the Catskills. "They were sweethearts, they came together as a package," recalls Sylvia Tucker, then the camp's manager. The couple made a few hundred dollars for the summer plus tips from the parents. "Peter was a very aggressive young man," says Tucker. "He would get the boys to do things, clean up their bunks."

When Peter Guber married Lynda Gellis in a lavish New York City wedding in 1965, he forged an alliance that enhanced his prospects. "Marrying Lynda was an elevation of Peter's status," says a friend who has known them for twenty years. Lynda's confident, forceful personality balanced Peter's anxious nature; she would be a strong ally and confidante as he negotiated the rough-and-tumble business world. "Lynda was the motivator, the driver," says the longtime friend. "In another age, Lynda Guber would have made it on her own, but she came from an era when women weren't pursuing careers."

The couple settled into a New York City apartment, the Gellis family helping financially while Peter attended New York University law school by day and studied toward a master's degree in business administration at night. Their first daughter, Jodi, was born in 1968.

As he was finishing law school, Guber considered becoming a Wall Street lawyer, a congressional aide, or a judge's clerk. But as he interviewed with New York and Washington law firms, he was encouraged by the NYU business school to meet with corporate recruiters as well. Three companies were conducting interviews: a lumber firm, a toothpaste manufacturer, and Columbia Pictures. Guber soon found himself heading up to the corporate headquarters of Columbia Pictures Industries at 711 Fifth Avenue for lunch with the motion picture studio's head, Stanley Schneider.

Peter had no particular interest in film nor any strong attraction to the glamour of Hollywood. But he did have a fascination with media technology. During graduate school he had traveled to Japan and on a tour of an electronics firm he had viewed a protoype for a video-cassette player. "I went into this room and there was this box," he said later. "A guy put up a screen, connected a wire from the box to the screen and all of a sudden there was *West Side Story*. I couldn't believe it. I even stood up and waved my arms in the air so I could expose the hidden projector. I came back to school totally excited and no one would believe me."

To Guber's professed astonishment, Columbia was keen to recruit him. He was flown to Los Angeles to meet West Coast studio executives. The company was willing to pay off $29,000 he owed in student loans and offered him a salary of $450 a week, three times the highest bid he was getting from law firms. Weary of the cold weather in the Northeast, Peter liked the idea of living in California sunshine.

Guber signed on to work as an assistant and management trainee at Columbia Pictures, the film division of Columbia Pictures Industries. He was given a parking space at the studio's Hollywood lot on Gower Street and Sunset Boulevard, and moved his family into a rented house in the Hollywood Hills.

# 7

## COLUMBIA, THE FIRST TIME

PETER GUBER arrived in Hollywood in 1968. He dedicated the next eight years to maneuvering his way up the executive ladder at Columbia Pictures. This time of profound social and political change was punctuated by several watershed events: the assassinations of Martin Luther King, Jr., and Robert Kennedy; Woodstock; the shooting of students at Kent State; campus protests over the Vietnam War and the bombing of Cambodia; the Watergate break-in and the downfall of a president.

It was a troubled time for Hollywood, too. The movie industry struggled to adapt to the shifting Zeitgeist and the tastes of the new youth market. As the sixties ended, Hollywood was in an economic slump caused partly by what could be called *Sound of Music* fever. Hoping for more mega-hits like Julie Andrews's 1965 classic, the studios were spending—and losing—fortunes on overblown, outdated musicals such as *Hello, Dolly!* and *Paint Your Wagon.*

Columbia was faring better than many of its competitors. The studio won thirty-five Academy Awards in the sixties with a prestigious roster of hits, including *Lawrence of Arabia* ('62), *Dr. Strangelove (or: How I Learned to Stop Worrying and Love the Bomb)* ('64), *Cat Ballou* ('65), and *Guess Who's Coming to Dinner* ('67). Having opened a production office in London in 1965, Columbia was well served by British filmmakers who crafted *A Man for All Seasons* ('66), *Georgy Girl* ('66), *To Sir with Love* ('67), and *Oliver!* ('68).

When Guber arrived, it looked as if Columbia might have

66

discovered the knack of pleasing both older and younger audiences. In 1968, it scored a blockbuster with the musical *Funny Girl,* Streisand's film debut. The folks who adored it would hardly pay to watch a bunch of pot-smoking bikers search for the real America—but another crowd made *Easy Rider* an unexpected hit for Columbia in 1969.

Columbia Pictures had lowly origins but it always managed to make pictures that transcended its humble beginnings. The studio had been co-founded by Harry Cohn and his brother Jack in 1924. In the decades preceding World War II, each of the major studios manifested a distinct personality that reflected the taste of its founder. MGM made glossy star-driven musicals such as *The Wizard of Oz;* Fox favored highbrow literary fare, including *Jane Eyre* and *The Grapes of Wrath;* Warner excelled at socially conscious films and gangster pictures; Paramount was identified with Mae West and W. C. Fields.

Harry Cohn had been dubbed "His Crudeness" by Frank Capra, whose films boosted Columbia's status and earned it a slew of Academy Awards. Cohn was paradoxically both vulgar and discerning, and Columbia cranked out films from schlock to classics. It never boasted a stable of glittering stars, although Rita Hayworth and Glenn Ford made several pictures there. Disparaged as "the germ of the ocean," Columbia also gave the world *It Happened One Night* ('34), *Mr. Smith Goes to Washington* ('39), and *From Here to Eternity* ('53). It was home to the Three Stooges.

The lady with the torch was a fittingly enigmatic symbol for Columbia. She could be a madonna or a harlot. Certainly she had been born in tawdry circumstances, in the heart of Poverty Row, a strip of B-movie studios that lined Sunset Boulevard between Beachwood Canyon and Gower Street. Columbia made its home there until 1972, when it relocated to the Burbank lot in a co-venture with Warner Bros.

In the fifties, Columbia had forged relationships with powerful independent producers such as Sam Spiegel, who was responsible for *On the Waterfront* ('54) and *The Bridge on the River Kwai* ('57), and Stanley Kramer, who made *The Caine Mutiny* ('54). In the sixties, Otto Preminger, Sidney Lumet, Arthur Penn, Ted Kotcheff, Fred Zinnemann, Sydney Pollack, David Lean, and William Wyler all made movies for Columbia. By the end of the decade, when Peter Guber arrived, all of this was

67

fading. Despite the studio's success in the late sixties, the venerable producers and directors were aging.

Guber soon learned one of Hollywood's eternal lessons: Nobody can predict with certainty which films will succeed. Salesmanship—the ability to convince people that one understands what ingredients combine to make hit movies—is a supreme advantage. Guber knew he was a fast talker. "He can sell anything to anybody," says *Forrest Gump* co-producer Steve Tisch, who was Guber's assistant in the early seventies at Columbia. "It's like the classic line, 'If you don't need a new television set, don't talk to Peter Guber. He'll sell you one.' "

Hollywood has always attracted driven, narcissistic young men. Eccentricity and excess—even dishonest or abusive behavior—are tolerated as long as profits result. Budd Schulberg depicted the prototypical young Hollywood hustler in his 1941 novel *What Makes Sammy Run?* Psychoanalyst Franz Alexander described Schulberg's character of Sammy Glick, in his book *The Age of Unreason,* as a "ruthless careerist, obsessed by the one idea of self-promotion." As a junior executive at Columbia, Guber approached Sammy's level of obsessive competitiveness.

He also displayed tendencies that would become more pronounced as his career matured. He was brilliant, manipulative, seductive, and virtually without close friends. Chronically anxious, he sought solace in New Age pursuits. He craved respectability, grabbing credit for success and fleeing from failure. Many of these traits are common in Hollywood, but Guber took them to the outer limits.

Above all, Guber was preoccupied with acquiring wealth. In an industry where greed is not unusual, his determination to squeeze every nickel for himself out of every deal was striking. "I was finding my way around a giant toy store," Guber said about his first days at Columbia. "I thought everyone was a genius. The whole profit motive, the way they saw the marketplace—everything. Of course, after six months I thought everyone was a fool."

From the first day he reported for duty to the stucco executive building on the Gower lot, Guber elicited a mixture of contempt and grudging admiration. He threw himself into his job as assistant to Jerry Tokofsky, a former producer who was head of the creative affairs department. Creative affairs was responsible for evaluating scripts and overseeing actors, directors, and producers working on the lot.

"Peter was a little hyper," Tokofsky recalls. "What was great is that, if I came into the office in the morning and I had twenty-two things I was thinking about, and wanted to explore them, I'd say, 'Hey, Peter, do this.' He'd go away and come back and they'd be done—and he'd take them one step further."

Guber's initiative and organizational skills were indeed impressive. Up until then, computers had been used only for the studio's payroll. He created computer files on working actors and writers, entering pertinent information regarding their credits, asking price, temperament, and more. He also pleased Tokofsky by drafting actors to tape-record summaries of scripts for his boss to listen to while driving to work.

One area in which Guber quickly carved out a niche was new entertainment technologies. Ever since his appetite had been whetted on his school trip to Japan, he had been fascinated by electronics. He was always running out to buy the latest gizmo on the market; a Columbia colleague recalls Guber excitedly inviting people into his office to see his first electronic calculator.

In 1969, Guber attended a reception given by the Sony Corporation at the Beverly Hills Hotel. Sony was demonstrating its new consumer video-cassette machine, which utilized a three-quarter-inch tape like that used by television stations. Guber was starry-eyed. "I have to write about this!" he cried. Dashing back to the office, he called Paul Schrader, who was at the time editing a small film journal called *Cinema*. Guber feverishly wrote an eleven-page special supplement for the magazine entitled *The New Ballgame*.

*The New Ballgame/The Cartridge Revolution* is a 15,000-word prediction of future shock, an analysis of how home video would transform American business, culture, and lifestyles. "This revolution will assuredly occur," Guber wrote, hinting at the information superhighway to come two decades later. "The impending . . . revolution will have an enormous impact on the motion picture industry, as well as every other American institution: music, theater, publishing, politics, sex, journalism, religion, and big business. Financial empires will rise and fall; the 'home entertainment center' will become the backbone of the national economy."

Guber asserted that the video industry would have to come up with a standard tape format. He could not have foreseen

69

that Sony would fight an expensive, humiliating, and ultimately futile battle to ensure that its Betamax system would set that standard, but Guber did observe that "Sony has no strategy towards software programming for its cassettes." And he anticipated the buzzword of the nineties—"synergy"—by pointing out CBS/Motorola's advantage in being able to exploit a television library, publishing house, and record company through home video.

Speculating that home video would threaten theatrical exhibition, Guber wrote that "the only advantage the exhibitor will have is the social experience." Theaters, therefore, should offer patrons more attractions, such as restaurants and bars, and experiment with innovations in projection and sound. "The neighborhood house as we know it will likely be extinct," he predicted.

He was prescient on several points: that weaker films would soon not be released theatrically but would comprise a straight-to-video market; that cassettes on sports, education, and home repair would enter the marketplace; that film libraries would be exploited in new formats and thus rise in value.

Guber also envisioned that the new technologies would create a "great new pornographic market." Here he let his imagination run wild: "One can make their own home movies, tapes and films as well as find distribution for them. Thus home nudies with neighborhood actors and actresses are a certainty."

*The New Ballgame* created a stir in Hollywood and even in New York. "We sent 25,000 reprints to Wall Street," Schrader remembers. The article represented Guber's statement of intent: He planned to help foment the high-tech revolution, to be at the center of the new world of entertainment. "A new industry is being born," he wrote, "and I want to help it become something more than a compendium of all the other mistakes this business has made."

DESPITE THE BUZZ over *The New Ballgame,* Guber was still just a flunky. Producer Ray Stark, who had been in post-production on *Funny Girl* when Guber started at the studio, called the eager newcomer "the kid." Stark was one of the most feared men in Hollywood, a behind-the-scenes godfather who demanded fealty and ruthlessly destroyed his enemies. He had been wheeling and dealing in Hollywood for years, first as an agent to such stars as Ava Gardner and Kirk Douglas, then as founder of the Seven Arts Company. In 1967 Stark had established his independent production company, Rastar, at Columbia.

Stark consolidated power by acting as a mentor to younger men, forging surrogate father-son relationships. Guber shined up to him and studied the way the producer dealt firmly with the high-strung Streisand, how he maximized his power by using it sparingly. Guber filed away lessons on bending others to one's will. "He was the best single producer and showman I met—old-fashioned Hollywood panache," Guber said of Stark. "And he was Machiavelli. He understood the workings and machinations of management, of creative talent, of directors, producers, and stars."

Guber understood that he stood to gain by standing in the aura of the master manipulator. "He gave me power by association," he said. "I became one of the fair-haired boys of the business through him. He taught me, too, about the impermanence of executives, and the fact that although they are impermanent, they make permanent decisions."

That impermanence was soon driven home. Before Guber had been at Columbia a year, Tokofsky was dismissed. "Bills for his expenses, flowers, massages, and girls were higher than the cost of making pictures," says Robert Lovenheim, then a junior executive with Guber at the studio. With his boss disgraced, Guber feared that he too would be tarnished. Tokofsky's successor, Gerry Ayres, was no fan of Guber. Eventually Guber was moved to business affairs as assistant to the head of that department, Chuck Fries.

In business affairs, the domain of contracts and legal documents, Guber's skill as a notetaker and listmaker came to the fore. Lovenheim notes that Guber already had picked up tricks that would serve him later: "Always seem important, and make yourself look good—even though he was just the assistant who came back and typed up the deal memo."

Guber swiftly catapulted himself out of the assistants' ghetto. In a round of corporate warfare, both Ayres and Fries were pushed out. "Who did this leave?" asks Lovenheim rhetorically. "The assistant! Peter, in a characteristically brilliant move, flew to New York on his own dime—as he made clear." There he

71

convinced Columbia motion picture chief Stanley Schneider to promote him. "Stanley did it; he wanted someone who wasn't going to give him any trouble," says Lovenheim.

Guber, now in charge of creative affairs, adopted a lifestyle befitting a rising young executive. He drove a candy-apple-red Corvette. He moved his family out of the rented house in Hollywood west to chic Bel Air, purchasing a ranch-style house on Brownwood Place for $79,000 in 1969. His second daughter, Elizabeth, was born in 1972. The same year, he headed the California Chapter of Young Republicans for Nixon.

With his bourgeois values, conservative politics, and natty sweater collection, Guber was an aberration. "He was Mr. Straight, Mr. Uptight," says one former Columbia colleague. Clouds of marijuana smoke wafted through Hollywood's executive suites, but Guber was not interested in getting high. He had trouble relating to hip young filmmakers like director Bob Rafelson, who made *Five Easy Pieces*.

In style, Guber foreshadowed the yuppie corporate warriors of the eighties. "What astounded me was that Peter already had kids, a wife, and a house in Bel Air," Lovenheim says. "In those days we were just experiencing the inflation of the Vietnam War. Peter was talking about how to refinance his house and I didn't even know anyone else who had a mortgage."

The town may have been awash in peace protests and free love, but the Hollywood social scene remained what it has ever been: a lubricant to business. Guber saw that the power he craved required social success. This was a disquieting thought: for all his gabbiness, Guber was uneasy with people. Lynda, more gregarious and more politically liberal than her husband, set about entertaining with gusto. As keen to conquer the Hollywood *beau monde* as her husband, she specialized in throwing "theme" parties, such as a Moroccan evening.

"I had to find something with which to befriend people," Guber said. "Everything was business. As I moved up in the business, the economic ladder, so the social ladder expanded, too." Guber called it "a despicable experience." But it didn't slow him down.

72  IN THE EARLY SEVENTIES, Columbia's fortunes had taken a turn for the worse. After posting record profits of $21 million in 1968 on $243 million in revenues, the company lost $40 million

in 1971. Following a slight upturn in 1972, it lost $65 million again in 1973 and teetered on the verge of bankruptcy.

Some of these woes were caused by factors beyond the studio's control: an overall decline in movie attendance; high interest rates; decreased fees for selling feature films to television; and competition from made-for-TV movies. But these also were the waning days of the Columbia patriarchy established by Harry Cohn. Abraham Schneider was chairman of the board and CEO of Columbia Pictures Industries. Schneider's brother-in-law, Leo Jaffe, was president. Both had started as accountants at the studio in the twenties and thirties. The motion picture division was run out of corporate headquarters in New York by Abe's son, Stanley Schneider.

Stanley Schneider kept promoting Guber. After his short stint as vice president of business affairs, Guber was named first to head of American production, then vice president of worldwide production. But Guber's advancements didn't give him much authority. "Stanley Schneider was running the company from New York, and he wanted no interference," Lovenheim says. "Peter had the [production head] title, he had Stanley's ear—and no power. Peter had a four-to-one shot of convincing Stanley of anything."

The problem, Lovenheim laments, was that "Stanley didn't have a creative bone in his body." A stodgy corporate functionary, Schneider had no vision for guiding the company into a new cultural and economic era. He'd ignore recommendations from West Coast executives and make movie deals with old cronies over dinner. "We'd read in the trades that we had a three-picture deal with some horrible outfit," Lovenheim remembers.

The graybeard filmmakers who got Schneider's blessing cranked out flop after flop. "They left behind a string of movies like *Hello, Dolly!, Goodbye Money!*" lamented Guber. "They were still in the mix long after they had been fashionable." One of these was the dud musical *1776* ('72), Jack Warner's adaptation of the Broadway show about the American colonies' declaration of independence from Great Britain. Another was *Lost Horizon* ('73), outrageously expensive for the times with a budget of $7 million, an excruciating remake of Frank Capra's utopian classic. Its characters, including Liv Ullmann and John Gielgud, burst painfully into song once they reached Shangri-la. "The director's wheelchair needs oiling," noted critic Pauline Kael.

73

To cut costs, Leo Jaffe had slashed overhead and dismissed some three hundred staffers in 1971, and top management took pay cuts. Columbia announced that it was selling the four-teen-acre Gower lot in Hollywood to relocate to Burbank, where it would share a lot with Warner Bros. The co-venture was the first time two major studios shared facilities and it would save Columbia money while giving it more space: The Burbank lot had some twenty-three soundstages, as opposed to Gower Street's fourteen.

While other employees were cleaning out their desks, Guber moved into an office in the new Columbia Pictures executive building, a two-story wood-and-glass structure built around an atrium on the eastern edge of the Burbank lot.

Although Guber attacked his new job with vigor, he was ham-pered at every turn. Determined to become a competitive buyer of literary properties, when he sniffed out what he thought was a hot book or script he still had no authority to write a check. He desperately wanted to bid on a project called *The Sting,* but Schneider refused to approve it. He was granted a degree of autonomy only with smaller pictures, and bought into some modestly profitable ones, like *The Lords of Flatbush* ('74) and *Aloha Bobby and Rose* ('75).

He pursued talent, too. He helped lure younger producers such as Larry Gordon and Irwin Winkler to the studio. When Guber heard that a young director had made an interesting TV movie for Universal, he instructed his assistant, Steve Tisch, to "call over to Universal and find a guy named Steven Spielberg." Tisch tracked down the twenty-two-year-old director of *Duel* and invited him over.

"When I was a kid starting out, trying to show my little seven-minute reel around town, Guber was a junior executive at Columbia," says Spielberg. "He was one of the only people in town that would look at it. And he let me hang out over there."

Later, Guber would describe himself as a bold and outspoken young upstart during this period of his life. "It was very difficult to deal with producers who had been in the business for ten, fifteen, thirty years," he said. "I was full of piss and vinegar, I said what I meant, and perhaps I wasn't diplomatic enough. That set a whole bunch of people off wrong."

But others viewed Guber as a maneuverer. Says Tisch, who worked for him from 1971 to 1974, "He was the kid, the golden

74

boy. As the head of the studio he didn't threaten the big old columns who supported Columbia Pictures. . . . He was deferential without being patronizing or condescending."

Guber's most inspired creation may have been his "directors' board." Behind his desk was a curtain that covered almost the entire wall. At the push of a button, the curtain drew back to reveal a six-by-eight board with a color-coded grid that displayed the working status of all the world's major film directors.

Tisch was the designated caretaker of the directors' board, and he updated it every Friday morning. By moving pushpins and wielding a little gun that stamped out names and titles on pieces of plastic, Tisch indicated which films were in production or preparing to shoot. Guber's colleagues were soon sneaking into his office to consult the board on which filmmakers were available.

Guber was not as orderly, however, in his interactions with people. "After a meeting with a writer or a director or an agent, Peter would dash off to another office—he had this to do, this set to visit," Tisch says. "And people would look at me and say: 'What was that? What happened in this meeting?' Peter could dazzle people. He was nonstop in terms of talking. He would just sort of leap up from the desk with a new idea and say, 'Let's do this, let's do that.' "

Many who were treated to Guber's enthusiasm never heard from him again. "People would be received with such exuberance that they'd walk away thinking they had a 'go' picture," says Peter Bart, who was then head of production at Paramount. "I'd say, 'Peter, half the people in Hollywood think they have a deal with you.' "

As the studio's financial health continued to decline, the rivalry among Columbia executives grew more intense. "People were rooting for each other's films to fail," Guber said. "There was a great deal of negative talk—backbiting and gossipmongering." Guber trusted no one. He did not forge the kind of enduring pragmatic personal loyalties that pass for friendship in Hollywood.

Bent on surpassing his competition—and with the energy and brainpower to do it—Guber was resented by his colleagues. But some were amused by his transparent self-seeking. "He would lean into you and say something that had the ring of insincerity to it, something flattering about how important you were to a project or something," says one executive. "It was

75

endearing in a way." Guber lacked the vengeful streak that drives many Hollywood players; he did not derive pleasure from inflicting pain. He simply wanted to finish first, and while he would do what had to be done, he also wanted people to think he was a nice guy.

In spite of his regular promotions, Guber was perpetually anxious, and he sometimes expressed that in ways his co-workers found bizarre. "The most vivid memory I have of Peter is of him coming into my office one evening," one recalls, "and I don't know what I was earning at the time, but he was making a lot more as head of production. And he was very worried about money. Maybe the stock market was falling or something, and he said, 'How am I going to feed my children?' He was white with panic—it was very strange. And I said, 'Peter, how can you say that?' Compared to us, he was making a lot—never mind the rest of the world. I said, 'What about all the children out there who really aren't being fed?' "

Guber's hyperactivity masked an insecurity which Lovenheim perceived as "fear of being broke, fear of not being accepted, fear that he's not really as cunning and cool and superbright as he thinks."

"For all his inner suffering, the narcissist has many traits that make for success in bureaucratic institutions," historian Christopher Lasch wrote in *The Culture of Narcissism*. Such institutions "put a premium on the manipulation of interpersonal relations, discourage the formation of deep personal attachments, and at the same time provide the narcissist with the approval he needs in order to validate his self-esteem. Although he may resort to therapies that promise to give meaning to life and to overcome his sense of emptiness, in his professional career the narcissist often enjoys considerable success."

Guber assuaged his feelings of worthlessness by pursuing New Age enthusiasms. Along with many of his Hollywood peers he was initiated into est, submitting to long days in hotel ballrooms without permission to use the bathroom. A kind of trendy California version of a Dale Carnegie course, est coated Western materialism with a veneer of Eastern spirituality. It promised to open the minds of devotees, who were told they deserved every gratification, including material success.

Guber got to be friends with est founder Werner Erhard,

and was soon parroting his jargon at Columbia. One colleague recalls Guber coming into his office after an est weekend. "He was very quiet, and his eyes weren't darting around the way they usually were. And he said very quietly, 'I want to work closely with you. I want us to be very open with each other.' " Guber's calm didn't last. Within a few days his colleagues found him as agitated as ever.

RAY STARK knew that something had to be done about Columbia, and that he was the man to do it. On May 6, 1973, the *Los Angeles Times* reported that the management-heavy, debt-ridden Columbia Pictures was ripe for a takeover. Stock was trading at $5 a share, down from $9 at the beginning of the year. With the studio's debt exceeding $160 million, the banks were threatening to force it to file for bankruptcy protection.

Stark staged a stunning coup by bringing in New York investment banker Herbert Allen to rescue the studio. New management was installed to Stark's specifications, including Allen & Co. executive Alan J. Hirschfield as president and chief executive of Columbia Pictures International, and former agent David Begelman as president of production.

Stark had finally toppled the dynasty that had held Columbia Pictures in its grip for fifty years and replaced it with a ruling family of his choosing. So stealthy were Stark's maneuvers that his name was scarcely mentioned in press reports of the management shuffle. But everyone in Hollywood knew that Stark was the architect of the deal. In Begelman's first year, Columbia declared a $50 million loss and its stock almost fell off the charts. But the studio was about to begin a dramatic recovery.

"When Herb Allen bought control of Columbia and Alan Hirschfield became CEO, they flew out to California," recalls Steve Tisch. "They asked Peter Guber to set up a meeting with the West Coast executives. The conference table was horseshoe-shaped, and Peter sat at the head of the table, opposite Hirschfield. And he asked that we go around the room and everybody introduce themselves and explain what their job is at the studio. When it got to my turn, I said, 'My name is Steve Tisch, and I come to the studio very, very early in the morning and I wind up Peter Guber.' "

As part of their mission to rehabilitate Columbia, Allen and Hirschfield spent several hours in Guber's office soliciting his opinion of all the projects originated by the old regime. "They're mostly dogs," Guber told them, startling his new bosses. He added that he thought only two of the films were worth making. One, he noted diplomatically, was a Ray Stark project. The other was *The Last Detail,* Hal Ashby's ribald sailor romp starring Jack Nicholson.

Guber has said that he was frank because he didn't care whether he kept his job. He was tired of Columbia and all its chaos, and he claimed to have other offers. Rumors around town had him jumping to Paramount. But Guber managed to impress the new bosses. When they cleaned house, Guber once again survived.

Begelman, the new studio chief, was a college dropout from the Bronx who dressed smartly and encouraged people to think he had a Yale degree. A savvy politician and deft handler of movie stars, Begelman and his partner Freddie Fields had previously owned one of the biggest talent agencies in town, CMA. Paul Newman, Barbra Streisand, and Steve McQueen were clients.

When Begelman moved into his plush new office in the Columbia executive building, one of his first moves was to call Peter Guber and Robert Littman—the only two production executives whose heads hadn't rolled—into his office. "There are only three people in this company that can make a decision on making a film, and they are sitting in this room," Begelman told them.

That number quickly dwindled, however. Littman didn't last long and he later acknowledged that he deserved to get sacked. "Peter used to work very, very hard," he recalls, "and I used to drink very, very hard." Guber was given the job of firing Littman, who appreciated the kindness he showed in delivering the bad news.

Begelman liked Guber, and valued his industriousness and intelligence. And Guber could be helpful in smoothing the transition from the previous regime. In August 1973, Begelman promoted Guber to vice president of worldwide production.

Hirschfield, the new chief executive, made clear that he would put a stop to out-of-control spending and fruitless deals. Rich contracts for producers were terminated. Stark, of course, had absolute immunity. In 1974, Columbia bought Rastar Productions, acquiring the rights to all of Ray Stark's films.

Meanwhile, Begelman focused on picking hits. In 1975, Columbia was on a roll with *Shampoo,* the Warren Beatty picture that Jon Peters later claimed was modeled on his life, and *Tommy,* The Who's rock musical. By the end of 1975 the studio, back from the dead, reported a $5.3 million profit.

Steven Spielberg's *Close Encounters of the Third Kind* was the biggest blockbuster of the Begelman era. The project came to the studio partly because producer Julia Phillips had a long-standing friendship with Begelman that had begun when he got her a job as an executive at First Artists. In her Hollywood memoir *You'll Never Eat Lunch in This Town Again,* Phillips recalled that Begelman instructed her to befriend Guber while making *Close Encounters.*

She arranged to meet Guber for lunch at the venerable Hollywood hangout Musso & Frank's Grill. At this meeting, Phillips observed one of Guber's curious traits: a habit of talking to women, even at business meetings, in the most graphic sexual terms. She recalled the conversation: " 'You know,' he says, 'if you put Chloraseptic on your cock you can stay hard all night.' Nice production meeting we're having here. The last thing I ever want to see is Peter Guber's penis, erect or not."

Later that day, Phillips posed with Spielberg for a *People* magazine spread. The magazine wanted to include a Columbia executive in some shots, so she phoned Guber. He arrived at the session almost before she could hang up the phone. "Boy, he came flying over in a hurry," Spielberg commented to Phillips. After this introduction, Phillips decided that she disliked Guber, and she told Begelman that he talked so fast that he must be on diet pills.

Guber had been telling friends for years that he was uncomfortable within Columbia's corporate structure. "After about three months, I knew I wanted to leave and produce motion pictures myself," he said. "But I hung in for eight more years." With Columbia back in the black, Guber now said he was getting restless again. If so, the timing was good because the new regime was beginning to sour on him.

Guber finally departed Columbia's executive ranks in 1975, telling everyone that it was his choice to leave. Begelman handed him a generous independent producer's deal. But the truth was that Begelman fired Guber. Guber may have been thinking about jumping—he maintained that posture throughout his career—but he was pushed.

"One of the myths Peter has spun is that he resigned from Columbia," says a former Columbia colleague. "As they started to get the company back on its feet, David could no longer handle the onslaught of agents, producers, and people in town who [thought they had a deal]. Peter would get on the phone and offer the same part to three different actors . . . and David tried to correct it with Peter several times. And Peter was in a massive denial about all of it."

"Peter asked me and my partner Harry Gittes to come to the Beverly Hills Hotel," recalls producer Don Devlin. "We went to see him, met him by the pool, and he said, 'They fired me! What am I gonna do? What am I gonna do?' We looked at him in amazement, and thought—how should we know? We weren't friends. We didn't socialize. He was like a frightened bunny."

GUBER LEFT COLUMBIA with an attractive résumé. By then he had already begun a career-long habit of handing out a curriculum vitae with a string of degrees after his name. In Hollywood, where moguls often lacked high school diplomas, Guber relished the cachet his higher education brought him. But he stretched the truth.

"Peter Guber is Vice-president of Columbia Pictures, holds B.A., S.S.P., LL.M., J.D., and M.B.A. degrees, and is a member of the New York and California bar associations. . . ." Or at least, so said the résumé that had been provided by the studio toward the end of his tenure there. In fact, Guber received his B.A. from Syracuse and two law degrees (J.D. and LL.M.) from NYU, but the others were tacked on for show. Guber claimed that the "S.S.P." was an arts degree he had received from the University of Florence. But Guber's Italian schooling consisted of his junior year at Syracuse's campus in Florence. He learned to speak passable Italian, but he received no degree.

NYU's archives indicate that Guber did not complete the credits to be awarded a Master's of Business Administration. Later he took some graduate courses at USC, but that institution's records also show that no degree was granted.

In crafting his image, Guber went to elaborate lengths in observance of his maxim "Perception is power." According to colleagues, a story circulated that he kept his own files on Columbia movies that were green-lit during his days at the studio. In each file he stashed two memos: one in which he recommended making the film; the other in which he cautioned against it. Once the picture opened, he discarded the "incorrect" version.

Guber's résumé further gave him credit for spearheading a number of prestige projects: "At the creative helm of Columbia, Guber originated and supervised the development and production of such films as *The Way We Were, Taxi Driver, Tommy, Shampoo,* and *The Last Detail.*"

Guber's claim to have "originated and supervised the development and production" of some of the most distinguished films Columbia made during his tenure far overstates his involvement. *The Way We Were* ('73), the romantic hit starring Barbra Streisand and Robert Redford, was a Ray Stark production and Stark wielded absolute authority over his films. Guber's job was to do what he was told. Columbia junior executive Roz Heller, whom Guber hired, persuaded David Begelman to green-light Martin Scorsese's *Taxi Driver.* Guber was assigned to oversee the production, but his authority was minimal. "I made *Taxi Driver* at Columbia and I was never involved with Peter," says its screenwriter, Paul Schrader. *Tommy* ('75) was a commercial hit for Columbia, but Guber's colleague Robert Littman was the executive who nurtured the film. And *Shampoo* ('75) was Begelman's baby all the way.

Of all the films listed, Guber could legitimately claim to have been a champion of *The Last Detail* ('73). At the first preview screening, Guber had nearly broken down in tears when the projector failed and half the recruited audience walked out. The movie earned Academy Award nominations for Jack Nicholson, Randy Quaid, and screenwriter Robert Towne. But generally, Guber was more a shepherd than a creator, or even an initiator, during his years at Columbia. He neither deserves credit for the studio's meager list of hits—nor blame for its disasters.

# 8

## PETER TAKES THE PLUNGE

No Hollywood tradition is more cherished than the golden parachute. Regardless of how poorly an executive has performed or how loathed he (or she) may be, if he is fired, custom dictates that the sting of his humiliation be salved by a generous compensation package and a flattering press release. With the approval of godfather Ray Stark, David Begelman handed Guber a three-year production deal with the studio and allowed Guber to say it was his choice. Only much later did Guber acknowledge: "I was run out."

In truth, Guber had been thinking about making a move for years. It galled him to see men who didn't seem that intelligent working less and earning more. He watched enviously as independent producers, including Stark, reaped big profits, glory, and power.

He had saved $19,000. With Columbia covering his overhead, he launched Peter Guber's FilmWorks. He set up shop in a two-story producers' building near the Hollywood Way entrance to the Burbank lot, which afforded him some much-desired distance from the Columbia executive building. Lynda decorated the office in shades of gray with pinstripe pillows that looked as if they were made out of the Cardin suits her husband wore.

Guber's first move was to pay $10,000 for the rights to the story of Billy Hayes, a young American he saw on the news who had escaped from a Turkish jail. He commissioned a book about Hayes's experience which he hoped eventually to adapt into a film. But first, sensitive to the talk that he had been pushed out of Columbia, Guber was determined to find a property he could get off the ground right away, "not only because my ego smarted at the thought of all the barracudas in the industry thinking the worst, but because without credibility I couldn't produce movies." Guber reasoned that he needed to acquire "a glossy, high-visibility property" that would give FilmWorks the image of power. "In Hollywood, as in other businesses, that image often *is* power," he said.

His next target was *The Deep,* Peter Benchley's first novel since *Jaws,* which Steven Spielberg had turned into the most successful motion picture of all time in the summer of 1975. Benchley had given *Jaws* producers Richard Zanuck and David Brown first crack. When Zanuck and Brown balked at Benchley's asking price of $1 million, Guber was ready to step in. The rookie producer persuaded Benchley's agents to give him a look at the 336-page manuscript.

The next day, Guber asked Begelman to purchase *The Deep* for him to produce. When his request was opposed by several Columbia executives, Guber let everyone know that Bantam had acquired the paperback rights for three quarters of a million dollars, and he circulated a list of competitors who were interested in acquiring the film rights. "After all, whatever you want looks that much better if someone else wants it too," he wrote later.

Hollywood producers are divided into two types: those driven by a passion for films and the filmmaking process, and those who view movies as product to be packaged and marketed. Guber placed himself squarely in the second category on his first film. "I wasn't crazy about the book," he admitted, "but I was crazy about the opportunity it presented. In the movie business, if you buy an important property with market awareness, that becomes a star of your film."

Guber's instinct in this instance was correct. The story of scuba-diving honeymooners in Bermuda who stumble on illegal drugs and Spanish treasure while exploring a shipwreck, *The Deep* wasn't strong on plot. But it had the makings of a titillating action picture, with deep-sea scenery, a menacing giant moray eel, and sadistic villains with a taste for voodoo. Guber cast Jacqueline Bisset, with her glorious appearance in a bathing suit foremost in his mind, as the heroine. Nick Nolte was signed to play her new husband, and Guber used all his

83

salesmanship to convince Robert Shaw—whose post-*Jaws* fee of $750,000 made him the most expensive actor in the cast—to portray a reclusive buried-treasure expert.

With big stars and a whopping budget of almost $9 million, *The Deep* would have been a highly ambitious first film had it been shot on land. But 40 percent of the action had to take place underwater and posed nightmarish logistical problems. Director Peter Yates insisted on filming on location rather than in a back-lot tank. The crew would be at the mercy of weather and the caprices of the sea. The action sequences, set in and around a shipwreck, required expensive special effects. After a month of filming in the British Virgin Islands, additional underwater sequences were to be shot in more controlled circumstances in Bermuda.

In July 1976, when Guber assembled his 100-person cast and crew at the luxurious Peter Island Yacht Club resort in the Virgin Islands, he was about to learn just what he did and didn't like about producing movies. He had enjoyed the brinkmanship of bidding for a hot literary property. Casting had been fun, too. But he would loathe the tedium, hazards, and physical hardships of production. He chronicled the ordeal in his book, *Inside "The Deep,"* "the true story of the greatest underwater adventure in the history of filmmaking by the man who produced the movie," as the cover line boasted. *Inside "The Deep"* is written in characteristic Guber style: upbeat, but with plenty of handwringing over every crisis.

"We have a long way to go and we're running horrendously behind schedule," Guber wrote at the conclusion of the first chapter. "But the excitement is overwhelming. . . . In spite of frequent attacks of panic, I am really up to my ears in making a major motion picture!"

The 151-day production was plagued by grim weather, jellyfish infestations, and island fever that was only partially relieved by drunken blow-outs. Cast and crew made a total of nearly nine thousand dives. Nolte learned diving quickly, then had a hair-raisingly close call when he ran out of air 80 feet down and had to make a fast return to the surface.

Bisset, terrified by the jellyfish and barracudas, took several weeks to gain the confidence to explore the deep without scrunching up her face on camera with anxiety. But when the first dailies were viewed, the transparency of her wet white

T-shirt gave everyone a boost. "All of us were ecstatic about this lovely and sensual sight," Guber wrote.

Although Bisset and Nolte were cool to each other at first, eventually they took to disappearing into her trailer together. This did not displease Guber, who was hoping for chemistry in the couple's love scenes.

While Guber would have preferred to stay dry—"I was deathly afraid of water," he admitted—Begelman ordered him to observe the underwater filming firsthand. After reluctantly taking diving lessons in the Peter Island Yacht Club pool, he donned mask, flippers, and tank, and took the plunge. One observer recalls that Guber was so nervous that he tried to talk while submerged, sending bubbles up to the surface. "I thought I was going to have a heart attack when I first dived," the producer said.

Guber was far more at home hyping his picture on dry land. He wrote postcards inviting journalists to view the underwater filming. Many were happy to travel to the Virgin Islands. "Guber insisted we take scuba-diving lessons," recalls Jim Watters, who wrote about the making of *The Deep* for the *Los Angeles Times*. Watters was treated to free meals, invited to dinner at Guber's bungalow, and upon returning to New York received a photograph of himself with the stars from Peter.

Guber oversaw every detail of the marketing campaign and release plan. Explaining the film's June 17, 1977, opening date to the *New York Times,* he said, "The maids and the blue-collars and much of industry get paid twice a month. They put their checks in the bank on the 15th, have them clear on the 16th and they're ready to spend by the 17th. That's why we opened *The Deep* on June 17."

Guber conceived the vertical poster design, tall and narrow, with bubbles rising and the logo on top, reminiscent of *Jaws*. He exploited images of Bisset in her revealing T-shirt to the maximum. Guber knew he had hit paydirt when he screened the first ten minutes of the film for exhibitors. "Well, the exhibitors went out of their minds when they saw Jackie," he exulted. "That T-shirt made me a rich man."

A paperback edition of *The Deep* was timed to coincide with the film's release. At a New York boat show, 700,000 visitors viewed the inboard-powered sport fishing boat used by Bisset and Nolte. There was a promotional tie-in with the Rolex Sub-

Mariner watch, the timepiece worn by the stars. Columbia's marketing manual even instructed exhibitors to encourage bartenders to concoct a rum drink called "The Deep": "It should be served in a tall vertical glass, simulating the tall, vertical ad look of *The Deep.*"

Columbia launched a "saturation buy" of television commercials while Shaw, Bisset, Benchley, and Yates worked the talk-show circuit. Meanwhile, a print advertising blitz hawked "an action-packed blockbuster which sprays excitement from the screen at gale-force velocity."

Guber drove *The Deep*'s marketing staff relentlessly. While conventional wisdom allows that publicity can only be as good as the product, publicist Sue Barton says Guber defied gravity. "I'd say Peter is better than his movies," she says. "He raises it to a whole new level."

All the effort made the film critic-proof. *New York Times* critic Vincent Canby called *The Deep* "even sillier than the Peter Benchley novel," while *Time* magazine pronounced it racist because all the bad guys were black. *New York* magazine's John Simon's intentions may have been scathing, but he surely helped entice viewers when he wrote that the first image on the screen was of Jacqueline Bisset's breasts—a "magnificently matched pair of collector's items." *The Deep* was a smash. In its three-day opening weekend it grossed more than $8 million, breaking industry records. *The Deep* became the second-highest-grossing film for 1977, behind *Star Wars*—a film that had redefined the term "blockbuster."

# 9

# CASABLANCA DAYS

Having proven himself with *The Deep,* Guber resolved never again to subject himself to the rigors of hands-on producing. He would function as an executive producer, doing what he liked and did best, packaging and promoting his films while hiring others to handle the filmmaking.

In fact, while *The Deep* was still in production Guber immersed himself in his preferred activity of dealmaking. On October 29, just days before his maiden project wrapped, Guber announced that he was merging FilmWorks with Neil Bogart's Casablanca Records to form Casablanca Record and FilmWorks. He would serve as chairman; Bogart would be chief executive officer. Both would share the title of president. Guber's three-year deal with Columbia Pictures would continue under the Casablanca banner.

From all appearances, Guber had chosen an ideal partner. Casablanca Records was a hot new label, the brainchild of one of the most flamboyant entrepreneurs in the music business. Neil Bogart, formerly Neil Bogatz, was a street kid from Brooklyn who made himself into a music mogul by inventing bubblegum music in the late sixties. A promoter above all else, he had managed and made millions for Buddah Records, scoring hits with the 1910 Fruitgum Co. and the Ohio Express ("Yummy, yummy, yummy, I've got love in my tummy").

Bubblegum died, and in 1974 Bogart made a deal with Warner Records chief Mo Ostin to start a new label called Casablanca. He based his company in L.A. and quickly signed the heavy-metal band Kiss, renowned for their sinister makeup and stage antics. But Kiss's satanic allure was lost on Warner Bros. and Bogart ended his relationship with the company the following year.

Casablanca would have gone bankrupt had Bogart not met Munich-based record producer Giorgio Moroder, who introduced him to a former gospel singer living in Germany named Donna Summer. Moroder produced a 12-inch, 17-minute dance single by Summer for Casablanca, the orgasmic "Love to Love You, Baby." It was a smash hit. By 1976, Bogart was riding the disco wave with Summer on his label. Other Casablanca acts were thriving, too, including the funk group Parliament.

But Bogart wanted more. Like many businessmen from a tough background, he craved legitimacy. In Hollywood, the top levels of the social ladder are dominated by movie moguls, and Bogart was determined to make his way onto the A-list. He was looking to buy himself a piece of the film industry—and it happened that his old friend Peter Guber was just then making a name for himself in Hollywood.

The link between Bogart and Guber was more complex than a simple friendship: It involved family. One of Lynda Guber's closest school chums from Brooklyn, Beth Weiss, had been Neil Bogart's first wife. The two couples had been friends when Peter was at NYU law and business schools and Neil was hustling his first million bucks in the record business. After Neil and Beth split up, Beth married Charlie Guber, Peter's older brother.

Some observers noted that in the early days of their company Bogart and Guber were like twins. Both grew up on the East Coast. They shared a natural ebullience and a carnival barker's flair for salesmanship. Their bond was warm and fraternal, fueled by ravenous ambition. Over dinner with their wives at a Chinese restaurant on Sunset Boulevard, Bogart and Guber shook hands and agreed to join forces.

With *The Deep* still in production and its box-office prospects uncertain, many people thought Guber got the better end of the deal in the Casablanca-FilmWorks merger. He was acquiring a substantial stake in a booming record company without bringing much to the table. Rob Cohen, who would soon produce *Thank God, It's Friday* for Casablanca, observes, "Peter traded something like five points in *The Deep* for 20 percent of Casablanca Records, which already had Donna Summer. What Neil wanted more than anything was to get into the movie business and he was willing to pay anything to get it."

In the mid-seventies Hollywood was just beginning to figure

out how to exploit tie-ins between movies, soundtracks, books, and other media. *A Star Is Born*'s marketing campaign had pioneered this kind of synergy. Guber had observed *Star*'s lessons closely. As soon as the ink was dry on the merger, he had Bogart put together the soundtrack for *The Deep*. Bogart talked Columbia into accepting Donna Summer as the title-track artist. With Bogart's expertise in radio advertising and distribution, Casablanca Records' $8.98 see-through blue vinyl soundtrack to *The Deep* went double platinum, selling 2 million copies.

In those first exhilarating days, Guber and Bogart spun grand ideas for marrying film and music and building an entertainment empire. They even talked about owning their own film studio one day. "It was like Camelot," recalls Joyce Bogart Trabulus, Bogart's second wife. "It was the best time of their lives."

There was some disharmony as Guber and Bogart combined their companies. Guber's FilmWorks staff reeled from the culture clash when they moved into Casablanca's offices on North Shelbourne Street in Hollywood. The music business, and especially Bogart, utilized far more outrageous marketing strategies than even Guber dared to dream up. Sue Barton, *The Deep*'s publicist, recalls, "I had a hard time when they couldn't figure out why I wouldn't send a dancing girl and balloons to see the *New York Times* film critic Vincent Canby. I would keep saying, 'You can't *do* that with film critics!' "

GUBER AND BOGART soon found themselves a new, deep-pocketed partner. Once again, Guber benefited from Bogart's allure. "We wanted to buy into a hot, creative record company," recalls Dr. Eckart Haas, a former executive with PolyGram International. "It was not Peter Guber who made us buy into the company—it was Neil Bogart."

At a glance, PolyGram seemed to be getting a good deal when it acquired nearly half of Casablanca Record and Film-Works in 1977. Casablanca reported gross revenues of $50 million and had sixteen gold and platinum albums. The price was never disclosed, but industry observers estimated that Poly-Gram paid between $10 and $15 million.

PolyGram and Casablanca made strange bedfellows indeed. Straitlaced and bureaucratic, PolyGram had been founded as a classical music label in the sixties. Jointly owned by Philips N.V. and Siemens, two industrial giants headquartered respectively in the Netherlands and Germany, PolyGram had begun moving aggressively into the American entertainment marketplace in the seventies. It acquired MGM and Verve Records and established the pop label Polydor. But its most critical move was buying the United Artists music distribution system, making it imperative that it invest heavily in pop to fill up the pipeline.

"They had a distribution system, and they wanted Neil to go for broke expanding it," says Joyce Bogart Trabulus. Bogart wasted no time spending PolyGram's cash. Casablanca relocated to three buildings at 8265 Sunset Boulevard and quickly grew from fourteen to two hundred employees. Casablanca executives were awarded such perks as Mercedes 450 SELs.

Bogart made sure that every visit to the Casablanca offices was a trip in itself. The parking lot, packed with Mercedes convertibles and Porsches, hinted at the extravagance within. In the lobby, visitors were greeted by stuffed camels, then led through rooms decorated in Moroccan style to look like Rick's Café in the movie *Casablanca*. There were palm trees, ceiling fans, Oriental rugs, and gold and platinum albums lining the walls. Donna Summer's wails pulsated throughout at maximum volume.

Even in a decade marked by excess, Casablanca was notorious. The host of the twenty-four-hour-a-day party was Neil Bogart, whose high spirits and paternal manner made him a beloved boss. Bogart openly indulged his sybaritic appetites on the premises and encouraged others to do the same. Casablancans didn't bother closing their office doors as they casually cut outsized lines of cocaine on their desktops.

Jeff Wald, Donna Summer's manager, kept an office at Casablanca. He and Bogart relished the fact that a couple of former New York street punks were now driving to work in Rolls-Royces: Wald's license plate read PS 79 BRONX; Bogart's PS 80 BRONX. "We had this interior decorator spending a million dollars on furniture," says Wald. "You walked into Casablanca and the size of the speakers just assaulted your senses, and there was cocaine on people's desks, and getting loaded. And by the time we got down to business, it was almost irrelevant."

Much of the business, such as it was, was conducted at Roy's, an unusual quasi-Chinese restaurant just down the street on

Sunset Boulevard. Bogart was a part-owner and the establishment was another setting for his movable feast. "There was more cocaine being tooted than Chinese food," says Wald. "They served egg creams and frozen Milky Ways and Snickers. Neil and I each had a booth with a little brass plate with our name on it, and a curtain that closed the booth, very chic then. It was about leaving hundred-dollar tips for waitresses. . . . It was about dope, it was about music, it was about parties, it was about spending money."

Although Guber, too, was an investor in Roy's, he did not adopt his partner's lifestyle. He conducted business there, but he skipped the other indulgences. Guber believed in showmanship as strongly as his partner, but his personal and business habits were more conservative. He might puff on a joint or drink an occasional glass of wine, but he was not about to give the appearance of losing control.

Guber's more corporate sensibility was reflected in the decor of Casablanca's FilmWorks offices, located on the ground floor beneath the record division. Guber's office was done in white, arranged like a living room, with a wet bar and stained-glass ceiling. As for the hijinks taking place upstairs at Casablanca Records, Wald maintains that Guber "put blinders on."

FOR A WHILE, Casablanca's profligacy went unchecked. PolyGram left Bogart and Guber to run the company as they pleased, largely because the parent company's coffers were bursting. A worldwide boom in pop music and the disco phenomenon boosted PolyGram's American operations, especially its RSO label. Meanwhile, Casablanca made two successful films with hit soundtracks, *T.G.I.F. (Thank God, It's Friday)* and *Midnight Express*—the Turkish prison escape saga that Guber had acquired. *T.G.I.F.* was Bogart's baby and *Midnight Express* was Guber's; both featured music that won Academy Awards.

*T.G.I.F.* was not so much a movie as an excuse to put out a disco record and get Donna Summer in front of a camera. When the Bogarts had visited the Gubers in Bermuda during production of *The Deep*, the two couples brainstormed over plot lines for a film designed to capture the zaniness of the early days of disco. Back in L.A., Bogart and Guber told Columbia that they were putting a disco script into development.

Meanwhile, Rob Cohen, head of the movie division at Mo-

91

town, was under the impression that *he* was making a project called *Disco* for the studio. "I made a deal with Begelman to make a $2 million disco film for Columbia," says Cohen. "The deal closed on a Friday. On Monday, Columbia executive Bill Tennant called and said, 'The deal is off.' He said, 'I can't talk about it; complain all you want.' " When Cohen phoned Begelman—a friend of Motown chief Berry Gordy's—Begelman explained that Guber had asked him to kill the rival disco project. Guber had an exclusive arrangement with Columbia, so Begelman felt he had to cancel Cohen's deal.

Determined to salvage his project, Cohen picked up the phone and called Guber. "I don't think you have a script," he began. "I have a script and you have a studio—we can merge." Cohen had struck a chord. "In less than fifteen minutes, Peter and Neil Bogart were in my office here at Universal," he remembers. Bogart strode in wearing a black leather jacket, a silk shirt, and gold chains; Peter was well groomed in a handsome hand-knit sweater. The three quickly shook hands on a deal whereby Motown and Casablanca would go fifty-fifty on the film. "Peter cut his teeth on the *T.G.I.F.* deal in terms of how to jump in on the action," says Cohen. This was the beginning, he says, of "a pattern of his parasitic action."

Bogart wanted to produce the soundtrack so badly that Casablanca paid $500,000 to buy out Motown. The album would include Motown stars Diana Ross and The Commodores, as well as Casablanca's Donna Summer. Cohen would produce the film while Bogart trumpeted to anybody who would listen that they were making "the *American Graffiti* of the seventies." Guber did not involve himself in production.

But after the picture wrapped, Guber weighed in with an inspired suggestion. Cohen remembers: "Peter came to me and he said, 'Wait, I got an idea for the beginning! I got an idea for the beginning!' You know, he talks really fast. He said, 'You see, we open on the Columbia lady, right? She's up there on her pedestal with her torch stickin' up in the air, and she steps down and she does a couple of disco steps, and then she climbs back up on her pedestal and grabs the torch, and we start the movie!' "

When the picture played in theaters, Guber's gag opener "brought the fucking house down," says Cohen. "And I used to sit back and say, 'If you can keep Peter an ally and just let him come in for those flashes of brilliance, he will spike up the promotion of any movie to a level that no one has ever seen before.' "

Guber and Bogart concocted a *T.G.I.F.* promotional orgy. When it was all over, the three-record soundtrack featuring The Commodores, Patti Brooks, Thelma Houston, and Santa Esmeralda, along with divas Ross and Summer, went platinum. Bogart's buy-out of Motown paid off as Casablanca raked in profits. Donna Summer's version of Paul Jabara's "Last Dance" would win the Academy Award for best song.

Meanwhile, the box-office take was $20 million—enough for a substantial profit since the film cost little more than $2 million to make. When it came to splitting up the spoils, however, Cohen claims that Casablanca and Columbia employed creative Hollywood accounting methods to avoid paying Motown. "They declared it as $6 million in the hole," he says. "They said they spent $3 million on advertising. There are so many ways to pad it. . . . There was no way to prove they didn't spend it."

The premiere of *T.G.I.F.* at New York's Broadway Criterion theater in May 1979 held special significance for Bogart. It represented the realization of his dream to produce feature films and he was celebrating on his hometown turf. But Bogart's partner was not by his side for the occasion. At the exact moment that *T.G.I.F.* premiered, Guber was at the Cannes Film Festival, attending a screening that was equally important to him, the debut of *Midnight Express*.

If *The Deep* had satisfied Guber's craving for commercial success, *Midnight Express* fulfilled his need to be respected. To be sure, the true story of a young American charged with drug smuggling and incarcerated in a brutal Turkish prison was a grim, risky choice for adaptation to the screen. "I could have played it safe," Guber pointed out, "and put together a movie starring a rubberized gorilla. But I wanted to make *Midnight Express* because I liked the story."

Taking executive producer credit, Guber had put together the elements of *Midnight Express* skillfully, hiring several rising young filmmakers who were still inexpensive. Oliver Stone, then in his early thirties with several unproduced scripts but no screen credits, was hired to adapt the novel and would win an Oscar for best screenplay. "Peter was very forceful in delivering his opinion of where the movie should be, and what the story was that was interesting to him," Stone remembers.

Guber also signed up the unknown Alan Parker, a former

93

advertising man, to direct. Parker went on to make *Fame, Missis-sippi Burning,* and *The Commitments.* David Puttnam and Alan Marshall were drafted to produce. Puttnam would be responsible for *Chariots of Fire* and *The Killing Fields* in the eighties, and then serve a brief, unhappy stint as chairman of Columbia Pictures. But in 1977 Puttnam was a British producer who needed money. He declined Guber's offer to serve as president of Casablanca FilmWorks, but agreed to make movies for the company.

"Guber left us alone to make the film," Parker says. "We re-created Istanbul's Sagmalcilar Prison in an old fort in Malta, where the film was made in fifty-three days. Guber visited once briefly with a press junket of journalists. I cut the film and finished it at Shepperton Studios, and Alan Marshall and I took the finished film to show to everyone in L.A."

Guber's visit to Malta yielded the kind of anecdotes that Hollywood insiders have long collected about him. Realizing that without big stars he had to milk every promotional angle he could, he brought along Billy Hayes—whose life story was the basis for the film—to show him off to the press. Included in the Hollywood lore is a Guber postcard story, which comes in at least two versions. As one source from *Midnight Express* remembers, "It was a big joke because a flurry of postcards hit the town. He showed up for one day, went to the production office, and sent postcards." A different source says that Guber sent a boxful of postcards with the inscription: "Worst location. Love, Peter"—which had been written after he had returned to Los Angeles. According to this version, he had the postcards shipped to the production office and mailed there so that people in California would see the foreign postmark.

Puttnam found that Guber was absent in more ways than one on *Midnight Express.* When Columbia president Daniel Melnick pressured Parker and Puttnam to remove a homosexual shower scene, Puttnam dug in his heels and refused. When he tried to get Guber on the phone to fight with the studio, Guber refused to take his calls. Puttnam finally dispatched a searing telex from France which accused Guber of disappearing when the heat was on. The standoff reportedly grew so ugly that locks were changed to keep Puttnam out of his office at Columbia. Ultimately the issue was resolved when Melnick's girlfriend liked the shower scene and the filmmakers were permitted to leave it in.

*Midnight Express* was a tough sell: a violent, harrowing tale with homosexual overtones in the prison scenes. Guber decided to open the movie in Europe to build awareness before bringing it to the United States. Avoiding the summer competition from such popcorn fare as *Grease* and *Jaws 2*, he took *Midnight Express* to Cannes, where it was well received, then opened it in Britain and waited for an October release in the States. Despite his efforts to give *Midnight Express* the aura of a serious film, *The New Yorker*'s Pauline Kael called it "muted squalor with a disco beat in the background, all packaged as social protest."

But *Midnight Express* proved an estimable hit, pulling in $34 million. When awards season rolled around it cleaned up, boosting revenues further. Besides garnering Oscars for best screenplay and score, it received nominations for best picture, best director, and best supporting actor for John Hurt. It also picked up six Golden Globes.

Guber was full of pride as he donned his tuxedo to make the rounds of the award ceremonies. The executive producer was so puffed up by his success, in fact, that Puttnam was irritated. "David was angry, felt totally betrayed because Peter took all the credit for it," says Bob Lovenheim, Guber's former colleague at Columbia.

Since then, Puttnam and Parker say they have put bad feelings behind them. "We who make the films are always sensitive to credit taken by people who sit behind desks in L.A.," Parker says diplomatically. "Peter Guber's role in *Midnight Express* was quite considerable and I have nothing but praise. . . . His smartest move was to put us all together and leave us alone to get on with it." As for Guber's tireless grandstanding for the picture, he jokes, "Someone did try to burn down a cinema in Holland where *Midnight Express* was about to play, and it garnered a lot of publicity. But I don't think even Guber would claim credit for that."

"Peter is a great kicker-offer of things," says Puttnam. "I don't think Peter has ever pretended to be a hands-on producer, and that's to his credit. He did a fantastic job of promoting the movie. Alan Parker and I learned a lot."

Despite present magnanimity, when Puttnam was making films for Casablanca he was put off by what he saw. The company's relentless emphasis on hype over substance was repugnant to Puttnam, the hands-on producer who cast himself as a

95

lover of cinema-as-art. He thought Guber and Bogart were merely on a get-rich-quick mission. He and others who worked for Casablanca were appalled by the company's chaotic management, which had failed to develop a slate of projects that would be ready to go into production after *The Deep, T.G.I.F.,* and *Midnight Express.* In 1978, just one film went before the cameras, director Adrian Lyne's *Foxes.* The same was true in 1979, when only *Hollywood Knights* went into production. Casablanca seemed to be always making announcements in the trade papers about projects in the works that never materialized.

This was a troubling loss of momentum for a company that had gotten off to such an impressive start. Other "mini-studios" such as Lorimar and Orion, which in fairness had been around longer than Casablanca, were averaging at least a half dozen films a year.

One person was fingered by many as the source of most of Casablanca's difficulties: the company's mercurial president, Bill Tennant. Before Guber had been fired from his Columbia job, he had hired Tennant as an executive there. Tennant, a former literary agent, happened to be the person who identified Sharon Tate's body after the Charles Manson murders. Tennant had been a faithful ally, helping Guber shove Cohen's original disco project aside. He had been rewarded when Guber installed him as Casablanca's president.

Guber—with his dislike of hands-on film producing—wasn't enjoying the task of running a company, either. After much complaining to friends about how much he hated the day-to-day grind, he had entrusted management of the film division to Tennant while he pursued other ventures. It was a disastrous decision.

Smart and charming when he wanted to be, "Bill was Peter's henchman," recalls one insider from the days when Tennant worked for Guber at Columbia. Tennant had gotten Guber out of sticky situations. When people left pitch meetings thinking they had a deal, Tennant got on the phone and disabused them.

At Casablanca, Tennant played the same role. Guber was like a top, spinning from one project to the next and avoiding unpleasantness whenever possible. "Peter had two rules," says Lynda Obst, who began working as an executive there in 1979. "One: Don't tell me anything good about anyone else's movie. Two: I don't give bad news."

Several former Casablanca employees remember Tennant's presidency as a reign of terror and an administrative disaster. He had a severe cocaine habit and frequently exploded into fits of rage. Tennant kept the door of his office locked, buzzing in staff or visitors with a button underneath his desk.

The junior staff, which fell victim to Tennant's abuses, was a talented group handpicked by Guber. Along with Obst, a former editor with the *New York Times Magazine,* there were Craig Zadan and Barry Beckerman; all three would later become producers. When employees called Tennant's problems to Guber's attention, Guber remained passive.

"At first I thought Peter was just not aware," says one source. "I'd say, 'Do you know what he's doing to the company, to the talent, to us?' And Peter would answer, 'I hear you, but he is the president of the company, and do what you can to get along with him.' "

"Every week Bill would say, 'Peter is no longer in charge, I'm in charge,' " recalls Obst. "Then Peter would call and say, 'Bill is a little erratic. Don't listen to him.' It was a banana republic." At the time, Obst was working on developing *Flashdance,* a project Tennant hated. *"Flashdance* defines the kind of movie I don't want to make," he told her. The story about a young blue-collar girl who dreams of being a dancer didn't appeal to Guber, either, who told her that he wouldn't finance it with PolyGram's money.

As Tennant's drug problem worsened, he was involved in a bizarre incident at actress Angie Dickinson's house. Dickinson called the cops when Tennant showed up in his boxer shorts late one night and began pounding on her door. According to Dickinson, Tennant believed that someone was chasing him and ran around her yard screaming until the cops came. He was later reportedly homeless, living in a doorway on Ventura Boulevard.

It seemed inexplicable that Guber, who seldom ingested anything stronger than Perrier, had chosen Bogart and Tennant—two drug addicts who couldn't control their own behavior—as his closest associates. He had established a pattern for his career: alliances with men who indulged their aggressive and self-destructive impulses. Whenever one of his partners finally destroyed himself, Guber survived and moved to the next opportunity, pocketing plenty of cash.

"Peter needs a bad guy around him," says a source intimately

97

acquainted with Guber's business dealings during the Casablanca/PolyGram era. "Peter's instinct is to accomplish something and to get it by any means necessary. His instinct further is not to have any such action ascribed to him. He always has to have somebody around him who can take the onus of having been the bad boy. And I think there is something in Peter's character that requires him to appear to the public to be the number-one good guy."

While he permitted the film division of Casablanca to drift, Guber was launching new enterprises to build the company into the empire of his and Bogart's dreams. He started Casablanca BookWorks, a short-lived division that was intended to help finance literary material that would be profitable and also provide material for screen adaptation. BookWorks placed seven authors under contract. Guber also announced the formation of KidWorks to produce children's records and books.

Of all his new endeavors, Guber was most enthusiastic about a foray into the New York stage scene. Like Ray Stark and, later, music entrepreneur David Geffen, who would produce *Dreamgirls* and *The Little Shop of Horrors,* Guber fancied himself as a presence on the Great White Way. He hired Craig Zadan, a former executive with Joseph Papp's New York Shakespeare Festival, to run the venture, called Casablanca StageWorks.

In 1980 StageWorks mounted a production of *Bread and Circus* at New York University. (Guber's alma mater donated facilities, and students worked on the production.) As his Broadway debut, Guber made overtures to back a new version of *Frankenstein,* to be directed by Tom Moore and produced by Joseph Kipness. Guber was excited about introducing film-marketing ideas to Broadway, where promotional techniques had hardly changed in thirty years. But *Frankenstein*'s producers were frightened by Guber's jargon about tie-ins and building awareness. "That's not the way it's done here," he was told. Guber withdrew and emerged unscathed when the show bombed on Broadway in 1979. Later, Cameron Mackintosh would apply the kind of marketing Guber proposed with great success to *Cats, Les Misérables,* and *The Phantom of the Opera.*

98          Guber also cultivated relationships at the Shubert Organization, the biggest producer on Broadway, and was offered a partnership in the company. Chairman Gerry Schoenfeld and

president Bernie Jacobs were eager for an infusion of money that Casablanca could bring, but they were seeking a silent partner. Guber wanted to invest on a show-by-show basis. Talks reached an impasse and Guber walked away.

While Guber's neglect and Tennant's mismanagement were largely to blame for Casablanca's stalled film production slate, Guber's strained relationship with Columbia didn't help either. He had submitted a number of projects which the studio did not green-light. He blamed the continuing turmoil and executive turnover which plagued Columbia. But the situation was exacerbated when Guber battled for profits he believed he was due from both *The Deep* and *Midnight Express*.

In April 1978, at a seminar on dealmaking at the Century Plaza Hotel, he complained bitterly that almost a year after the release of *The Deep*, "I've seen zero dollars in profitability for my company." His dilemma was a function of clout: When his Columbia deal had been made, he was a rookie who could not command a percentage of the gross profits of his pictures. Instead, he worked for a fee and a cut of the net profits, which rarely materialize, thanks to the studio's famously elastic accounting practices. Guber complained publicly that he had received "a screwing" at the studio's hands, and vowed that he would finance his films independently and become a gross-profit participant.

In June 1979, Casablanca Record and FilmWorks severed its exclusive relationship with Columbia, exercising a provision releasing it from its three-year contract if there was an eighteen-month period in which it hadn't begun production on a film. Meanwhile Guber had persuaded PolyGram to increase its investment in Casablanca FilmWorks, bankrolling the film division to the tune of $100 million. He cut a new two-tier production and distribution deal with Universal Pictures boss Ned Tanen that gave Casablanca more independence as well as a bigger portion of the pie.

"There is nothing standard about the new deal with Universal," he crowed to a trade reporter. "We are really in control of our own destiny."

IT WAS INEVITABLE that Casablanca Records would come crashing down. By 1979, disco was dying and the label's talent roster had lost its sheen. Kiss and The Village People had peaked.

In his expansion fever, Bogart had signed dozens of mostly forgettable musical acts: Brenda and the Tabulations, Suzanne Fellini, Four on the Floor, Love & Kisses. Then Donna Summer sued Casablanca Records and both Bogart and his wife for $10 million, alleging that they had defrauded her. They denied the charges and the case was ultimately settled. By then, Summer had fled to Geffen Records.

Casablanca continued pressing and overshipping records. Bogart squandered money on parties, promotions, and drugs. In 1979 PolyGram bankrolled a huge party in Palm Springs and hired Henry Kissinger to speak. "It was like the money was never going to end," recalls Jeff Wald. "It just came in handfuls or buckets."

PolyGram was slow to grasp that Casablanca was a sinkhole, perhaps because Bogart had a way of seducing emissaries from the home office into joining the fun. A straitlaced accountant would arrive from Europe, and in no time Neil had him sporting gold chains and driving a Mercedes convertible. But when they finally took a good hard look at the bottom line, PolyGram executives were stunned. Along with the wasteful spending and drug excesses, there were mutinous songwriters and artists. "Most of the people at Casablanca as artists or producers were not really paid right," says Bob Esty, who worked there as a disco producer. Finally, he says, PolyGram "realized it was all done on smoke and mirrors." While Bogart had lured the talent to his label with honey, Esty says, he bullied and intimidated when deals went sour. "Neil was a fun guy but a killer," he remembers. "You didn't cross him."

By early 1980, PolyGram had decided that Bogart had to go. It was an agonizing moment for Guber. He loved his partner, his dark twin, who by this time had been diagnosed with cancer of the kidney, possibly linked to his drug abuse. Bogart had been Guber's soulmate and springboard, but now he was a liability. "Peter was very ambitious, and was very much concerned that Casablanca's reputation and Bogart's fate would reflect negatively on him," says Wolfgang Hix, then president of PolyGram. "And on our side, we were interested to continue with Guber, whereas we wanted to separate from Bogart. So our interests ran parallel."

Guber made the sensible decision and dumped his partner. On February 8, 1980, PolyGram forced Neil Bogart to resign as president of Casablanca Records, the company he had founded, buying him out for a reported $15 million.

Bogart gave angry interviews to the press. Guber had deserted him, he charged. Meanwhile, Guber was in the Netherlands negotiating his deal to be chairman and half owner of a new company, PolyGram Pictures, the spin-off of Casablanca FilmWorks. It was to be a fifty-fifty partnership in which Poly-Gram would provide the war chest. Guber would make the movies and serve as CEO.

Guber brought in Gordon Stulberg, the lawyer who had negotiated his deal with PolyGram and a respected former executive with 20th Century Fox, to be chief operating officer of PolyGram Pictures. Bill Tennant—who was still in place at the time—would join the new company as president, but he would last less than three months. Dr. Eckart Haas, newly named president of the PolyGram Group's film and television division, announced that the new company would receive funding in the "nine figures."

# 10

## KARMIC BROTHERS

B<small>Y THE LATE</small> 1970s, Jon Peters and Barbra Streisand were part of a Malibu Beach crowd that included Neil and Joyce Bogart. They lived across the street from each other in the Colony, an exclusive enclave of multi-million-dollar cottages nestled so close to a private beach that almost every year the winter rains threatened to sweep them into the Pacific. A twenty-four-hour guard station ensured the privacy of the Colony's star inhabitants, who included Cher, Linda Ronstadt, and Johnny Carson. Sometimes Neil would join Jon on a morning walk on the beach, taking two Quaaludes before he started.

Peter and Lynda Guber, who rented a Malibu retreat, occasionally put in appearances on the beach party scene. As Bogart was declining, Guber was on the rise. The eighties would be a comfortable time for him. Hollywood generally followed the ethos of Wall Street—and now it would add its own twist to the covetousness of the go-go years. On the social scene, it became cool again to talk about money. But at Malibu parties on summer nights, moguls and would-be moguls applied the jargon of est and therapy to their endeavors, adding a spiritual overlay to the pursuit of wealth.

Although he was better acquainted with Bogart, Jon had crossed paths with Guber several times. Peter and Lynda went to parties at the Malibu ranch during the *Star Is Born* days and Lynda had hit it off with Streisand. As a junior operative at Columbia, Guber had tried to cultivate a relationship with Streisand. "Peter had a crush on Barbra," Jon remembers. "Barbra told me that before I knew her, Peter would call her late at night and talk dirty to her on the phone."

Guber may have dismissed Jon in those days, but Jon had

come up in the world. He still needed Streisand: His production deal at Orion hinged on the understanding that Streisand would appear in one of the three pictures he was to produce. But now Streisand was determined to make a very personal project—and it was a choice that would doom her relationship with Jon. He would find himself in need of a new partner.

Barbra was insisting that she would make *Yentl*, a script she had developed based on an Isaac Bashevis Singer short story about a Polish Jewish girl who pretends to be a boy so she can study the religious texts. Streisand had been obsessed with *Yentl* for years. During one of her first nights with Jon, she had astonished him by acting out the role of the yeshiva boy. In November 1979, Orion announced that Streisand would direct *Yentl*, while Jon Peters would co-produce the film with Joan Ashby.

Jon was opposed to the project—a period piece set in Poland with distinctly non-rock songs by Marilyn Bergman. He also resented the time that Barbra was devoting to Jewish studies in preparation for the role. But Streisand had made it clear to Jon that she would not be starring in any more piffle like *The Main Event*, the 1979 comedy about boxing that Jon had pushed her to make.

As Barbra asserted herself, Jon became restless. There were reports that he was having affairs even as he tried to bully her out of making her dream project. "Barbra, you have one year left before you turn into an old bag," he yelled at her one night in front of a group of friends gathered at the Carolwood house for a screening. She started to cry. But this time, she was ready to strike out on her own.

Although they would remain somewhat involved personally and professionally, the love affair and business relationship were effectively broken when Streisand made *Yentl* without Jon. It was as the romance was fraying that Jon and Barbra attended parties at the Gubers' Bel Air home.

Friends noticed Jon and Peter circling each other, engaging in a kind of courtship. Lynda Guber encouraged the ritual, which took the form of boasting about money. She wanted Peter to find a replacement for Bogart. Familiar with her husband's constant anxiety, she knew that Peter needed a fearless partner. At one gathering, observers listened to Jon and Peter bragging to each other about real estate bids they had made,

103

casually tossing out numbers in the millions of dollars. "You could see them falling in love, saying to each other, 'Aren't we incredibly rich and entrepreneurial?' " says one regular Guber partygoer.

In May 1980, Jon Peters, Neil Bogart, and Peter Guber announced the formation of a new company. The trades revealed little about the enterprise except that it would be involved in film, music, television, theater, and publishing. Bogart—at loose ends after his ejection from Casablanca—would run the company's music division. Jon would make movies. Guber would lend his name to the company while he remained CEO of PolyGram Pictures, with all his projects exclusive there. The company was named Boardwalk; in Monopoly, Bogart explained, the Boardwalk was "the most expensive property on the block."

The stated purpose of Boardwalk—to increase the dealmaking clout of the three partners—was a flimsy excuse to form a company. But Boardwalk served the needs of each member of the triangle. And as with most threesomes, in the end there would be room for only two.

By now, Bogart was in free fall. Boardwalk represented his chance to rise from the ashes of Casablanca Records and the PolyGram debacle. He knew it would be his finale: He was suffering from cancer and his prognosis was poor. Jon needed someone to replace Barbra. The person whose motives were at first glance the most opaque was Guber. Given his revised deal at PolyGram, he didn't need to start a new company. But Boardwalk was a way to allay his guilt over having conspired with PolyGram to dump Bogart. Peter knew Neil was dying and that Boardwalk would be his last hurrah. And it could be a convenient escape vehicle if things got too hot at PolyGram.

Just as Boardwalk was launched, Bill Tennant resigned the presidency of PolyGram Pictures. His drug abuse had caught up with him and he was unable to continue working; he would eventually enter a treatment program and successfully rehabilitate himself (Tennant says he has been drug free ever since). Guber had lost his bad cop. Gordon Stulberg, the COO of PolyGram Pictures, was a principled professional who wasn't 104  suited to fill Tennant's role. At PolyGram, there was a vacuum waiting to be filled by Jon Peters.

Meanwhile, Guber was putting a bright face on the reconstituted PolyGram film company. That May, he attended the Cannes Film Festival with Stulberg and vice president of business affairs David Saunders. Bill Tennant had been scheduled to come but didn't turn up. Guber wanted a splashy debut for PolyGram Pictures and he spent plenty of the company's money to get it. A hundred first-class hotel rooms were booked as stars and filmmakers attached to PolyGram projects were flown in. Dudley Moore arrived to promote *Dangerously;* director Franco Zeffirelli and producer Keith Barish hyped *Endless Love;* John Frankenheimer flacked *The Pursuit of D. B. Cooper.*

All were present at a black-tie dinner PolyGram hosted at the posh Majestic Hotel on the Croisette. The company brass from Germany was there and so were dozens of reporters. Sylvester Stallone dropped by on his way to Budapest to star in *Escape to Victory.* Guber had succeeded in throwing an A-list party.

A PolyGram executive recalls that Guber hired Dennis Davidson Associates, a publicity outfit, to organize the company's promotional events. Guber ordered that everything be laid on in the highest style, from the best accommodations to an extra fish course at a huge dinner party. When Davidson mentioned the mounting costs, Guber replied, "I don't care."

Eckart Haas says PolyGram didn't mind footing the bill. After Bogart's excesses, Guber seemed prudent in comparison. But Haas remembers that Guber took up residence in a private yacht that he had chartered during the festival.

Guber returned from Cannes ebullient. But considering his inconsistent attention to the company during its previous incarnation and the fact that he had created another distraction by forming Boardwalk, some doubted whether he would do better this time. "I told everyone at Cannes and I'll say it again," he told *Variety.* "I am fully committed to PolyGram Pictures. I own half the company. It's my primary loyalty and three years from now, I will still be working there."

In the past, Guber had expressed irritation at having to cede profits to Columbia Pictures. Now, with PolyGram backing him, he was hellbent on getting the money he felt he deserved. Every time a film went into production, he would get a producer's fee plus a cut of gross profits.

But this was not enough. PolyGram was to learn quickly that Guber's loyalty pledges were conditional. "I don't care whether it's his wife, Jon, or Sony, or anyone else," says a source with intimate knowledge of Guber's dealings with PolyGram. "Peter owes allegiance in the final analysis to deal with himself as first priority. In his mind his job in this world was to protect himself, and he did it extremely well."

Having drafted his attorney Stulberg to run the business side of PolyGram Pictures, Guber needed a new lawyer. Paul Schaeffer would be another of his bad cops. "Peter always had an entourage of people like Paul Schaeffer, who was another 'twin brother,' " says Haas. Schaeffer's mandate was to exploit every opportunity to make Guber richer. Guber and Schaeffer applied constant pressure to PolyGram to cough up more money. "There was a permanent renegotiation of his contract, or his perks, or whatever, that drove us crazy," Haas says. "There was hardly any particular business deal which didn't somehow result in a discussion of his own contract." Haas says PolyGram had no reason to suspect that any of Guber's activities strayed beyond legal bounds; it was a matter of taking advantage of every loophole, maximizing his leverage.

Stulberg confirms that Guber's compensation was in a constant state of flux. Guber's producer fee soared above the industry norm to $750,000 for a picture wholly financed by PolyGram; reportedly he also eventually received an amazing 12 percent of the box-office gross.

An executive who worked at Universal, which had begun to distribute PolyGram films, reports that Guber was also hardline in dealings with that studio. "Business executives at Universal marveled at how Peter Guber's office sent expenses down to the last parking receipt so every dime was covered," says the executive there. "The whole studio was struck by the lavishness of the [PolyGram] overhead."

The same source says that Guber would tell anyone—with the exception of the PolyGram executives who were footing the bill—that his objective was to "build a portfolio," to get his name on as many pictures as possible. This observer sums up the Guber modus operandi: "Find a company, move in, make it his own and move out. . . . He departs, having used that company to make movies with his name on them."

During this chapter in his career, Guber would not justify PolyGram's faith in him—or his liberal expenditures—by producing hit movies. Astoundingly, even after they realized that they would be devastated by the financial results, PolyGram's European executives remained somewhat in his thrall. Guber was able to convince them that he felt a keen responsibility to make good on their investment. But Guber's commitment is questioned by a business associate. Asked if Guber showed any sense of obligation to PolyGram, this insider answers with a flat, unhesitating "No."

"I understand the position that some people are taking," says Wolfgang Hix, who still serves as a consultant to PolyGram in Germany. "They say, 'That Guber is so damned clever that he always has these silly foreigners who allow him to personally make lots of money and they are losing their shirts.'"

But Hix justifies PolyGram's view of Guber by comparing him with the other show business characters that the company had encountered. "If you compare three names—Jon Peters, Peter Guber, and Neil Bogart—well, Guber is on an entirely different level. He is not only a very creative guy, but you can talk on other subjects with him. He is a much better educated person, and that makes it easier for him to communicate with foreign executives and foreign managers. . . . With Guber you felt, well, you can talk to this guy; what he is saying makes sense and he is not humming a tune all the time and snapping his fingers and doing crazy things. If you went into Neil Bogart's office, with the camels—it was very, very strange. It was a very weird situation."

"I must say I'm still impressed by the man," says Eckart Haas. "He's extremely bright." But Haas's opinion has been some-what leavened. "He was extremely motivated and motivating and aggressive and full of ideas—mostly full of ideas about what is good for himself," Haas says. "And certainly when it came to his ambition to do major movies, he was much more inclined to gamble with third-party money than with his own money."

IN THEORY, Jon Peters was supposed to develop projects for Boardwalk. Instead, he dove into PolyGram business, collaborating with Guber on movies. Guber made no announcement about Jon's role at the company and staffers were baffled by the sudden presence of this hurricane in their midst.

"When Jon came to work at PolyGram, he and Peter insisted on sharing an office," says Hillary Ripps, who worked as Jon's assistant. "They sat together at a long glass desk, the two of them on the phones. They really liked to be around each other."

"Karmic brothers," they called themselves. Each had such

abundant energy that he had always had trouble finding people who could keep up. Now they had each other. Peter could talk a mile a minute, spewing out ideas, and Jon was right there with him. Peter was galvanized by Jon's self-confidence, his sense of entitlement about making millions of dollars—and by his ruthlessness toward anybody who would stand in his way. "I call it the Rasputin syndrome," says a source who worked for them both.

Their relationship was emotionally intense. People sensed their excitement in each other's presence. Some even perceived a homoerotic undercurrent, though no one has ever suggested that they were lovers. The rush they felt in each other's presence wasn't about sex—or it wasn't only about sex. "Money is their drug," says a longtime associate. "No doubt about that. Money and power."

Jon and Peter described their relationship in unusually affectionate terms, even for men who had been initiated into the New Age. "We had an incredible loving, bonding, caring relationship," Jon Peters says. They would explore that relationship in joint therapy sessions. Their involvement was so intimate and consuming that Lynda Guber, who had encouraged their friendship, complained to friends that she felt left out.

Inevitably, Jon picked fights with Neil Bogart and drove a wedge between him and Guber. "Jon completed Peter," says producer Rob Cohen. "If you can have your surrogate, your alter ego, destroy everything in your path so that you can walk in on rose petals, that's a great thing."

And Peter fulfilled Jon's needs, too. "Peter was my credibility," Jon says. "He was a lawyer. He was in the club. He knew all the right people. Everyone thought he was talented. And he helped me, he taught me. He was like my father. I didn't have much of a family, and he made me feel like a part of his family."

Guber had found his soul mate—if only the PolyGram brass could be convinced to accept the newcomer. It wasn't an easy sell. "Guber forced Jon Peters into the picture," says Haas. "Peter said, 'Either you agree that he comes in or I commit suicide, jump out of the window,' or whatever. It was a power sell. We didn't like Jon too much; we had a lot of difficulties with him. . . . We insisted that Guber was our partner and not Jon Peters."

But Guber won. "Peter said, 'Jon is my partner, I want him

to be my partner in law and in fact in PolyGram Pictures,' and they went along," Stulberg says.

Guber and Peters agreed that they would jointly own what had initially been Guber's 50 percent stake in PolyGram Pictures; Jon brought profits from *Caddyshack,* a big hit in the summer of 1980, to the table. With their arrangement settled, they quickly dissolved their partnerships in Boardwalk, leaving the dying Bogart as the sole owner. They had not produced a single picture or television show for Boardwalk.

TOGETHER, GUBER and Peters shoved projects into the pipeline at PolyGram Pictures. Although Guber wanted to make classy films, their operating philosophy was to churn out lots of movies with mid-range budgets, ideally with soundtracks that could be released on PolyGram Records (now run by Bogart's successor, Harvey Schein). Because they split a $750,000 producer's fee each time a movie went into production—a sum that was supplemented by a stake in the box-office and music sales—it was in their best interest to make as many movies as possible. "It doesn't matter if the movies make money," Jon told his former assistant, Laura Ziskin. "We make a fortune."

A fair number of crises and catastrophes are usual for independent film companies, but PolyGram Pictures was more trouble-prone than most. Jon and Peter got off to a rocky start with major personnel problems on their first two movies—both of which had been Bill Tennant's brainchildren.

*King of the Mountain* was based on an article in *New West* magazine about kids who raced cars on Mulholland Drive, the scenic but hazardous highway that runs along the ridge of the Santa Monica Mountains above Los Angeles. Brad Davis, the star of *Midnight Express,* was cast in the lead role as a beer-drinking garage mechanic who races his car by night. But when shooting was about to begin, Davis abruptly dropped out. His agent, David Eidenberg, told *New West* magazine that the movie had not jelled. "What they were starting was a merchandising idea, and they never got it any further," he complained. A PolyGram source says Davis had to be replaced by Harry Hamlin because of Davis's active drug addiction. (Davis later admitted he had been a heroin addict; he died of AIDS in 1991.) 109

The company also made an adventure film called *The Pursuit of D. B. Cooper,* the true saga of a hijacker who bailed out of an airplane in 1971 with $200,000. "It's no coincidence that Peter Guber was attracted to the story of a guy who disappeared out of an airplane with lots of cash and was never seen again," jokes a former PolyGram executive.

Tennant had signed up *Manchurian Candidate* director John Frankenheimer, but after seeing some lackluster footage shot in the Grand Tetons, Guber and Peters fired him in June 1980. Frankenheimer immediately slapped PolyGram with a $12 million lawsuit for breach of contract. Buzz Kulik, who had made *Brian's Song* at Columbia, was hired—and fired—next. Roger Spottiswoode was finally brought in to finish the film.

Jon focused on music, taking over the soundtrack for Franco Zeffirelli's *Endless Love* and for the horror spoof *An American Werewolf in London*. John Landis, who directed the latter, wanted to use original recordings of classic pop songs about the moon: Elvis's "Blue Moon," Creedence Clearwater Revival's "Bad Moon Rising," Van Morrison's "Moondance." Peters assigned staffer Adam Fields the task of securing the music rights. Presley had never allowed the use of his recordings for a movie other than his own. When Fields was told that Colonel Tom Parker would consider the request, Jon Peters cooked up a scheme to impress Parker with his seriousness of purpose.

"You tell Colonel Parker I'm on safari in the Congo," he instructed Fields, "and I'm going to call him on Friday from Africa." On Friday, Jon assembled a group of junior executives in his office and put a handkerchief over the speakerphone. As he dialed Parker, he ordered everyone to make "caw-caw," and "ooh-ooh-oooh" jungle noises. It is not known whether Colonel Parker fell for the ruse, but in any case he wasn't impressed. There would be no Elvis song in the werewolf flick.

Nonetheless, Jon Peters soon became the dominant force at PolyGram Pictures while Peter Guber grew more passive. "Peter would tend to accept a path that Jon would want to follow," says Stulberg, "because Jon was so, uh, unequivocal about his feelings."

Jon's behavior followed his old pattern. While he liked to say, "I'm the people guy; Peter's the detail guy," his people skills were as raw as ever. When junior executive Ron Rotholz disagreed with him in one meeting, Jon tore Rotholz's shirt to shreds. On another occasion, Barry Beckerman was arguing with Guber about something when Jon overheard the discussion and leapt in. "You can't talk to my partner that way," he shouted in Beckerman's face. The next day Beckerman found a dozen bottles of organic shampoo on his desk as a peace offering. Producer Joel Silver, a volatile man himself, also clashed with Peters during his short stint as a PolyGram executive. Silver was heard muttering about hairdressers and saying, "I'm either gonna quit or I'm gonna kill that guy."

Guber and Peters dissipated what goodwill their staff felt for them by being ungenerous with money, praise, and credit. High-level types such as Schaeffer and Stulberg, whose loyalty was key, were well compensated. But junior employees were paid little and often worked long and hard on a project with the understanding that they would see their names on it, only to be denied credit at the final hour. After Adam Fields did most of the work for Jon on the *Endless Love* soundtrack, featuring Diana Ross and Lionel Richie, he was denied the executive producer credit Jon had promised him. Instead, Guber and Peters took the credit for themselves.

Guber was especially miserly, ranting about the price of Perrier water and not allowing his staff to subscribe to all the trade publications. The staff joked about the insincerity of Guber's est jargon. "He used to say things like, 'I want to share something with you,' " one former employee says, "and you know it's the one thing he's incapable of doing."

Jon called his old assistant, Laura Ziskin, and asked her to come in for a job interview. She remembers that when she sat down with Guber in his office, "he said, 'I wish you were a guy. If you were a guy we could go to New York and get laid together.' He said, 'I never make a pass at women I work with.' " Ziskin noticed that he was writing his name—"Peter Guber, Peter Guber"—over and over on a yellow legal pad on his desk. She was relieved to have a good excuse for turning down a job at PolyGram: Jon and Peter's offer did not top the salary she was making at Kaleidoscope, a company that made trailers for upcoming films.

For all their stinginess with employees, Jon and Peter treated themselves royally. Jon and Hillary Ripps flew on the Concorde to London to observe filming of *An American Werewolf.* One employee remembers a day when PolyGram's head of business affairs, Jim Johnson, questioned a grocery bill in the thousands of dollars from a Malibu store that Peters had submitted for reimbursement. "When I'm at [home], all I do is think about movies," Peters told Johnson.

Stulberg, who had been hired by Guber to administer Poly-Gram Pictures, found that his authority was eroded. "Jon became the embodiment of the company," he says. "I couldn't make the decisions. I had terrible fights with Jon, and Peter would back Jon. That was on the administrative side. And on the creative side, Jon simply made more of the decisions than Peter because in personality he was just out front all the time and Peter let him get away with it. I never forgave Peter for abdicating authority to Jon. It affected me, it implicated me, and I didn't need it. I had had a very good career in film. PolyGram was my unhappiest chapter."

In 1981, as Guber and Peters's pictures were ready to open in the theaters, PolyGram's executives in Europe began to experience déjà vu. The red ink was flowing again. "We had a string of pictures that fell on their ass," Stulberg says.

*King of the Mountain,* PolyGram's debut feature, grossed a disastrous $2 million at the box office. The rest of the year produced one disappointment after another. *Endless Love,* a high school melodrama starring America's sweetheart, Brooke Shields, opened in July and made only $15 million.

In November, PolyGram took a big financial hit with the ill-fated *Pursuit of D. B. Cooper. Variety* said the film was "doubtless a law-enforcement ploy to lure the skyjacker out of hiding: surely after seeing this mess he will want to surface and sue somebody." Joel Silver, who had pushed the film over budget while trying to rescue it, was fired after working exactly six weeks at PolyGram. (PolyGram settled its lawsuit with John Frankenheimer for an undisclosed high-six-figure sum.)

In July 1981, Guber and Peters decided it was time for some public relations spin. "We're just trying to have some fun and make the days be enjoyable," Guber blithely told the *Los Angeles Times* in an interview at PolyGram's Sunset Boulevard offices. He put a bright face on the company's financial prospects. "We've both made people hundreds of millions of dollars in revenue," he said. As for the partnership with PolyGram, "The good thing about our situation is that we have no bosses. . . . We're in control of our own lives. We can afford now for it to be fun. That doesn't mean it won't be hard—it just doesn't have to be a drag."

112

Meanwhile, Jon threw out vague allusions to all the deals he and Guber had percolating. *Flashdance* was in the works at Paramount. *A Chorus Line* and *Batman* would be in production soon. There were television projects and foreign sales galore. Guber and Peters had their own music company, Jon pointed out, and their own real estate firm. They were in the process of buying a piece of their own bank, Bel Air Savings and Loan. And in the fall, PolyGram would move into plush new offices on the MGM lot in Culver City.

Their act did not fool the German executives who were staring at the balance sheets. The $100 million the parent company had committed to PolyGram Pictures the previous year was rapidly evaporating: Production costs for the 1981 releases were said to total nearly $40 million.

That December, *The Hollywood Reporter* highlighted the "growing pains" at PolyGram Pictures. The company appeared to be unstable, since Lynda Obst had recently departed to go to work for Mary Tyler Moore, Barry Beckerman had quit, and Joel Silver was fired. Friction was said to be building with the European owners.

Guber was working to convince them to take a long-term view. He pointed out, correctly, that new markets for entertainment were on the verge of exploding, meaning that a library of films would become a valuable asset. But given the company's track record—and the fiscal climate in the entertainment business in 1981—his partners at PolyGram didn't feel comfortable. Box-office revenues in general were flat. The cost of making motion pictures was rising alarmingly: from 1979 to 1982, the average negative cost rose from $6 million to $9 million. Interest rates skyrocketed from 6 percent to 15 percent. Television networks were paying less for pictures, shrinking one of the largest ancillary markets. The era of video and pay television that Guber anticipated had not yet dawned.

All in all, PolyGram's European managers lacked faith in the idea that a cash drain today might mean profits down the road. "You lived or died on opening weekend," says Michael Kuhn, currently the CEO of PolyGram Filmed Entertainment. "Guys in Hamburg or Bonn listened on Friday nights to guys in Hollywood telling them they'd lost $10 million." In January 1982— after "six dogs in a row," as Kuhn remembers—Philips and Siemens cut their losses. By then, PolyGram International reportedly had poured away $80 million into its fledgling film division.

Guber and Peters walked away from PolyGram Pictures in good shape. Taking advantage of the urgency with which their backers wanted to escape, Guber negotiated a deal that allowed him and Jon to take away several valuable film properties, including *Batman*. "Our brief was to get out of the motion picture business as quickly as we could," says Haas. "Had we had more time, we would have saved a lot. It was a question of getting out in weeks rather than months."

As of January 15, 1982, Guber and Peters were no longer PolyGram officers with equity in the company. PolyGram retained a stake in the films that Guber and Peters took with them—most significantly a piece of *Batman* that assured the company of 7.5 percent of the gross.

With the end of PolyGram in sight, Barry Beckerman had pitched the *Batman* script to Frank Wells at Warner. He came back to Jon and Peter and said, "Not only do they want *Batman*, they want everything else we have, too." Jon, who had been eager to get rid of "the Germans," as he called them, raced over to see his old friend Terry Semel. He quickly made a deal to produce *Batman* for Warner.

Guber and Peters established their own company, the Guber-Peters Co., in 1982. They still had a relationship with Universal but it wouldn't last long. Frank Price, who took over from Ned Tanen as head of the studio in 1982, knew Guber because Price had run Columbia during the Casablanca era. "Everyone knew the day Frank Price took the job as head of Universal, Peter Guber started to pack," says a former Universal executive. "He was not going to be able to put his methods over on Price. . . . This was a hostile environment, and it was time to find a new host body."

Meanwhile, Gordon Stulberg stayed behind to dismantle PolyGram Pictures and mop up the mess. He oversaw the release of the remaining features and tried to recoup as much money for the parent company as possible. Costa-Gavras's *Missing*, a political thriller about a man who searches for his son who has disappeared in Chile, turned out to be a critical success in spring of 1982. The film received a best picture Oscar nomination and won the award for best screenplay adaptation; Jack Lemmon and Sissy Spacek were nominated in the best actor and actress categories. *Missing* was a moderate success at the box office, grossing $18 million. But because Guber had

114

not expected it to perform, he had allowed Universal to finance it, shrinking the up side for PolyGram.

On balance, Guber and Peters almost invariably guessed wrong when deciding whether PolyGram should wholly finance its films—increasing both its risk and its potential payoff—or share the burden with a studio.

The one film that would have turned the tide for PolyGram had Guber believed in it was *Flashdance,* Lynda Obst's pet project. After Guber refused to finance the picture, it was sold to Paramount, which reimbursed PolyGram for $225,000 in development costs. When Jon arrived at the company, he took a shine to the story about a female welder in a Pittsburgh factory who becomes a dancer. While Obst envisioned it as "a female entitlement film," Jon endorsed the chance to get lithe young women dancing in sexy clothes before the cameras.

Dawn Steel, then a production executive at Paramount, picked up *Flashdance* and ran with it. She hounded a reluctant Adrian Lyne to direct it and hired Don Simpson and Jerry Bruckheimer to produce. While credited as executive producers, Guber and Peters were not involved in the production, although Jon was instrumental in bringing aboard Jeffrey Hornaday as choreographer and Phil Ramone as music director.

*Flashdance* was not just a hit, it was a phenomenon, grossing more than $180 million domestically. Irene Cara's version of Giorgio Moroder's theme song "Flashdance . . . What a Feeling" won an Oscar and boosted sales of the soundtrack into the stratosphere. There ensued the usual Hollywood discussion of who really gave birth to the project, with each of the players promoting his or her own part. Guber and Peters whined publicly that they were not receiving their due. "I knew it would be a *Rocky* for women," Jon boasted in an interview with the *Los Angeles Times,* in which he advanced the false impression that he had developed the screenplay. He did not even mention Lynda Obst.

"Thank God I've got bank credit," groused Guber, "because if I had to depend on screen credit, I'd be in trouble."

From PolyGram's point of view, the silent hero in the *Flashdance* saga was Gordon Stulberg. In making the deal with Paramount, Stulberg had fought hard to hang onto the soundtrack rights for PolyGram—which were ultimately worth $9 million to the company.

PolyGram enjoyed a much-needed financial boost from *Flashdance* in 1983, ironically as the film company was being sold off piece by piece. The PolyGram Group did not return to profitability until 1985—thanks to the compact disc. By then, its overall losses in the United States were estimated at $220 million. "With the combination of the studio failing and the record industry recession," says Michael Kuhn, "the company lost a fortune."

While PolyGram was being buffeted by the movie business, Neil Bogart had achieved his dream of scoring one last hit on his last record label, Boardwalk: Joan Jett's "I Love Rock 'n' Roll" was a best-seller. When he died of cancer of the kidney and colon in May 1982, Jon Peters and Peter Guber paid their respects at his funeral, as Donna Summer—by then an artist on Geffen Records—sang hymns.

# 11
## JOINING THE WARNER FAMILY

AFTER POLYGRAM, Warner Bros. was like a warm, soothing bath. In 1982, Jon and Peter set up shop in Building 66, a one-story stucco bungalow beneath the water tower on the Burbank lot. It felt like a homecoming to Jon. He had friends here —some in high places. In the Spanish-style executive building, near the circle drive gate on Olive Avenue, Terry Semel, now president and chief operating officer, occupied a big corner office. Semel, who had started as a salesman at Disney, had replaced studio president Frank Wells, who astonished Hollywood by taking a break from his career to climb the Himalayas.

Semel's relationship with Peters and Streisand had helped him maneuver out of distribution to the more glamorous production side of the business. He and Jon had worked and played together. Now he was running a studio in a budding partnership with chairman and chief executive Bob Daly, who had come to Warner in 1980 from CBS. Daly and Semel would become one of Hollywood's most stable and successful management teams. And as Semel flourished, so would Guber and Peters.

More than any other studio, Warner Bros. nurtured a family atmosphere. The big daddy was Steven Ross, the dynamic silver-haired chairman of Warner Communications Inc. Ross's personal and business style was unabashedly extravagant. He pampered the Warner stars and producers, flying them on the corporate Gulfstream 3 jets for weekends at company retreats in Acapulco and Aspen. Ross was a close friend of Streisand's, and Jon had long been studying his imperial style, planning to emulate it one day.

The boys' club was thriving in the eighties. Despite the presence of a few women, the power at Warner Bros. and at every other major studio belonged to men. The members of the club partied together, kept each other's secrets, and helped each other amass wealth. Jon called Semel his "best friend," shared stock tips with him, and cut him in on real estate deals. Semel knew all about Jon Peters—he had been along for the ride on *A Star Is Born* and Jon had hidden under his desk after punching out Frank Merino. But Daly and Semel weren't put off by Jon's antics. Jon Peters made them laugh.

They didn't have to wait long to see him in action. Jon and Peter's first project at Warner was *Vision Quest*, a coming-of-age drama about a teen wrestler played by Matthew Modine. Jon and music producer Phil Ramone had become aware of an unknown singer-dancer from New York who was then signed to Sire Records, a subsidiary of Warner Bros. Ramone took the singer—Madonna—to dinner at Streisand's house on Carolwood, where she played some of her European videos. They were impressed with her self-possession and sexy fishnets-and-crucifixes style.

After testing Madonna in a New York studio, Jon decided he wanted her in *Vision Quest*. She recorded the ballad "Crazy for You" and another song for the film. As it happened, the opening of *Vision Quest* was scheduled to coincide with the release of Madonna's *Like a Virgin* album for Sire. Warner Bros. Records chief Mo Ostin didn't want Jon to release "Crazy for You" as a single because it would distract attention from the release of an album by an artist whom the company was grooming to be a major star. Ostin went to Bob Daly and asked him to pull the Madonna tracks from the *Vision Quest* album.

Daly summoned Jon and Peter to his office and told them they had to lose the Madonna music. As Peter watched in horror, Jon leaped on top of Daly's desk and began jumping up and down, thundering in protest. Daly ran from the room.

Warner caved; Madonna's music stayed in the *Vision Quest* soundtrack. "Crazy for You" became a number-one single. No one has jumped onto Bob Daly's desk since.

118 GUBER AND PETERS had arrived at Warner Bros. at an opportune moment. The entertainment business was expanding globally and Warner needed on-the-lot producers to keep mov-

ies flowing into its distribution pipeline. In the early eighties, new markets for movies—cable, video, foreign theatrical—were blossoming.

The blockbuster mentality had reached a fever pitch in Hollywood. The studios hungered for hits that would not only top $100 million in box-office revenues but spawn sequels and a merchandising bonanza of toys, lunch boxes, and T-shirts. But the game demanded big stars and breakthrough special effects as well as imaginative "event" marketing. A strong opening weekend was essential, and that required expensive saturation television advertising. Meanwhile, star salaries were rising and production costs were climbing much faster than the rate of inflation. Steven Spielberg's *Jaws*—the picture that helped create the prevailing blockbuster fever—had a $10 million budget in 1975; it would have cost more than $40 million ten years later. And while Spielberg's film opened in just 409 theaters, major films now routinely opened on 1,000 screens or more.

For every smash hit—*Raiders of the Lost Ark, Fatal Attraction,* or *Ghostbusters*—a studio had to survive many losers. In 1989, Spielberg decried the blockbuster syndrome that he had inadvertently helped to foster. "There's anxiety everywhere," he observed. "There's a palpable tension. Everything has to succeed—or else. I'm telling you, it's viral."

For Guber and Peters, this nervous environment created opportunity. With the studio footing the bill, they would make a slew of movies, casting big stars and taking risks on popular books that were difficult to adapt to the screen, such as *The Color Purple, The Witches of Eastwick,* and *The Bonfire of the Vanities.*

The Guber and Peters modus operandi was still the same: Hire executives to oversee script development and filmmakers to make the movies. They would swoop in when a film was completed and apply their astute promotional instincts to marketing. They aspired to be not so much filmmakers as entrepreneurs who owned a film company. They liked to announce how much money they were making. An employee remembers Peter remarking, "Today is Tuesday, November the 7, and we just made $7 million."

"All Jon did was talk about all the money he made," says Roz Heller, who worked for Guber-Peters as an executive in the eighties. "I said, 'Jon, you're talking to *me*. I remember when Barbra was teaching you how to read.'"

119

The Guber-Peters Co. branched out into an array of new enterprises. It launched a television division. It bought a piece of a Spanish-language entertainment weekly called *Mundo Artístico*. It played the stock market, set up a separate real estate company, and invested in a shopping mall. Guber and Peters each owned a 5 percent stake in Bel Air Savings and Loan. While they attended board meetings, they were not involved in the day-to-day management of the bank. When they sold their shares in 1986, they had tripled their money in four years, getting out just before the country learned that many savings and loans were lemons that had been squeezed dry. (Bel Air, however, managed to stay afloat under a new owner.)

Despite all the distractions, Guber and Peters worked their way toward becoming A-list producers—at least, by superficial measures—managing to get their names on a lot of movies. But many within the industry were unimpressed. Some of their detractors were envious; others dismissed them as "not real producers," merely packagers. "They're used-car salesmen," said a famous director who made a picture with them in the eighties. "Occasionally one of their cars wins a race, but most of them don't make it out of the lot."

Guber and Peters undeniably had a special talent for getting studios to green-light their projects. "A lot of people get paralyzed in the decision-making process," says Roger Birnbaum, who was president of their company in 1986. "They didn't. Jon would say, 'I have a dream,' and Peter would say, 'I know how to get it done.'"

Guber generally stayed in the office working the phones, pursuing material and talent, cultivating relationships around town. He grew a ponytail and cut a slick figure in his designer suits and white socks with soft loafers. He made endless lists on yellow legal pads and spouted maxims to colleagues and employees. The lessons hadn't changed since his early days at Columbia. "The perception of power" was what mattered, he instructed. "People move toward power."

"There is nobody in town that can move a project faster than Peter Guber," says Stan Rogow, who was associate producer of the disastrous *Clan of the Cave Bear* at Guber-Peters in the mid-eighties. The adaptation of Jean M. Auel's caveman bestseller starring Daryl Hannah had been dropped by Universal. "Guber set it up the next day at Warner Bros. Before we were

120

asked to leave the Universal offices, we had new offices at Warner," says Rogow.

Jon preferred to work at home, communicating with his partner by phone and taking meetings in Bermuda shorts by his pool. But he pitched in when Guber was trying to lure someone into a deal. They were a relentless tag-team, attacking their quarry with an onslaught of cajoling phone calls and gifts. Guber favored classy engraved silver *objets* from Tiffany; Peters made carefully chosen donations to charity.

When radio personality Rick Dees said something nice about *Dreams,* a Guber-Peters television show, Jon sent him a cake in the shape of a Hollywood star with Dees's name on it. For other business acquaintances, Jon felt a gift with a pulse might be more appreciated. He was a longtime friend of the notorious Madam Alex, Hollywood's premier madam at the time. A former assistant remembers one such transaction: "Jon was courting a head of a record company for a soundtrack deal and for that guy's birthday, he sent a hooker."

Jon also used his relationship with Madam Alex to help Streisand when she was preparing to play a call girl in her 1987 film, *Nuts.* He arranged a meeting between Streisand and a gathering of Alex's "creatures," as the madam called the comely young women who served her clientele. The lesson took place at Alex's home and happened to coincide with Drexel Burnham's annual investors' meeting, known as the Predators' Ball. Jon was amused when he heard complaints that several girls were busy in the tutorial with Barbra while Drexel customers were kept waiting at the Beverly Hills Hotel.

JON AND PETER secured their position at Warner Bros. by stroking studio executives, seeking promotions for those who helped them, and neutralizing those who didn't. "They knew instinctively how to court middle management," says Stan Rogow.

Mark Rosenberg had been named head of production in July 1983. A former left-wing political activist, Rosenberg was an intellectual by Hollywood standards. His tastes ran to films with a social message; his pet projects at Warner included *The Killing Fields* and *Greystoke: The Legend of Tarzan, Lord of the Apes.* Rosenberg was not Jon and Peter's style, but other Warner executives were. Jon's former aide, Mark Canton, was a senior vice president. Bruce Berman, Guber's former assistant at Casablanca, was now a vice president of production, as was Allyn Stewart, a clever young woman who would become a staunch Guber-Peters ally and an intimate friend of Guber's.

Unlike Rosenberg, Canton wasn't wracked with doubt about wasting his intellectual talents as a studio executive. He adored working for Warner Bros. A sign on his office door announced that the "Friend of Comedy" dwelled therein. The diminutive Canton championed many of the studio's light summer movies. His ambition and lowbrow taste made him a target of ridicule: His detractors called him "Friend of Comedy, Enemy of Intelligence." But in the early eighties many of Canton's pet projects performed better at the box office than Rosenberg's. Among them were *Risky Business, National Lampoon's European Vacation,* and *Pee-wee's Big Adventure.*

Canton wanted Rosenberg's job and Jon and Peter wanted him to have it. Jon knew that Mark Canton would remain his loyal slave if he rose in the studio hierarchy—Canton was easily dominated. "I created Mark Canton," Jon would bellow around the Guber-Peters offices.

Jon lobbied Semel and Daly to fire Rosenberg and put Canton in charge of production. And Canton wasn't bashful about hounding his bosses. His fiancée, an aspiring producer named Wendy Finerman, reportedly told agents that they should send material to Canton rather than to Rosenberg.

The engagement party that Jon Peters threw at his Beverly Hills mansion for Canton and Finerman in 1985 was one of those surreal movie business affairs that occur when a shift in the power structure is in the wind. The guest list included executives, directors, and producers in the Warner Bros. "family," many of whom had already seen the handwriting on the wall for Mark Rosenberg.

"We walked in and practially died," recalled one person who attended the bash. "It was like Tara in the middle of Beverly Hills." Jon's backyard had been lavishly tricked out for the party, with some outlandish touches. A chimpanzee in a Warner Bros. T-shirt was perched on the branch of a tree. An orangutan sat nearby in a wheelchair.

With a crowd including Warner bosses Daly and Semel gathered around the pool holding their wineglasses, Mark Rosenberg slipped and fell into the water. A moment that would have embarrassed anyone was especially cruel for Rosenberg, who was extremely overweight and was unable to pull himself out of the pool in his drenched clothing without completely losing his dignity.

"Mark fell in the pool! Mark fell in the pool!" cried Jon and Canton, hugging each other and jumping up and down.

"It was this wonderful, ugly Hollywood scene," says a source who witnessed it. Another person who was there remembers: "Not only was it ugly then, but for the next several days everyone talked about it. It was really revolting. They [Peters and Canton] were vile."

On September 25, 1985, the trade papers announced Warner Bros.' promotion of Mark Canton to president of worldwide theatrical production. Rosenberg was departing to establish an independent production company at Universal with director-producer Sydney Pollack. With Canton's promotion, Jon and Peter had effectively installed their ideal functionary in the top production job at Warner. He was like an obsequious little brother, timid and unimpeachably loyal. "Mark was their whipping boy," says an observer.

An excellent cheerleader and company man, Canton would almost invariably support Jon and Peter on creative decisions, increasing their leverage over filmmakers and running interference with Semel and Daly. When Jon battled with director Harold Becker over music and casting on *Vision Quest,* and later with George Miller over the special effects in *The Witches of Eastwick,* Canton backed Jon. On the London set of *Batman,* Canton would be at Jon's side in disputes with director Tim Burton. And he helped convince Semel and Daly to authorize more money for the action sequences.

Jon and Peter's rapport with Canton was unusual in one sense. Within their own company, they consistently had trouble keeping male employees. They had better luck with women. In December 1986, Stacey Snider was hired as director of development at Guber-Peters. Snider was a twenty-six-year-old UCLA law school graduate, brainy and attractive. She had previously worked for *Flashdance* producers Don Simpson and Jerry Bruckheimer. She had also been a roommate and close friend of Wendy Finerman, now Mark Canton's wife, when she was an undergraduate at the University of Pennsylvania.

Snider was a godsend: a dutiful worker with good taste in material, eager to please. Peter imparted to her all his wisdom

123

on developing and producing films. Snider became the closest thing Guber had to a protégée. He was headed for the top, and she hitched her wagon to his and went along for an eight-year ride.

This would not come without its price. Although talented enough to make it on her own, Snider is one of many women in Hollywood—where the power is concentrated in the hands of males—whose advancement has been inextricably linked to powerful men. When she went to work at Guber-Peters, Snider and Mark Canton became intimate friends. Jon and Peter had bound Canton more closely to them than ever before.

AMONG SUPPORT STAFF, Guber-Peters was known as one of the toughest places in town to work. The assistants and secretaries were paid little and worked hard with little acknowledgment. "It was like boot camp," says Missy Alpern, an assistant to Guber for seven years.

"They weren't very good at pampering their employees," concurs Stan Brooks, who was vice president and later president of the television division between 1985 and 1989. "They ran a very frugal company. I remember an employee having a fight with the office manager over whether they would let us have real milk in the refrigerator, as opposed to non-dairy creamer. The word came back: 'Buy your own milk.' "

Guber was forever on the lookout for ways to save money— for himself and Jon. In the mid-eighties, Guber-Peters had deals with various studios around town that allowed the company to charge expenses. Although such arrangements are routinely exploited to the maximum by Hollywood producers with the full knowledge of the studios, Peter took them to the outer limits. He drove the assistants to bill the studios for every penny he could wring out of them. "That's one of the secrets to their success," says Brooks. "They never spend their own money. They're always spending someone else's money."

At least three former assistants recall that Guber devised inventive ways to fob off personal expenses. He told his secretary to tell a printer that he would not pay for the programs for his daughter's bas mitzvah until the bill was resubmitted with the notation "for scripts printed." First-class plane tickets were billed to more than one studio. Another assistant says that she saw a form submitted to Warner requesting more money so

124

that she could be given a raise—which she never received. "Peter Guber got a raise," she says.

Peter's most ingenious scheme for getting someone else to subsidize his lifestyle was the financing of his boat. Ever since he made *The Deep,* he had been interested in underwater filming. In partnership with his old friend Al Giddings, *The Deep*'s renowned underwater expert, he produced *Mysteries of the Sea,* a two-hour prime-time special for ABC. The show won an Emmy. Guber and Giddings collaborated on a home-video cassette called *Underwater Symphony* for MCA which combined music and ocean images.

In June 1982, Peter purchased an 80-foot steel ketch made in New Zealand which he transformed into a luxurious filmmaking vessel. No expense was spared to make the *Oz* a sumptuous living environment. Angelo Donghia, the designer of the S.S. *France,* decorated the interior. Picasso ceramics adorned the dining area and George Hurrell portraits of Loretta Young and Robert Taylor hung in the galley. A hot tub was built into the ship's fantail.

The motor-sailer was outfitted to serve as a high-tech filmmaking platform. "The boat is a creative environment—inspirational, clean, well-lit," Guber told *Nautical Quarterly.* "The idea is not to rough it; it's to be able to do your work and do it well."

Guber made full use of his yacht for pleasure and business. He hired John Bill as the boat's skipper and Bill's wife Carol also joined the crew. "With a boat like that, you need a full-time crew," says Bill.

Bill would sail the *Oz* to the Caribbean or Hawaii and meet Guber and his family, who would fly in for vacation cruises. Guber loved being on the water and became a competent sailor. In normal circumstances, the *Oz* would have been an extravagance, but Guber made the boat earn its keep. "We did a fair amount of corporate entertaining," says Bill. When the *Oz* was docked at the Marina del Rey in Los Angeles, it was rented out for private charters and for film and commercial productions. By registering the *Oz* as a charter vehicle, Guber was able to write off renovations and operating costs.

But he managed to make the deal even sweeter. In 1984, Guber and Peters launched their television division. They teamed up with a company called Centerpoint, whose president was an old friend of Jon and Peter's named Tom Tannenbaum. Tannenbaum had access to $100 million in financing from Sentry Insurance, a Wisconsin-based company that wanted to get into the glamorous world of Hollywood.

The Guber-Peters Co. produced a series for Centerpoint called *Dreams,* a spin-off of *Flashdance* that was canceled after four episodes. They also made a television movie starring Mr. T which went $1 million over budget—an extraordinary overrun. Then Guber came up with the idea for *OceanQuest,* a series which amounted to filming blond former Miss Universe Shawn Weatherly in a bikini sailing around the world on the *Oz.* Weatherly would visit the Caribbean, Baja, and Hawaii, where she would learn about buried treasure and become acquainted with marine life.

Guber sold his friend Brandon Tartikoff, president of NBC, six hours of *OceanQuest* for a $600,000-an-hour licensing fee. At the time, the going rate was $800,000 an hour, so Tartikoff was getting a programming bargain. But *OceanQuest* cost $875,000 an episode to produce, so Centerpoint had to kick in $275,000 per episode.

The *Oz* was chartered by Centerpoint for most of the year the series was filmed, from 1984 to 1985. Guber would fly in whenever possible to meet Weatherly and the crew, joining them in La Paz for a Baja episode and in Cuba when *OceanQuest* was invited there by Fidel Castro. Al Giddings had struck up an acquaintance with Castro, an avid diver. The Cuban dictator dove for *OceanQuest*'s cameras in a segment filmed outside of Havana Harbor and along the island's north shore. He posed for photographs with Guber.

"*OceanQuest* cost a fortune," says Tannenbaum. Meanwhile, he wasn't sure that Sentry Insurance understood the kinds of deficits that could be involved in creating television programming. "They were an insurance company from Wisconsin," he says.

"Centerpoint lost a lot of money," acknowledges Stan Brooks, "But they were an extremely badly managed company. They had overhead up to the sky well before they had any revenue." But Tannenbaum says, "Peter told me Guber-Peters made a lot of money on Centerpoint."

126

*OceanQuest* premiered on NBC in August 1985. The series ultimately put Centerpoint out of business and Sentry Insurance Company, having lost millions in its brief but traumatic foray into Hollywood, went home to Wisconsin.

In December 1987, Guber sold the *Oz* for $1 million.

IF THE GUBER-PETERS Co. didn't make much of a mark in television, many of its movies were forgotten just as quickly. Its first film at Warner, *Vision Quest,* had been a $12.9 million bomb. In 1985–86, five of the company's six films were dismal failures. *The Legend of Billie Jean* pulled in only $3 million. *Clue,* a film based on the board game that was made for Paramount, didn't win audiences and grossed only $13.9 million. Guber's old friend Peter Bart co-produced *Youngblood,* a romance set against a hockey backdrop with Rob Lowe and Patrick Swayze, which grossed $14.1 million. *Head Office* was an embarrassing comedy despite a cast that included Judge Reinhold, Danny DeVito, and Wallace Shawn; it brought in a mere $3.3 million. And *Clan of the Cave Bear* didn't even reach $2 million at the box office.

But one film was a $95.1 million bull's-eye: *The Color Purple,* director Steven Spielberg's adaptation of Alice Walker's best-selling novel about a southern black family in the first half of this century. While Guber and Peters owned the rights to the novel, Spielberg had the clout to produce the film at his own company, Amblin Entertainment—and to write a clause into his contract which barred them from the set.

It was Carol Isenberg, the wife of Peter's childhood friend Jerry Isenberg, who had approached Guber about buying the rights to *The Color Purple.* Afterwards, Guber brought Warner recording artist and producer Quincy Jones aboard to compose the score and co-produce the film. Warner executive Lucy Fisher and Amblin boss Kathy Kennedy got Spielberg interested in the project. Kennedy and her husband, Frank Marshall, co-produced the film with Jones.

"They were never on the set, they were never in the cutting room," Spielberg says. "The first time I saw them was at the screening of *The Color Purple* at Todd-AO dubbing studios, when I showed it to the Warner Bros. executives. So I never had any kind of collaboration with them."

That didn't stop Guber and Peters from trumpeting in their 127 company bio that they "created" *The Color Purple.* And when they wooed other filmmakers, they would drop Spielberg's name, implying that they had been close collaborators. It didn't bother Spielberg enough to stop him from producing a second film with Guber and Peters, *Innerspace*. Based on an idea of Guber's and directed by Joe Dante, the movie starred Dennis Quaid as a Navy test pilot who is miniaturized in an experiment and accidentally injected into the body of a grocery clerk. The movie grossed a respectable $34 million but was still a disappointment, since Warner had anticipated a major hit.

*Innerspace* was in the works at the same time as *The Witches of Eastwick,* an adaptation of John Updike's novel. As the "literary" partner, Peter Guber intended to oversee *Witches* and Jon Peters was supposed to be the point man on *Innerspace*. But even though Spielberg was not directing *Innerspace* himself, Amblin personnel issued an edict that they would not work with Jon Peters. Guber was obliged to switch his jurisdiction over to *Innerspace,* leaving Peters to make his mark on *The Witches of Eastwick.*

JON AND PETER'S personal activities were often more colorful than their movies. Just after he left PolyGram, Peter's marriage to Lynda had hit a rough patch. Eventually he rented a house in the Malibu Colony and lived there alone for a year.

"He was devastated when he and Lynda separated," says a close acquaintance. "He was a mess emotionally." Adds another friend, "He'd be calling me from all over the world—he was miserable, he was really hurt by it." Just as Peter and Lynda were separating, Lynda's younger brother Sam was killed in a motorcycle accident in West Hollywood. Sam was a sweet, troubled young man who had once worked for Peter, including as an assistant on *The Deep*. His death deepened Peter's emotional distress.

The Gubers reconciled about a year later—soon after Peter paid a visit to his attorney to discuss what kind of a settlement would be required in a divorce. "He was told he'd have to give her half his assets," says a source who was in the office when Peter returned from his meeting with the lawyer. "He called Lynda up and said 'Hi, honey. I'm coming home.' " A friend of Guber's recalls him saying, "I can't do this—I can't wipe out everything I've ever worked for."

Peter and Lynda apparently agreed to hold the family together and continue raising their children under one roof.

"I was devastated when my father died," says Jon Peters. "It was like my world kind of ended." Jack Peters, a truck-stop cafe owner who suffered from heart trouble, died in 1955, when his son was ten.

As a boy growing up in the San Fernando Valley, Jon won a second-place medal in a local swimming meet. Before he was expelled from junior high school and sent away to youth detention camp, he excelled at gymnastics and boxing.

Jon Peters and actress Lesley Ann Warren got matching haircuts for their May 1967 wedding in the penthouse suite of the Sands Hotel in Las Vegas. During the marriage, Peters moved from hairdressing into show business for the first time, helping produce a stage version of *The Threepenny Opera* in which Warren starred.

*Above right:* Peters picked up his haircutting scissors to give Kris Kristofferson, Barbra Streisand's co-star in *A Star Is Born,* a trim. Peters was jealous of the folk-rock star, who had previously dated Streisand, and the two battled on the set.

OPPOSITE:
*Top left:* Although *A Star Is Born* was savaged by the critics, Jon and Barbra were vindicated in the court of public opinion: The movie was a $100 million hit with a smash soundtrack and Peters and Streisand picked up four Golden Globe awards.

*Top right:* Peters spearheaded *A Star Is Born*'s sultry ad campaign, lining up photographer Francesco Scavullo to shoot the poster of Barbra Streisand and Kris Kristofferson in a *Gone With the Wind*–goes–naked clinch. Here, Peters and Streisand attend the premiere in December 1976.

*Bottom:* Steve Ross *(left)* was the powerful and magnetic chairman of Warner Communications, Inc., later Time Warner. His open-handed manner of dealing with stars like Streisand endeared him to many in Hollywood. He was Jon Peters's idol, and once Peters took the helm at Sony's studio, he tried to mimic Ross's lavish style.

Peter Guber's first move as an independent producer was to pay $10,000 for the rights to *Midnight Express,* the story of Billy Hayes, a young American who had escaped from a Turkish jail after being incarcerated for drug smuggling. Ever the promoter, Guber brought Hayes *(right)* to the Malta location of the film.

Guber joined forces with music mogul Neil Bogart *(right)* in 1976, merging their two companies into Casablanca Record and FilmWorks. Bogart's excessive spending on parties and drugs came to epitomize the excesses of the disco era—and caused Guber and their financial backer, PolyGram, to cut him loose in 1980. Bogart died of cancer of the kidney in 1982.

In the marketing campaign for his first production, *The Deep*, Guber fully exploited the appearance of star Jacqueline Bisset in all her wet glory. "That T-shirt made me a rich man," he said.

Jeff Wald, pictured with his former wife, Helen Reddy, managed disco diva Donna Summer and other major music acts. He got to know Peter Guber during the wild days at Casablanca Record and FilmWorks. After overcoming a ruinous cocaine habit, he worked for Jon Peters and Peter Guber during their brief and tumultuous tenure at Barris Industries, later called Guber-Peters Entertainment Co.

Lynda Guber enjoyed the perks of being a Hollywood wife. The marriage suffered some strains, but the couple stayed together. After her husband got the top job at Sony, she was set up in her own production company at the studio, though her only relevant experience was co-producing a yoga video.

...an | John Hamlin | Peter Guber | Jon Peters

Burt Sugarman gave Guber and Peters a rude introduction to the world of financial "players." Terren Peizer, a lieutenant of junk-bond king Michael Milken, matched the two, pictured here with Sugarman *(left)* who had a controlling stake in a cement company and a television firm best known for producing *The Gong Show.*

Debauchery reigned on the Rolling Hills golf course location of *Caddyshack* in Fort Lauderdale. Here producer Peters clowns with stars Chevy Chase, Ted Knight, and Rodney Dangerfield.

When Peters and Guber signed their partnership agreement in 1980, Peters's relationship with Streisand was waning and Guber was looking for another "dark twin" to replace his ailing former partner, Neil Bogart.

Peters and Guber got credit as executive producers of *Rain Man,* but they visited the set only once. The producing chores were handled by Mark Johnson, who got the honor of accepting the Oscar for best picture. At the Governors Ball following the awards, Guber and Peters borrowed a statuette from screenwriter Barry Morrow, who had won for his script, and posed for the cameras.

As the hands-on producer of *Batman,* Jon Peters pushed director Tim Burton to incorporate more action and romance into the film, making it more commercial. From left, Burton, Peters, Jack Nicholson as the Joker, and Michael Keaton as Batman on the London set.

"My sweetheart hoodlum" was actress Kim Basinger's nickname for Peters, who romanced her on the London set of *Batman* in 1988. During the shoot, Basinger, who played photographer Vicki Vale, could be seen at night ascending the elevator in the St. James Club hotel to Peters's suite, toothbrush in hand.

After several years in which Warner Bros. spent about as much as it made on the Guber-Peters relationship, Warner co-chairmen Bob Daly and Terry Semel (*far left,* pictured with Peters, Guber, and Mark Canton, then president of production) were thrilled when *Batman* brought in huge profits and created a franchise.

Peters and Guber were attending a party at the Playboy Mansion in the late eighties when Peters spied a blond Playmate-in-the-making across the room. Future *Baywatch* babe Pamela Anderson looked like a "little peanut," recalls Peters, who became her lover and protector off and on for several years.

*Above right:* Peters met Swedish supermodel Vendela in 1990, when he lured her to Los Angeles with the ruse of giving her a talent deal at Columbia. Before she arrived at her hotel, Peters filled her room to overflowing with orchids, and a romance was kindled.

*Below left:* After Sony lost an expensive battle to introduce the Betamax format as the standard for home video, Akio Morita, co-founder of Sony, concluded that the company would have prevailed if it owned entertainment software. The decision to acquire CBS Records and Columbia Pictures, the "synergy" strategy, fit his vision of Sony's future.

*Below right:* Sony's president, Norio Ohga *(left)*, established a warm relationship with the company's number-one corporate officer in America, Michael Schulhof *(right)*. Ohga assumed more responsibility after the Betamax fiasco in the seventies, and always wondered whether he could make a success of Morita's vision of marrying hardware and software.

Michael Ovitz, the superagent to the stars, ushered Sony, and later Matsushita, into Hollywood. He angled for the top job at Sony's studio but asked for richer terms than even Sony was willing to pay. The Japanese balked, but the Sony deal would propel him into a new career as agent-*cum*-dealmaker.

Walter Yetnikoff, the irreverent chief of CBS Records, helped to engineer the sale of the music company to Sony. His next ambition was to acquire a film studio. As Sony closed in on its deal to buy Columbia Pictures, Yetnikoff was flown on the company jet for rehab at the Hazelden clinic in Minnesota.

Jets were a constant theme in the Guber-Peters partnership. They coveted the Warner jet, quarreled with Bert Sugarman over the company plane during their partnership with him, and finally got full jet privileges.

*Above right:* Alan Levine, a lawyer whose practice had focused on television, landed the number-two job as COO at Sony's new studio despite Jon Peters's objections. Generally disparaged as a colorless figure without executive experience, he demonstrated surprising survival skills.

Columbia president of production Michael Nathanson *(left)* had survived several regimes at the studio when Peters and Guber became co-chairmen in 1989. He became one of Peters's most loyal soldiers after undergoing a brutal hazing at his hands. Three years later, Peters returned that loyalty, supporting Nathanson when he was publicly swept up in the Heidi Fleiss scandal.

Michael Medavoy *(right)*, pictured here with Mark Canton *(left)* and Guber, had worked for years making quality films under financial constraints at Orion. Taking over as chairman of TriStar represented the end to his personal and professional money worries. But Guber cooled to Medavoy after Warren Beatty complained that the TriStar chief was off boating on the Nile as the studio opened *Bugsy*.

Patricia Duff Medavoy, seen here with Peters, complained that decorating her Coldwater Canyon mansion gave her chronic fatigue syndrome.

COURTESY OF JON PETERS

A lifelong Republican, Peter Guber jumped with both feet onto the Bill Clinton bandwagon. TriStar chairman Michael Medavoy introduced candidate Clinton (shown here with Guber and his wife, Lynda) to Hollywood.

Peters and Guber pose with Michael Jackson, who signed a $60 million deal with Sony in 1991 encompassing films as well as music. Although most Hollywood insiders believed that Jackson's persona was too weird for him to become a film star, Peters was developing *MidKnight,* a fantasy project about a superhero, for him. *MidKnight* was shelved after Peters left the studio.

SAM EMERSON

SCOTT DOWNIE

PHOTOFEST

FRED PROUSER/SIPA PRESS

*Above left:* Jon Dolgen *(left)* had a reputation as a tough boss, but when he took over as president of Sony Pictures his efforts to bring expenditures under control were largely stymied. He warned that the studio might literally "spend itself to death."

*Above right:* Producer Steve Roth found the script for *Last Action Hero* and brought it to Columbia—only to be elbowed off the project when Arnold Schwarzenegger signed on. When the Heidi Fleiss scandal erupted, the studio tried to divert attention from its executives by pointing to Roth, an admitted Fleiss client.

*Right:* Arnold Schwarzenegger and Mark Canton, all smiles at the June 1993 premiere of *Last Action Hero* in Westwood, would both come to regret that they had overhyped the film. "It's probably the greatest action movie of all time," Canton crowed a few months before it was humiliated at the box office by *Jurassic Park.*

After Hollywood madam Heidi Fleiss was arrested in June 1993, Columbia was rocked by a scandal in which its executives were publicly linked with call girls. Her arraignment at the downtown Los Angeles municipal courthouse on August 9 was a major media event.

With his wife, *Forrest Gump* producer Wendy Finerman, looking on, Columbia-TriStar chairman Mark Canton blows out candles on his birthday cake at the premiere of *First Knight* in June 1995. With a budget of more than $70 million, *First Knight* was another in a long line of Columbia's overpriced, disappointing movies.

Mickey Schulhof was Sony's top-ranking non-Japanese executive. A physicist by training, Schulhof was believed by many in the entertainment industry to have been seduced by Hollywood glamour in general and Peter Guber in particular. He stood by as the expenditures mounted.

He moved back into their Brownwood residence, which was transformed into a sprawling ranch on two and a half acres with a barn for his daughters' horses. The house had been added onto so many times that "it was an architectural nightmare," says a friend. "Every square foot was used for babbling brooks, Moroccan smoking dens, and Art Deco living rooms."

The Gubers broadened their reach when they bought a ranch in Aspen for almost $6 million in 1987. The 648-acre spread encompassing aspen groves, meadows, and streams lay in the middle of an elk migration route on Owl Creek Road. Guber named the property Mandalay after Kipling's poem of the same name, which his mother had read to him as a child.

The Gubers drove local workmen hard to build—in four months—an 11,000-square-foot house of rustic wood and glass with three family bedrooms, three guest suites, a screening room, and a gym. They furnished it in Ralph Lauren Santa Fe style with pony-skin couches, an elk head over the doorway, and Edward S. Curtis sepia-toned photographs of Plains Indians. "The house was overdone," says a source who has attended parties there. "If Ralph Lauren walked in, he would edit."

Peter and Lynda designed Mandalay as a family retreat where they could spend time with their daughters, as well as a showcase for entertaining. They began hosting one of Aspen's toniest annual parties on the Saturday before New Year's Eve. Hollywood's finest would turn out, including Goldie Hawn, Jack Nicholson, Michael Douglas, Barry Levinson, Mike Ovitz, and Terry Semel. Snowmobiling was on the agenda, and guests could borrow gear from a downstairs storeroom which housed bins of sweatsuits, down coats, and powder suits.

As their children were growing up, Lynda cultivated interests of her own. She traveled to India with her closest friend, Carol Isenberg. She produced *Yoga Moves,* a home video for MCA. Despite her New Age explorations, Lynda still reveled in being a Hollywood wife, borrowing jewels on a floater policy from Frances Klein in Beverly Hills when she was required to show up at black-tie fundraisers with her husband, then returning them the next morning.

While Hollywood whispered about Lynda's love life, Peter went his own way. He continued his peculiar habit of blurting out his sexual proclivities in graphic detail to women he hardly knew in business situations. "I think Lynda gives Peter what he

129

wants, which is that she runs a good house, she's right in the social stream of things," says a friend who has known the couple for decades. "They are cut out of the same cloth, they really are. They understood each other. I know they came close to divorcing but she won't let him go and he won't let her go. . . . Lynda is a very conniving, manipulative woman and Peter is the same way."

Jon Peters continued his bachelor's life. He became involved in a volatile, on-again-off-again relationship with tall-and-blond interior designer Christine Forsyth; they married in 1986 and split again in 1987. When they were apart, Jon was as active as ever on the romantic front. Upon meeting a new prospect, he would send her a flower arrangement that barely fit inside her door, tell her to throw away her size 29 jeans in favor of size 27s, and get her started on a regimen of buttocks exercises because "every woman needs help there." He would send her to Azzedine Alaïa in Beverly Hills for skintight dresses and set her up with a therapist. Jon kept pop psychology books, such as *Men Who Hate Women, & the Women Who Love Them,* beside his bed.

At a soiree Jon and Peter attended at the Playboy Mansion in the late eighties Jon met future *Baywatch* babe and pinup goddess Pamela Anderson. Anderson had flown down from Vancouver Island to test for a Playmate spread. "I saw this little peanut standing in the corner," said Peters, who began talking to her and found her adorably sweet and naive. He advised Anderson not to pose for the pictorial: "You don't need to take your clothes off—you're *magic*," he told her. She ignored his advice, but they began a romance that would continue intermittently for years.

Jon had not yet learned to control his temper. Early one morning in July 1985, two workmen came to his Aspen ranch to collect $110 for landscaping. "Mr. Peters came out wearing a bathrobe and carrying an old-style, pearl-handled six-shooter," says Tom Stephenson, the police officer who investigated the incident. "He proceeded to point it at them, yelling and screaming at them to get off the property." James Bates, nineteen, and Thomas Aley, twenty-five, filed suit for $22 million, saying Peters squeezed the trigger four times. Jon settled out of court, reportedly paying Bates and Aley $60,000.

Even as his career as a producer blossomed, Jon continued

130

to devote himself to the acquisition and development of real estate with the zeal he had brought to remaking the ranch in Malibu. He bought a home in Beverly Park, a development of fourteen multi-million-dollar estates with twenty-four-hour guards in Beverly Hills just off Mulholland Drive. He filled the house with Remington sculptures, added a koi pond, and planted seven hundred trees, some of which required hauling by helicopter. He built a petting zoo and raised potbellied pigs and miniature horses.

By the late eighties, Jon had also begun buying and selling in Montecito, a wealthy community just south of Santa Barbara. Gene O'Hagan, a realtor there who worked with Peters, says he often watched Jon engage in protracted negotiations over expensive properties, whipping brokers into a frenzy of false hope. "He works these people to death and then gets in the car and says, 'It's a piece of shit. I don't want it,' " O'Hagan says. "Jon doesn't mind making $8 million, $10 million offers when he has no intention of doing anything about it."

O'Hagan concluded that Peters simply liked to generate confusion. "Jon is a man who can drive through an intersection, cause a fifteen-car accident, go out the other side unscathed, and then wonder why everybody else is such a bad driver," he says. "If you really want to analyze the character, Jon only works in chaos. If it's all laid out, he can't even think. If there's hysteria, screaming, arguments—he walks through like an altar boy."

Over the years, the Montecito community learned to dread Peters's maneuvers, O'Hagan remembers. In 1985, Jon acquired a beautifully landscaped house and brought in crews to plant mature trees. "Within a week of escrow closing, there were fifty- and sixty-foot semis, bumper to bumper, with these huge trees," O'Hagan recalls. "It was like bringing coals to Newcastle when you bring trees to Montecito. Then he put in another pond. The town was on its knees." There was a drought at the time and the community was trying to conserve water, but Jon created "this greenbelt that looked like Costa Rica, blithely paying any fines that were levied."

In 1988, O'Hagan remembers, Peters bought another house with a breathtaking ocean view. "As you panned around from the patio, there was a stand of eucalyptus trees—rather old —that blocked out maybe 20 degrees of a 180-degree view,"

131

O'Hagan says. The trees stood on an adjoining property and the owner, who had bought the house from music entrepreneur Irving Azoff, had not yet taken possession of the property. Jon had the trees cut down and sent his new neighbor a check for $50,000. Eventually, he trucked in tons of dirt to raise his land so that the view would be improved. Meanwhile, he gutted the house, then changed his mind about the renovation and left it boarded up. But the year after Jon bought the property for about $3 million, O'Hagan says, he sold it for $7 million. While Jon usually exaggerated the bargain prices that he paid for houses and the windfalls that he reaped when he sold, O'Hagan maintains that in this case he legitimately benefited from the last gasp of the real estate boom.

Jon's extravagant antics fueled an ongoing debate in Hollywood: Why did Peter Guber need Jon Peters? Apparently, they sometimes asked themselves the same question.

"They would fight every day, break up every day," says a former Guber-Peters employee. "That's been their style— screaming continuously." Frustrated by his partner's unwillingness to talk about his feelings, Jon insisted that Peter join him in weekly therapy sessions.

The truth was that Peter did need Jon as Jon needed Peter. One former Hollywood studio chief explains: "Peter in his heart has always wanted to be Jon, and Jon has always wanted to be Peter. Peter is an emotionally locked-up guy who would like to be fucking [television actress] Nicollette Sheridan but can't because he's a nice Jewish boy. And Jon always wanted to be taken seriously."

"They are incredibly different, almost antithetical," says their former television executive Stan Brooks. "One is like a machine, the other is like an animal. One is mind and the other is heart. And that's why they're so good together."

## 12

# MEN AT WORK

DURING THEIR YEARS together, Jon Peters and Peter Guber developed a modus operandi that became well known in Hollywood. Guber would go to almost any length to get literary material that he wanted, even if it meant grabbing properties from others who had nurtured them. Peters was usually less involved in pursuing books and scripts, but from time to time he would swoop down on projects in the works and wreak havoc. He also added a spark of creativity, just as he had done on *A Star Is Born*.

When Guber wanted to make a film about the story of murdered primatologist Dian Fossey in the mid-eighties, for example, he found himself competing with another producer. Arne Glimcher had been in lengthy negotiations with Fossey before her death and was preparing to make a film about her life at Universal. Guber quickly moved to knock his rival off track.

He set up a competing version at Warner, commissioned a quickie script, and dispatched a Warner executive to scout locations in Rwanda. He secured the cooperation of various agencies and wildlife organizations. But his most original move was reserved for the Rwandan government, whose blessing was needed to film in the gorillas' protected mountain habitat.

Roger Birnbaum, then the newly named president of Guber-Peters, flew to Washington to meet with the Rwandan ambassador. "I sent a letter to the president of Rwanda and we offered him the Humanitarian of the Year Award—we *made this up*, you know," says Birnbaum, laughing. "We offered them the world premiere of this movie in Rwanda. It was unbelievable."

"I was just outraged," says Glimcher. "I thought, 'These pirates are jumping on my movie,' and they were." But eventually, Glimcher had to yield. Universal and Warner agreed to an unusual joint venture—using the script by Anna Hamilton Phelan that Glimcher had carefully developed. And when *Gorillas in the Mist* opened in September 1988, Guber's name was emblazoned on the screen as executive producer.

None of this should have come as a surprise to anyone who knew Guber. "He doesn't come to you with a great reputation," said *Gorillas* director Michael Apted at the time. "You think, Guber-Peters, well, that's on the cusp of Hollywood sleaze here. . . . But they take these literary properties and make them into commercial entities. So it's sort of like this mixture of class and sleaze." In the case of *Gorillas,* which featured a bravura performance by Sigourney Weaver, that mixture resulted in a disappointing $24.7 million take at the box office in 1988.

On a couple of projects, Guber and Peters combined their special skills, with memorable results. On such occasions, they would leave a trail of traumatized producers and directors in their wake. Both left their imprimatur on *The Witches of Eastwick,* Updike's best-seller about a trio of small-town New England witches who tangle with the devil. That the story was about Satan seemed fitting; no one who worked on the film would forget how Guber and Peters bedeviled them from the beginning.

ROB COHEN was in the middle of a divorce and his career wasn't going well either. The aspiring filmmaker had recently directed a flop called *Scandalous.* He was broke and in desperate need of work. "I got a call from my lawyer, Tom Pollock, saying, 'I have something interesting for you, but God help you,' " he remembers. Cohen's friend, Matthew Robbins, had signed to direct *The Legend of Billie Jean,* a story about a young Texas brother and sister who become outlaws. Cohen was being offered the job of line producer, but there was a catch: It was a Guber-Peters production. Cohen was still smarting over the way Guber had horned in on his disco movie, *T.G.I.F.,* but he needed the cash. "I'll take it," he said.

Weeks later, Cohen sat down for breakfast with Guber at the Parker Meridien Hotel in New York before a *Legend* casting session. "It's great to be back working with you," said Guber. "Do you have anything else you're interested in?"

"Well, there is a book I'm trying to get made," replied the

134

unwary Cohen. "I've gotta tell you Warner Bros. has already passed on it. It's called *The Witches of Eastwick.*"

Cohen had heard about the project in February 1983 during a dinner party at producer Don Devlin's house in the Hollywood Hills. Devlin had told Cohen that he had read an advance copy of the book and thought it might make an interesting vehicle for his old friend and former roommate Jack Nicholson.

Cohen and Devlin put their heads together to figure out how to adapt the book to the screen. It dealt with dicey material, including homosexuality and cancer. The heroines weren't sympathetic. "What if the women aren't harridans?" mused Cohen. "What if they're good?" He envisioned the story as a primal battle of the sexes. Daryl Van Horne (the devil) would visit Eastwick with the intention of impregnating the three women. The part where the witches give a young girl cancer would be excised. "I ran all over town for the next few weeks, taking the book to every studio," Cohen said. No one nibbled.

But now, Guber responded with enthusiasm. "I love witches!" he exclaimed. "I used to love them when I was a kid!"

Guber instructed Cohen to go back to Warner Bros. to discuss development of the project with executives Mark Canton, Lucy Fisher, and Lisa Henson. After a successful meeting, Cohen remembers, he called the agent that was handling the book rights. He was informed that Guber had just optioned the book for $50,000 in his company's name.

"They bought the book out from under me," says Cohen. He was outraged: For the second time, he thought, Guber had essentially stolen a property from him. "I had trouble getting Guber on the phone so I went over to his office at Warner. He presented a deal to us which was essentially a line producer's deal. It was, 'Take it or leave it.' " Guber and Peters would get a producing fee of as much as $750,000, while Devlin and Cohen would receive $250,000. "Peter, I don't know how you can do this to me," Cohen remonstrated. "I thought we were going to be partners. We've been friends, we've already made a movie together. How could you?"

Cohen says Guber couldn't look him in the eye. "He said, 'Rob, this is the best I can do, I can't do any better.' That's the last time I saw Peter Guber on the entire project," Cohen says.

Cohen began working with screenwriter and Pulitzer Prize–

135

winning playwright Michael Cristofer, developing the script along the lines that had been discussed. Jon Peters presided over the next script meeting at Warner.

After the screenwriter went off to write a first draft, Cohen traveled to Corpus Christi, Texas, to make *The Legend of Billie Jean*. Cohen butted heads with Jon when Cohen refused to fire the director, who was sending dailies back to Burbank that Jon didn't consider sexy enough. "Every script was analyzed based on cock, pussy, killing, rock 'n' roll, and what movie was a hit last weekend," Cohen says. "That's the Jon Peters view of movies. He would say, 'What I love about Billie Jean is, you know, she's got this pussy. She's young, and she hasn't had any cock. She's probably a virgin. She's out there and this guy tries to rape her.' I'm telling you, it was *like* that." When Cohen defied Peters, Jon fired him, calling him a "Judas piece of scum," then rehired him half an hour later. The film bombed.

A year later, Cohen (who had landed a job running the Taft-Barish company) received Cristofer's first draft of *Witches*. He and Devlin loved it, but Warner didn't share their enthusiasm. Devlin ran the script over to Nicholson's house. "If we can get the right director, I'm in," the star said. Cohen learned that George Miller, the brilliant Australian director of the *Mad Max* trilogy, was available. Miller read the script and expressed interest, saying that he would make the movie as a comedy.

Cohen and Devlin informed Warner and Guber-Peters that Jack Nicholson and George Miller were both interested in *The Witches of Eastwick*. A few days later, Cohen got a call from Cristofer. "When are you going to Paris?" he asked.

"I don't know what you're talking about," Cohen replied.

"I just got a call from Lucy Fisher, and she said I'm supposed to go to Paris and meet George Miller. I assumed you're supposed to go too.'" Cohen called Fisher, who told him that Warner had decided to send Guber to Paris to close the deal. She added that Cohen would get a call shortly from Warner business affairs director Jim Miller about changing his and Devlin's credit on the film from producer to executive producer. Now that a script had been delivered that was attracting big-name talent, Guber and Peters were shoving aside the team that had nurtured *Witches*.

"Without legal cause, they threw both of us off the film," says Devlin. "We had to renegotiate our deal so that we were no longer the producers—they were. Mark Canton, president of Warner Bros., hired his own brother [Neil] as line producer. . . . We were treated abominably, subhumanly."

Cohen's lawyer, Tom Pollock, advised them that they couldn't win a lawsuit since their contract allowed Guber-Peters to pay them to go away. All Pollock could do was negotiate an increase in their fee from $250,000 to $300,000 each in exchange for their points in the film.

It was all over for Cohen and Devlin; now it was director George Miller's turn to step into the line of fire. *Witches* was about to get the Jon Peters treatment. Having grabbed the material and secured the talent, Guber disappeared. The production would descend into contentious chaos punctuated by chair-throwing, tears, and recriminations.

Looking back, Miller realizes that he had not done his homework. "I heard that Steven Spielberg had it in his contract that he would never have to meet Guber and Peters on the set of *The Color Purple*," he says. "I should have seen that as an early warning sign. . . . All I had to do was ask Steven. [Guber and Peters] said, 'We've worked with Steven, we had a great time with him,' and all this bullshit. Of course, he never even [dealt with] them."

*Witches* got off on the wrong foot when Warner pressured Miller into making key casting changes in the final hour. Miller had promised the part of Alexandra, the lead witch who sculpts fertility idols, to Susan Sarandon. The studio insisted on Cher for the part. Miller was obliged to ask Sarandon to play the number-two witch, Jane. Michelle Pfeiffer was brought in as Sukie, witch number three. Sarandon had the impression that Cher had demanded the lead role. "Susan wouldn't talk to me, she wouldn't look at me, she was crying a lot, she was smoking like crazy," Cher says. "And I didn't know [why]. I thought it was just her erratic behavior. I didn't know any of the back story."

Meanwhile, Miller was resentful that the rock diva had been forced on him, though she had acquitted herself well in *Mask* and *Silkwood*. "George Miller wanted anybody but me in his movie," Cher says. He shook her confidence. "Like, on my birthday," she says, "I'll never forget this—we've got a picture of me in my hotel room on my bed. They're bringing a cake in to me, and I'm sitting there crying because George Miller told me that I'm not sexy enough to play Alexandra."

137

The film was shot in the Massachusetts town of Cohasset, whose spare clapboard Yankee architecture and steepled church provided the right backdrop for the fictitious Eastwick. The director's vision was "basically a fairly ironic, eccentric comedy of manners," says Miller. He was eager to pit the rakish Daryl Van Horne, who describes himself as "a horny little devil," against the three formidable women who learn that they have special powers, including the ability to levitate and conjure thunderstorms. Van Horne seduces them one by one, but then he pays a price. Miller was striving for wit. Jon Peters had something else in mind. He saw *Witches* as a special-effects extravaganza. Warner decided to let the two men fight it out, figuring that Jon would provoke Miller into making a less decorous but more commercial movie. The studio was footing a big bill for the talent, including $6 million for Nicholson, and it wanted its money's worth.

The script was not set before shooting began. Jon hired Ron Bass to write some revisions, which Miller rejected. Miller admits he was feeling his way along as he shot and did not know how he wanted to end the picture. But although he was often unsure how to proceed, there was one thing he knew: He didn't like Jon Peters's ideas. "Jon had aspirations to be creative," says Miller, who is a physician by education. "It's a problem, because he's genuinely thought-disordered. The mind can't focus very clearly on one issue. You know, it's coming from fifteen different directions." Miller says that Peters's suggestions always pivoted around "the last movie he saw, or this week's grosses. If *Aliens* was out, it was, 'Oh we've got to make it like *Aliens.*' And the next week it's a Whoopi Goldberg movie, and he's saying, 'We've gotta turn it into a Whoopi Goldberg movie.' "

Peters in turn found Miller's indecisiveness intolerable. "I just wanted him to act like a director," he said. Jon was driven wild with frustration when he watched Miller nervously consuming Dove bars on the set while trying to decide how to resolve creative dilemmas.

With their director and producer at war, the three actresses felt ignored and insecure. "They made stupid mistakes," says Cher. "Like we're spending millions and millions of dollars on a movie, and they didn't have enough money for all of our costumes. Half of Sue's wardrobe I brought from my closet

138

because they had no money for us. Michelle's wardrobe came from second-hand stores. My wardrobe, most of it came from my own closet."

The female stars started to make their own demands. They believed that the script portrayed them as interchangeable, and insisted on revisions that would distinguish them as characters. They threatened to quit if the script was not amended.

"The women had begged to be in the movie," says a source at Warner. "And suddenly it became, 'How can we say these stupid words?' . . . They sensed confusion and panicked, and then misbehaved badly. The more they were quitting, the more fun it was for Jack. Jack would stir them up and would sit there and laugh."

The actresses saw things differently; they did not consider Nicholson the provocateur. "The women were so unimportant that they didn't really give a shit about us," says Cher. "And our only ally in the whole thing was Jack. And Jack went head-to-head with everybody."

As the shoot progressed and the conflicts between Peters and Miller grew sharper, Jon took out his anger on whoever strayed into his path. He threw a chair once during a meeting with Sarandon. "He was really rough on Sue," says Cher, "really disrespectful." He barred Sarandon's daughter Eva from coming to the set, then brought a group of visitors—including Barbra Streisand—to watch the cast work on a particularly difficult day, enraging the actresses. Peters infuriated Cher when he tried to placate her by offering her jewelry. "What do you think I am, a whore?" she retorted.

One day a scene was shot that required Cher to be covered with writhing snakes. "Which one is Jon Peters?" she inquired, entertaining the crew. "Here he is," she said, pointing to a reptile. "And the little one is Mark Canton."

Jon had been reluctant to mix it up with Nicholson, the only person on the movie who was clearly above him in the pecking order. But he shocked everybody by eventually losing his temper even with Jack. "We all just about shit," says Cher. "It was at the end of the movie. I think he was finally just running on fumes."

The scene was a big powwow among the actors, director, producers, and executives around a conference table at Warner. An ending still had not been agreed upon and there was 139 considerable pressure to wind up the film. The meeting hit a sour note when executive Lucy Fisher, who was expecting a baby at the time, told a complaining Cher, "You're lucky to have this job." Enraged, Cher balled her hand into a fist. "I almost hit her," Cher admits. "Because she was just so mean to us. . . . And Sue [Sarandon] grabbed my hand and said, 'She's pregnant!' "

In this environment, Jon exploded at Nicholson. "You know, you *can* talk to me this way," Nicholson responded evenly. "But if you keep doing this, I'll turn off. And if I turn off, you'll be in a lot of trouble."

The studio seemed unable, or unwilling, to address the problems. On occasion Guber would show up on the set but produced no discernible effect. "We all knew it was very dire if Peter Guber came," says Cher. "I don't know if he actually did anything. Jon Peters at least would scream and yell, and you knew what he was thinking, and you knew who he was and what he meant. Peter Guber—you never knew what was going on with him. I mean, he'd just smile."

As the end of filming approached, Jon forced Miller to shoot footage against the director's will. The budget ballooned as new scenes, mostly special-effects sequences, were filmed. Many would never be used. Miller blames Peters for the budget overruns. "Jon's ambition to be creative is so incredibly wasteful of money," he says. "It was at least 30 percent over budget because of his direct interference."

Michael Cristofer had written two possible endings, but as the film had become much bigger everyone knew they were too slight. "The struggle was, do you make it a witty ending or a special-effects tour de force?" says Miller. He favored the former; he wanted to shoot the final confrontation between Daryl and the witches in the kitchen of his mansion, where Daryl would reveal that he was a demon. Jon had another scenario, which Miller considered ludicrous. "It was like *Friday the 13th:* some ridiculous scene of the three women emerging out of a pool," he says. "And I kept trying to say, 'People, this isn't going to work. This is just nonsense.' "

Miller says he and Nicholson—who had approval of the movie's ending—were certain Jon's version would never be used. But "a wall of money came down" from the studio, so Miller caved in and shot the scene. As soon as the producers and

Warner executives looked at it, it ended up on the cutting-room floor. The climax that appears in the finished film features a 50-foot-tall Daryl Van Horne peering into the kitchen from outside the windows as the mansion shudders ominously. It was close to what Cristofer had originally written.

After a final row, Miller called Terry Semel and told him he would no longer deal with Peters. Jon responded as he often did when he had pushed too hard. "He does probably the most insulting thing he possibly can—he showers you with gifts," Miller says. "I mean, the most extravagant gifts you can imagine. I'm talking about thousand-dollar gifts, and fruit baskets. And then follows up the gifts with phone calls saying, 'Have you forgiven me?' I mean, the gifts are worse than the insults. He doesn't have the subtlety to understand that."

Polly Platt, the production designer on *Witches*, says that Warner should have ensured that everyone agreed on an ending before shooting began. "I think a great picture went down the drain," she says. "As a filmmaker, it breaks my heart to see what I saw—and I don't blame Jon Peters alone. Where was Guber? Where was everybody as we were struggling through that film? Toward the end, it was just grotesque."

As for Cohen and Devlin, the "executive producers" of *The Witches of Eastwick* were invited to attend its premiere in Westwood in the summer of 1987. They both loved the finished film: It was close to the script they had developed. Cohen says he called Guber the next day and congratulated him. Then he called Peters. "What did you have to do with it?" Jon said. "I rewrote every fucking line in that script."

The movie opened to mixed reviews. Janet Maslin of the *New York Times* wrote that *Witches* "brings a lot of special effects to bear upon a story of seduction that is much too frail to support this kind of gimmickry." Nonetheless, it was a $64 million hit. George Miller, despite being deluged with offers to direct prestigious studio films, felt so burned by his experience that he did not direct another picture for five years. He refused to return to Hollywood until 1992, when he made *Lorenzo's Oil*, which he also wrote and produced, for Universal Pictures. The picture, starring Susan Sarandon, is a harrowing true story about a gravely ill child. It did not succeed at the box office. But Miller's contract with Universal assured him complete creative control, and no studio personnel on the set.

141

# 13

## DANCING AT
## THE PREDATORS' BALL

THOUGH JON AND PETER liked to boast about their wealth, they knew they were relative pikers in the superheated environment of the eighties and hungered for a much bigger score. The question was how to get there. They had made diverse investments but they had not become tycoons. Jon Peters had an idea that there was one man who could help them fulfill their dreams. That man was Michael Milken, the junk-bond king whose fame was growing despite his efforts to keep a low profile.

Without being sure who Milken was, Jon figured that he was worth knowing. Frank Wells, who had left Warner Bros. to climb mountains, had since joined the Walt Disney Company as its president and chief operating officer. He took Peters to Milken's offices at Drexel Burnham Lambert.

They arrived at four-thirty one morning, an hour when Milken frequently received those seeking an audience. Wells was the kind of smart, self-assured, well-connected client who interested Milken. Jon Peters was hardly of Frank Wells's stature; he couldn't hope for Milken's attention on his own. He was just a movie producer whose fortune was paltry by Milken's standards.

Like Jon, Milken had grown up in the San Fernando Valley, but otherwise the two had little in common. "Sex, drugs, and rock 'n' roll wasn't Mike's thing," a former colleague from Drexel remembers wryly. But Jon had "force of personality" and famous friends. Maybe he wasn't a total write-off. Milken assigned Terren Peizer, his young protégé, to take charge of this questionable prospect.

142

Peizer was twenty-five years old when he arrived in Los Angeles in 1985 to start his job at Drexel Burnham Lambert. Dark and good-looking in a small-boned, delicate way, he had the sheen of someone who spent time in the gym and in expensive clothing stores. A former salesman at First Boston, Peizer had gained Milken's favor and confidence. Peizer was given a favored position next to Milken at his large X-shaped desk and a starting salary of $3.5 million a year with other perks thrown in.

To his fellow salesmen, Peizer's adulation of Milken was too bald—he almost seemed to want to become Milken. Since their voices sounded similar, Peizer would sometimes pretend to be the junk-bond king on the phone. At one point, he pasted a tiny picture of himself in a family photograph that Milken kept on his desk and started calling his boss "Dad."

When Peizer arrived in Los Angeles, he stayed at the Beverly Wilshire Hotel, near the Drexel offices, while he looked for a place to live. One weekend afternoon as Peizer was working beside the hotel pool, he received a phone call from Jon Peters. "I gotta meet you," Jon said. "I gotta talk to you."

At that point, Peizer was working with Ted Turner, who was exploring the idea of buying all or part of MGM/UA. The studio belonged to investor Kirk Kerkorian, who was making an industry out of selling it in bits and pieces. The once-venerable studio still seemed to mesmerize investors, and Jon was not immune. In that first phone conversation with Peizer, Jon said maybe he could get a piece of the MGM/UA deal, buying studio operations that didn't interest Turner. Peizer agreed to have dinner with Jon that Sunday, and the two got together at 72 Market Street, a fashionable Venice Beach restaurant.

To Peizer, Jon seemed to be the one who was obsessed with Michael Milken. He had a fierce hunger to become a "player" in the world of business. He started calling Peizer several times a day and taking him everywhere. They spent weekends in Santa Barbara or Aspen. Jon got his young friend into Helena's, a hot club favored by entertainment sybarites such as Jack Nicholson. He introduced him to women. And of course, he introduced him to Peter Guber.

Peizer was having a wonderful time with his new friends but he had no illusions about their financial skills. Jon would pester him to explain what he did at Drexel and then quickly lose

143

interest when Peizer went into detail. "Jon had it in his mind that you buy a private company and then you bring it public and then you cash out and make millions of dollars. It was just that easy," Peizer says. And Peizer doubted he could convince any investors to bankroll Guber and Peters in a play for a company. Given their lack of experience, he figured, they would be hard to sell as a management team. They made a great impression as producers and promoters but not as top-level executives, he thought.

But perhaps something could be worked out. Maybe their friends would ante up some money to back them. From the beginning, Barbra Streisand's name was bandied about, and Steven Spielberg's. And then there were Warner executives Terry Semel and Mark Canton, who had the kinds of résumés that Peizer needed to get a deal working. "I always did think that if a studio came up for sale, Jon and Peter needed some executives to lend credibility to their team," Peizer says.

Peizer and his new Hollywood friends toyed with various ideas for months. Jon tried to get Warner to finance the purchase of the Six Flags amusement park, which he planned to rename Guber and Peters's Six Flags. (Eventually, Warner did purchase a controlling interest in Six Flags but sold it in 1995.) Other schemes came and went: buying the short-lived De-Laurentiis Entertainment Group, or RKO, another struggling company. Nothing materialized.

As time went on, Peizer's primary relationship gradually shifted from Jon to Peter. "Peter was rational. Peter was presentable. Peter was articulate," he says. Jon was mercurial—and he had a habit, maybe amusing, maybe annoying, of trying his luck with women that Peizer had dated. Peizer concluded that Peter represented his only hope of doing some sort of business deal for his friends.

But Guber was restless. He was talking to Columbia Pictures, then owned by Coca-Cola, about becoming an executive there again. He had to get away from Jon, he told Peizer. Their personalities weren't meshing. "Peter wanted to go to Columbia. Jon wanted to be an industrialist. It clashed," Peizer says. Peizer urged Guber to wait. "Don't go," Peizer told him. "Do something bigger first. You can always do that."

With the pressure mounting, Peizer finally came up with an idea—an idea that he would later describe as "my joke." He would set Guber and Peters up by teaming them with a relatively small but hungry Drexel client, someone who had a bundle of Drexel-raised money burning a hole in his pocket. One evening in 1987, Peizer joined his friends on Peter's boat for dinner. He brought along Burt Sugarman, an eccentric and ruthless businessman who would give Jon and Peter a rude introduction to the world of players.

SUGARMAN WAS a Los Angeles native who had started out in the car business. As a teen, he had won a state drag-racing championship. He got a degree in finance at USC and started selling used cars. At twenty-four, he saw a photo of a Ghia and went to Italy to buy one. He became the U.S. distributor and started selling fast cars to the Hollywood set. Eventually, Sugarman was selling Maseratis and Excaliburs to the stars, and dating some. He nearly married Ann-Margret (she bailed out at the last minute) and got into the entertainment business in partnership with her manager, Pierre Cossette. They produced a television music special in 1970, but the partnership lasted only a couple of years. "I wanted to make shows and he wanted to be Howard Hughes," Cossette told the *Wall Street Journal* later.

Sugarman's biggest success was *The Midnight Special,* a late-night TV show that featured big rock acts: The Rolling Stones, Chicago, The Temptations. But Sugarman was still hungry. In 1982, he bought a controlling stake in Giant Group, a publicly held cement company in Columbia, South Carolina. Sugarman told friends that he loathed the cement business so much that he burned his clothes after visiting the factory, but Giant provided him with a springboard from which to embark on new financial adventures. He started making runs at other companies.

Not many months before Sugarman met Jon and Peter, the Securities and Exchange Commission (SEC) had decided it didn't like the look of him. His early activities as a Drexel protégé aroused suspicion. He was investigated for various securities law violations but the SEC never brought charges.

Even as he pursued his other investments, Sugarman kept his appetite for the entertainment world. He had produced a few films which got some favorable reviews but didn't perform particularly well at the box office. In 1987, he decided to try a

145

more commercial approach. He bought a controlling interest in Chuck Barris Productions, a company that produced game shows, including *The Gong Show, The Dating Game,* and *The New-lywed Game.* The company had been run by Barris and his partner, Bud Granoff, for some twenty years. The syndicated television business had its ups and downs, but Barris and Granoff had stayed together and made out well until they had a bitter falling out. Barris sold his shares to Sugarman, leaving Granoff with a new partner.

Granoff didn't stay at the company long, but several things bothered him while he was still there. For one thing, he was annoyed that Sugarman had used some of the company's money to buy a $5.5 million Gulfstream jet. "We needed a Gulfstream like I needed an accordion," Granoff complained. He also objected when Sugarman got Barris to pay him $1.15 million for his collection of old television programs—*The Midnight Special* and a couple of game shows. Granoff thought the properties were worthless and found that he "couldn't get a nibble" from television stations when he tried to sell the shows.

Granoff was baffled again when Sugarman hired Jeff Wald—Neil Bogart's old crony. Wald was clearly being groomed to run the company after Granoff left. Wald was short, barrel-shaped, hot-tempered, and profane. He knew nothing about the television syndication business.

Wald's reasons for taking the job weren't at all mysterious. He was short of money and, for once, short of confidence. At forty-two, he was operating for the first time as an adult without the crutch of drugs. Wald had been married to singer Helen Reddy for eighteen years. He was her manager well before she became famous with her anthem, "I Am Woman." But Reddy wasn't Wald's only client. At various times, he managed Chicago, George Carlin, Flip Wilson, Sylvester Stallone, and Crosby, Stills and Nash. He claimed credit for packaging Donna Summer into a mega-star ("I sent her to Francesco Scavullo for pictures and Bob Mackie for gowns," he says).

He was a high roller in the high-rolling show business world of the seventies. But after years of mind-boggling drug abuse, Wald finally collapsed one day. At the brink of death, he underwent major surgery (his cocaine-ravaged face literally had to be pinned back together). When he emerged from the Betty Ford Clinic, Wald was deeply in debt and jobless. He knew Sugarman

146

because Reddy had been a host on Sugarman's *Midnight Special* television show. And he desperately needed a job.

Despite his ignorance about the syndicated television business, Wald saw no mystery in Sugarman hiring him. Even after his drug habit left him ruined, Wald felt that he brought something to the table. "I was an A player in this town, socially and otherwise, and Burt was a B player," he says. "I mean, socially, he wasn't Jeff Wald. My relationships were much broader and deeper than his."

At the time, Sugarman was raising $60 million through Drexel, and he told Wald that he planned to parlay the money into something bigger. Terren Peizer was the man who would make it happen. Sugarman had met Peizer at Drexel's Predators' Ball, its annual conference of clients, in 1987.

"He had a tenacity about him, an intensity," Peizer says. "I had these two relationships going side by side. So I had this thought: 'Here's Burt Sugarman with two publicly held companies doing what Jon would like to be doing. Jon and Peter were doing what Burt wants to do.'"

The deal made sense. Peizer wouldn't have to convince anyone other than Sugarman to invest in Jon and Peter. If Sugarman acquired the Guber-Peters production company, Jon and Peter could bring some glitz into Barris's distinctly unsexy game-show business. And Jon and Peter had some high-profile projects in the works, including *Rain Man* and *Gorillas in the Mist*. There was talk—as always—that Streisand could become an asset to the company.

The partnership had both a certain logic to it and an equivalent recklessness. Perhaps Guber might have noticed that Sugarman's interests were so varied—from metals to cement to television programming—that he looked more like a forager than a builder. Perhaps he might have worried about the SEC investigation of Sugarman's conduct. Perhaps he might also have fretted about giving up the freedom that he and Jon enjoyed within their own company, where they didn't have to share fees with anyone and didn't have to file reports with the SEC or answer to shareholders.

For whatever reason, Guber did hesitate. To Peizer, Guber's behavior seemed irrational. One evening he drove over to Peter's house to convince him of the benefit of the partnership. He couldn't believe he had to make this pitch; he felt that he was giving Jon and Peter a spectacular gift. He was putting them into the big show, giving them the platform of a publicly held company that had Drexel-raised cash on hand. At their production company, they were splitting around $7 million before taxes in their best year—hardly real money, to Peizer's way of thinking. And there were years in which they made less than half that amount. For the nine months before the deal, their revenue was down to $152,000.

Jon and Peter had everything to gain from the Barris deal, Peizer told Guber. They were movie producers, but what tangible assets did they have that could be worth millions of Sugarman's dollars? He showed Peter a sheet of yellow legal paper on which he had sketched out the premise of the agreement with Sugarman. His conclusion was underlined: "Sweetheart Deal."

For the purposes of the deal, Peizer made the assumption that Guber and Peters's production company was worth about $50 million. Based on Drexel's valuation of the company, Jon and Peter would receive Barris stock and short-term notes, making the deal worth nearly $30 million based on the stock's value at the time. Peizer expected to get a piece of the action: According to him, Jon and Peter had named him an officer of their company and pledged 20 percent of the stock to him.

Guber and Peters didn't share Peizer's understanding. They told Peizer to forget about a 20 percent share in their company unless he was willing to quit his job at Drexel and come to work with them. Peizer—who was making millions at Drexel—was stunned. He felt that Jon and Peter had broken an unwritten rule by trying to revise their agreement with him. And he couldn't believe that they were so jealously guarding a share in their meaningless company. "All of a sudden, they're starting to believe their own story," he marvels. "All of a sudden, their little fees from making these movies wouldn't be going all to them. All of a sudden, they don't own the company. Well, guys, your company isn't worth anything."

According to Peizer, he gave back his entire stake in Guber-Peters and washed his hands of the matter. " 'Do I want to be involved with these unsophisticated people?' " he asked himself then. "I think they didn't realize what I had just done for them," he says. "They're very greedy. Very greedy." As he bowed out, he figured the new partners would need plenty of

148

luck to make it together. "I got off the phone thinking, 'This thing will never work,' " he adds. "I didn't think their chances of survival were too good without their marriage counselor. Jon and Peter didn't understand Burt's world and they needed someone to explain Burt's world. Constantly."

IN DECEMBER 1987, the Guber-Peters Co. announced a merger with Barris. "We're a real studio now," Jon boasted to the *Los Angeles Times*. "I want to build another MCA." It was a grand dream: MCA, the parent of Universal Studios, was a sprawling entertainment empire worth billions. Jon may have made a big leap, but still his past haunted him. The *Times* couldn't resist observing: "That would make quite a climb for the 41-year-old seventh-grade dropout and reform school graduate who began his show-business career as Barbra Streisand's hairdresser-boyfriend-manager."

But carping aside, Jon had taken a step toward becoming a player. "He amazed me with his gumption and—for a guy with his lack of education—his business sense. I doubt Jon could tell you what cash flow is," says Stephen Weinress, a financial analyst who was alone in endorsing and promoting Sugarman's companies during this period.

Weinress remembers attending a meeting of prospective investors shortly after the deal was announced. The setting was corporate and those invited to attend were staid business types. One participant asked about Jon and Peter's vision for the company. Jon responded. "He said, 'This might be a little seed right now but it's going to germinate into a fucking sequoia,' " Weinress recalls. "Everybody in the room just about popped out of their chairs. That was his last appearance before the investment community."

Peizer's sweet deal had included one key provision that would turn increasingly sour to Jon and Peter: Sugarman would retain the power to vote all their shares. So, even though they were executives and shareholders who had authority, on paper, to run the company, Sugarman had the ultimate power to call the shots. "They basically just got jobs," says one former Sugarman associate. "Effectively, they really were employees. They had nothing to say, whether they liked it or not."

149

It wasn't long before the Guber-Peters/Sugarman partnership started to show signs of strain. There were fights over the usual issues: money and control. Sugarman may have told Jon and Peter that they would run the company, but they would soon learn that he wasn't the type to keep his hands off.

The company had two shows on the air when Jon and Peter joined: *The New Newlywed Game* and *The Dating Game,* and there was an effort under way to revive *The Gong Show,* one of Barris's biggest hits. Meanwhile, Sugarman seemed to be spending Barris money liberally, but not on the empire-building deal that Jon and Peter had in mind. Instead, he was pursuing other costly adventures—flying around on his jet, sending the bills to Barris. Gadding about on a Warner Bros. jet was one thing. Now that Jon and Peter were owners, those big bills were being paid out of their pockets.

The combination of personalities became increasingly combustible. "Peter was always quiet and Jon was always shouting and Burt was always quiet and you thought somebody was going to get killed," says Chris Bearde, an original *Gong Show* producer who was hired to help update the show. "[Burt] had this cement factory and there was this joke going around that someone would end up in cement."

The new partners made their first public appearance together on a June afternoon to announce a talk show featuring Kenny Rogers. Rogers had turned down other offers to do talk shows, but his manager, Ken Kragen, says Sugarman and his partners had been persuasive. "The big inducement was movies," Kragen says. "They dangled a lot of very juicy things in front of us. [Jon] was very grand about all of this and left us with this incredible impression about how successful we were going to be." And then, Rogers had other reasons to succumb. "They offered him a ton of money," Kragen says—a couple of million dollars just to do a pilot. "They were big spenders," he remembers.

The Guber-Peters-Barris contingent had called a press conference at Spago, the trendiest of Hollywood restaurants. Guber told the reporters that he, Peters, and Sugarman were making their first appearance to announce "the most important project that we'll do this year."

But the show of unity almost turned into a fracas. Jon had carefully planned the announcement and dispatched Jeff Wald to Kragen's office earlier that day to relay the details. When Wald arrived, he was surprised to find Sugarman already there, delivering his own set of instructions. "And Burt shouldn't have been there," Wald says. "I mean, he shouldn't have been involved at that level. . . . And so when the thing happened at Spago and it wasn't the way Jon wanted, Jon came up to me, furious. Not swinging, but loud and angry. Saying, 'What happened?' "

Wald explained that Sugarman had overruled his instructions.

"Jon grabbed Burt and punched him in the chest," Wald says. "Right in Spago. Right in the fucking front room of the restaurant. Took his breath away pretty good. At which point, Peter and I pushed Jon and Burt into the men's room. It was really bizarre, to tell you the truth. You know, there's like two hundred members of the press in the other room. There were all the cameras and shit in the other room and this is going on like twenty-five feet away. So, I mean, Peter and I just fucking freaked."

After all the fighting, the Kenny Rogers talk show never materialized. Wald maintained that Sugarman had offered Rogers so much—$12 million in the first year—that the company could never have made money. There weren't enough television stations interested in the show to justify going into production. "We lost our ass," Wald said. "We spent a ton of money and time and effort, but Burt had made this impossible deal."

SINCE THE MERGER was consummated, it seemed, almost nothing had gone right. All Jon wanted was to get on with his plan of building another MCA. But that dream had been expensively sidetracked as Sugarman pursued another quarry. He was waging an expensive battle for control of Media General, a Richmond, Virginia, based company that owned newspapers, television stations, and cable systems.

In February 1988, Barris and his Giant Company launched a $1.75 billion takeover bid for Media General. The company was controlled by the conservative and powerful Bryan family, and financial analysts quickly concluded that Sugarman's chances of success were, as one put it, "nil." Nonetheless, Sugarman pressed ahead.

The battle was costly, embarrassing, and futile. Wald, who had been an active political fundraiser in his day, was asked to use some of his political connections to help in the attack. He

151

felt particularly put upon. He had told Jon and Peter that he thought Sugarman was abusing the company. He told them that Sugarman had gotten the company to overpay him for the old *Midnight Special* reruns, and said Sugarman asked the company to pay for trips on the corporate jet that appeared to have nothing to do with business and everything to do with his girlfriend and, later, wife, *Entertainment Tonight* anchor Mary Hart. Wald refused to sign some of the checks to cover these expenses.

"Here I'd survived being a drug addict," Wald explains. "I'm not going to get my tit caught in a ringer in terms of being one of these schmucks in a public company that screwed up." He turned to Peter for counsel. Peter told him to do what he thought was best. Wald took that evasive answer as a sign that Guber respected his judgment.

However restrained Peter's response, both he and Jon were feeling victimized by Sugarman. The jet, which was costing the company thousands of dollars, became something of an obsession. For once, someone else's extravagance was the problem. Chris Bearde, the *Gong Show* producer, remembers going to meetings that were supposed to be about programming and finding instead that he was listening to endless bickering. "[I was] sitting there with my stupid pieces of paper and these guys are on about this fucking jet," he remembers. "They were talking about jets more than they were talking about show business. It was very frustrating. There was this crackle in the room. When you walked out, it was such a relief."

Weinress, the financial analyst who had supported Sugarman for so long, later said he assumed that Guber and Peters knew all along that Sugarman was taking advantage of the company. "None of this should have been a surprise to Jon and Peter," he says. None of it was secret. Weinress acknowledges that he also was aware of Sugarman's activities even while he was promoting the company. "I defended everything," he says. "I'm realistic enough to know that there's so much crap going on in this business, I'm jaundiced about it." And as far as Jon and Peter were concerned, he says, Sugarman's "self-dealing and all that other stuff . . . only became an issue when they wanted to get him out."

By the end of Barris's fiscal year in May 1988, the company's revenue was off 33 percent; its operating income was down nearly 50 percent, to $14 million. Its television shows were failing. Old syndicated television hands like Chris Bearde and Bud Granoff blamed Wald in part for wrecking the company. "He didn't have enough knowledge of syndicated television," Bearde explains. "You can't just walk into this. Bud Granoff was the ultimate master of being able to schmooze those television station guys. . . . Jeff doesn't have that ability. You get people who dislike you in those stations and they'll destroy a show. That's what happened with Jeff and Burt." Wald countered that the shows were worn out and impossible to sell.

According to the company's lawyer, Terry Christensen, Jon and Peter became fearful about what their shareholders would make of Barris's dealings. The wild ride of the eighties was drawing to a close. The SEC was known to be cracking down on Sugarman's patrons at Drexel. Fear was in the air. "Jon and Peter were always worried about shareholder lawsuits," he recalls. "They had never been in this situation and I think their inclination was not a bad one, which was, 'Let's get real cautious here.' "

By July 1988, the Guber-Peters-Barris team seemed to have one last chance at making something out of their misbegotten marriage. They were poised to make the big move that Jon and Peter had been longing to make: The partners announced that they would pay Kirk Kerkorian $100 million for 25 percent of that coveted property, MGM. The plan called for creation of a new MGM, with Peter Guber as its chairman and chief executive and Jon Peters as president and chief operating officer. The majority of the new company would still be owned by tycoon Kirk Kerkorian.

Since MGM's crown jewel—its library of films—already had been sold to Ted Turner, no one was quite sure what the Barris partners were getting for their money. The only obvious answer was the Leo the Lion logo. And Jon and Peter and Wald all dived right in, dashing around with Leo the Lions plastered on sweatshirts and gym bags.

The big play quickly turned into an embarrassing debacle. Two weeks after it was announced, the Barris partners backed out without explanation. *Variety* cited unconfirmed reports that Guber-Peters-Barris couldn't arrange financing for the transaction. Others speculated that the would-be acquirers changed their minds when they got a closer look at what they would

153

be buying. Attorney Terry Christensen, who interestingly also represented Kerkorian in the transaction, says the amount that the Barris partners proposed to put in diminished during the negotiations. But according to him, the deal collapsed because the Barris team—mainly Peter Guber and Burt Sugarman—simply couldn't decide what to do. (Jon says it wasn't that the group couldn't decide, but that he raised questions about whether the three partners could service the debt if they managed to arrange the financing.)

Perhaps Jon and Peter were wise to hesitate, but staying out was expensive, too. The deal collapsed at a cost of $5 million to Barris, according to Wald. And in October 1988, Barris's financial news got worse. The company reported a net loss of $6.9 million for first quarter of fiscal 1989. Revenue had dropped 13 percent. The company cited investment setbacks: It had lost money on various stocks. *Forbes* quoted a money manager's analysis: "Barris has turned into an investment company that doesn't have control of its destiny."

Jon and Peter may have had some interest in being part of an investment company, but hardly one that was losing money and respect. On the other hand, they weren't doing much to help. *Caddyshack II* had bombed and *Gorillas in the Mist* was heading for a lackluster performance. Relations among the partners were at an all-time low. Sugarman was no longer speaking to Wald; they communicated by way of correspondence sent to Peter Guber.

Guber appeared to be in a funk. Wald thought he seemed thoroughly worn out with his adventure as chairman of a publicly held company. Wald remembers Peter telling him at one low point, "It's like Christmas and your kid gives you a tie and you hate the tie and you've got to wear it."

As the situation degenerated, the task of brokering peace fell to Gary Winnick, a former associate of Michael Milken's who had brokered Sugarman's first introduction to Drexel. Winnick now ran his own investment firm and he had a stake in what went on in Barris: He owned about 4.9 percent of the stock—as much as he could own, under government rules, without disclosing his position to the public. He was an adviser to Sugarman and eventually Jon and Peter also turned to him for counsel.

A big, beefy man with a street-smart style, Winnick was always

154

much amused by the hypocrisy of the Hollywood set. He tried without luck to impose a cease-fire on the warring parties. But now, just a year after the partnership had been announced, Jon and Peter had had enough of Sugarman. The company had started to attract unflattering attention in the media. In an article in its November 1988 issue, *Forbes* said Guber and Peters were "reportedly furious that Burt's stock deals have all soured and they would like either to wrest control of Barris from Sugarman or get their company back." With Sugarman holding all the voting power in the company, was he likely to walk away? As *Forbes* put it: "Fat chance."

This was not the kind of press that Jon and Peter wanted. But walking away wouldn't prove easy for them, either. Their deal with Barris had been set up so that splitting off their old company would have heavy tax consequences for them. They had to get Sugarman to leave. Weinress, the financial analyst who had soured on Sugarman, suspected that Jon and Peter had enough unflattering information about Sugarman to get him out. "He didn't want to be embarrassed," Weinress says. "Let's be real. Mr. Sugarman's reputation is not what I call the best. They would have raked him over the coals."

Some of Sugarman's associates dismiss the idea that he would have been intimidated by Guber and Peters. But he might have heeded Winnick, who had concluded that Barris was self-destructing and told Sugarman that somebody had to go. Sugarman was willing but he didn't want to suffer. With the stock that he had bought at $13 a share now trading at about $7, Sugarman told Winnick, "I'm not taking a loss."

Winnick took on the daunting task of finding a buyer who would pay a premium for the company. Soon after, he found himself discussing the problem with Larry Horowitz, an investment banker working out of San Francisco. Horowitz was a man of varied background: he was a medical doctor who had been a top aide to Senator Ted Kennedy in Washington before becoming involved in investment banking. Horowitz came up with Frank Lowy, an Australian shopping mall and television magnate.

Guber was dispatched to Australia to practice his legendary salesmanship on Lowy, who was willing to buy at a high price. That meant Sugarman was out.

Why would Lowy pay $13 a share for a company trading

155

much lower? Perhaps he was hoping to mimic fellow Australian Rupert Murdoch, who had bought 20th Century Fox. Meanwhile, Jon and Peter had a hit. *Rain Man* picked up four Oscars the week before the deal was announced. "Just keep it in mind, it was the eighties," Christensen says. "Thirteen dollars a share —what the hell? It was probably borrowed money."

Guber wasn't thrilled with Lowy, who now became chairman of the board of the company, now named Guber-Peters Entertainment Co. "I gathered when Frank took over that Peter was not wildly happy about having an Australian mall developer," says a board member brought in by Lowy. "On the other hand, he was so anxious to get rid of Sugarman that it represented a great achievement for him."

BY APRIL 1989, the Guber-Peters-Sugarman relationship was a memory and Jon and Peter had a new partner, or perhaps a new boss. According to Christensen, they were in for a rude awakening. The new marriage would be even briefer than the partnership with Sugarman.

"It turns out Lowy was as opinionated as Burt but with a much rougher edge," Christensen says. "Jon and Peter immediately saw that this is from the frying pan into the fire. They expected a lot more distance from Lowy. And he shows up at a board meeting and starts talking about what the budgets are going to be and what the reporting relationships are and basically acting like a CEO."

But Lowy was in for some surprises, too. Jon and Peter had come up with their biggest hit, but when *Batman* was released, says a board member, the Lowy camp was shocked to discover that Warner got most of the money. Peter Guber's knowledge and understanding of the movie world were "kind of dazzling to those of us that weren't familiar with it," that board member continues. But there were aspects of Hollywood arcana that were less appealing. "I had the feeling he was hiding the ball a lot of the time. His communications were somewhat minimal. [Lowy] was having a hard time getting used to the Hollywood way."

Under Gary Winnick's tutelage, Guber started looking for new ways to make something out of the company. They toyed with the idea of buying the New Jersey Nets basketball team. Guber went to Japan to attempt to arrange a financing agreement with Fuji. Somehow Jon and Peter's situation had to improve. "They were at a point in their lives when they had money, they had success, and this is not fun," Christensen says. "They thought it wasn't fun with Burt. They knew right away it wasn't fun with Frank Lowy."

One Saturday night, not four months after Lowy bought into the company, Winnick picked up a rumor that Sony was poised to buy Columbia Pictures. And Winnick had an idea. Maybe an opportunity was there. The next morning, he phoned Peter Guber at home and asked, "Who do we know at Columbia?"

Peter had his relationships at Columbia but he and Jon had a much closer friend, surprisingly perhaps, at Sony. Not a Japanese friend, but an American one: the thoroughly outrageous head of Sony's record company, Walter Yetnikoff. And Yetnikoff, though he was staggering toward collapse from substance abuse, was the right friend to have.

# 14

# HIT MEN

By the time they were plotting how to horn in on the Columbia deal, Guber and Peters had "made" the two huge hits that would immeasurably enhance their résumés. *Rain Man* and *Batman* provided them with credentials that would help them sell themselves. These films created the impression that Guber and Peters had such brilliant commercial instincts that maybe they could even run a major studio.

As usual, the two men had displayed some of their greatest skill by picking two properties that would turn red-hot. They had virtually nothing to do with making *Rain Man*—the story of a slick car salesman and his autistic brother—though they weren't shy about taking credit when it turned out to be a hit.

*Batman* was the first and only blockbuster the Guber-Peters Entertainment Co. could legitimately call its own. Of course Jon and Peter had appropriated ideas and elbowed aside others who deserved credit. Old habits are hard to break. But Jon Peters, though he incited havoc on the set, put his imprint on the movie, and in this instance, when style mattered more than substance, he succeeded in creating a phenomenon.

These films catapulted Guber and Peters to a new level. Only Hollywood insiders knew that appearances were deceiving.

Neither Guber nor Peters had initially shown much interest in *Rain Man,* though they allowed one of their employees to acquire and develop the original screenplay. Michael Ovitz, then widely known as the superagent to the stars, is the man credited by everyone involved as the powerhouse who eventually packaged the picture and got it made with his own clients —Dustin Hoffman, Tom Cruise, and director Barry Levinson.

Barry Morrow, a television writer, had come up with the story of a cynical salesman (Cruise) who discovers he has a brother (Hoffman) when their father dies. In early 1986, he presented the idea to Roger Birnbaum, then president of Guber-Peters and Stan Brooks, who was running the company's television operation. "When Barry pitched it to me, the first words out of my mouth were, 'This is the best story I ever heard,' " Birnbaum recalls.

Birnbaum and Morrow offered the project to Warner, which passed because it had a similar movie, *Forrest Gump*, in the works. (To its sorrow, Warner later dropped *Gump* because it thought the project had been preempted by the success of *Rain Man*. The record-breaking *Gump* was made and released—almost a decade later—by Paramount.)

United Artists president Robert Lawrence embraced *Rain Man* in the first pitch meeting. "It was this thing that Roger and this television writer had," he remembers. "I bought it fifteen minutes into the pitch."

Guber was unenthusiastic. He told Birnbaum that he believed the best movies were based on books. "I remember he was annoyed at me because I kept saying, 'I have this great movie I want to make called *Rain Man*,' " says Birnbaum. "He said to me, 'You go work on *Rain Man*, I'll go work on *Contact*.' " (*Contact*, based on a Carl Sagan book, languished for years.)

Birnbaum spent eight months developing the script with Morrow. As president of Guber-Peters, he had a piece of the company, and his contract guaranteed that he would get producer's credit and a percentage of the profits if the picture was made. He was passionate about getting it done. "This was my baby," he says.

When Ovitz got Dustin Hoffman and director Martin Brest interested in the script, Birnbaum and Morrow met them at a diner in Malibu. At the conclusion of the meeting, Hoffman threw his arm around Birnbaum and said, "We're going to do this movie together, and it's going to be great."

Birnbaum got into his car with Morrow and dialed Guber as they pulled out of the parking lot. "Remember that little movie you said was nothing?" he asked his boss. "Well, Dustin Hoffman just committed to doing it with Marty Brest." Guber told Birnbaum to come to his house with Morrow first thing in the

159

morning, saying he wanted to go over some important script points.

Birnbaum and Morrow arrived for breakfast at Guber's house promptly the next day. Guber told them he had thought of the perfect way to wrap up the movie. Morrow's draft concluded with Hoffman's character, the autistic Raymond, being brought back to Los Angeles by his brother; the last sequence was of the brothers sitting on a hill outside of Dodger Stadium watching a baseball game.

"I've got this ending which is going to be really sensational," Guber told them excitedly. "What will happen is, Raymond will come back and his brother will get him to pitch in the Dodger game—and he'll win the game for the Dodgers! And it will be big, it'll be huge!!"

"I could see Barry Morrow's complexion turn translucent," recalls Birnbaum. "He was stunned. But I had been in story meetings with Peter, so I was very, very aware of his attention span. And so I said, 'That's a very interesting idea. We'll go back and we'll work on that.' And we left and we got into my car and I said, 'Forget about it. He won't remember it after tomorrow.' "

Meanwhile, Birnbaum was being wooed by United Artists to become its president of production. He says that when he came to Guber-Peters, he had been assured by his bosses that they would let him out of his contract if such an opportunity arose. Although he liked and respected Guber, he was having serious difficulties working for Peters. One particular incident cemented his resolve to take the UA job.

In a meeting with screenwriter Randy Feldman, who was working on *Tango & Cash* for Guber-Peters, Birnbaum had volunteered some ideas. "Shut up! I didn't ask you to speak in this meeting!" Peters yelled at him. "I'm the producer of this movie, I don't need you to speak." Birnbaum walked out of the room.

A few days later, Peters called Birnbaum and asked him to do something for him. "I didn't want to do it, because I thought it was immoral—probably it was illegal too—but I honestly don't remember what it was," Birnbaum says. "And I said, 'No, that's your mess, you do it.' He said he was going to come down to my office and break my jaw. I said, 'I'm right here.' Of course, I never expected to see him." But Birnbaum guessed wrong.

160

"He came barreling into my office and he grabbed me by my shirt, pulled my face up to his, and he said to me, 'I am worth a hundred million dollars, motherfucker. What have you got?' And I said, 'I have self-respect.' "

Birnbaum went to Guber and said he could no longer work at the company. "I said, 'I'm getting out of here, and I don't even know why you're still with this guy—this guy is an embarrassment.' At that point he practically begged me to stay. I said I would consider it if Jon was gone. How can you work in a place where the guy doesn't respect your creative ideas and threatens you with bodily harm?"

According to Birnbaum, Guber and Peters finally agreed to let him out of his contract but to maintain his participation in the films he developed, specifically *Rain Man*. "They said, 'Don't worry. These are yours, and we're still gonna take care of you, and you'll still get credit and still get paid on these projects.' And so in a very naive way I said, 'Great,' and we broke the contract." Birnbaum went off to United Artists.

Hoffman was notoriously finicky, known for micromanaging any project in which he was involved. Brest fell by the wayside because of differences with Hoffman and it fell to Ovitz to shop the project to other directors, which went on for nearly a year. Meanwhile, screenwriters Richard Price, Michael Bortman, Kurt Luedtke, and David Rayfiel all took expensive swipes at the script. Jack Nicholson was considered to co-star with Hoffman, but Tom Cruise was looking for a serious dramatic role and he committed to the project.

Spielberg wanted to work with Hoffman and he spent several months honing the script, but then left reluctantly because he was committed to direct the third *Indiana Jones* installment. Sydney Pollack came and went, saying he didn't see how to make the movie work. (The miracle was that Pollack even considered working with Hoffman: The two had quarreled furiously during the making of *Tootsie* a few years earlier.) Finally, Ovitz brought in Barry Levinson.

Spielberg told Levinson the film would be a hundred-million-dollar winner. "That was my last line to him after he debriefed me at a restaurant in Westwood and I gave him everything—all my notes, everything that I had developed," Spielberg says. "I just poured them out to Barry—what he used or didn't use was his call."

Like others associated with *Rain Man,* Spielberg had seen nothing of the executive producers during the time he was involved. "Peter Guber, he wasn't even around," he remembers. "I never had a single meeting with him in the five, six months I worked on the project. Never had a single meeting with either of those guys, as it was with *The Color Purple.*" Levinson's longtime associate, Mark Johnson, took over the producer's duties.

The executive producers visited the *Rain Man* set just once, winging in on the Warner jet when the production was in Las Vegas. They chatted with Levinson, Cruise, and Hoffman. Jon reportedly asked Hoffman, "Are you playing the retard or the other guy?" The unit photographer took pictures of Jon and Peter with the stars; then they dashed back to Los Angeles in time for a Lakers playoff game.

When it was time to sell the movie, Guber came on the scene. "Peter was involved in several marketing meetings and was quite helpful," says Johnson. "I actually learned a lot from Peter in those meetings. His enthusiasm was so overwhelming, I think he was helpful in bullying UA into spending more money than they otherwise would have on marketing the movie."

Johnson was satisfied. But for Roger Birnbaum, the horror was about to begin. He asked Guber and Peters about his promised credit; he hoped his name would appear in the executive producer slot alongside theirs. After all, he had done much more than they had to get the film made. Guber and Peters weren't forthcoming.

"Jon would say, 'It's okay with me; you've gotta ask Peter.' And I'd go to Peter, and he said, 'It's okay with me; you've gotta ask Jon.' And you know, they played that game until I realized they were just bullshitting," Birnbaum remembers. Guber and Peters declined to share, but Levinson was more generous: He gave Birnbaum a special credit at the end of the film.

"*RAIN MAN* BELONGS to a lot of people," producer Mark Johnson told nearly a billion viewers from the stage of the Shrine Auditorium when he collected the Oscar for best picture of 1988. He thanked the long list of people who had contributed to the winning project before it fell into his hands. Levinson

162

won as best director; Dustin Hoffman was named best actor; and Barry Morrow and Ron Bass got best original screenplay awards. Mike Ovitz heard his name cited appreciatively several times from the stage. Johnson thanked Ovitz and his associate Rosalie Swedlin for "standing by this for weeks and years." He also thanked Guber and Peters "for being exactly what executive producers should be, and supporting us all the way."

Even film aficionados probably don't remember that Mark Johnson produced *Rain Man*. But they may have a vague recollection that Guber and Peters were associated with the film. They might recall a photo of Jon Peters and Peter Guber brandishing the bronze statuette on Oscar night. The executive producers hadn't collected the Oscar themselves, but at the Governor's Ball following the awards ceremony they borrowed Barry Morrow's and posed with it for the cameras.

In another picture Guber is laughing heartily, his bow tie a bit askew; Peters, in a string tie, has his left arm thrown around his partner's shoulder. The picture ran as the double-page opening spread of a flattering article in the *New York Times Magazine* in 1989, and it was frequently reprinted.

Upon returning home after the ceremony, Birnbaum was consoled to find a little plastic Oscar, left on his pillow by his wife, with "producer of the year" inscribed on it.

A few weeks later, Mark Johnson got a phone call from Peter Guber, who asked to borrow *Rain Man*'s cache of awards so he could have them photographed. Johnson bundled up a Golden Globe; a People's Choice Award; a Donatello, the Italian equivalent of the Oscar; the Golden Bear from the Berlin Film Festival—and sent them all over to Guber.

Although he has seen Guber and Peters repeatedly take credit for *Rain Man,* Johnson says it doesn't worry him. "I was the one who won the Oscar," he says. "They didn't." He is confident that industry insiders know that he produced the film.

He also came out ahead financially. According to the deal worked out by Ovitz, only the four biggest guns got gross points: Cruise, Hoffman, Levinson, and Johnson. Cruise was guaranteed at least $3 million; Hoffman was promised at least $5.8 million; and Levinson made do with $2.5 million. With Ovitz calling the shots, this was one deal that Guber was not able to rig in his favor: Ovitz had forced Guber and Peters to give up their gross points. They had to settle for splitting a $500,000 fee.

Birnbaum, still nursing some bitterness, says it wouldn't have taken much for them simply to acknowledge in the credits that he had played a key role in making *Rain Man,* and to give him some financial token. "I always liked Peter and I was heartbroken when he did what he did to me," he says. "It was like, 'What else do you need in this world?' If they'd given me what I deserved, and what I was due, would it have changed their lives at all? No. Would they have respect from one more person in this business? Yes."

EVER SINCE he was a child, Michael Uslan had been obsessed with Batman. Growing up in Cedar Grove, New Jersey, he dreamed about writing *Batman* comics as he built a collection of thirty thousand comic books. He taught an accredited college course on comic books at Indiana University and in 1974 his dream came true: He was hired by D.C. Comics Inc., the home of Batman.

Uslan set his sights on producing the definitive *Batman* movie. To gain experience in the movie business, he took a job in the legal department of United Artists in New York. He met and formed a partnership with producer Ben Melniker, who had been an executive at MGM for thirty years and had worked on such films as *Ben-Hur* and *Doctor Zhivago.*

As originally created by Bob Kane in 1939, the character of Batman was a dark, brooding figure who stole through the nighttime shadows of Gotham City to avenge evil. While the character had already been the subject of several feature films, most people remembered the sixties television series starring Adam West as Batman, a camp classic complete with ill-fitting tights and chintzy sets. Uslan and Melniker persuaded D.C. Comics, which resented the silly portrayal in the television version, to sell them licensing rights to make a series of *Batman* movies. D.C. president Sol Harrison was convinced that Uslan would preserve the integrity of the character.

Melniker and Uslan took a step that would doom them— even as it advanced their project—when they pitched their idea to Casablanca in 1979. They knew they needed to ally themselves with producers who had the clout, and the financial backing of a company such as PolyGram, to get their film

164

made. They met first with Casablanca executive Barry Becker-man. "I went into Peter's office and said, 'We're buying this,' " Beckerman recalls. Guber was instantly enthusiastic. "I love it! I get it!" he said.

As usual, Guber was full of promises to share money, credit, and creative control. Melniker and Uslan entered into a joint-venture agreement with Casablanca in November 1979. The contract was complicated and full of contingencies, but it guaranteed Melniker and Uslan 40 percent of whatever profit Guber and Peters received. It also stated that they "shall be accorded credit as the producers of the picture."

When Peters joined PolyGram Pictures in 1980, he met with Melniker and Uslan at the Carlyle Hotel in New York and asked them for a memo outlining their vision of the film. Uslan provided him with a single-spaced, nine-page memo, dated November 6, 1980.

"No longer portrayed as a pot-bellied caped clown," Uslan wrote, "Batman has again become a vigilante who stalks criminals in the shadow of night." He recommended that Robin's character be eliminated or whittled down, and that the story focus on Batman's attempts to vanquish a villain called "the Joker." Uslan even suggested casting for the Joker: Jack Nicholson.

Unfortunately for Melniker and Uslan, Guber and Peters never stayed in one place for long. First, Casablanca evolved into PolyGram Pictures. That company's distribution deal with Universal disintegrated. For the next several years, Melniker and Uslan fought to stay in touch with Guber and Peters about the status of *Batman,* but were fobbed off on underlings (who were happy to listen to their ideas).

When Guber and Peters affiliated themselves with Warner in 1982, they kept the original producers in the dark about the terms of the new deal on the project. Melniker and Uslan were never permitted to see documents and they assumed that the terms of their original deal would still apply. Later, they would find that Warner did not consider itself bound. The studio spent hundreds of thousands of dollars on several versions of the script, and directors Joe Dante and Ivan Reitman were attached at different times. Nevertheless, *Batman* was languishing in 1986 when Roger Birnbaum became president of Guber-Peters.

It was Warner production executive Bonni Lee's idea to

165

revive *Batman* as a vehicle for twenty-nine-year-old wunderkind Tim Burton. Burton's strikingly offbeat visual style and humor had first been revealed in his live-action short *Frankenweenie,* which he made when he was an animator at Disney. Lee had showed *Frankenweenie* to Mark Canton, who lured Burton to Warner Bros. to direct *Pee-wee's Big Adventure.* Now Burton was making *Beetlejuice* for the studio, a unique comedy about a group of newly dead characters, starring Michael Keaton and Geena Davis.

Burton was a haunted-looking fellow with a pale face framed by a nest of black hair. He dressed in black and rarely spoke in complete sentences. He shared a fondness for ghoulish imagery with Danny Elfman, the composer who scored his movies. Burton referred once to "the severe manic depressive psychopathic side" of his personality. But Burton had long been a *Batman* lover. He adored the bat iconography—operatic, he called it—and he loved the idea of making a dark, psychological study of the superhero. Sam Hamm, a young screenwriter and comic-book freak, was brought in to draft a new script. Melniker and Uslan got to meet with Burton twice, and provided research and ideas. For the next year, Burton, Hamm, Lee, and Birnbaum worked on a *Batman* script that eventually was green-lit by Terry Semel and Bob Daly. Filming was to start in October 1988 at the Pinewood Studios in London.

One day, Melniker and Uslan read in the trade papers that *Batman* was going into production—and that Guber and Peters were taking credit as the producers. When they contacted Warner head of business affairs Jim Miller to inform him that the studio was breaching the Casablanca agreement, they say that Miller told them if they did not sign an amended contract, they would be thrown off the picture entirely. On September 8, 1988, they signed a new contract which gave them nominal credit as executive producers, stripped them of creative involvement and consulting rights, and granted them 13 percent of net profits. As all but the rankest amateurs in Hollywood know, net points are generally worthless. But Melniker and Uslan say that Miller told them, "If you don't like it, you can bring a lawsuit."

166     While Melniker and Uslan fretted that Guber and Peters had betrayed them, Burton was getting an earful about Guber and Peters from *Witches of Eastwick* director George Miller. "I always

heard [*Witches*] was a total nightmare," says Burton. "I tried not to listen too much."

In the beginning, Burton didn't see much of Jon Peters. "When I first started the project, Peter Guber was the one I dealt with most," he recalls. "He's very smart. He talked too fast for me to understand sometimes. It kind of made me hyper."

For the key role of production designer, Burton chose Anton Furst, whose work on Kubrick's *Full Metal Jacket* he had admired, to create a moody Gotham City and spiffy high-tech Batgear. Because the director had never made a big-budget picture or shot action, the studio wanted to surround him with an experienced crew.

In early casting discussions Burton considered square-jawed heroic types such as Tom Selleck to play Batman. Jon Peters favored Michael Keaton, arguing that the actor had the right edgy, tormented quality. Having directed Keaton in *Beetlejuice,* Burton was persuaded. Jon faced considerable resistance to Keaton from Semel and Daly, but they finally agreed.

Despite a reputation for instability, *Blade Runner* star Sean Young was cast as the photographer, Vicki Vale. Burton had comedian Robin Williams in mind as the Joker, but had some problems signing him. Canton and Peters had their hearts set on Jack Nicholson, whose star power would lend *Batman* enormous cachet. Warner executive Lucy Fisher, who had developed a good relationship with Nicholson on *Witches,* brought Burton to meet the star.

At Nicholson's house off Mulholland Drive overlooking the San Fernando Valley, Burton and Nicholson discovered that they shared a fascination with animation. But Jack needed wooing. Jon Peters jumped in with a different type of salesmanship. Gotham City and the Batmobile were under construction in London. Wouldn't Nicholson like to zip across the Atlantic with Jon on the Warner jet to see the sets—and while they were at it become acquainted with some of Britain's loveliest young roses? Jack said he wouldn't mind, and Peters reserved the Warner Gulfstream 3.

It was Jon's impression that the actor seemed a bit frayed, so he planned a few restorative surprises for their trip—notably a personal trainer and a masseuse. After the jet took off, Nicholson worked out with the trainer and had a massage before sampling the caviar with which Jon had stocked the aircraft.

167

When he returned to Los Angeles, Nicholson told Peters he'd be the Joker—and then cut himself a deal for a $6 million fee plus a hefty stake in the film's gross earnings. Eventually he would make a reported $50 million.

Tim Burton soon got a taste of what George Miller had experienced. Burton had expected to shoot the Sam Hamm script, but found to his dismay that Jon, backed by Warner, wanted extensive revisions. The protagonists in Burton's movies—*Edward Scissorhands* and *Ed Wood*—have generally been twisted, troubled souls on the fringes of society. Left to his own devices, Burton would have made Batman a lurking loner. But a superhero who needed Prozac and who couldn't get a date was hardly Jon's idea of entertainment. He bore down on Burton to make a Batman who was exciting and tantalizing to women. "He's supposed to be Batman, not Wussman," Jon complained.

Burton and Peters were opposites: the delicate, easily spooked artist versus the explosive entrepreneur. As Burton stood on the back lot at Pinewood Studios outside of London, gazing at sets which filled nearly ninety-five acres and nine soundstages, he felt overwhelmed. He had four months to make a special-effects extravaganza that had to make every kid want to wear a Batcape next Halloween. Warner was already nervous about the $30 million budget and would become more fretful as that climbed to $48 million. "Torture," Burton called the *Batman* shoot later. "The worst period of my life."

Burton was appalled by the way Jon Peters bullied the crew and fired and rehired people. There was a running joke on the set about how many chauffeurs came and went. Jon alternately tyrannized and coddled the young director, and Burton developed mixed feelings about him. "Before I met Jon," he says, "people said, 'Watch out—Jon's this, Jon's that, he's not creative.' And I definitely argue that point. He is creative, and he did have some good ideas. . . . I was not seduced by Jon. What I responded to in Jon was just the insanity, the nuts quality. I loved that somebody just said whatever they thought. You don't hear people doing that."

Burton's frailty worked in his favor. Everyone on the set wanted to protect him, including Jon. "Mark Canton and I felt he was one of the most talented directors and we really cared for him," says Jon. One evening after Peters and Canton had been trying to impress upon him that the movie needed more pathos and romance, Burton ran off the soundstage crying. They chased him down and soothed him, told him what a great job he was doing. "We loved him up, took care of him," Peters says.

A major crisis faced the filmmakers early in the shoot when Sean Young fell and broke her arm on a horseback-riding excursion with Michael Keaton. Back in Hollywood, wags speculated that someone may have pushed the high-strung actress off her mount. In script read-throughs, Young's colleagues had found her difficult and Nicholson reportedly had warned Warner Bros. that he had doubts about her.

With Young out of commission, Burton wanted Michelle Pfeiffer to play Vicki Vale. But Keaton had just broken off a romance with Pfeiffer and the actor thought it would be awkward for them to work together. Jon called Canton, then in L.A., and the two settled on Kim Basinger, the beautiful blond actress from *9½ Weeks*.

Basinger was whisked to London with her hairdresser husband. Jon took the couple out for dinner early in the shoot and was angered by what he considered to be her husband's verbally abusive treatment of the star. He reached across the table and grabbed him by the neck, and they nearly got into a brawl. Thereafter, Peters considered Basinger fair game. He was a free man—his marriage to Christine Forsyth had ended. Once Basinger's husband left town, the actress began an affair with Peters that lasted the duration of the shoot. Peters would later boast to friends that he did Basinger a great favor by getting her away from her husband.

"My sweetheart hoodlum," she called Jon. Some nights Basinger could be seen in her pajamas leaving her hotel room in the St. James Club, toothbrush in hand, and heading up to his penthouse suite to spend the night. As Christmas approached, a *Batman* set decorator was called in to dress the suite in festive seasonal style and deliverymen carted in gifts from Jon to his female lead.

Peters took care of Basinger on the set, too, making sure that Burton shot plenty of close-ups. He was particularly influential over a key scene in Vicki Vale's apartment in which Bruce Wayne tries to reveal to her that he is the mysterious Batman, only to be interrupted when the Joker bursts into the room. Jon wanted the scene to demonstrate the strong attraction between

169

Bruce Wayne and Vicki Vale—and to underscore Wayne's inner torment over his double identity. He also thought the confrontation between the Joker and Bruce Wayne wasn't dramatic enough in the script.

Peters summoned Burton to his hotel suite one night and the two improvised dialogue to expand the apartment scene. Jon played the role of Bruce Wayne and Burton was Vicki Vale. The next morning they blocked out the scene on the soundstage apartment set with screenwriter Warren Skaaren. Burton then rehearsed the new scene with the actors and all three contributed new ideas; it was shot the next day. Burton found the last-minute rewrites nervewracking, but he admits, "It's one of my favorite scenes."

One day, Anton Furst was summoned urgently to meet Jon in the production office. When he arrived, Peters was looking at poster designs commissioned by the Warner marketing department. "Jon was there with the artwork in front of him," Furst said later. "He said, 'Look at these.' One was sort of like Conan, or Robocop—the word 'Batman' spelled in *Conan the Barbarian* type. Nothing original, nothing you hadn't seen before many times."

"I want you to design the logo," Peters told Furst. "Drop everything. Drop the set design."

Furst came up with the simple but evocative Batsymbol that would become ubiquitous before the film opened. "I thought the logo should look like it was stamped out of the gear Batman wears," Furst said. "It became a sort of trompe l'oeil, it became ambiguous, so you had to look twice. But it was very definitely the Batsymbol, so there was no problem in people identifying it."

"That's exactly what we want," Peters exclaimed when Furst showed him his sketch. Peters wanted the poster to consist solely of the logo and the June 23, 1989, opening date: no title, no Jack Nicholson, no Michael Keaton. "I wanted to do, like, foreplay, to create the magic and myth of it all," Jon says. "I didn't want to give it away." He waged an all-out war with Warner. "I never thought he'd get away with no name and no writing," Furst marveled. "Jon told me, 'You'll never know the battle I had, right up to pinning people against the wall.' "

170

"Jon made the *Batman* campaign," says a Warner source. "It was Jon who insisted on no music in the first trailer." By bringing Furst into the marketing process, Peters unified all the film's visuals, including the merchandising tie-ins. He even turned down a $6 million offer from GM to build the Batmobile because the car company would not relinquish creative control.

During production, a *Wall Street Journal* article had reported that Batfans were unhappy with the casting of Keaton. In response, Jon rushed out the first trailer that played in theaters at Christmas—months before the film opened. It was simply a surreal assemblage of scenes from the movie, without music. It created enormous anticipation for the film.

When Jon tried to impose his will on the movie's climax, the results were less successful. He wanted a major action sequence to take place in the tower of the cathedral where Batman finally triumphs over the Joker. "Towards the end of the film Jon realized you couldn't just have Batman beating up the fifty-year-old Joker," Furst said.

Originally, the plot called for Vicki Vale to die at the end of the movie. Jon recognized that audiences would be horrified. Without telling Burton, who liked the original approach, Jon started working out last-minute revisions. The Joker would take Vicki captive and drag her up the cathedral bell tower stairs. Batman and Vicki would end up hanging off the tower by their fingers in a gothic cliffhanger finish. The specific action had not yet been delineated but the broad strokes of the idea were clear enough—and Burton hated the change.

By this time *Batman* was well over budget. But Warner was pleased with the rushes and Jon got more money to film a big ending. Furst told Peters that the new climax would require a 38-foot model of the cathedral for special-effects sequences. "Just the model alone cost $100,000," Furst said. "Jon said, 'Fine.' He observed that it was worth it. I think Jon has a pretty good sense of the broadstroke, whereas other producers would say '$100,000?' "

Because of the final-hour change, the sequence had to be largely improvised, which terrified Burton. "Here were Jack Nicholson and Kim Basinger walking up this cathedral, and halfway up Jack turns round and says, 'Why am I walking up all these stairs? Where am I going?' " Burton said later. "And I had to tell him that I didn't know. The most frightening experience of my life. I knew they had to go up to the bell tower and 171 they better do something up there. That was always a given. But what? Help me! Help me!"

Jon hired stunt doubles to play the Joker's heavies and maximize the mayhem. Meanwhile, Burton focused on getting some kind of footage with the lead actors that he could cobble into a coherent sequence. He was ultimately pleased with *Batman's* climax, but he doesn't recommend that kind of last-minute hysteria. "There was just no time for me to work on it," he says. "I was basically reacting to other people's ideas and then trying to come up with stuff of my own. Hollywood is a very control-oriented place, and if people want to feel in control, a very easy way to bring control back to yourself is to create chaos. Because if you're the one creating chaos, then you're the one who has to fix it. And on some level, that may be true with Jon."

Before *Batman* wrapped, Jon had made himself unpopular with much of the British crew. A major reason was that he had taken them off the payroll during a three-week Christmas break. It is customary for crews to be paid over holidays and members of the company were especially irked because the movie had such a lavish budget. And Jon was living in high style.

Money was also the issue in a flap over the top-of-the-line black leather crew jackets, which displayed the *Batman* logo on the back. Nicholson had made a verbal agreement with Jon to split the cost of the jackets over and above the $10,000 allotted in the budget. But when a bill arrived for $100,000, Jon reneged.

*Batman's* production manager, Nigel Wool, told Nicholson that it would cost him $90,000 to cover the cost. Nicholson stormed over to Basinger. "Tell that guy whose cock you've been sucking for the past six months that he's an asshole for not paying for the jackets!" he snapped. That, at least, was the story that made the rounds in Hollywood for months.

Warner absorbed the cost of the jackets.

A MAKE-OR-BREAK ATMOSPHERE prevailed at Warner before *Batman's* opening, where there were rumors that executives' heads would roll if the movie was a box-office disappointment. On the night of Thursday, June 22, Guber and Peters, along with Semel, Daly, and Canton, were buoyed by news reports of kids in sleeping bags outside Westwood theaters, waiting for the box office to open the next morning.

By that Saturday evening, the studio brass had received re- ports that ticket sales across the country were exceeding their wildest dreams; *Batman* might even break records for the big- gest opening weekend ever. That night Wendy Finerman threw a birthday bash for her husband, Mark Canton. Terry Semel, Bob Daly, Jon Peters, and Peter Guber convened for the occa- sion in a celebratory mood. Canton took a call in his kitchen as the party preparations were under way. He was stunned to hear the voice of Warner Communications Inc. chairman Steve Ross on the other end of the line. At the time, Ross was nursing along the merger of Warner with Time Inc. The gloss of a huge hit could only help that process. "Congratulations," he told Canton. "You may be responsible for making the merger hap- pen." It was a vintage Ross feel-good move. Canton was ecstatic that Ross had called him at home to pat him on the back.

On Monday morning, the trades trumpeted joyful news: *Bat- man* had taken in $42.7 million at 2,100 screens, breaking every record in motion picture history. Within ten days it grossed more than $100 million, another record.

In predictable Hollywood style, a chorus of voices claimed credit. The loudest was Jon Peters, who blustered to anyone who would listen that he had written, directed, cast, and single- handedly marketed the film. "Jon contributed a lot," screen- writer Warren Skaaren observed in 1990. "And I hear a lot of stories of Jon saying he wrote it and directed it and acted in it. And that's just sort of who Jon is, and he's hilarious. I'll say this: He never poisoned it for me. He'd come in and throw things up in the air, and you'd say, 'Gee, I wish he hadn't done that, because it will take a while to put back together.' But he was always trying to make the film better."

Tim Burton would go on to make *Batman Returns* without Peters, who by that time had moved on, leaving the most lucra- tive cinematic franchise of all time behind at Warner. The sec- ond *Batman* movie would be darker—and much less profitable —than the original. Warner executives regretted that Jon Pe- ters was not around to lighten up the moody vision of Tim Burton.

The original *Batman* producers, Ben Melniker and Mike Uslan, filed a breach-of-contract suit in Los Angeles County 173 Superior Court on March 26, 1992, in which they claimed to be "the victims of a sinister campaign of fraud and coercion that has cheated them out of continuing involvement in the production of *Batman* and its sequels, denied them proper credits, and deprived them of any financial rewards for their indispensable creative contribution to the success of *Batman.*" A Superior Court judge threw out their case, which is now on appeal. In the meantime they have had to console themselves with their executive producing fees of $300,000 apiece. Seven years after the release of *Batman,* with total revenues topping the $2 billion mark, Melniker and Uslan have not seen a penny more than that since their net profit participation has proved worthless. According to Warner Bros., *Batman* is still in the red.

# 15

## WALTER AND NORIO

With *Rain Man* and *Batman* in their résumés, Peters and Guber presented themselves to Walter Yetnikoff to see if he could help them achieve their dream of running a major studio. Their timing was perfect. The head of Sony's music division was a key man in the company's quest for a studio. He couldn't get Sony to close a deal unless he also could present the Japanese with American management for the new company. Yetnikoff, a friend of Jon's from the Streisand days, was a brilliant, vulgar, substance-abusing executive whose dominance at CBS Records hadn't fulfilled his ambitions. For many years, he had cast a jealous eye on Warner boss Steve Ross.

Ross, who had parlayed a funeral home business into a global entertainment empire, was perhaps the most envied man in the entertainment industry. He was far more richly rewarded than Yetnikoff could ever hope to be as the head of a record company. Ross had a lavish salary and compensation package that would translate into a payment of $193 million in 1990, when he engineered the merger between his company and Time Inc. He led a life of wealth and comfort that was the envy of his many rivals. Warner had a fleet of jets and vacation houses in Aspen and Acapulco. Ross used those perks to coddle members of the Warner "family" like Streisand and Spielberg. To Yetnikoff, Steve Ross was the model, the apex of achievement.

"I wanted to be Steve Ross. Oh, absolutely," Yetnikoff says. "I wanted to have dominion over an empire." In pursuit of that goal, he became an ardent advocate of the match between Sony and Columbia Pictures. When the deal was done, Yetnikoff expected to run the Sony film and record companies.

In aspiring to become another Ross, Yetnikoff seemed to lack not brains but temperament—not to mention temperance. Ross was polished; Yetnikoff seemed to delight in his own crudeness. He was notorious for his profanity and his explosive, erratic behavior. He was shrewd in business but he seemed to feel that corporate codes of conduct were made to be broken. He wore his shirts open, showed up to work at noon, and once fell asleep, or pretended to, at a CBS shareholders meeting.

One of his trademarks was making a constant issue of his Jewishness. Perhaps because he had worked so many years at CBS—an exceptionally white-shoe, WASPy place—Yetnikoff had become a caricature of himself. His super-Jew routine must have been particularly irritating to CBS founder William S. Paley, who had distanced himself from his Jewishness. But Yetnikoff had a knack for getting away with things—and he had risen at CBS Records.

"He's the first executive to really act like a star—by that I mean the temper tantrums, the *geschreiing,*" said Allen Grubman, a leading music industry attorney who owed much to Yetnikoff. He recounted a heated negotiation with Yetnikoff: "I look up and a plate whizzes by my head and smashes against the wall behind me. 'Did I see what I think I just saw?' I ask. Walter cracks up."

Yetnikoff was known for his predilection for bosomy blondes, his "shiksa farm." They were just another entry on the long list of Yetnikoff indulgences. His relationships with women were marked by an almost compulsive urge to shock. "I'm a bit of a male chauvinist pig," he has confessed.

As Walter rose at CBS Records, his out-of-control act began to seem less like an act. But he managed a long reign as top man. He was not an especially good administrator and he wasn't known for his ability to find new talent, but he was famous for his relationships with major artists. He was especially close to Michael Jackson, Barbra Streisand, Billy Joel, Bruce Springsteen, and Cyndi Lauper.

"I think I have a heavier case load than most psychiatrists," he told *Rolling Stone* in his heyday. "My role is rabbi, priest, guru, banker for sure, adviser, counselor, friend, psychotherapist, marriage counselor, sex counselor, you name it."

176  Yetnikoff was dogged by some of his business connections. CBS Records was the leading user of independent record pro-

moters—freelancers who were hired to ensure that certain records got played on the radio. The indie promoters were not only extremely expensive, but suspicions always followed them. There were accusations about kickbacks, payola, and ties to organized crime.

Yetnikoff had other friends whose reputations were dubious. Notable among them was Morris Levy, a record-label owner with links to the Genovese family of New York. In 1988, Levy was convicted on extortion charges and sentenced to ten years in prison. Long before that, Levy had befriended Yetnikoff, who used to visit his farm and even invested money in one of Levy's racehorses. (Levy also sold shares to CBS recording artist Billy Joel and Yetnikoff's protégé at the record company, Tommy Mottola.) Yetnikoff says he started doing business with Levy at CBS's behest and never ran into any problems with him.

In 1967, when Yetnikoff was a young staff attorney at CBS Records, his company had negotiated with Sony to set up a joint venture in Japan. The new company was headed by Norio Ohga. The son of a wealthy lumber trader, Ohga was a classically trained musician with an aristocratic aura. Ohga and Yetnikoff struck up an improbable friendship that would last for decades.

Ohga had had pleurisy as a child and had been exempted from wartime service on health grounds. He spent World War II at his father's summer house in Numazu City, southwest of Tokyo, studying singing. After World War II, Ohga became a student at Tokyo National University of Fine Arts and Music. While there, he offered Yamaha a critique of the company's pianos. The chairman of the company was impressed and offered him a job, but Ohga refused. "I was a vocalist and wanted to remain one," he said.

Ohga's opinions soon attracted attention. In 1947, he wrote a letter to Tokyo Tsushin Kogyo, a fledgling company that would become Sony, criticizing the company's pride and joy: the first reel-to-reel tape recorder. "A ballet dancer needs a mirror to perfect her style, her technique," he complained. "A singer needs the same—an aural mirror." The outspoken student was invited to visit, where he encountered Sony cofounder Akio Morita. Ohga didn't know who Morita was and

177

might not have cared if he did. He argued with him audaciously. "The staff was amused by his brashness," Morita remembered. He acknowledged that Ohga was correct—the machine had too much wow and flutter.

Morita hired Ohga as a consultant. Inside the young company, Ohga was dubbed "the tough customer." He made an early tape recording of his school orchestra with himself as baritone soloist in Brahms's *German Requiem.*

In 1954, Ohga left for Germany for three years of vocal training. Morita retained him on salary, instructing him to keep Sony informed of developments in electronics there and telling him, "When you come back, maybe you can help us once a week." When the company developed its transistor radio, Morita sent one to Ohga in Germany.

When Ohga returned to Japan, he kept singing, giving concerts with his wife, pianist Midori Matsubara. Five years later, he joined Morita on a business trip to Europe. Morita planned to woo Ohga again but he didn't broach his subject until the two were on board the S.S. *United States,* sailing from Southampton to New York. At that point, Morita recalled later, he had Ohga captive for four days and ten hours. The two had little to do but eat and talk. "Ohga, a strapping, barrel-chested fellow with a resonant voice, criticized Sony in beautiful tones," Morita remembered. "And I was most interested in what he had to say. He didn't pull any punches. 'Your company is full of engineers,' he said, and from his tone of voice I could tell he didn't mean it as a compliment. 'Since these engineers started the company,' he continued, 'from their point of view they think it is right that they should continue to run it. But from an outsider's point of view, the company is old-fashioned and poorly run.' It was a fresh point of view, and startling, because we still thought of ourselves as quite daring and original managers."

"All right, you join us and you will be one of the management team," Morita challenged him. But Ohga held out, insisting that he wanted the freedom to be an artist. Morita promised that he could perform and work for Sony full time. After they returned to Japan, Morita got his wife, Yoshiko, to appeal to Ohga's wife, Midori (the two women had been high school classmates). Finally convinced, Ohga started as general manager of professional products.

Less than two years later, he gave up his operatic career when he became director of all of Sony's tape recorder business. He was shooting up the Sony ladder. In 1961, he became head of Sony's design center—the unit that created the sleek look that gives Sony products their visual identity. The job gave Ohga a chance to exercise his artistic sense as he molded Sony's image.

In 1964, when he was thirty-four and had been with the company only seven years, Ohga became a member of Sony's board. His ascent was "something unheard-of in traditional Japanese companies," Morita recollected with obvious pride. In his first year, Ohga smashed another Japanese tradition by hiring almost forty people away from other companies. He was reputed to be hot-tempered and reluctant to give praise—even to himself. But he was behind some of Sony's biggest coups. That year, for example, he got Philips to release its patent on cassette recorders. While the Dutch company viewed the device as an office machine, Ohga saw the potential uses in the home and car. The end result would be one of Sony's greatest hits, the Walkman.

Yetnikoff met Ohga and Morita when he traveled to Tokyo in 1967 to work on establishing the CBS/Sony record company. "We went over to the Sony offices and these two funny guys come out and they're wearing Sony uniforms, short blue jackets," Yetnikoff remembered. "I said, 'This is ridiculous.' " But somehow they got along. Ohga was amused by Yetnikoff, calling him "the funny American."

A couple of years after the joint venture was established with a million-dollar investment on each side, Yetnikoff became head of CBS International. He and Ohga met often. Yetnikoff would travel to Japan two or three times a year and he helped the joint venture set up a lucrative record club. Ohga came to the United States and visited Yetnikoff's house in Great Neck. (At the time Yetnikoff was still on his first marriage.) "Once he was very tired and my wife put him to bed in our bed," Yetnikoff recalls. "He had his glasses on. She had to take his glasses off. It was that kind of homey, cozy kind of thing."

Ohga was straitlaced. "Ohga was the reverse of a party animal," Yetnikoff says. "He was very serious, a classical musician, conductor. He was not the type that would go out with us at night. He once had a brandy with me in Germany and got whacked from one brandy." But Ohga was not prissy or ascetic, 179 as Yetnikoff also remembers. "He could fly airplanes and race cars. I don't know that he was that good at all of it but I would say, 'Oh, Ohga, you're a great racing car driver. You probably drove for the emperor.' Stuff like that. . . . He could cook, you know, make bouillabaisse. He thought I was very smart and we were friends."

The relationship was unusual—"an odd friendship for a Westerner and a Japanese—particularly if you go back ten, twenty years," Yetnikoff says. "We would talk about things like, 'When a man gets older, he should change his character and try to improve himself.' . . . And he would tell me about his personal problems. Very, very unusual for a Japanese. He wanted to have children—that kind of conversation. Boy-boy conversation, or man-man. I would try to talk him into adopting a child."

At that point, Yetnikoff was hardly working on improving his character. On his trips to Japan, he would venture into Tokyo's seamiest district. "I think they sent tails out after me in Tokyo 'cause I would go out, into the night, fucked up," he says. "They were afraid I would go out into the night and I wouldn't come back."

Sony and CBS had their business disputes, as Yetnikoff recalls. One of the biggest was over home taping of recordings, which created a conflict between Sony and CBS. CBS contended that Sony was creating taping technology that harmed its record business by allowing consumers to make free copies of records at home. For Yetnikoff, this set up an awkward situation: He was dispatched to relay CBS's displeasure to the chief executive of Sony, Akio Morita. Yetnikoff found Morita somewhat intimidating. "I called him Mr. Morita," Yetnikoff says. "I never even called him Akio."

On the other hand, Yetnikoff remembers, "I would go to Japan and pull on his hair." And that's not all. "I once called Morita in the middle of the night because he had given an interview to *Playboy* magazine saying the problem with American business is that there are no John Waynes left. I called him at three o'clock in the morning. I woke him up. He said, 'Ho, you wake me up. It's three o'clock in the morning.' I said, 'You want John Wayne? John Wayne doesn't sleep.' "

180 The executives remained friends and made money together. By 1987, the joint venture was generating $730 million in sales

and more than $100 million in pretax profits. The friendship was mutually beneficial. As Yetnikoff rose at CBS Records, he would arrange for Ohga to receive bonuses and stock options. Ohga would extol Yetnikoff's brilliance at CBS.

However ambitious Yetnikoff may have been, Ohga had his own appetites. He resolved to make the new venture the largest record company in Japan. Not only would he succeed, but he would later be instrumental in introducing a new format developed jointly by Sony and Philips engineers: the compact disc. Despite opposition from record manufacturers, Ohga got help in this effort from two classical artists: Seiji Ozawa and Herbert von Karajan. He used the Sony/CBS joint venture to launch the new technology. It was a successful experiment in using software to introduce an innovation in hardware, a model for the type of synergy that Sony hoped to find in Hollywood.

WHEN YETNIKOFF was still head of the CBS Records International division in the seventies, he and Irwin Segelstein, head of the domestic company, went to dinner at Barbra Streisand's place in Malibu. "This guy shows up in tennis shorts," Yetnikoff remembers. "And he sits down, cross-legged on a chair, and he's eating with us and I know it's her boyfriend." Jon Peters and Walter Yetnikoff hit it off. As Jon became more involved in Streisand's career, he felt that Walter was backing him up on some of his ideas. They started to play together and dream together.

Once, Yetnikoff, Jon, and Warner executive Terry Semel used the Warner jet for a trip to Hawaii. Someone lit a joint and started passing it around. The pilot emerged from the cockpit to tell his passengers to stop. Peters invoked the name of the powerful Warner chairman. "Steve Ross told us we could have this plane so you just do what you're told," he said.

"Fine," the pilot responded. "I'm turning around and when we get back, you can tell Steve Ross that *he* should fly the airplane." The joint was extinguished.

Jon and Walter talked often of building empires together. "Jon Peters and I did this every day for ten years," Yetnikoff says. "It was not very serious. It was jerk-off time . . . I was interested in doing business because of what I call his effervescence. These conversations were like pie in the sky. They were all over the lot." If that were true, Jon didn't think so.

181

And while Yetnikoff wasn't exactly banking his career on the outcome of these talks, he says, "If something had come up, I definitely would have jumped at it." Meanwhile, he dabbled in Hollywood. At one time, he tried to talk CBS into buying Fox. Then he had an idea to put Springsteen into a movie about a rock star in Japan. "It was called *Final Encore,*" Yetnikoff recalls. "It was about a rock star who's in Japan, who goes wacky and goes to a Buddhist monastery." He approached his friend Ohga about getting Sony to put $3 million toward the project. "If I tell CBS you'll come up with money, they'll go along," he told him. Sony agreed but Springsteen didn't and the project was dropped.

In 1984, Yetnikoff persuaded CBS to allow him to produce movies on the side. Disney gave him a three-picture deal. Yetnikoff was one of three executive producers on the film *Ruthless People.* He got CBS Records artists Billy Joel, Bruce Springsteen, and Mick Jagger to contribute songs to the soundtrack album. The movie was a hit but the soundtrack wasn't. "It's a comedy," Walter lamented. "Where do you put the music in?" Eventually he and Disney released each other from that contract.

Yetnikoff told *Esquire* magazine at the time that he wanted the movie deal because "the *goy* upstairs"—that was the way he referred to CBS chief executive Thomas Wyman—"won't let me make any money." It was an overstatement, of course, but by the mid-eighties, Yetnikoff was becoming obsessed with wealth. He was hardly poor, making $550,000 a year with hefty annual bonuses, interest-free loans, and other perks. But he had watched as other powerful music moguls—David Geffen and Irving Azoff—had made millions by investing in their own record labels and management companies. They were entrepreneurs, while Walter remained an employee. He couldn't even get a corporate jet while his counterparts at Warner were flying all over the place.

Meanwhile, Walter's employer was undergoing a significant change. Financier Larry Tisch, who had started buying up CBS shares when a takeover offer by Ted Turner made the stock interesting, accumulated a controlling interest in the company. In September 1986, he became president and chief executive. Wyman, "the *goy,*" was out and Tisch, a dedicated Jew, was in charge.

Even so, it didn't take Walter long to decide that he detested

Tisch, whom he dubbed "the evil dwarf" and even "the kike upstairs," according to journalist Fredric Dannen. Apparently Tisch returned Walter's sentiments with interest. He was a moneyman with an eye on the bottom line. Walter's high-rolling tastes, his flair for drama, his extravagant Jewish routine left Tisch cold. If Walter hoped to get his long-coveted jet out of Tisch, he was in for a disappointment. Instead, Tisch closed off Yetnikoff's kitchen and executive dining room in a cost-cutting measure.

Tisch was besieged with questions from news media about Yetnikoff's connections with independent promoters. As an owner of television stations, CBS could have been particularly vulnerable to federal regulators: If the company didn't behave itself, its broadcast licenses might be at risk.

Though Tisch asserted that CBS Records wasn't for sale, he had apparently considered the idea from the start. Yetnikoff aside, Tisch was inclined to sell off parts of the company that didn't relate to its core business—and he concluded that the network and record company had little to do with each other. "Nothing happened that was beneficial to the network because of CBS Records and vice versa," he told the *New York Times*. True, the record division actually pulled in more profit than the network in 1986, the year Tisch took over. But the business was cyclical, he observed. And while the record company was a part of the CBS corporate identity—Paley had bought it in 1938 and regarded it as his "baby"—Tisch wasn't sentimental about a business that could cause trouble and might also fetch a handsome price.

Soon after he took charge, Tisch was approached by Drexel-backed investor Nelson Peltz (in league, coincidentally, with Jon Peters and Peter Guber, then deep into their romance with Terren Peizer). Peltz expressed an interest in CBS Records. Tisch agreed to sell at a price that struck Peltz as high—$1.25 billion—but he said he wanted further information about the division.

Tisch didn't consult or even inform Yetnikoff of the offer. Walter found out about it by accident. The news wasn't particularly welcome. Yetnikoff had just finished telling an interviewer for *Esquire* that rumors of Tisch selling the company were "empty talk and bile," adding that Tisch "assured me there was nothing there." The news of the prospective sale was enough

183

to trigger one of Yetnikoff's famous bursts of temper. But soon he began to reconsider.

Tisch invited Yetnikoff to come up with his own offer, as long as the price was $1.25 billion and the deal was concluded by the end of the year—a critical tax consideration. For a month, Yetnikoff tried to arrange a management-led buy-out. Finally he turned to his old friends at Sony.

He caught Mickey Schulhof, then vice chairman of Sony's American operations, at Teterboro Airport in New Jersey. He made his pitch: Sony could buy CBS Records for $1.25 billion, but time was of the essence. He added that he wanted a $50 million pool "for me and the *mishpocheh*"—his "family" of executives. Schulhof called Tokyo from the airport. Within twenty minutes, Morita and Ohga approved the deal. Making such decisions at breakneck speed was hardly the Japanese way, but Sony considered itself a maverick. And it had an appetite for the world's largest record company.

Sony was thinking synergy. After getting burned in the seventies when its Betamax video recorder succumbed to the inferior but cheaper VHS format, Sony had concluded that control of software, or programming, might give it an edge as it introduced new hardware technology. "If I owned a movie studio, Betamax would not have come out second best," Morita told Yetnikoff. Sony might have prevailed if it could have put out a stream of its own popular movies in the Betamax format. In 1986, Sony was developing the digital audio tape recorder. Linking the new technology with the world's biggest record company might make the new recorder much more attractive to consumers. (The digital audio technology, overshadowed by the compact disc, never caught on.)

The morning after Sony agreed to the deal, Schulhof and his advisers went to Yetnikoff's apartment and cobbled together an offer. Yetnikoff, no early riser, was still wearing his bathrobe when he called Tisch to present the offer. To everyone's shock, Tisch's response was noncommittal.

The next day, Tisch called Morita and explained that Paley, the eighty-six-year-old CBS founder, had opposed the deal. The CBS board was unreceptive. The Japanese were stunned. "I was so surprised," Norio Ohga told the *New York Times Magazine*. "The head of the company said they would sell to us. Then we start to negotiate and the board of the company said, 'No, no, no. This is just Mr. Tisch's idea.' It was a very unusual circumstance. We have never seen such a thing. The president wanted to sell, but not the board. . . . Such a headache!"

THE DEAL WAS DEAD, at least for the immediate future. But Yetnikoff had glimpsed independence. He launched a campaign to convince Tisch that a sale was desirable and even necessary. "In those days, I had a hard-on for Larry Tisch," he remembered. Walter acknowledged that he tried "a lot of hijinks" to annoy Tisch—and simultaneously to create the impression that without Yetnikoff, there was no CBS Records.

"Yetnikoff played Tisch like Jascha Heifetz," says one powerful executive at another entertainment company who observed the events. Not that Tisch needed much encouragement. In the interim, Disney had weighed in with an offer for the record company and Tisch was starting to salivate. Tisch called Schulhof and offered to sell again, but the price had changed. Instead of $1.25 billion, he was asking $2 billion. Schulhof dashed to Tokyo: Tisch wanted an answer in two days.

Once again, Sony stepped up to the plate even though Yetnikoff, who was in Japan for a Michael Jackson tour, told them the price was too rich. Morita called Paley to assure him that Sony would take the best possible care of the record company, would give him an honorary title, and would make a contribution to the Museum of Broadcasting in his name. Sony was certain it had a deal; but Tisch once again balked. The board wouldn't make a decision for at least a month and wanted to hire consultants to study the future of the record industry.

"We couldn't believe it," Schulhof said. "We couldn't understand why a company that is the world's largest record company, that basically makes the future of the record industry, needs an outside consultant to tell them . . . the future of the industry."

When the month elapsed, the board convened and refused once again to sell. Tisch began to toy with the idea of spinning the record company off and selling stock in it. Sony and Yetnikoff were frantic. But a few days later, everything changed. On October 19, 1987, the stock market crashed. Tisch, a pessimist, believed that the plunge signaled a permanent turn for the worse for businesses everywhere. The idea of spinning off the record company no longer seemed viable. Maybe Sony

185

wouldn't be so eager to spend an extravagant $2 billion for the record company anymore. He called Schulhof to ask.

For the third time, Sony said yes. But first, Schulhof demanded that Tisch pledge in writing that he and Paley would urge the board to approve the deal. Tisch complied and the deal was quickly agreed upon. This time, it went through—but not before Tisch exacted a little more tribute from Sony. Having gotten his price, he also demanded that CBS be allowed to keep the record division's fourth-quarter earnings. Sony tried to draw the line. But when Tisch appeared willing to drop the deal over this dispute, Sony capitulated.

In the first reports of the deal, analysts concluded that the price was too high. But the deal would prove to be brilliant— so much so that when Sony subsequently decided to buy a movie company, it would hardly worry when some of the same critics once again said Sony was paying too much.

Yetnikoff bought himself a new Jaguar. He boasted in the press that he was responsible for driving Tisch to make the sale. But he concedes now that he had overstated the case. "I encouraged Larry Tisch to sell the company in every way I could think of," he says. "But I didn't induce it. Black Monday induced it."

This was the first major Japanese purchase of an American company—and CBS Records was a particularly American company. Originally the Columbia Phonograph Company, its first stars were John Philip Sousa and the U.S. Marine Band. It was the label of Duke Ellington and Bessie Smith; Bob Dylan and Bruce Springsteen; Michael Jackson and Barbra Streisand. It recorded musicals from *My Fair Lady* to *A Chorus Line*. Naturally, some in the industry expressed concern about the implications of Japanese ownership.

But as far as anyone could tell, the Japanese were invisible. Yetnikoff remained in control, assuring reporters that Sony was not only a hands-off owner, but "a better company and a better caretaker" of the records division than CBS. He was looking forward to becoming another Steve Ross.

"We're looking to buy a studio," he told Fred Goodman of *Rolling Stone* in 1988. "I might become chairman of the board. Then I don't have to talk to people like you any more."

It happened almost as Yetnikoff predicted. But by the time it did, Yetnikoff's bad habits had practically killed him. Just as he was poised to take over a combined music and film enterprise, Yetnikoff fell victim to himself—and to the many enemies he had made. Like an unholy Moses, Yetnikoff was never to enter his promised land.

# 16

# THE SONY STORY

"I was born the first son and fifteenth-generation heir to one of Japan's finest and oldest sake-brewing families," Akio Morita wrote in his biography. The Morita family of Kosugaya village had been making sake for three centuries.

The family had a taste for innovation that went back several generations. Akio's great-great-grandfather had toyed with the idea of producing Western-style wine and had invited a Frenchman to advise him on the project. At the time, Japan was ending two and a half centuries of isolation and Western ideas were in vogue. Although the vineyard produced a small amount of wine, the experiment ultimately failed. The rootstock that had been imported from France was infected with parasites that destroyed the vines.

When Akio's father came of age, the family business was suffering from neglect. His ancestors had been more interested in collecting art than minding the store. But by the time Akio came into the world in January 1921, his father had succeeded in reestablishing the family's wealth. Akio was brought up rich in a rambling house with its own tennis court. The family lived on one of the best streets in Nagoya, an industrial town where the Moritas had moved as Akio's father began rebuilding and modernizing the business.

Morita's mother, though she dressed in the traditional kimono, was unusually assertive and something of an iconoclast, according to her eldest son. She was keenly interested in his education, and though the house was packed with family members and servants, she gave the boy a room of his own with a bed instead of the tatami mats that most of the others in the house used. "I was being modernized," Morita recalled later, "even as a child."

Akio's mother loved Western classical music and played Enrico Caruso recordings on her Victrola. When Morita was in junior high school, the first electric phonographs were imported and his father paid a small fortune to get one of them. Years later, Akio would vividly remember hearing a recording on the new machine for the first time: Ravel's *Bolero*. He was bowled over and became obsessed with the technology that made the improved sound possible. Akio became so fascinated by his own experiments with electronic gadgets that he nearly flunked out of school.

Though the family had an iconoclastic strain, Akio felt that his father was too conservative and that his attitude toward business was somewhat joyless. Akio was being groomed to take over the family empire, and even as a child of ten or eleven, his father would have him sit through tedious board meetings. "As a young boy in middle school," he said later, "my holidays were consumed by business, business, business."

But Akio was far more attracted to gadgets than account books. To his father's disappointment, he studied science instead of economics. While he never became a great student, he always shone in physics.

By the time he entered Osaka Imperial University, Japan was at war. Morita was keen to avoid combat. He enlisted in the Navy, taking the route that seemed most likely to keep him in school. The strategy worked until early 1945, when the war intensified. Even then, Morita stayed out of the line of fire. He spent much of his time in a country house in the small town of Zushi, putting his mechanical and electronic skills to use on research projects. In one such effort, he was part of a group that was trying to develop a heat-seeking missile. This project led to his fateful meeting with Masuru Ibuka, a civilian who was thirteen years older than Morita. Ibuka worked at the Japan Measuring Instrument Company and had developed an amplifier that could be used to detect submarines.

The war went relatively easy on Morita. When the first atomic bomb was dropped, he was lunching with his Navy colleagues and heard only that "a new kind of weapon that flashed and shone" had been used on Hiroshima. With the fighting over, he returned home to find that his two brothers also had survived unharmed. The family's home and even its offices and factories were intact.

When the war ended, Morita was invited to join the faculty

189

- at the Tokyo Institute of Technology. He reestablished contact with Ibuka, who was opening a new lab in Tokyo. Ibuka set up shop in a bombed-out department store in the heart of the city, named his company Tokyo Tsushin Kenkyusho, or Tokyo Telecommunications Research Laboratories, and began to cast about for ideas. He wasn't sure what the company should do. His colleagues offered various suggestions, not all technology-based: building a miniature golf course or selling bean-paste cakes. The company tried to develop a rice cooker, but never invented a successful model. Finally, it started making heating pads, which sold well and provided some ready cash. But Ibuka had larger ambitions. He created a device that could convert AM radios to short-wave receivers, which had been illegal during the war and were much coveted. The product was a hit.

Morita had read about his old acquaintance's doings in a newspaper and went to visit him when he arrived in Tokyo. Though he thought the offices looked "pathetic," he was struck by Ibuka's enthusiasm. And though Ibuka told him money was tight, Morita suggested that he might work with his old colleague part time. The two men had talked about starting a company together, and in March 1946 they decided to try to put the plan into operation.

They started Tokyo Tsushin Kogyo: the Tokyo Telecommunications Engineering Company. Morita's father, having finally given his blessing to his son's abandonment of the family business, was liberal with loans to get the new company on its feet. Morita was eager to get away from his teaching obligations and was thrilled when he read a newspaper report that all teachers who had served in the military were to be purged. When nothing happened, he went to the head of his school and urged him to start the purge.

Free at last, Morita joined his new company, which relocated from the department store to a dilapidated wooden building with a leaky roof. The company started selling phonograph parts, but Ibuka and Morita were looking for something more exciting. Their concept was to build a company that would be "an innovator, a clever company that would make new high 190 technology products in ingenious ways," Morita said. Ibuka considered and discarded so many ideas that he began to have credibility problems inside his own company. But then he saw something new: an American tape recorder. He showed it to his colleagues and convinced them. This was it.

"Our strategy from the beginning was not only to build a machine, but also to make and sell the recording tape, because we knew there would be a continuing market for tape from our customers who brought recorders," Morita said. Building the mechanism was easy, but devising a usable tape was not. As they set out trying to find suitable material, Morita and Ibuka made experimental tapes by hand, cooking up the magnetic coating in a frying pan and painting it on with fine raccoon-bristle brushes.

In 1950, they went excitedly to market with a new machine —rather bulky and heavy at 75 pounds, and quite expensive. The concept of the tape recorder was very new in Japan. "Almost no one knew what a tape recorder was and most of the people who did know could not see why they should buy one," Morita said. "We could not sell it."

To Morita, one of the biggest lessons of the tape recorder fiasco was that he had to learn about marketing. The notion that a good product would simply attract customers had been dispelled. Ibuka was the technical genius who could create the product, but Morita would have to learn how to convince people that they needed what the company was peddling. Gradually, Morita and his partners got the hang of it. They started selling their recorders and trying to build smaller, lighter, and cheaper models.

The new company got a big break because it had teamed with another Japanese firm to buy the patent to a widely used recording technique that had been developed in Japan. Morita's fledgling company was aggressive about asserting its ownership of this technology and soon found itself tangling with a much larger American firm that was importing machines to Japan without paying licensing fees to his company. Morita's firm took the unusual step of going to court to secure an injunction. In 1954, after a three-year battle, Morita's company won the right to earn a royalty on every tape recorder sold in Japan and to export its recorders to the United States without paying fees. "It was my first negotiation with the Americans," he wrote later, "and it ended so well that I began to feel new encouragement about the future."

191

□

THE COMPANY had grown to about 120 employees when Ibuka became fascinated by another new American invention, the transistor, which would revolutionize the company. "Miniaturization and compactness have always appealed to the Japanese," Morita said. "Our boxes have been made to nest; our fans fold; our art rolls into neat scrolls; screens that can artistically depict an entire city can be folded and tucked neatly away." The American inventors had thought the transistor's only use for ordinary consumers would be in hearing aids. But Morita and his associates envisioned a new radio, small enough to fit in a shirt pocket. Pursuing a license to the new technology, Morita made his first trip to the United States, and initially, he felt ill at ease. "Everything was so big," he marveled. "I thought it would be impossible to sell our products here."

While the company worked to perfect its radio and tape recorder, Morita was mulling over another project. In his travels abroad, he decided that the company's name was unwieldy. Americans couldn't pronounce the original Japanese, even when the name was shortened to Totsuko, and the English translation was too clumsy. Morita wanted to build an international enterprise like the Dutch giant Philips, and he thought the company needed a name that would be recognized and remembered around the world.

In the United States, he noticed that many of the biggest and best-known companies had acronyms as names, such as ABC, RCA, and AT&T, and that they used those letters as their corporate logos. He decided that the company's name should be short so it could also serve as its symbol. It had to be pronounceable anywhere in the world. The new transistor radio would be the first product to bear the name.

As Ibuka and Morita pored over dictionaries looking for ideas, they came across the Latin *sonus,* for "sound." "The word itself seemed to have sound in it," Morita said. And it had a number of positive associations: It sounded like "sunny." And it sounded like "sonny" or "sonny boy," English words which were used in Japan as slang for a cute boy. Morita fancied himself something of a sonny boy in those days. But the word "sonny" would have been pronounced *sohn-nee* by Japanese tongues, which means "to lose money" in that language. That seemed a poor choice. Morita came up with the idea of dropping a consonant and making the vowel long. The name

192

"Sony" was chosen. There was another consideration: Japanese goods were still considered cheap and inferior. While Morita said his company did not exactly want to conceal its true identity, it didn't want to emphasize it either. The name "Sony" served that purpose.

By 1957, Sony had its first "pocketable" transistor radio, although in truth the gadget still was too large to fit into a standard man's shirt pocket. But Morita and his colleagues were wedded to the pitch, so they devised a simple solution: Sony salesmen wore specially made shirts with pockets that were slightly larger than usual. "We never said which pocket we had in mind," Morita explained later.

The Japanese economy began to boom in the late fifties. Ibuka and Morita were well connected and they installed a prestigious and powerful board, which helped the new company get financing. As Sony established itself at home, Morita kept his eye on the international market. At one point, he turned down a large order from Bulova for transistor radios to be sold in the United States because the company insisted on putting its name on the product. "I am now taking the first step for the next fifty years of my company," Morita told the astonished Bulova buyer. "Fifty years from now I promise you that our name will be just as famous as your company name is today."

Already Sony was getting a reputation as the "guinea pig" company, Morita said. If it developed a product that looked like it would do well, other bigger companies rushed their own versions of the new device to market. "It is flattering in a way, but it is expensive," Morita said later, noting that over the years, larger companies had followed Sony innovations from the transistor radio to the VCR, from Trinitron color television technology to the Walkman, from hand-held video cameras to compact disc systems and more. The company had to emphasize new products, pouring resources into research and development.

Morita sought out mentors in the United States who helped him learn American business conventions. "Most Japanese businessmen who visited the United States in those days tended to be clannish and learned about the country from the other Japanese businessmen who had preceded them," he said. "Despite a couple of years of living in a foreign country, these Japanese businessmen were still strangers; following their ad- 193 vice was like the blind leading the blind. I was learning about America from people who were right at home in America and had 20-20 vision." For years, Morita would find that his confidence in American advisers was well placed. Though some of Japan's business titans regarded him as an upstart—and a rather loud and self-satisfied one, at that—Morita must have found it easy to console himself with the thought that they were envious.

Soon Morita was commuting to the United States. With slightly less than half of the company's products going overseas, the company created Sony Corporation of America in February 1960. Sixteen months later, Sony became the first Japanese company to offer stock in the United States, in the form of American Depository Receipts. The process required Sony to jump through a number of American regulatory hoops that didn't exist in Japan. The Americans were particularly puzzled, Morita recalled, by provisions in Japanese contracts that provided for the parties to discuss their differences if some unforeseen circumstance interfered with either side's ability to fulfill the terms. This was common in Japan, where many companies did business without contracts, but it looked worrisome to the Americans. After a wearying struggle, the offering went forward and Sony raised $4 million in its first outing.

Meanwhile, Morita decided he needed to immerse himself in the American experience to be effective. He sublet a twelve-room apartment in New York opposite the Metropolitan Museum of Art and started to live the life of a Westerner. His two sons, who spoke no English, grappled with the mysteries of baseball at Camp Winona in Maine. His wife, also learning a new language, adapted herself to the American custom of entertaining in the home (and later wrote a book on the subject). Morita set about building up his empire. But the family didn't stay in the United States for the planned two years. When his father died suddenly, Morita felt his place was in Japan. Yet his appetite for Western culture remained strong. When Sony erected its own building in the heart of Tokyo's Ginza district, he decided to install a replica of Maxim's of Paris, copying the decor, menu, and wines.

194    Morita traveled extensively. While Sony acquired a company plane—something unheard of in Japan—Morita still often flew commercial, carrying aboard a small box of sushi and a bottle

of sake. Meanwhile, the expansion continued. Sony created a European branch a year after Sony Corporation of America was established, and in 1971 the company opened a showroom in Paris on the Champs-Elysées.

As early as 1963, Morita had outlined a philosophy about entering foreign markets. In a newspaper interview, he explained that it was essential to have a sales and marketing team in place and to know the market well. "My view was that you must first learn the market, learn how to sell to it, and build up your corporate confidence before you commit yourself," he said. "And when you have confidence, you should commit yourself wholeheartedly."

IN 1974, Sony was preparing to introduce an exciting new invention: the home video-cassette recorder. Morita invited representatives from rivals Matsushita, JVC, and RCA to see it. The others came away feeling that Morita's message was typically arrogant: "Morita's attitude was, 'We completed this one, so why don't you follow?' " complained a spokesman for one of the rival companies. "There was no [room] for advice or joint development."

Sony took its Betamax to market. But two years later, after Sony had sold 100,000 machines, Morita was shocked to learn that JVC was introducing its own machine using the incompatible VHS format. JVC was a Matsushita subsidiary and Morita took the extraordinary step of petitioning the eighty-one-year-old Konosuke Matsushita, a revered figure in Japanese business, to have JVC recall the machines and reconfigure them to Sony's standard. Matsushita declined. Sony struggled to save the Beta format, though in what some considered a symptom of Sony's arrogance, it insisted on keeping its prices higher than the competition on the grounds that its quality was better. The effort to save the Betamax failed and Sony was forced to abandon it. The experience was a lasting humiliation that only heightened Sony's sense of competition with Matsushita.

Sony lost out on a booming business. Over the next several years, there was a creeping perception that Morita was past it. In the early eighties, Sony president Norio Ohga, then in his fifties and nearly ten years younger than Morita, assumed a greater role in day-to-day operations. In defeating the Betamax, Morita's countrymen had pushed a bitter pill down his throat.

"We didn't put enough effort into making a family," he later said sadly. "The other side, coming later, made a family."

Sony rebounded with the Handycam, the lightweight video-camera. But the Beta fiasco was an episode that Morita would never forget. Sony needed to diversify beyond the fickle consumer electronics business. It was hard to keep "living from magic show to magic show," as *Fortune* magazine put it. Sony didn't want to rely on inventing new products that nobody knew they needed and then watching competitors come up with cheaper imitations.

Ohga pressed ahead with measures designed to change the Sony mix: Instead of looking to consumer products to generate 80 percent of its business, Sony pursued a "50-50 strategy," aiming to sell less to consumers and more to businesses. It broke with its own tradition by selling components to other manufacturers, plunged into work-station computers, and built its semiconductor facilities.

But another notion was burned into Morita's consciousness: If you controlled the software, the public would have to accept your hardware. Morita, who had been so deeply impressed by the Dutch electronics giant Philips N.V., once again gazed upon that company with a jealous eye. "Philips is our greatest competitor," he said in an 1988 interview. "And Philips benefited from software—it owned PolyGram Records, and that helped its compact discs." If Sony had put dozens of great films—movies that it owned—on its tape format, the Betamax might have survived. With that in mind, Sony bought a record company and started to patrol for a movie studio.

While Morita was prepared to drive relentlessly toward his goal of creating a company that exploited a synergy between hardware and software, Ohga had doubts. "Morita always had a consistency of vision," says a Sony source. "Ohga, the tactical operations guy, always wondered whether he could make Morita's vision work."

MICHAEL OVITZ HAD qualities that seemed to make him a perfect choice to be Sony's guide into Hollywood. He was acknowledged to be the most powerful man in the entertainment industry. His firm, Creative Artists Agency (CAA), represented an enviable roster of the biggest stars, including Tom Cruise, Steven Spielberg, Dustin Hoffman, and Robert Redford. But

196

Ovitz had transcended the role of agent. He was becoming a man who had to be consulted in every major negotiation. With rare exceptions, none of his agents dared to defect to rivals. Some went to work for studios, but Ovitz insisted that his permission be sought before an agent was even approached about taking a position elsewhere. One hapless studio executive who disregarded the rules and asked an agent if she wanted to work for him without getting Ovitz's permission to broach the subject found that the powerful Ovitz punished him by declining to speak to him for a year. This penalty was imposed even though the executive never hired the agent in question.

Ovitz had an affinity for things Japanese and had studied aikido. His own company was built on a Japanese model of loyalty and cooperation, unlike any other institution in Hollywood. CAA agents were sometimes called the "Moonies" of the business, famous for walking in lock-step. And when CAA was ready to build its own gleaming headquarters—a curved, fortresslike building designed by I. M. Pei—Ovitz had a *feng shui* ceremony performed to ensure that his yin and yang were in the right places. Among Ovitz's favorite sources of insight into the Japanese way was Edwin Reischauer's book *The Japanese Today.*

From his reading of Reischauer, Ovitz had to be aware of the pitfalls that awaited his Japanese clients. "Westerners seem to [the Japanese] a little rough, unpredictable and immature in their frankness and ready display of emotions," Reischauer wrote. "In the West unpredictability in a person may be seen as amusing or spirited, but to the Japanese it is a particularly reprehensible trait. . . . The Japanese have a strong aversion to most open displays of emotion, whether of anger or love." Such sensitivities clearly would be trampled in Hollywood.

The Japanese decision-making process, as Ovitz well knew, was incompatible with the way the entertainment industry works. "Americans, accustomed to a relatively dictatorial top-to-bottom style of decision making, are surprised to see in Japan decisions that appear to come from the bottom up," Reischauer wrote. The careful consultation that would precede a decision is called *nemawashi*, he explained, "a term literally denoting cutting around the roots of a plant before it is transplanted. . . . From this may emerge a consensus."

This approach slows the decision-making process and it is

inimical to the Hollywood way of doing business, which is fast and autocratic. Hollywood is not a hothouse where seedlings are gently nurtured. Plants are ripped from the soil. If they die, you buy more.

Over the years, Sony had seemed somewhat "foreign" to some of its Japanese rivals. The company had bucked tradition by raiding executives from competitors. Its hierarchy was less stratified than those of other big concerns. But after the Betamax disaster, Sony seemed to make an effort to conduct itself in a more Japanese manner. In his 1986 book, *Made in Japan,* Morita suggested that some American practices compared unfavorably with Japanese business traditions. He inveighed against lavish display. "We do not believe in posh and impressive private offices," he wrote a decade before he would undertake his adventures in the movie business. "Too often I have found in dealing with foreign companies that such superfluous things as the physical structure and office decor take up a lot more time and attention and money than they are worth."

His insight was sound, but Morita would not follow his own advice. If Sony had become somewhat more traditional at home, the company would follow Morita's old formula of adapting itself to what seemed to be the American way when it ventured into the studio business. Morita had reason to congratulate himself on his understanding of American culture: The company had done well in the United States and its acquisition of CBS Records had been a success. None of this would prepare Sony for the culture shock of Tinseltown.

In his book, Morita stressed the need for companies to create a sense of family, "a shared sense of fate among all employees." In Hollywood—where it has been observed that the assets walk out of the door each night—there is a paradox at work. No industry is more reliant on the particular skills of individuals, yet true loyalty between the employer and the employed is rare indeed. And if Morita expected the managers that he would install at his entertainment company to bond with Sony, to view their fates as linked with the company's, he miscalculated greatly.

# 17

# SONY GOES SHOPPING

THE BETTER THINGS went for Walter Yetnikoff, the crazier he got—and things were going very well as the eighties wound down. Even though CBS Records had hit a major slump in 1988, the Japanese owners had not lost faith in him. Sony was confident, so confident that it had started shopping for its movie company. Yetnikoff pushed for a deal. With a studio, he believed that Sony could exploit all sorts of synergy with music and video, not just hardware. "I thought Sony could be very good at managing a movie studio, 'cause I thought I was going to manage it," he says.

The dollar dropped 50 percent against the yen between 1985 and 1989. This was a good time to shop. While the Reagan administration economic strategy was intended to make American goods cheaper abroad, some analysts foresaw that the falling dollar would make U.S. properties cheaper for the Japanese.

And Yetnikoff concedes that his ego was involved. "I was generally floating above the human race," he remembers. "Issuing orders, coming up with strategies, running the show. I am whacked . . . cruising into the bottom. And the drunker I get, the better business gets. How do you account for that?" (Yetnikoff generally referred to himself as "drunk" although he also was said to be abusing drugs.) As Sony's intentions became serious, Yetnikoff made the introduction to Ovitz, the superagent. Considering Ovitz's power in Hollywood, cutting him in on the studio purchase was good policy.

Ovitz occupied a singular and dominant place in the entertainment community, but the chance to broker a deal for Sony would surpass anything that Ovitz had done before. He would be playing on a global stage, dealing in billions of dollars.

When Ovitz got Yetnikoff's call, he was amused but also intrigued. The idea of Yetnikoff aspiring to be another Steve Ross, standing astride an entertainment empire, seemed a little ridiculous to Ovitz. But whatever Yetnikoff's shortcomings, he was offering Ovitz a stupendous opportunity. Sony was big game. Ovitz was not one to miss a chance to expand his portfolio. And maybe he would be more than a marriage counselor. Maybe Ovitz could find a way to work around Yetnikoff and run things himself.

Over the next several months, Morita and Ohga had a series of getting-to-know-you meetings with top executives at major studios. Some were arranged independently, some with Ovitz's help. They talked with executives at Paramount, Fox, and MCA/Universal. Sony didn't intend to attempt a hostile takeover but it was willing to entertain any other kind of business combination or partnership with a studio. Ovitz knew that Coca-Cola was interested in selling Columbia, but he didn't necessarily intend to steer Sony—his prize client—into Columbia's arms. Nonetheless, he didn't have that many wares to show; there are only a half dozen major studios in the world. If it came down to Columbia, there was a delicate personality matter that had to be handled.

Victor Kaufman, the straitlaced president and chief executive of the company, wasn't on speaking terms with Walter Yetnikoff and hadn't been for years. The feud went back to the days when Kaufman ran TriStar, a film company created in 1983 by three companies: HBO, Columbia, and CBS. Kaufman and Yetnikoff had gotten into a bitter fight over the use of a Willie Nelson tune in a TriStar film called *The Songwriter.* Though CBS was part owner of the studio, Yetnikoff had demanded royalties for use of the song in the video version of the film, threatening to sue and even warning that he would try to block TriStar from making a planned stock offering if Kaufman didn't comply. Eventually, CBS chief executive Thomas Wyman intervened and overruled Walter. But Yetnikoff and Kaufman remained adversaries.

TriStar had merged with Columbia since then and Kaufman ran the combined Columbia Pictures Entertainment. If Sony were interested in making a deal with Columbia, Kaufman could not be circumvented. No matter how much it would annoy Walter to sue for peace, he had to do it. Ovitz called

200

Kaufman and asked him to meet with his old adversary. Kaufman, never one to lose sight of business objectives, was happy to comply. "The day Yetnikoff came over and made peace was the day I knew Sony might buy Columbia," he says. "He said he had mellowed and all those kinds of things. It was time to put the past behind us."

With that chore handled, Sony's top American executive, Mickey Schulhof, went with Yetnikoff to meet with Kaufman. Over lunch they talked about possible joint ventures. Nothing came of the talk, but that suited Kaufman and his allies fine. They may have been dressing up Columbia Pictures for sale but they were in no hurry. The stock was still trading around $8 a share, partly because the merger of Columbia and TriStar left the combined company with about $1.6 billion in debt on its books. Columbia's owners were happy to take the time to goose up the price a bit before making a deal.

Sony continued its explorations. Ovitz was enthusiastic about MCA/Universal—a company that had a strong library, valuable real estate, a couple of theme parks, a publishing house, and Hollywood's most stable management team. The company's powerful chairman, Lew Wasserman, was getting on in years and there were endless premature rumors that his demise was imminent. "Mike was in love with MCA," one Sony adviser told *The New Yorker.* "He said, 'You have got to be able to see the potential. It has this great film library. It has mystique and magic. Wasserman is like royalty in Los Angeles—you don't understand what that kind of clout and prestige is worth.' " But Wasserman wasn't ready to sell just yet. And with the price likely to be around $6 billion, the transaction might have been too rich for Sony anyway.

MGM/UA was cheaper. The company had lost much of its luster thanks to Kirk Kerkorian's wheeling and dealing. A serious flirtation began, starting with a meeting between Morita and Kerkorian at Ovitz's house. The meeting was cordial, if not particularly substantive, and Morita's advisers went to work trying to ascertain the value of the company—a task that proved difficult. Kerkorian had a $1 billion–plus price tag on his company. After poring over the company's records, Sony agreed to meet Kerkorian's price, at first.

Then Kerkorian attempted to impose some conditions which struck the negotiators on Sony's side of the table as unreason-

201

able. He wanted to keep the MGM name for his hotel business and to continue producing films under the company's famous lion logo. "One of the conclusions we came to was that [Kerkorian] really didn't want to sell," Schulhof said later. "He wanted to sell a piece and then hold on and start up again." Considering Kerkorian's track record, no conclusion could have been fairer. Sony was already nervous about Kerkorian and the quality of financial information it was getting. The deal fell apart.

Ovitz tried a last run at MCA, without luck, and then turned to Columbia. The studio had its problems, of course. Its movie division was in a quagmire. Its library wasn't considered one of the industry's best: founder Harry Cohn had been slow to introduce color because of the cost. There were a lot of B-titles. But there was plenty of fodder for a software-hungry acquirer. On the film side, there were bright spots—the classics like *It Happened One Night, Mr. Smith Goes to Washington, On the Waterfront, The Bridge on the River Kwai,* and *Lawrence of Arabia.* And there was a clutch of relatively recent hits, including *Close Encounters of the Third Kind, Tootsie,* and *Ghostbusters.*

The company had a vibrant television operation, rich in half-hour sitcoms that were cash cows when sold into the syndication market. At the time, its hits included *My Two Dads, Designing Women,* and *Married . . . With Children.* Its game shows —*Jeopardy!* and *Wheel of Fortune*—also generated an impressive profit reliably, every year.

In November 1988, Schulhof called Kaufman and asked if he could pay a call at his office. Kaufman was happy to oblige. As Kaufman recalled the meeting, Schulhof initially said Sony was interested in acquiring something less than outright ownership of the studio. Sony was interested in buying Coca-Cola's 49 percent share, leaving Kaufman and his management team in place as it had done with Yetnikoff, when Sony acquired CBS Records. Kaufman kept his eye on the ball. "I said, 'Forget about me and management; it's not relevant.' And I said Coke would never consider selling just its shares and not treating the public in exactly the way they're treated. If that's what you want, you'll be turned down." Schulhof responded that Sony was open to the idea of buying the whole company.

That was the answer Kaufman wanted to hear. He had not been entirely sincere when he said he didn't care whether Sony

202

kept him around—at the time, he was inclined to stay—and certainly his pride would have been wounded if Sony didn't at least ask. He knew he could make it a condition of the deal that Sony at least extend his contract. But about a month into the negotiations, Kaufman began to rethink the situation.

He knew that if Coke sold the company to Sony, the price would be so high that making a success of the venture would be difficult. Naturally, if the company lost money, Kaufman would take the blame. He also suspected that he eventually would run up against Schulhof, who would want to take the reins of the entertainment operation. Finally, it was absolutely unthinkable that he would have to work with Walter Yetnikoff. Kaufman's second-in-command, Lew Korman, was opposed to staying if the company was sold. He believed that it was imprudent to work for managers who were half a world away.

One Saturday afternoon late in 1988, about a month into the negotiations, Kaufman went to a theater matinee. During intermission, he suddenly knew there was no way he could stay if Sony bought Columbia. He called Korman at home and said he had changed his mind, that he and Korman definitely should leave if Sony bought Columbia-TriStar. Kaufman was convinced that he wouldn't survive more than a year if he tried to remain at the studio. The following Monday, he passed the word to Sony through Coke and its investment bankers. Sony made no effort to dissuade Kaufman. Doubtless Yetnikoff was delighted to see him take himself out of the equation.

Kaufman wasn't going to get too soppy about Columbia and TriStar, even though he had devoted years to Columbia and had founded TriStar. He was an asset-creating technician, a man whose pulses were quickened by imaginative new financing techniques. He took less in salary than other executives, preferring to be paid in stock. It was a longer-term strategy with potential for the big payoff.

WHEN SCHULHOF HAD approached Kaufman about the studio, Kaufman immediately referred him to the man who could make the deal. In a sense, after all, Herbert Allen, Jr., was Kaufman's boss.

Allen had effectively been running Columbia since he 203 bought his board seat in June 1973. He was a scion of the Allen & Co. banking house, which was co-founded by his uncle

Charles. In his famous 1982 exposé *Indecent Exposure,* David McClintick described how producer Ray Stark had befriended Charles Allen in the 1950s. The two had much in common. Both wanted to make more money in show business and both had innovative ideas for doing it. "And both shared a business attitude, common in the hurly-burly world of Hollywood and certain sectors of Wall Street, which accommodates occasional association and conduct of business with people of questionable reputation," McClintick wrote. In the late fifties, Stark served on the board of a company that licensed films for television; the chairman of that company, Louis Chesler, had ties to organized crime figure Meyer Lansky. But Ray and Charles felt that "[t]here was nothing wrong with dealing with rogues . . . so long as one did not dirty one's own hands in the process," McClintick wrote. "Charlie and Ray stayed clean."

Ray was friends with Charlie but he became even closer to Charlie's nephew, Herbert Allen, Jr. Some speculated that Herbert became a kind of substitute for Ray's own son, who had apparently committed suicide. Ray and Herbert spoke to each other daily at least. Stark once told *Esquire* magazine, "If I were a woman, I'd marry Herbert."

Herbert Allen had entered the family business upon graduating from Williams College in 1962. He had a well-established reputation as a ladies' man (and was twice married and divorced). Rich and good-looking, Allen dated the most beautiful actresses and models in New York, though he seemed to set impossibly high physical standards for his women. "He would mull over fine points of physique with cronies and would shun a woman for such minor failings as exposing what he considered to be too much of her gums when she smiled," McClintick reported.

That approach was like a paradigm for Herbert's style. He enjoyed life's pleasures but recoiled from sloppiness and excess. He was fastidious and controlled, a creature of habit, an early riser, a conservative but meticulous dresser. His office was appointed like a gentleman's library with American Impressionist paintings on the walls. He tried to keep the surface of his antique desk bare.

204    Herbert had become president of Allen & Co. at twenty-seven. There were those who were unconvinced that he was up to the challenge and feared he had been given too much

responsibility too soon. In fact, in the early seventies, the company became involved in a number of deals that led to scrapes with the Securities and Exchange Commission. These appeared to be the logical extension of Herbert Junior's forebears' tolerance for doing business with rogues.

Allen said as much to the *New York Times* at that time. "We trade every day with hustlers, shysters, deal-makers, conmen," he said. "That's the way businesses get started. That's the way this country was built." (Some years later, he disavowed the quote.)

When Columbia got into financial trouble in 1973 and Stark became alarmed that the studio might go belly up, Charlie and Herbert Senior were reluctant to get involved. But Herbert Junior bought a 6.7 percent stake for $1.5 million. He was named to the board and soon assumed effective control. Within a few years, the studio achieved the highest profits and revenues in its history. And Stark—a successful producer of profitable but generally forgettable films—always had very favorable deals for himself.

Peace never reigns long in the movie business. In the late seventies, Columbia was ripped by a spectacular scandal that occurred after David Begelman, the studio president who had fired Peter Guber from his job at the studio, was caught forging checks. He was forced to take a leave from the studio and an epic power struggle ensued. Stark wanted to protect his friend Begelman and reinstate him in his job. Studio chairman Alan Hirschfield felt that a public company couldn't keep a confessed thief like Begelman in a top executive position.

(During this period, Herbert Allen pleaded Begelman's case by arguing that his departure might cause promising young producers—namely, Peter Guber and Jon Peters—to leave. At the time, Guber had produced *The Deep* and Peters was making *Eyes of Laura Mars.* "You better get the next Streisand movie!" Allen warned Hirschfield. Concerned, Hirschfield visited Jon and Barbra, but found that they didn't mention Begelman at all. Instead, Jon asked for an introduction to Hirschfield's financial advisers.)

Begelman was reinstated briefly, during which time he dramatically sweetened Guber's production deal. Finally, Hirschfield managed to eject Begelman, but having taken on Ray Stark and Herbert Allen, he too was forced out.

205

Columbia Pictures was in for a rough ride. Hirschfield was replaced by one of Herbert's schoolmates from Williams College, Fay Vincent. Vincent knew nothing about show business; he was an official at the Securities and Exchange Commission. (He later became commissioner of baseball and was fired in a dispute with the team owners.)

David Begelman was replaced as head of the film division by Frank Price, who had been a successful television executive at Universal and had yearned for years to get into the movie business. And at first, Price appeared to have a golden touch. During his tenure, the studio released an enviable string of films, achieving a mix of prestige and success or both with movies like *Gandhi, Tootsie,* and *The Blue Lagoon.*

But before long, Kirk Kerkorian appeared as an unfriendly suitor. He acquired a 25 percent interest in Columbia and had to be bought out at a hefty price, pocketing about $60 million for his trouble. Herbert Allen hadn't been amenable to an attack from Kerkorian, but he wasn't necessarily opposed to selling the studio, always maintaining that he would accept a "ridiculous" price—somewhere between 50 and 100 percent more than the prevailing value of the studio's shares—if someone offered it.

Someone did. In 1982, Coca-Cola paid $752 million, about $70 a share for stock that was trading around $40. Coke said control of the studio would be left in the hands of Fay Vincent and Frank Price—always, of course, with Herbert Allen and Ray Stark in the background. Allen & Co. got a $5 million fee for investment banking services, and Allen and the firm also made about $40 million in cash and Coke stock. All that, and Herbert Allen still remained a force at Columbia. His offices were a few floors down from Columbia's at 711 Fifth Avenue in New York. He was a Columbia director and was to become an influential member of Coca-Cola's board. It wasn't a bad day's business for Herbert Allen.

Even though Frank Price got to keep his job, the advent of the Coke era didn't go unnoticed at the studio. Price's office promptly sent out a memo forbidding the use of anything the color of Pepsi blue in interior decor on the lot, banning all non-Coke soft drinks—even Perrier—from the lot, and finally decreeing that anyone planning a studio event at resorts or hotels had to make sure that no Pepsi products were sold at the site, even from a vending machine. Price later said the memo was written and circulated in error by an overzealous secretary.

Price's memo played into Hollywood's already unfriendly attitude toward Coke. The entertainment community didn't much like the idea of a soft drink giant buying one of its vaunted brand names. "For some reason, people didn't think Coke was good for the industry or Columbia," one former Columbia executive says. "People in Hollywood were not treating them as insiders, in a sense. Hollywood reacts to anyone who might be bigger than they are. If you're not part of the community, if you don't physically live there, if you haven't been through the wars together, you're going to be attacked."

Price found it difficult to get along with his boss in New York, Fay Vincent. The problems between Vincent and Price were always about money. Despite Price's impressive slate of films, Vincent says, Price lost as much on bad movies as he made on the good ones. "It's hard for someone like Price to confront the fact that *Tootsie* doesn't make up for six bad films," Vincent says. "We had to deal with publishing numbers, and the Prices of the world could give interviews about all the hits he made. It bothered Frank to have failures and things go wrong. Then he wouldn't come to work and he'd stay home and talk to Ray Stark ten times a day."

Price saw it differently. He thought Columbia was being stifled by too many managers imposing too many demands with too little understanding of the realities of the business. "Once Coca-Cola was in the picture, we had a corporate headquarters in Atlanta, another in New York, and Columbia located on the West Coast," he says. "We had a lot of layers there."

While Vincent complained that Price wasn't moving pictures into the pipeline fast enough, Price complained that Coca-Cola was pushing him too hard, seeking to boost production from twelve films a year to twenty. "I probably have one of the best records for turning out hits," Price says. "To pick up the pace and get to twenty, it would take me about three years. . . . The key to it is signing deals with talent. I had to have Sydney Pollacks, Ivan Reitmans, Larry Kasdans. They wanted to do it right then. And they did it after I left. If you look at the results, suddenly the hits vanished. You can't step up production that quickly unless you ignore what your hit ratio is going to be. I'll 207 go as fast as I can and make hits."

By October 1983, Price was out. His short-lived successor was the man who was running Ray Stark's production company, a former agent named Guy McElwaine. The dapper McElwaine was well liked by men and women, going through so many wives that one acquaintance joked that McElwaine had "a prenuptial tearpad." But McElwaine released an abysmal string of losers. He also provided more fodder for Coca-Cola jokes. In 1985, when Coke introduced with much hoopla the "new" Coke, Hollywood was amused. "Look at this company," people said. "They change the formula of Coca-Cola but they keep Guy McElwaine." As it turned out, McElwaine didn't do much better than the failed soft drink. He got the boot in April 1986 after less than three years.

Columbia hadn't had a blockbuster in a couple of years. Its last big successes were pictures left over from the Frank Price regime—including the huge hit *Ghostbusters*. McElwaine also left behind a box-office surprise, but it was hardly a pleasant one: The studio was stuck with *Ishtar,* a legendary disaster starring Warren Beatty and Dustin Hoffman. The film cost about $40 million, considered a scandalous amount at the time. It became a symbol of excess in the film business. But, of course, it was soon supplanted by more expensive flops.

With McElwaine out, Fay Vincent decided to embark on a bold experiment: He hired David Puttnam, the charismatic British producer of *Chariots of Fire* and *The Killing Fields* as well as Guber's *Midnight Express,* to run Columbia. Puttnam didn't have much executive experience and he had never produced a major hit, although he had accumulated a number of Oscars. But he came in with much fanfare, boasting that he would make modest, artistic, and socially conscious films, nothing like the overpriced garbage cranked out by the other studios.

If he had walked softly, or if he had made hit movies, he might have lasted longer. Hollywood, with its unslakable thirst for elegance and legitimacy, has always adored a British accent. Puttnam's Oscars and his high-flown talk gave him a certain cachet in the creative community. But the men in the executive suites are invariably hostile to outsiders who second-guess the way business is done. Puttnam, an upstart foreign producer who had never even worked for a movie studio, was very much an outsider, an outsider with a big mouth.

As Puttnam's rhetoric alienated his competitors, they waited eagerly for him to fail. They didn't have to wait long. He quickly made several serious strategic errors. Perhaps the worst was antagonizing Ray Stark by questioning his generous long-standing deal with the studio. He reportedly attacked Bill Murray in a speech as an example of a typical spoiled creature of Hollywood, possibly a fair statement but an impolitic one. And he clashed with Bill Cosby, a television superstar whose potential on the big screen was about to be tested at Columbia's expense through the ill-fated *Leonard Part 6*. Cosby had been a Coke spokesman and had good relationships with executives in Atlanta. Like many in Hollywood, he decided he loathed David Puttnam.

Puttnam was naive in failing to grasp the significance of these men and their relationships. Cosby had his friends at Coke headquarters; Murray was essential if the studio were finally to make a long-dreamed-of *Ghostbusters* sequel; Stark may have been an old man, a dinosaur, but he was powerful. He was still close to Herbert Allen. Stark alone was an enemy who could do serious damage.

And Puttnam committed the biggest sin of all: He failed at the box office. Hits would have saved him even if he had slapped Stark's face and spit on Cosby's shoes. Without them, he was doomed.

By now, Coke was beginning to tire of its adventures in the screen trade. "When you make the margins they do selling sugar and water," one leading Hollywood dealmaker said later, "the entertainment business isn't worth it." Not that the company had suffered financially over the long haul: When it first bought the studio, some financial analysts questioned the rich price but soon concluded that Coke had made itself a pretty good deal. And Coca-Cola had made some shrewd acquisitions, buying some success by acquiring Embassy Television, which produced successful sitcoms, including *Who's the Boss?*, and Merv Griffin Enterprises, home of the profitable *Wheel of Fortune* and *Jeopardy!* Coke's entertainment operations achieved an industry-high operating profit in 1986. But the money was coming from its television division, not from movies.

"I never got the film studio working properly," Vincent says. "I never had a guy running it who could do a good job. . . . The [television] acquisitions were very good and we did reasonably well with what we had. But we didn't set the world on fire."

Coke knew that sustaining its momentum would be expensive. Growing by buying up more companies would be costly, especially since Coke's own previous purchases had helped to drive up prices. In September 1987, a big story broke with little warning: Coke was spinning off Columbia Pictures Industries and merging it with TriStar. The resulting company, which would be called Columbia Pictures Entertainment, would include the two studios, each producing its own slate of films, as well as Columbia's mighty television operation and the chain of theaters owned by TriStar. Coke, which owned 100 percent of Columbia and 40 percent of TriStar, kept a 49 percent stake in the new company.

Victor Kaufman, head of TriStar, had been summoned to Coke's Atlanta headquarters on a moment's notice and informed of the change. TriStar wasn't an especially glamorous match for Columbia; since Kaufman started the company in 1983, it had not won much respect in the creative community. TriStar had launched a few prestige films (*Places in the Heart*, for example). But TriStar movies were generally middle-of-the-road, forgettable popular entertainment, with virtually no major hits. Kaufman insisted on approving the movies but his instincts never proved particularly good.

Coke's decision to merge Columbia and TriStar was dubbed "the 49-percent solution" for the amount of stock that Coke would hold in the new company. But the soft drink giant was only beginning to back away from its venture into show business. Its executives had learned a lesson frequently taught to outsiders drawn to the glamour of the entertainment industry: The movie business has a way of generating a lot of bad press. Negative publicity—whether from a flop like *Ishtar* or from the type of scandal that brews too easily in Hollywood's wealthy and permissive environment—can have a disproportionate impact on the parent company. The entertainment business was a small part of Coke's operations, but Coke chairman and chief executive Roberto Goizueta said the company was too often "judged by how the movies are doing in the theater." He had learned one of Hollywood's central lessons—a lesson that Peter Guber had learned years earlier. In the movie business, he concluded, "perceptions are more important than fact."

210

□

THE MARRIAGE OF Columbia and TriStar was the end of David Puttnam. His job was eliminated, and he was paid handsomely to go away. Fay Vincent, the man who had hired him, was exiled to a vaguely defined position overseeing bottling properties—Coca-Cola's equivalent of Siberia. Victor Kaufman took the reins amid reports that Columbia stood to lose tens of millions on upcoming Puttnam movies that America wouldn't want to see.

At Columbia Pictures Entertainment, Kaufman had his work cut out for him. There were write-offs and layoffs ahead. He warned that profits would be limited or nonexistent as the company worked to right itself. But rumors swirled: that the new management wasn't up to running the company, that the studio was slated to be sold and wasn't open for serious business. The grapevine buzzed with reports that the acquirer might be Sony. While some analysts were warning shareholders to get rid of the stock, Herbert Allen spent the summer of 1988 quadrupling his holdings in Columbia Pictures.

With two motion picture units to run, TriStar and Columbia, Kaufman left David Matalon, the head of TriStar's unglamorous movie-making unit, in place. Finding someone to take the Columbia job wasn't so easy. Many in Hollywood assumed that whoever "ran" Columbia Pictures would answer to a committee of Herbert Allen, Ray Stark, Victor Kaufman, and Kaufman's number-two man, Lew Korman. No one who could demand autonomy would consider taking the job. And there was a question of security, since many suspected that Coke intended to sell the newly created company.

Dawn Steel wasn't in a position to fret much about autonomy. She was a feisty and petite woman with a famous mane of honey-colored hair. And she was out of a job. She had been dumped as head of production at Paramount Pictures while in the hospital giving birth to her first child. The idea of making a spectacular rebound by getting the top job at Columbia had its allure. And Kaufman was happy to provide plenty of support, allowing her to bring her baby to the office.

Steel was attractive, with the sleek look that a collection of Armani jackets can confer. She was a tough but occasionally insecure New Yorker who had got her start by creating and marketing novelty toilet paper. She succeeded until she got into trouble with the Gucci people for trademark infringement.

She came to Hollywood, got a lowly marketing job at Paramount, and started up the ladder. She made an impression in the production department through her early support of the project that would become *Flashdance.* Eventually, she was promoted to head of production by bosses who made it humiliatingly and publicly clear that she was getting the job by default. Then, when she was having her baby, Paramount dumped her.

At Columbia, she had a difficult job awaiting her. Puttnam's leftover films—the unreleased *Me and Him,* about a talking penis, for example—were costing the studio more than $100 million in write-offs. (The mere notion of a talking-penis film might have been enough to make the image-conscious Coke eager to sell the studio.) It would take months to put a new slate of movies together. Steel tried to get a handle on her new job. She managed to launch the long-delayed *Ghostbusters II* as well as the third installment of the successful *Karate Kid* series. To establish her bona fides with the creative community, she okayed the risky and expensive *Casualties of War,* a grim tale of rape and murder in Vietnam. Even the casting was a gamble, since Michael J. Fox would be playing against type in this gritty drama.

Meanwhile, Steel was miserably unhappy. First, she was caught in the middle of a disabling strike by the Writers Guild of America. Rumors were constant that Columbia Pictures Entertainment would be sold or that her job would be reorganized out of existence. "People kept saying, 'How long are you going to be there? Is it stable?' . . . It was like being Sisyphus for me, pushing a rock up a mountain," she says.

Steel took it out on her employees. She was famously difficult to work for and there was constant talk about her abusive behavior. One story circulated that she had shrieked orders at a secretary who had fallen ill and was being carried out of the office on a stretcher.

Steel denied everything but acknowledged that her reputation was suffering: She even had a recurring nightmare that all her former assistants had appeared on *Geraldo* to talk about the horrors of working for her. Some of her fears were confirmed when *California* magazine featured her in an article about the 212 worst bosses in the state. Her picture appeared on the cover with the caption "The Queen of Mean."

When Steel's slate of movies started to come out, the results weren't great. Green-lighting *Ghostbusters II* was considered a no-brainer—indeed, some industry observers speculated that Coke was just waiting for the film to boost profits to assist it in selling the studio. But the sequel didn't perform up to expectation, and neither did another, *The Karate Kid III*. And *Casualties of War* was an expensive bomb. Needless to say, Steel wasn't getting any happier in her job.

Before she would really have a chance to make or ruin her name at Columbia, Steel would find that the rumors of an impending sale were true. The news created uncertainty about her future, but the blow was cushioned. When he hired her, Victor Kaufman had offered Steel a chance to take less in salary and more in stock. She took the stock. With a deep-pocketed buyer finally arriving on the scene, Steel was about to make millions. She was only one of many who would become rich as a cyclone of money started to blow through Hollywood.

# 18

## THE DEAL IS DONE

IT WASN'T REALLY FAIR, Walter Yetnikoff said later, to throw Sony's Mickey Schulhof into a negotiation with Herbert Allen. Not that Schulhof wasn't impressive in many ways. He had a Ph.D. in physics from Brandeis University. He could fly planes. He shared with his boss, Norio Ohga, not only an interest in airplanes but in art and ham radio. Ovitz found him polished and graceful. A massive wall closet in his office at Sony headquarters in New York contained a showcase of high-tech toys: laser discs and compact disc players.

But when it came to negotiating the purchase of Columbia, Yetnikoff and many others were sure that Schulhof was no match for Herbert Allen. "To have Mickey Schulhof against Herbert Allen is almost a crime," Yetnikoff says. "Herbie Allen and Mickey. This is not fair. This is like putting my Labrador retriever Thunder against a Chihuahua. This is stupid."

By now, Allen was a powerful fixture in the entertainment community—a link between Wall Street and Hollywood. The annual summer conference that he hosted in Sun Valley, Idaho, was a place where communications moguls, moneymen, and financial players met to talk business at morning seminars, and to talk more business as they played golf and tennis in the afternoon. While the suspicion that Columbia had been gussying itself up for a sale had become widespread by the middle of 1989, some wondered whether Allen would be willing to part with the studio after seventeen years. His friends doubted that he would suffer many pangs. "If an offer was received acceptable to Coke and advantageous to the other shareholders, he would sell in an instant," said John Heyman, a British film financier and a friend of Allen's at the time.

214

Schulhof's mother was German and his father was Czech. They had fled the Nazis and settled in a small apartment in the Bronx. His father, Rudolph, started a business that would become the country's largest publisher of Catholic greeting cards and Mass folders. By the late 1940s, he had moved the family to an exclusive Long Island suburb. Mickey was a reserved child, according to his brother Thomas, preferring ham radio to sports. He grew up imbibing conversation about business and the arts. His parents assembled an extraordinary art collection that included Cy Twombly, Alexander Calder, and Ellsworth Kelly. Rudolph became a trustee of the Guggenheim, and his wife, Hannelore, became a trustee of the Brooklyn Museum. She played the violin in the Great Neck Orchestra, and insisted that her children visit museums and attend symphonies. Mickey was sent to learn French in Geneva and Tours.

Mickey's two younger brothers went into the family business, but Mickey pursued his interest in science, doing research for a time at Brookhaven National Laboratory. During his relatively brief academic career, he published twenty-seven papers. But he always intended to meld his interest in science with a career in business.

In the early seventies, Rudolph and Hannelore were vacationing at Round Hill in Jamaica where they met and dined with Clive Davis, then president of CBS Records. The connection led to a job for Mickey, who was hired as an assistant to the vice president of operations. (At the time, Walter Yetnikoff was still working his way up the CBS Records ladder.)

A couple of years later, Schulhof told Davis that he was ready to move on to a company where his background in physics might be an asset. Davis introduced him to Harvey Schein, then president of Sony USA. Schein hired him as his assistant and Schulhof advanced quickly. By 1975, Sony had made him a vice president—the youngest to hold that title in the American operation. At one point, Norio Ohga learned of Schulhof's interest in flying and asked him to make a recommendation about a plane for the company's use in the United States. The two men began to bond.

In 1979, one of Schulhof's younger brothers was killed in a midair collision in a chartered plane. Mickey's father asked him to help with the family's greeting card business. Sony founder Akio Morita showed patience and tenacity—just as he

215

had done when the young Norio Ohga insisted on pursuing his singing career before settling down with the company. "Look, I'm the eldest son also," he told Schulhof. "In Japan, we have obligations, too. You go and help the family business as much as you want, but I won't let you leave Sony." So Sony installed a telephone line at the family firm and Schulhof worked there, remaining a Sony employee, for four years.

Schulhof returned to the Sony offices and joined the board of the CBS/Sony joint record venture that Walter Yetnikoff had helped set up in 1967. So when Yetnikoff wanted Sony to buy CBS Records, he naturally broached the idea first with Schulhof. When that deal was made, Mickey was drawn into Sony's foray into the entertainment world.

Not everyone at Sony loved Mickey. Some in Tokyo distrusted him. Some were jealous of his influence and some resented the idea that Sony was beginning to gamble on Hollywood. "These guys [in Japan] tilled the fields in the hardware business a long time to earn capital as a manufacturing company," said a source associated with Sony. "Now, do they want to put that capital at risk on the movies?" But those forces were overruled. Now Sony's choice had come down to Columbia, and that meant Herbert Allen.

Of course, Schulhof wasn't dealing with Allen alone—at least, not at first. He had his well-paid advisers, including Michael Ovitz. And on Wall Street, he had the Blackstone Group, an investment banking firm that had seen Sony through its acquisition of CBS Records as well as the failed MGM/UA talks.

Blackstone's chairman was Peter G. Peterson, a former Secretary of Commerce during the Nixon administration and a former chairman of Lehman Brothers. Blackstone was small, but Peterson's connections helped it snag some high-profile clients. He was particularly admired in Japan, where his role as chairman of the Council on Foreign Relations gave him prestige. He was close to Sony chairman Akio Morita.

Peterson, however successful and connected, had a way of getting on some people's nerves. Many of his colleagues respected him but didn't much like him. He treated them autocratically, summoning them to his office unexpectedly and requiring them to wait outside for long periods. After he had founded Blackstone, *Barron's* dubbed Peterson "the Cadillac Cassandra" because he berated the public for overconsumption while living a jet-setter's life in Manhattan. "The Peterson who rebukes us for our dependence on foreign creditors is the same Peterson who cashes a fresh $100 million check from a Japanese securities firm bent on snatching up American goodies," *Barron's* wrote.

"The thing with Pete is that he's not an intellectual," economist Arthur Laffer said. "He doesn't have a commitment to ideas. The ideas are a vehicle to make him rich and famous."

But Sony only had reason to feel good about Peterson and Blackstone. The acquisition of CBS Records had gone well. It was natural to turn to Blackstone again about its purchase of a studio. But there was a problem: Blackstone would be dealing in the entirely unfamiliar and financially idiosyncratic world of Hollywood.

Setting a value on Columbia required some sophisticated analysis and some educated guesswork. What was the value of projects in the works? Would *Flatliners,* a movie about medical students doing life-after-death experiments, be dead on arrival or would it earn millions? Kevin Costner in a picture called *Revenge*—wouldn't that be a sure bet? Would a television show that the critics liked, *The Famous Teddy Z,* survive? That was where Ovitz came in. He and his associates at Creative Artists Agency were assigned the task of educating the Blackstone delegation, helping them appraise the studio and projects in the works. They had performed the same role when Sony was considering the purchase of MGM/UA. It was Blackstone's job to put the pieces together and come up with a fair price.

Nothing was going to happen fast. In the early stages of the discussion, Sony and Coke were miles apart, with Sony starting off in the low 20s per share. Allen, acting as Coca-Cola's representative in the matter, was asking for as much as $35. And he gave Sony's advisers the impression that he would walk away if his price was not met. On-again, off-again discussions dragged on for a year. To the Columbia side, it seemed agonizingly protracted. But the Japanese were daunted by the high price mentioned by Allen. "There was no basis for realistic dialogue," says a source familiar with Sony's thinking.

And unbeknownst to the Columbia side, negotiations stalled because Norio Ohga had a serious heart condition. "Every time we would build to making an offer, [Ohga] would get sick," that insider said. "We couldn't move without him." Ohga had at least one and possibly two serious heart attacks during the year when the talks took place. One of them occurred while he was in Germany; this episode was not disclosed to the public, as would be customary in the United States. An associate said Ohga later confided that he had made up his mind to proceed with the Columbia purchase as he was being wheeled out of intensive care. Another Sony source says Morita also had major surgery that was never disclosed.

In July 1989, at a meeting of the international Sony board in Cologne, Morita and Ohga approved the concept of buying Columbia if Schulhof could find a manager to run it. Sony had made a practice of installing American managers to run American operations. The company wisely assumed that it was especially important to put a native in charge of an American entertainment company.

A lot of cooks were working on this project, and all of them wanted to see a deal happen. Peterson knew that this was his client's objective, and Blackstone's multi-million-dollar fee was dependent on a consummation of the courtship. Yetnikoff's goal was to become Steve Ross. And Schulhof, perhaps, was already tempted by the possibility of supplanting Yetnikoff as the head of Sony's growing entertainment business.

Then there was Michael Ovitz. Making this deal happen would be a watershed for him and for Creative Artists Agency. It would prove that Ovitz could broker a multi-billion-dollar transaction in an international arena. So the sale in itself was worthwhile to Ovitz. But his interests hardly ended there.

If Sony bought Columbia, Ovitz would seek to ensure, at the very least, that whoever ran the studio would be amenable to buying his agency's talent. Everyone in Hollywood had to do business with CAA, but some were more enthusiastic about it than others. Better to have a hearty customer like Warner than another frugal Disney, which tried to circumvent CAA's rich deals as often as possible.

And maybe there would be even more in it for Ovitz. As Sony shopped for a studio, its executives began to respect and trust him. He had no experience as a studio executive, but Ovitz exuded an aura of such competence that most people simply assumed he could do the job. As the negotiations wore on, Sony reached the same conclusion.

Ovitz hired Robert Greenhill of Morgan Stanley to represent

218

him in the negotiations. The matter had to be kept absolutely secret. If word got out in Hollywood that Ovitz was considering a move, his position would be damaged. The stars from whom he derived his power might get nervous that he wasn't fully committed to them. His associates at CAA might start jostling for power. So Ovitz had to keep things quiet or deal with some unpleasant consequences if the negotiations didn't pay off.

In some ways, Ovitz's interest in the job seemed a bit out of character. He occupied an almost mystical place in Hollywood. Why would he want to run Columbia and TriStar when it seemed that he already had de facto control over almost all the studios? If the deal was sweet enough, however, it would make sense. Ovitz was a titanic success at CAA and he was emerging as a dealmaker, but he was still an agent living off a percentage of fees paid to the talent. Talent could be fickle. And without a change, Ovitz could not launch himself into the financial stratosphere like Michael Eisner, the chairman of Disney, or the envied Steve Ross.

Greenhill and Ovitz made their presentation to Sony. The Japanese were stunned by its dimensions. For Ovitz, nothing would do but the deal of deals—a deal that reflected Ovitz's position in Hollywood. He would ask for everything: huge compensation, total control of the company, a significant amount of stock, an enormous acquisition fund to buy new businesses. MCA and Paramount and Warner all had publishing divisions —why not the new Sony entertainment company? Hearing the Ovitz wish list, Sony executives felt somewhat betrayed, according to one source close to the negotiations.

As soon as it became apparent that Sony wasn't going to meet his terms, Ovitz tried to ensure that history would record that he had turned the job down. As rumors about his negotiations circulated, Ovitz steadfastly denied that he ever wanted to work for Sony. The word was that he had sought a very rich deal, but Ovitz implied that he had asked for a lot to induce Sony to drop him. Asking for the moon was just a polite way of saying no, he suggested.

WITH OVITZ OUT of the picture, Schulhof and Yetnikoff became increasingly nervous about finding competent management. At one point, Schulhof even asked Herbert Allen to advise him about possible candidates. Allen said he would be willing to make suggestions but warned him that he represented Columbia's interests, not Sony's.

Finding someone with the brains, guts, and instincts to run a studio has always been difficult. The job calls for an individual who can make constant decisions involving hundreds of millions of dollars. Business sense isn't enough; a studio chief needs to have some intuition about what will entertain the fickle public and some rapport with temperamental actors and directors. Indecision is intolerable: The distribution system is a gaping maw that needs to be filled with one picture after another. Aside from movies, there are television operations, home video, theaters. Overhead roars along at more than $100 million a year. Failures are public.

Those few who have demonstrated an ability to achieve consistent success are jealously guarded by their employers and given handsome long-term contracts. The A-list players—Bob Daly and Terry Semel at Warner; Jeff Katzenberg, then at Disney—weren't likely to jump ship, especially considering the stigma involved in going to work for the first Japanese owner of a Hollywood studio.

Sony was faced with a daunting challenge. But before its management problem could be solved, Walter Yetnikoff was sidelined. His doctor warned him that his substance-abuse problems were going to kill him—soon. On August 13, 1989, the Sony jet delivered Yetnikoff to the Hazelden clinic in Minnesota.

Mickey Schulhof was left to press ahead with the search. He tried to communicate with Walter, who was living in a barrackslike setting with one pay phone in the hall of his dormitory. "I had crotch rot," Yetnikoff remembers. "I was dripping from my nose. I had high blood pressure. I'm on the verge of dying. And they're calling me on the pay phone. The unit has 120 guys. You can imagine in rehab, people have some problems. And they're calling me: 'Who's going to run the company?' "

When he got Walter on the phone, Mickey said he planned to proceed with the purchase of Columbia even though the management issue still wasn't resolved. Yetnikoff wasn't happy to hear it. He also was undergoing a metamorphosis in rehab. "Two or three weeks into it, he went spiritual," says one of

Sony's advisers. "The man became a monk. He got so ethereal, so philosophical. It was a bad movie."

Yetnikoff emerged from rehab after a month's stay, on Sunday, September 10. It was a pristine day and he was a changed man, infused with gratitude for the green grass and the shining sun. Still, there was business to be done. Sony was moving toward closing a deal to buy Columbia and there was no management in place. Usually, Hazelden's graduates are advised not to dive back into their old lives, but Walter showed up at the office the next day. The first thing he did was command his staff to join hands and recite a prayer.

Schulhof hadn't committed himself to hiring anyone, but he thought he had a candidate from a short list provided by Ovitz. It was Frank Price, the man who ran Columbia in the early eighties and made a slew of prestige hits, but not a great deal of profit. In some ways, Price was eminently presentable. He had been at the helm of Columbia before, and he had run Universal. He could claim credit for *Tootsie, Out of Africa, Ghostbusters*. Though he had grown up poor in the Depression, his family moving from city to city as his father looked for work, Price had made himself into an urbane, attractive executive, a carefully groomed man who looked good in a board room. "Frank is a self-created invention," marveled one former Columbia executive. "You would think he grew up as a privileged child, going to Choate."

But Price had been fired from Columbia and then from Universal. The complaint was always the same: He was too slow and he didn't communicate. "He lost the willingness to make movies and he would not talk to his boss," says one high-level Universal executive.

After Price left his studio job, his old friends at Columbia gave him an exceptionally rich production deal with autonomy and power to make up to six films a year. But after three years, he had failed to put a single picture into production. Price maintained that the strike by the Writers Guild had hampered him. And he was fastidious about the projects he wanted to make, working and reworking them. An executive who worked at Price's company remembers how his excitement ebbed as projects failed to materialize. "Every day we met and talked about things we had read. For a while, it was very exciting because you wanted to believe you were onto something that

the rest of the community just didn't understand," he says.
"You develop [material] intelligently—slowly, but intelligently
—and eventually you would reap extraordinary rewards. But as
the months went by, as we seemed to be at a stage where things
really weren't moving forward, it became problematic to conduct business with agents." Finally, the executive remembers,
"paralysis set in."

Price had done Ovitz some well-timed favors in the past.
Many executives and agents thought he had helped Ovitz on a
couple of occasions by getting individuals out of Ovitz's way.
One was Guy McElwaine, the affable former agent who had
succeeded Price at Columbia. When Coke fired him from his
studio job, the rumor mill held that McElwaine was going to
become an agent again. Many in Hollywood believed that Ovitz
wanted to avoid the competition, since McElwaine had been
quite influential in his day.

Price, then running Universal, had handed McElwaine a
lucrative deal to give the studio an option on films he might
want to produce. MCA president and chief operating officer
Sid Sheinberg, Price's boss, was incensed, according to sources
familiar with the episode. Price disputes that he offered the
deal as a favor to Ovitz. "Guy had been my head of production
at the time I was head of Columbia, so we worked together
extremely well," he says. "Therefore, a production-type arrangement with him would have been the logical thing to do."

While many in the industry had concluded that Price was
not decisive enough to run a studio, Ovitz apparently had not
lost faith. With Sony searching for a studio chief, he had put
Price on his list of candidates. Price met with Schulhof and it
is easy to imagine the two hitting it off, Schulhof relieved,
perhaps, to find someone from Hollywood who seemed so polished. But trouble lay ahead. If Frank Price was Ovitz's candidate, he would hold little appeal for Walter Yetnikoff. Walter
would feel uncomfortable with a studio chairman who had
such strong ties to Ovitz.

So when Schulhof took Price to lunch in Yetnikoff's office a
couple of days after Walter's return from Hazelden, Walter was
not in a hospitable mood. Price found him volatile and easily
distracted. The lunch ended unceremoniously when Yetnikoff's
barber appeared. Walter donned a kimono and sat down to have
his hair cut. The search for management was to continue.

It seemed that a test of wills was developing between Yetni-

222

koff and Ovitz. As the pressure mounted, Walter decided to seek out his own candidate, someone who might not have been anyone's first choice but whom he might reasonably expect to control. The day after the lunch with Price, he phoned Peter Guber.

Jon Peters, having already heard about the brewing deal, had called Walter to remind him of their many conversations about running an empire together. They had talked about it on a cruise that they had taken together a year earlier in the Virgin Islands. Despite that prompting, Yetnikoff would later maintain that he was clear in his own mind about one thing.

When Yetnikoff had mentioned to Ovitz that he might call Guber, Ovitz responded with a warning: Jon Peters and Peter Guber had a long-standing relationship with paternalistic Warner. They had just signed an extremely favorable five-year production deal there, with the bloom of *Batman* still on them. If you want to speak to them, Ovitz said, you must approach Steve Ross first to enlist his support. There was reason to think Ross would go along. He had agreed, back when Jon and Peter had made their abortive offer for MGM, to let them out of their contract if the deal went through.

And Ross would probably have let them go again, if they had asked properly. He knew better than anyone that Jon and Peter had been an expensive fixture at Warner. "Steve would have been happy at that moment to make a deal," said one insider. "He was a good guy, he didn't want anyone to dislike him. He had a mega-overhead with them. They were working half-days." But Ross was a man who had to be asked; obeisance had to be paid, or he would react with fury, like an indulgent father faced with the ingratitude of a favored child.

Naturally, nothing could be more repugnant to Walter Yetnikoff than the idea of going to Steve Ross on bended knee to ask permission to speak to Jon and Peter. If anything, he might have liked the idea of handing Ross—the man he had regarded with such bitter jealousy for so long—an unpleasant surprise. He ignored Ovitz's advice.

With Yetnikoff proceeding on his own, Ovitz's involvement in Sony's acquisition of Columbia Pictures came to an end. According to two Sony sources, Ovitz received an $11 million fee. And shortly thereafter, he was retained by Matsushita to broker its acquisition of MCA.

□

WALTER YETNIKOFF called Guber in Los Angeles on a Thursday and Guber was in Manhattan in time for dinner on Saturday night. Yetnikoff laid out his cards: Sony was going to buy Columbia Pictures Entertainment and needed someone to run the company. "When I have this conversation, am I talking to you and Jon, or am I talking to you?" Walter asked. "Your call."

"You're talking to both of us," Peter responded. "We're a team."

It might have seemed a peculiar answer. Peter had been complaining about Jon on and off for years, and in the preceding weeks one knowledgeable source maintains that he was secretly plotting to bring about some kind of divorce with Steve Ross's help. But now, handed an opportunity to walk away, Guber didn't take it. "He went into his normal rap," Yetnikoff remembers. " 'Oh, our talents are synergistic. . . . Jon is the one that can always go get Jack Nicholson. We work together. We're partners.' "

This wasn't some colossal failure of nerve. By demanding that he and Jon come as a team, Peter was following through on a strategy he had blocked out with his advisers: to get Sony to buy their company—formerly Barris, now renamed Guber-Peters Entertainment Co. (GPEC). The company was foundering. Not only did Peter stand to make tens of millions on his stock if Sony bought GPEC, but other shareholders—among them Gary Winnick, the former Drexel salesman who had joined the Guber-Peters board, and Australian financier Frank Lowy—would see a handsome return on their investments.

Yetnikoff coached Guber on what to expect when he met Schulhof the next day. That Sunday, Schulhof came in from East Hampton and arrived at Peter's suite at the Regency shortly after noon. Peter was casual in flannel shirt and jeans and he hadn't shorn his ponytail for the occasion. But Peter Guber had been born for this moment. What took place appears to have been a vintage seduction.

"I was immediately attracted to him," Schulhof said later. "I found him very sympathetic. I subsequently discovered that he and I are both amateur radio operators . . . and that he has had an interest in technology that goes quite far back." During the first few hours, "the chemistry was wonderful. I didn't hear anything that made me feel uncomfortable at all." Schulhof also was enchanted to learn that he and Peter were almost exactly the same age, born just months apart in 1942.

At about 6:00 P.M., Schulhof called Pete Peterson at home and asked him to come over. Peterson brought his partner at Blackstone, Steve Schwarzman. Within a few short hours of his first meeting with Guber, Schulhof was completely hooked and Schwarzman also was bedazzled. "He really is one of the most captivating, bright, driven, creative, charismatic, intuitive people I've ever met," he gushed.

By midnight, Peter had introduced the key element of his deal—that Sony buy his company. He carefully mentioned the fact that he had some obligation to Warner in the form of a newly signed five-year contract. After the long search for management, Schulhof and his team apparently weren't in a mood to fret over details. They were caught up in making sure that Jon and Peter were going to solve their problem, which meant drawing the outlines of a deal and sending Guber on the road to complete the sales job with the top men at Sony.

Peter flew back to Los Angeles on Monday and frantically put out the word: The deal was heating up! Winnick got a call as he was driving south on the San Diego Freeway, en route to a meeting of Republican fundraisers. The host had a collection of antique cars that Winnick was particularly keen to see. But first things first: Winnick turned around and headed back to Jon Peters's house.

Early the next morning, Jon and Peter clambered aboard Frank Lowy's 727—loaned for the occasion—with a batch of advisers from the Guber-Peters Entertainment Co., including Gary Winnick, general counsel Terry Christensen, and Alan Levine, the lawyer who represented Jon and Peter personally. Christensen was the high-powered entertainment lawyer who had long been associated with financier Kirk Kerkorian and had run Kerkorian's holding company, Tracinda. He also had been hired by Burt Sugarman as counsel to Barris. He had represented both sides in Barris's ill-fated run at MGM. After Sugarman's departure, Jon and Peter had asked him to stay on.

The men sat excitedly discussing their prospects for a deal until the last leg of the flight, when the plane flew into a violent storm. The flight became genuinely terrifying. As the plane bounced and dipped sickeningly in the turbulence, everyone fell silent until they landed safely at Teterboro.

Most of the contingent that arrived on Lowy's jet headed for the Regency except for Winnick, who always stayed at the Plaza Athénée. That evening, they went to Sony's offices at 9 West

225

57th Street for their first formal meeting. Waiting for them were Schulhof, Yetnikoff, and several Japanese executives and their advisers: investment bankers from Blackstone and lawyers from Skadden, Arps, Slate, Meagher & Flom.

The Guber-Peters team had decided that it might be prudent to exclude Jon from this first formal encounter. "One guy with a ponytail was enough," Winnick thought. Jon and Peter's strategists had agreed that their hand would be strongest if Sony committed to them—which meant buying Guber-Peters Entertainment Co.—before they signed a deal with Coke. "Once they did a deal with us, they were very likely to do the Columbia deal," Christensen explained later. "But it also gives us the most leverage if the whole Columbia deal was sort of riding on our shoulders."

Steve Schwarzman initiated the negotiation by lowballing. Blackstone thought it could recommend that Sony pay $7.00 or $8.00 per share for Guber-Peters Entertainment Co., he said. The stock was trading at about $11.50. Winnick objected: "First of all, you're missing a digit." Schwarzman drew Winnick aside and asked his price. Winnick replied: $22.50.

"You're kidding," Schwartzman said. But Winnick had a ready reply. Frank Lowy, the investor who had bought out Sugarman, had just recently paid about $13.00 a share, he said. Lowy was thrilled with the company, Winnick continued. He wasn't a seller. He would have to be bought out at a premium.

Yetnikoff was in a belligerent mood, smoking a Nat Sherman cigar as was his custom. One of the conferees remembers one seemingly irrelevant tirade, possibly intended to assert Walter's primacy over the lawyers and investment bankers. "Walter says, 'Who in this room has ever run a company?' And Terry [Christensen] says, 'I was chairman of Tracinda.' [Tracinda was Kerkorian's company.] And Walter says, 'What was Tracinda? . . . That's not a company.' So Pete Peterson says, 'Well, I was chairman of Bell & Howell.' And Walter says, 'You're a fucking asshole.' Walter says Peterson is responsible for him getting screwed on his contract [when Sony bought CBS Records]." Walter kept insulting Peterson with Schulhof seated, uncomfortably enough, between the two. The Guber-Peters team was dumbfounded. What was going on? Who cared what had happened to Walter's contract? They took a recess.

The meeting stretched past midnight. At some point Jon

Peters, who had been excluded from the session, grew impatient and burst into the room—leather jacket, ponytail, and all. One of the Guber-Peters team glanced nervously at the Sony executives to see their reaction. "These doors come flying open," he says. "We thought it was a terrorist attack. I see the two Japanese guys look at each other and do a little oy-oy-oy." The Guber-Peters team urged Jon to take a seat and stay quiet.

Despite these disruptions, the first round of talks went well. The Guber-Peters team said Jon and Peter would want some share in the studio's profits—and a piece of any increase over the company's current value. Christensen thought the Sony team seemed pleasantly surprised that they weren't asking for more. By the time the meeting broke up, there seemed to be the outlines of an agreement.

But as the meeting adjourned, Schwarzman drew Christensen aside. Christensen remembers the conversation this way:

"I think we have the parameters of a deal," Schwarzman said. "Now what we'd like to do is set that aside and negotiate with Columbia. . . . Then we'll come back and finalize everything with you."

This was precisely what the Guber-Peters team wanted to avoid. "Let me give you my thoughts on that," Christensen said amiably. "Number one, you guys are great. We had a great meeting. It's amazing that we were able to come to an agreement so fast, create this deal so quickly. So we think you guys are wonderful, we have a lot of respect for you, we wish you all the luck in the world."

"What does that mean?" Schwarzman asked.

"We're going home," Christensen said. "You're the big guy. You're paying the billions. You go do it the way you want to. . . . That's your call. But we don't have a deal. We don't have a little bit of a deal, we don't have a potential deal. Because unless we do it now and get it done, we have nothing."

"You can't do that," Schwarzman protested. "You can't put us in that position. Here we came to an agreement with you. It's going to work out great. You can trust us."

"We do trust you," Christensen said. "But we're not doing the deal that way. You have to do us first. You put our deal to bed, then you do Columbia. We have public shareholders; they're going to get excited, the stock's going to run up. We don't want to be responsible for that. We're going to blow our

Warner relationship. We don't want to do that. We're not doing anything until we have a deal in place. . . . So you have to do our deal first and if you want to do Columbia, go with God. We just don't have any deal at all. Nothing."

"Nothing?" Schwarzman asked.

"Nothing."

The next morning, Christensen saw Schwarzman at breakfast. The Sony team had discussed the Guber-Peters position after the previous night's meeting had broken up, Schwarzman said, and everyone had been furious. Sony couldn't possibly do the Guber-Peters deal first, he said. But he asked whether they would agree to allow Sony to negotiate both deals simultaneously.

"That's a pretty big concession on our part," Christensen replied. "There's something that I was thinking about last night that I should have raised. If we're going to concede that, I'm going to raise it." As a quid pro quo, Christensen said, Sony should commit to guarantee a minimum $100 million bonus pool for Jon and Peter to divide after five years.

When the two sides reconvened later that morning, the Sony side agreed to do the Columbia acquisition and the Guber-Peters acquisition simultaneously. Christensen's proposed $100 million bonus was reduced to $50 million—a figure that must have exceeded Jon and Peter's wildest dreams. The next piece that had to be resolved was price. Evaluating the company as generously as possible, Sony's advisers were finding it impossible to consider offering more than $10 or $12 a share. The Guber-Peters team continued to insist on a number in the low 20s.

The negotiations dragged on for a few days. As the talks continued, Peter was dispatched to meet the Sony elders. Once again, Jon stayed behind.

"We certainly didn't want to take a lot of chances that Jon and the Japanese would not hit it off," Christensen says. "We felt they knew that Jon was an unusual guy, a volatile guy, but they were prepared to accept that because it was definitely part of the package. But why test it? It would be very easy for them to be upset." They had accepted Yetnikoff, he observes. "He was their volatile guy. They had their Schulhof-Yetnikoff team, sort of a Guber-Peters kind of team. They didn't need another one, or at least you didn't want it to be in their face."

Jon, convinced that he was the architect of all that was taking

place, agreed to stay in the background. And in a way, his vision
of himself was not unjustified. He had been the one agitating
for change and adventure from the start. He was the one who
didn't know fear. He was the one who had pursued Michael
Milken and had ultimately got himself and Guber into partnership with Sugarman. No matter how poor the match had
proved to be, no matter how absurd the goings-on at Barris, it
had positioned them as managers in a publicly held company.
It made them credible candidates for the Sony job. Jon's ability
to imagine anything except limits to his own potential had led
him and Peter to this opportunity.

Now it was Guber's turn to shine. He flew to Pebble Beach,
California, where Morita was attending a conference on U.S.-
Japanese relations. "I always need someone around me to make
me feel excited and young," Morita once told a friend. "It
helps me keep my engines going." One can only imagine the
kind of charge Morita would have gotten from the electrified
and electrifying Peter Guber. The two talked for four hours,
and once again, Peter made his sale. Morita said Guber was
"like a whirlwind" and concluded, "I think he's a Sony man."
From there, Peter had to meet Norio Ohga. He flew from
Monterey to Los Angeles, where he caught a Japan Airlines
flight to Tokyo.

Meanwhile, Herbert Allen was wondering what was going on
with Sony. He pressed Schulhof to come to a resolution, hinting that he might otherwise have to convene Columbia's board
to entertain some expressions of interest from other unspecified purchasers. After Peter's successful Saturday meeting with
Morita, Schulhof called Allen to tell him that Sony might be
ready to act soon.

Allen may have had other buyers but none was willing to bid
anywhere near the amount—in the high 20s—he was hoping
to get from Sony. At most, he thought he might have gotten
$20 a share from Fox when Rupert Murdoch considered merg-
ing his studio with Columbia. But one Fox source said Murdoch felt he had been generous by suggesting $15 a share.

With the nudge from Allen, Mickey Schulhof called Ohga in
Tokyo. If he liked Guber, he said, Ohga should get the Sony
board together the following Monday to finalize its offer for
Columbia. Peter arrived in Tokyo and spent the next day with
Ohga. Guber wooed and won again.

That day, Mickey Schulhof set a price for the Columbia stock

229

on the phone in a brief conversation with Herbert Allen. Sony, which had started out talking about paying $15 a share, according to one source familiar with the discussion, agreed to pay $27. It was a handsome price for stock that had never traded above $17 in fiscal 1989 and had dropped as low as $7 in the first quarter of 1989.

The next day, the Sony board met and approved a $3.4 billion offer for Columbia Pictures. Throwing in the $1.6 billion in debt on Columbia's books, the deal was valued at $5 billion.

One source familiar with Sony's reasoning says the company felt it had little room to maneuver. "There was a sense if [Sony] walked away from the deal that Herbert wouldn't come back at $20," he said. And with so few major studios in existence, the company reasoned, Columbia had enhanced value because it was, after all, a scarce asset.

Once again, Morita pushed to have his way. "Ohga expressed financial concern and Morita would say, 'Don't worry about it. We can always recover money. The opportunities like this come once in a lifetime,' " a Sony source remembers.

It was a fine day's business for Coke, which would get $1.55 billion in cash for its stock ($509 million after taxes). While many analysts insist that Coke's venture into show business was a mistake and contend that Coke had never made a success of the studio, Allen disputes that view. He maintains that Coke made plenty of money when it ran Columbia and then made more when it sold its stock. And Coke benefited Hollywood, too, he adds, by building up the studio. "From the standpoint of the entertainment community, they owe a lot to Coke," he says. "And from the standpoint of Coca-Cola, they owe a lot to the community."

Allen & Co. made out well, too. It sold its stake in Columbia Pictures Entertainment for $70 million—and collected a $30 million fee from Coke for negotiating the deal. Anyone who had stock in Columbia Pictures Entertainment had reason to rejoice. When Coke had spun off the entertainment company in 1987, shares were valued at $7.44. Now the shareholders were getting more than three times that much from Sony. Victor Kaufman made more than $22.4 million on his stock; Lew Korman made $13.5 million; Dawn Steel, who had run Columbia for a year, and Jeff Sagansky, who now ran TriStar, each made about $7 million. The industry joked that Sagansky's take was more than TriStar's profit from movies during the previous four years.

Most entertainment executives agreed that Sony paid far too much for Columbia Pictures Entertainment. Several sources close to the deal blamed Pete Peterson and the Blackstone Group for endorsing a price that, as one executive close to the negotiation put it, "had no relationship to the worth of the entity."

"Sony . . . has apparently decided to accept Columbia's projections that it will substantially improve its results and its cash flow in 1990," the *Wall Street Journal* reported skeptically. For the first quarter of the year, the studio's earnings had been down 53 percent, to $2 million. But a knowledgeable Sony insider says that Blackstone led Sony to be overly optimistic about the studio's earning power. "Where Ohga has frequently criticized Blackstone . . . has been in the quality of their projections," that source says. "They put together high, medium, and low [projections] and they blew it in all three areas. They simply didn't understand the business."

There was ample opportunity for finger-pointing. Some argued that Ovitz hadn't educated Sony properly and had been overeager to get the deal done. Some said the eagerness, and therefore the blame, lay with Sony.

Paying a stiff price for Columbia was only the beginning of Sony's misadventure. "The overpayment wasn't the cardinal sin," observes one source on Columbia's side of the negotiation. "It was all that followed. It's like Vietnam. It's what happens when you get into the wrong place with the wrong advisers."

THE DEAL was not a hit in Japan, where it was feared that it would heighten tensions with the United States. Buying an entertainment company was emotionally charged. Eishiro Saito, the head of the Keidanren, Japan's politically powerful alliance of businesses, made comments to one of Japan's biggest newspapers that seemed a barely disguised shot at Morita. "Japanese tend to advertise and boast about purchasing foreign businesses and properties," he said. "This is not good."

Once Sony's board approved the offer for Columbia, Morita paid a visit to Keiji Shima, then the powerful chairman of

231

the Japanese public broadcasting company, NHK. Although his four television channels competed with five commercial networks, NHK had exclusive rights to give politicians airtime during campaigns. He was close to leaders of the ruling parties. The short, stocky Shima wielded so much power that he was known as "the Emperor."

Morita was driven in his limousine to a restaurant where Shima awaited him in a private room. The two sat cross-legged on tatami mats and Morita told Shima that Sony was moving forward with the purchase of Columbia—at the time, the most expensive foreign acquisition ever of an American company.

"Morita-san, you're making a big mistake," Shima reportedly said.

Morita was stunned.

"Making movies is different; it's a special kind of business," Shima continued. "You don't understand Hollywood. It won't work. You're asking for trouble. You're getting into a business that you won't be able to control. Don't do it!"

# 19

## STEVE ROSS'S REVENGE

As the Columbia board met to consider Sony's offer, Schulhof's team was still hashing out the purchase of Guber-Peters Entertainment Co. Jon and Peter's negotiators, led by Terry Christensen, had been fighting hard over the price. Both Sony and GPEC had consulted investment bankers to evaluate the company and Sony was coming up with numbers no higher than $13 or $14, which was already a stretch. GPEC's side presented numbers in the 20s, which was beyond a stretch.

The discussions were tricky because of a peculiar problem: Part of GPEC's value was attributable to its share in the anticipated *Batman* sequels. But since the rights belonged to Warner, GPEC wouldn't get to produce those films if it were sold to Sony. So right off the bat, Sony was being asked to pay for something that it wouldn't own if it bought the company. Naturally Sony objected, but Christensen insisted that Jon and Peter had an obligation to their shareholders to seek compensation for this asset, which presently belonged to Guber-Peters Entertainment, after all. That was "a big hurdle" for the Sony side, Christensen says.

Finally, Christensen had a conversation with Schwarzman. "Let's just talk turkey here," he said. "We can have ten more investment bankers come in and they can get a range from one to a thousand. But we're not agreeing to less than $17.50. So that's what we're going to do. And if you want, we'll keep negotiating at $20, $21 . . . But our price is $17.50 and that's how this is going to end up."

Sony gave in. Guber-Peters Entertainment would be sold for $200 million, about 40 percent above its assessed market value. The company had lost $19.2 million on revenue of $23.7 mil-

233

lion in its previous fiscal year. Now, Peters and Guber stood to make more than $55 million on their stock. Their old friend Terren Peizer from Drexel Burnham Lambert had positioned them to get rich when he had set them up with Burt Sugarman in Barris. He might have had more time to relish his triumph had not the federal government's investigation into the financial practices of Drexel and Michael Milken been going full bore at the time. Peizer was a government witness, a move that earned him the enmity of Milken's defense team. And that, in turn, would become a matter of concern for Jon Peters and Peter Guber, though not quite yet.

Meanwhile, Sony had also agreed to give Guber and Peters a compensation package stuffed with goodies. They were to receive $2.7 million in annual salaries, rising to $2.9 million over five years. There was a profit-sharing provision. Guber and Peters were to receive an 8.08 percent share of any increase in the company's value over a five-year period, potentially a staggering number. Finally, Sony pledged to create a $50 million bonus pool at the end of five years. By the time the cake was iced, Jon Peters and Peter Guber would have made themselves one of the richest deals in entertainment industry history.

Before the deal was ready to sign, a critical point had to be resolved: Jon and Peter were under contract to Warner. They acknowledged this fact, but said Warner executives had a long-standing oral agreement to release them from their five-year deal to produce films there. Sony had sense enough to be wary of an oral agreement that didn't bind anyone, if it even existed. So Sony tried to negotiate a provision that would terminate the purchase of Guber-Peters Entertainment Co. should Warner refuse to release Jon and Peter.

If Christensen were to fight that, it would suggest that he anticipated serious trouble from Steve Ross. So he went along, contending that in the unlikely case that Warner made a fuss, Jon and Peter had a strong legal case for obtaining a release from their contract. "They just said, 'Don't worry about it,'" Schulhof commented later.

Still, Sony worried. Its negotiators wanted to allow a short time frame—a few days after the deal was announced—for Peters and Guber to get their release from Warner. Christensen fought for more time. If Warner put up a fight, he argued, a short deadline would give all the advantage to Warner in a

234

negotiation. Of course, leverage wasn't his only concern. He also hoped that Sony's tender offer for Columbia Pictures Entertainment would be well under way before Jon and Peter had to resolve their situation with Warner. The deeper Sony was into its Columbia purchase, the greater the bond to Jon and Peter.

The final round of negotiation came down to three points, but according to Christensen, two of them were merely window dressing. The sole concession that Christensen wanted to win was time—as much as possible for Jon and Peter to get their release from Warner. Christensen's partner, Barry Fink, battled Sony's lawyers at the Skadden, Arps offices all night over the three points, and at seven the next morning the weary Guber-Peters team returned to Sony. Christensen opened the meeting by listing the points in dispute. "On point number one, we give up," he said. "On point number two, we give up. On point number three—the timing—you should give up." Sony agreed to extend the deadline to October 25, a month away.

WHILE THE PARTIES haggled in New York, Peter Guber returned to Los Angeles to begin the delicate and critical process of bidding Warner farewell. On Monday, September 25, he sat down to lunch with his old friend, Warner president and chief operating officer Terry Semel, at the Burbank studios. He told him that he and Jon had made the deal of a lifetime.

Peter had come hoping to make a quick strike. He had brought with him a release form that had been drafted a year earlier, when Jon and Peter made their abortive run at MGM. Warner had been willing to sign then and Peter obviously hoped Semel wouldn't see any difference now. On the form, "MGM" was crossed out and "Columbia" written in. But if Peter had imagined that Terry Semel would be foolish enough to sign the revised release, he was doomed to disappointment. Semel wouldn't sign until he spoke to studio chairman Bob Daly and, of course, Steve Ross, who by now had expanded his empire by becoming co-chairman of the recently merged Time Warner.

The two men would later differ on exactly what was said at the lunch. But whatever words were uttered, Peter left the lunch with his release still unsigned. Semel and Daly immediately put through a conference call to Ross. And when they

235

told him that Jon and Peter were planning to make a break for Sony, his reaction was everything that Jon and Peter might have feared.

"When Steve heard about it, I tell you, he had a nuclear explosion in his office," says one well-placed source.

Everyone familiar with the situation was certain that Ross's attitude would have been different had Jon and Peter consulted him earlier in the process instead of handing him a fait accompli, and using Terry Semel as the messenger. Ross surely felt he had been exceptionally generous to these two. He had given them one of the richest contracts in town. And in August, he had listened to a presentation from Peter Guber, who had shown him a video about Guber-Peters Entertainment and asked him for advice on developing the company. He agreed to review financial information about the company and try to help out. Ross had done everything he could do for this pair and now they were abandoning him without so much as a courtesy call.

The day that Guber had lunch with Semel, Jon Peters was leaving for New York. His mission was to win Steve Ross's blessing. He was too late. When he called Ross the next day, Ross refused to meet with him. Jon later said that he pleaded with Ross and "reminded" him that Daly and Semel as well as production chief Mark Canton had repeatedly given their opinion that Guber and Peters had every right to accept an offer like Sony's. According to Jon, Ross referred to them with an obscenity and replied, "Tell them that they don't have a job. You can take them with you." (Warner disputed this aspect of Jon's account.)

That evening, Ross and his wife Courtney went to an American Film Institute dinner in Washington, and sat at the same table with Mickey Schulhof. Naturally, the talk turned to contracts. "In Japan, there aren't even written agreements," Schulhof said. "People do things on handshakes and the Japanese system seems to work."

"Yes," Ross replied coolly. "But here we rely on the sanctity of contracts." Later, he said he meant his comment to be a pointed warning. But Schulhof said he remembered only some "vague comment about contracts," a remark that struck him as "very oblique, very minor."

Clearly, Ross's "warning" had little impact. The following

236

morning, Columbia's board approved the sale to Sony and Schulhof signed the required papers. That afternoon, he signed the deal to buy Guber-Peters Entertainment. Jon and Peter signed their lucrative employment contracts. Christensen said the negotiators celebrated with "a stack of sandwiches and two bottles of champagne split amongst thirty people."

By now, of course, Sony had an inkling that Warner was preparing for battle. Schulhof jetted to Paris for a wedding that weekend but arranged for the first meeting with the Warner side the following Monday.

WHEN THE DEALS were announced, the reaction was stunned disbelief all around. Not that the purchase of Columbia was such a shocker: that had been rumored for some time. But now the long-anticipated first Japanese incursion into Hollywood was reality, and the fact that the price was high only exacerbated the public's anxiety. The Japanese seemed rich and invincible. *Newsweek* magazine published a cover depicting the famed Columbia lady as a kimono-clad Japanese, with the headline JAPAN INVADES HOLLYWOOD. Inside was a poll showing that Americans now dreaded Japan's economic might more than the Soviet Union's warheads. The purchase of Columbia was more than another mega-deal of the eighties; it was a political issue: The poll showed that 43 percent of Americans opposed the sale, with only 19 percent approving it.

Sony's mode of announcing the deal didn't help matters. The *Wall Street Journal* reported that Sony held a press conference in Tokyo for Japanese journalists only. While U.S. reporters repeatedly were denied access to top Sony officials, Norio Ohga talked to the Japanese group for almost an hour about the synergies that Sony hoped would emerge from the deal. The article went on to describe Japan's "kisha club," a favored group of Japanese reporters from major news services, which operated "more like a news cartel than a reporters' club." The system reflected "a strong Japanese preference for harmony over unbridled competition," the article said.

Sony, with its much-touted internationalism, should have been the last company to exclude foreign reporters. But the company was still viewed as something of an upstart in Japan. Had Sony bucked the kisha-club system, it could have faced retaliation from the Japanese press.

237

Finally, Akio Morita held a news conference to answer the deal's critics. Denying that the purchase was a takeover of American creativity, Morita lamented that Americans still viewed the Japanese as "strangers."

"There are examples in the past where foreigners bought American movie companies," Morita complained, referring to Australian Rupert Murdoch, whose News Corporation owned Fox Inc. "But people criticize only when the Japanese make the purchase." Sony would boost the company's sales and profits, he said, as it had done with CBS Records. "By proving that [the acquisition] was a good thing for the U.S., we could ease the U.S.'s unneeded anxiety towards Japan," Morita said. "We think it's our mission to make the effort."

Morita also pledged that Sony wouldn't interfere with Columbia's management, even if the studio made a picture critical of the late emperor Hirohito, though people in Japan might not want to see it, he added. The promise did little to allay fears in the United States. "Such a film might make Morita bashing as popular in Japan as it is in the U.S.," *Fortune* magazine noted tartly.

The flames were fanned again by Morita's co-authorship of a book, *The Japan That Can Say No,* which urged Japan to be tougher in its dealings with the United States and reiterated some of Morita's criticisms of the American way of doing business. He and his co-author, politician Shintaro Ishihara, also contended that "racial problems" were to blame for America's distrust of Japan. The book was perceived as anti-American and prompted an outcry in the United States. Morita insisted that it wasn't meant for American audiences and tried to block an English-language edition, but copies of a quick Pentagon translation made the rounds in Washington. The episode did little to allay what Morita had called America's "unneeded anxiety towards Japan."

THE NATIONAL MEDIA hadn't focused on the purchase of Guber-Peters Entertainment Co. yet. But in Hollywood, the $200 million price tag was noted with surprise. Sony maintained that the cost of its extravagant purchases would be cut, eventually, by revenue still to come from earlier Guber-Peters films. (In an SEC filing, Sony said it expected eventually to get a total of $50 million from *Rain Man, Batman,* and *Gorillas in the Mist.*) But the price left even GPEC's own board members —especially the contingent headed by Australian investor Frank Lowy—"dumbfounded," according to one of those directors.

"We thought it was a dramatic overpayment," said another board member. "We thought Peter and Jon had cut one of the greatest deals of all time."

Also pleasantly surprised was an irate stockholder, a New York investor who had written several letters, copied to the Securities and Exchange Commission, complaining about the "indifferent, covert, and incapable management" at Guber-Peters Entertainment Company. He had written to Guber a few weeks before the sale congratulating him on the success of *Batman* and *Rain Man* but charging that "stockholders have been furnished no idea as to how those successes have affected their interests." He had got no satisfactory response from Guber but he was amazed and very pleased when the Sony deal was announced. "Those people at Sony have to be the dumbest bastards that ever lived!" he exclaimed later. "I just laughed and laughed."

STEVE ROSS wasn't laughing. He phoned Nick Nicholas, then president of Time Warner, fuming over Jon and Peter's defection. "He was embarrassed and humiliated because the Time Warner deal had just been announced," Nicholas says. "Now I'm not saying he said this, but it was understood: He always prided himself on being somebody who could deliver talent. And he saw that in delivering Warner to Time Warner, that's what he was basically doing. And even if they're not good talent, just name talent . . . it looked like the man who supposedly had control didn't have control." In fact, Nicholas doubted anyone at Time would have been especially concerned about Guber and Peters. But Ross was convinced that he was dangerously close to a humiliation and to setting an undesirable precedent. "He was goddamn angry," Nicholas says.

By the time Ross assembled his lieutenants a few days later for a strategy session at his elegant Upper East Side apartment, Nicholas remembers, Ross was thinking in pragmatic terms. "Steve immediately switched over from being humiliated to, 'How much can we get out of it?'" Nicholas says. Ross knew a stunning victory over Sony would be remembered far longer than any embarrassment over losing Guber and Peters.

239

Daly was there, along with Nicholas; Ross's financial adviser and privy counselor, Oded Aboodi; and attorneys Arthur Liman (who was also at this time occupied with the defense of junk-bond king Michael Milken) and Stuart Robinowitz. They gathered around the dining-room table, ate sandwiches, and devised their approach.

"The big strategy from Steve's point of view was, these are Japanese buying in and they don't want to be embarrassed," Nicholas says. "They are more vulnerable to the embarrassment of theft of talent than your ordinary American. If AT&T buys Guber and Peters, so what? AT&T is American. He wanted to take advantage of his belief that the Japanese would do anything to avoid press and noise."

Ross came up with a "wish list" of demands that he would attempt to impose on Sony. He had three key "wishes" and a fourth thrown in for good measure. On the serious side, Ross demanded real estate. Columbia owned and occupied 35 percent of the Burbank lot that was also home to the Warner studio. Ross wanted Sony to swap that property for a less valuable lot that Warner owned in Culver City on the west side of Los Angeles. Warner figured that Columbia's piece of the Burbank lot was worth about $25 million more than the entire Culver City lot.

Ross also wanted cable television rights to Columbia's library. But the jewel in the crown was CBS Records' valuable mail-order music business—its record club. Ross wanted half, and valued that share at $500 million. At the time some analysts considered that appraisal high, but it soon became apparent that Warner's estimate was reasonable.

Yetnikoff figured Ross got the idea from him. The summer before, Yetnikoff had raised the possibility of selling a half-interest to Warner, which owned the rights to so much music offered through the mail-order business that CBS Records was constantly having to negotiate and renegotiate the licenses. Yetnikoff thought that if Warner bought a half-interest, the mail-order business would get a steady supply of music and he could present Sony with a nice pile of cash in the wake of its purchase of CBS Records. The deal had broken down over price, which Yetnikoff said would have been $500 million. Now Warner was proposing to get its half of the business free.

Finally, as an extra, Ross intended to ask Sony to contribute

240

$20 million into a charity fund that would be distributed at Ross's discretion.

As he presented his ideas, several of his listeners were shocked. All told, Warner figured Ross's demands were worth $800 million. "Steve was not ranting and raving but everybody's looking like, this guy's nuts," says one of the participants.

Bob Daly, who would lead the Warner negotiating team, became upset. After all, he had a relationship of several years' duration with Jon and Peter. And it wasn't in his nature to humiliate an opponent. In this case, he thought Ross was pushing for a confrontation and he didn't relish the idea of presenting this list of tribute that Ross wanted to exact from Sony. "Daly and Steve started yelling at each other," says one observer. "Daly said, 'Goddamn it, that's just not reasonable.' "

Daly stalked out of the room and one of Warner's other strategists went over to Ross. "I said, 'Steve, why get him so goddamn mad?' . . . Steve winks and smiles and says, 'I've done this before.' Translated: It's like getting your soldiers ready before they go into the battle. It's pumping everybody up."

INDEED, THE ADRENALINE was coursing freely through everyone's veins in the first skirmish of the war between Warner and Sony, which took place at the Third Avenue offices of Sony's lawyers, Skadden, Arps. The Sony faction assembled: Schulhof, Yetnikoff, Guber, Peters, and their attorneys. Among those present for Warner were Nicholas, Bob Daly, and Terry Semel; Bob Morgado of Warner's record company; and attorneys Liman and Robinowitz.

Having reviewed Guber and Peters's contract, Warner made clear its view that they had breached it, that Sony was to blame, and that Sony would have to pay. Sony came back with the Guber-Peters view that Warner had promised to let them go. The meeting started unpleasantly and deteriorated from there. Yetnikoff was up to his usual shenanigans and Jon Peters was similarly antagonistic. Bob Daly would later tell an associate that this was the most hostile business meeting he had ever attended. At one point, Daly—perhaps still humming from his spat with Ross—became so annoyed with Yetnikoff that he said, "Well, fuck you!"

"I've been in lots of hostile meetings where people are civil. This was a different kind of hostility," Nicholas marveled later.

"I thought it was amusing. I just thought, 'Jesus Christ, who *are* these guys?' Guber distinguished himself by behaving normally."

Daly presented Warner's case dramatically, stating Guber and Peters's value to the company in the most hyperbolic terms. Having delivered what he hoped was a resonant speech, he excused himself and went to the men's room.

He was preparing to use the facilities when Jon Peters burst in. Daly cringed, flashing back to Jon's escapade when he had pulled a gun on a pair of workers in Aspen. For a moment, the chairman of Warner Bros. feared that the would-be chairman of Columbia Pictures was about to punch his lights out. Instead, Jon threw his arms around him in an emotional embrace. "You've never said that stuff to me before," Jon exclaimed, visibly touched. "Did you really mean it?" Daly could hardly say he did not.

Inside the conference room, tempers stayed hot. There was another bout when the session closed with nothing settled and Yetnikoff lingered in the room, trying to read the opposition's documents. "Why are you the last to leave?" Liman demanded.

Yetnikoff's reply was terse: "Fuck you, Arthur Liman."

Perhaps Yetnikoff was disappointed that Ross was not present to see him at his best, but he still enjoyed needling him in his absence. "Ross-o-rino later said to a bunch of people, 'Walter used foul language! I don't know how Sony can't control him.' Right, like Ross never heard me talk like this before?" Yetnikoff asked. "This spiritual I'm not. And Sony never heard me talk this way before? And as if Sony's gonna control what I have to say anyway. They like the way I talk. They paid for part of this shtick and theatrical stuff."

Whatever his progress in kicking his addictions, Walter's hubris was still roaring along. In fact, Schulhof and his advisers were nervous that Yetnikoff's style might not be working to their advantage in this negotiation. Walter didn't help matters when he took a swipe at Ross's wife, Courtney, who was then working on a documentary about Quincy Jones. It was up to Walter, as head of CBS Records, to give her permission to use clips of Jones protégé (and CBS Records artist) Michael Jackson. Though she had the impression that Yetnikoff had consented, Walter would not release the tapes when the time came.

Jon and Peter were working against a deadline. The Sony

purchase of Guber-Peters Entertainment Co. would go forward only on condition that Warner released them from their contract by October 25. After the first meeting, no one had any more illusions about Warner's attitude. With the two sides taking entrenched positions, Terry Christensen's mission was to get Sony to waive the condition and commit to buying Guber-Peters even if they couldn't get a release from Warner. While he was telling reporters that the waiver might not be necessary, he focused on getting it.

The Guber-Peters team met at Sony's offices and the contingent from Japan, Christensen noticed, was bigger than ever—at least ten people. Christensen told the Sony team that they had to drop the condition and buy Guber-Peters.

"They looked at us and they said, 'No way,' " he says. "And we said, 'You really have to. Because as long as this condition exists, Warner is not going to agree to anything because they feel that they have everybody hung up and now all the deals are hanging by a thread and they're the only ones that can solve it. . . . With Warner, all you need to do is give them an inch of leverage and they'll take it a thousand miles. We need to tell Warner that there is no condition between us, that we're all partners, that all these deals are done and whatever their best shot is, we're willing to take it. And that will bring them to the table.' "

Everyone agreed with Christensen's concept, up to a point. "They all agreed that we should stand as one," Christensen remembers wryly, "but they wanted to stand as one without waiving the condition."

The two sides argued for hours. "They said to me, 'Don't worry, we'll stand by you. Even if we have the condition, we won't exercise it,' " Christensen says. But he couldn't afford to quit now. "You have your own interests," he told Sony. "I won't have any less respect for you if you exercise your own interests but I have to take into account that you might do that."

As the argument heated up, Walter Yetnikoff moved to the other side of the table, and went from sitting with Schulhof and the rest of the Sony team to joining the Guber-Peters side. Now he addressed his colleagues at Sony from across the table. "You guys are a bunch of assholes," he said. "You don't know what you're doing. You've got Jon and Peter here, they are going to make you billions, and you're being assholes. You

243

should stand by them! You should waive the condition!" By now, Yetnikoff was shouting. The Japanese contingent didn't yell, as Christensen remembers, but argued heatedly with Yetnikoff. "It was total chaos," Christensen says. "Interestingly our guys—especially Peter—were getting genuinely distressed." Christensen called for a time out.

By now it was late at night and the corridors in the Sony offices were dark. Jon and Peter huddled with Christensen and Levine down a hallway amid the secretaries' desks. "This is terrible," Guber said. "This is not working. Let's give it up. Let's go home. This is just not right. . . . They're going to hate us. We're going to hate them. It's not going to work out. This is a bad idea."

"Peter," Christensen interposed, "they're about to give up."

"It didn't sound that way to me."

Christensen relented. "Let's run with this," he said. "You guys are upset. It's genuine. Let's send you back to the hotel. I'll hang around if they want to talk to me. But let's play this out. You're willing to go home. You're willing to walk away from the deal."

They returned to the conference room and Christensen once again slipped into the conciliatory mode he tended to adopt when he was about to issue an ultimatum. "Listen, we don't mean to cause trouble," he told the Sony team. "We see you guys are shouting at each other. This is not good. Jon and Peter are upset. They never meant to be part of this. They wanted to be part of a harmonious company. . . . We don't mean to cause any problems between you and Walter, who's our friend."

If Sony bailed out on its proposed purchase of Guber-Peters Entertainment Co., he observed, the GPEC stock probably would plummet. Shareholders would sue. And Warner might exact its revenge on Jon and Peter. But this fighting with Sony was simply too unpleasant. "We're going home," Christensen said. "We may sue you, we may sue Warner, we may do nothing, but we're going back to Los Angeles, and we're going to take the high ground and we're going to figure out what's best for us and our shareholders. We just can't sit here at your mercy."

With that, Peters and Guber walked out of the room and returned to the Regency. Christensen was preparing to leave, when one of the Sony executives pulled him aside. "Terry," he said, "you know that we really will stand by you."

244

"I don't want to start over and tell you whether I believe it's true or not, because I don't want to insult anybody," Christensen said. "All I know is, we can't rely on it." The Sony executive said he would call Tokyo and get back to him. With that, Christensen left, too.

According to Yetnikoff, he resumed the argument on Jon and Peter's behalf, insisting that Sony capitulate. Sony's lawyers resisted. Then, with his long-anticipated deal hanging in the balance, Yetnikoff laid it on the line. He called Ohga and told him: Accede to Jon and Peter's request or I will resign.

All of these jarring discussions must have been immensely stressful to the Japanese negotiators. In his book, Morita had observed the Japanese distaste for loud fights. "It is very difficult to fight in the Japanese language, because of the character and structure of the language," Morita wrote. "And the fact that it is very indirect and nonconfrontational forces politeness on you unless you want to get very rough. Most Japanese, hearing any Western argument, tend to overreact to such exchanges."

WHILE THE SONY SIDE was left to consider its next move, Christensen joined Jon, Peter, and attorney Alan Levine in Peter's suite at the Regency. It was past one in the morning. They had been through a long day and now it looked like their dream-of-a-lifetime deal might be collapsing. But before the commiserations could begin in earnest, the phone rang. It was Mickey Schulhof; he was coming over. They exchanged knowing glances. Sony was about to cave once again.

Sure enough, Schulhof said Sony would waive the condition. The company's only request was that Sony be allowed to dispose of the fight with Warner in its own way. Christensen said his team would step aside if Sony indemnified Guber and Peters from any liability for breaking their contract with Warner. Schulhof agreed. And Christensen was pleased to let Sony take over. After all, Sony would have only itself to blame for the result.

Sony announced on October 10 that it was waiving the condition and proceeding with the purchase of Guber-Peters, regardless of its dispute with Warner. Now, its only exit had been sealed. "They put themselves in a box and then worked very 245 hard at making that box smaller and smaller," Ross's adviser, Aboodi, gloated later.

Three days after Sony announced its plan to proceed with the purchase, Warner sued Sony for $1 billion for inducing a breach of contract. Sony countersued, alleging that Warner was interfering with its acquisition plans. (According to Christensen, the couriers who took Sony's suit to the court found Warner's couriers standing two places ahead of them in line.)

In the course of the litigation, Sony executives said they had been so convinced by Jon and Peter's assurances that Warner would sign a release that they never even looked at the Guber-Peters contract with Warner until October 3, after they had signed the team. Warner's counsel, Stuart Robinowitz, was stunned. "You wouldn't buy a used car without finding out something about it," he said.

Yet as Schulhof had told Ross at dinner some weeks earlier, this posture was not inconsistent with the Japanese manner of doing business. Akio Morita had repeatedly contended that the proliferation of lawyers hobbled American industry. "American businessmen seem to think it is natural always to be looking over their shoulders to see who is coming up behind them with a lawsuit," he had written in *Made in Japan*. In Japan, he observed, there were far fewer lawyers and much less litigation. "While the United States has been busy creating lawyers, we have been busier creating engineers," he said. The excessive reliance on lawyers, he added, created a climate of distrust in the United States. "In Japan, we customarily trust each other."

In court, however, Warner seized on the trust issue. Ross in court papers sounded a faintly xenophobic note by presenting Warner as a company that "maintains and nurtures trust with talent" better than any other studio, while depicting Sony as "an outsider to the American film industry" that had sought "by secret negotiations" to raid Guber-Peters. Ross accused Sony of "brazen and unethical conduct."

Yetnikoff responded in his own court filing that Steve Ross had revealed an anti-Japanese bias in comments to him when Sony bought CBS Records. Ross called that "a reckless, irresponsible and baseless charge" and accused Yetnikoff of "McCarthy-like tactics." He had nothing against Japan, he said, adding pointedly: "My animus is toward Mr. Yetnikoff and his colleagues here."

As papers were filed in the litigation, a few key differences in critical parts of the story emerged. For starters, there was the lunch at the Burbank studio, when Guber had first broken the news about the Sony deal to Terry Semel. In Guber's version, Semel "hugged and congratulated me and expressed joy that we had finally realized our longtime ambition of running and having an equity position in a major entertainment company."

In Semel's version, he had never congratulated and hugged Guber. Instead, Guber had boasted that the Sony deal would allow him and Jon "to make more money than anyone in the history of the motion picture industry." Semel said he had replied that the deal looked great for Jon and Peter but bad for Warner.

"I do not make oral agreements to terminate written contracts, especially when they involve key talent and millions of dollars," Semel stated. Further, he said, Guber confessed that day that he had never consulted Ross about his talks with Sony because he was afraid that Ross would call Akio Morita and kill the deal.

Sony maintained that once Warner had made its opposition known, it had reviewed the Guber-Peters contract and concluded that the two were precluded only from producing films at another studio, not from taking executive positions elsewhere. Warner responded that allowing Guber and Peters to run one studio while producing films at another was an absurd notion because it created obvious and intolerable conflicts of interest.

Guber and Peters also argued that Warner had stood ready to release them when they had made their abortive offer for MGM. Warner responded that those circumstances were entirely different. And Bob Daly noted that those agreements were made before *Rain Man* and *Batman,* when the two were not as successful as they later became. Guber disputed that, offering a twelve-point list of awards earned by films with which he and Jon were associated before making *Rain Man* and *Batman.*

The situation got nastier. Jon and Peter complained that Warner was pushing them off the production of the Sylvester Stallone–Kurt Russell film *Tango & Cash.* Warner denied the charge.

Negotiations between the parties weren't going well—not that Yetnikoff was an ongoing problem. His insults to Steve Ross's wife had not gone unnoticed. Schulhof told Yetnikoff

247

that Ross refused to talk at all if Walter was included. Whether this actually occurred or was a device that Schulhof used to get rid of Walter is unclear. Either way, Schulhof had taken another step toward supplanting Yetnikoff. Along with his advisers from Blackstone, Schulhof handled the talks himself.

By now, Nick Nicholas wasn't the only one who marveled at the bitterness in this conflict. "I've never worked on something where the emotions were so personalized and sustainable at such a high pitch for so long," Blackstone's Steve Schwarzman said.

Once again, Schulhof was in a negotiation in which he was at a clear disadvantage. Warner was dealing on its home turf, which was entirely unfamiliar territory to Schulhof. As talks with Warner went on, he had to fly to Los Angeles to get a look at the Culver City lot that Warner was proposing to exchange for Columbia's share of the Burbank studios. While anyone in Hollywood would have regarded the Culver City lot as inferior, Schulhof said he was taken by its history. The lot had formerly housed MGM. Schulhof later said how charmed he was that the old canteen from the days of Louis B. Mayer was still in operation. "They still have chicken soup there that Louis B. Mayer started," he exclaimed. "I had chicken soup at the lot!"

Schulhof called the lot "a small gem." But its historic past was a potential problem. It was designated a landmark and development was subject to strict regulations. Its office facilities were small. Renovations would cost a fortune.

Warner asked for a preliminary injunction forbidding Guber and Peters from moving to Columbia. A hearing was set for November 2, then moved to November 9. As the court date drew near, Sony was under considerable pressure to get the matter resolved. As Schulhof observed in court papers, Sony had some $5 billion tied up in the Columbia and Guber-Peters deals. The idea of assuming control of Columbia Pictures with no management in place was intolerable.

No executive on either side had been forced yet to sit for a deposition, and none faced the prospect with much relish. "It was not in anyone's interest—neither Warner nor ours—to see the kinds of things that would have come out," Schulhof said. "Those are things I can't discuss."

Sony was also reportedly beginning to worry that if Warner won a delay, Congress might get into the act. The idea of a

Japanese company acquiring an American studio had stirred up negative sentiment; the prospect of a congressional sideshow had little appeal.

Schulhof and Schwarzman continued talks with the Warner team, now spearheaded by Ross adviser Oded Aboodi and Warner general counsel Marty Payson. But there was an impasse that had to be broken. Once again, Sony would have to capitulate. Finally Ohga, accompanied by Schulhof, paid a visit to Ross in his office. "It was a very fine meeting in tone," said one who was present. "It didn't resolve anything but it was very civil." Nothing dramatic was said but the signal was unmistakable. Sony was ready to make a deal.

In mid-November, a settlement was announced. Warner had gotten everything on Ross's wish list except the contribution to the charity fund. The brilliance of Ross's initial game plan, as one Warner executive observed later, was that it allowed Warner to come out so far ahead without scorching the earth for Sony. Instead, Sony could reason that it had gotten a steady supply of product for its music mail-order business, a new lot of its own, and a distribution fee for product that would be shown on Warner cable.

Nonetheless, Hollywood was aghast at the amount Sony had paid, all told, for its studio and management team. *Variety* estimated that the settlement with Warner had brought the cost of hiring Guber and Peters to more than $1 billion. Factoring in the cost of Columbia Pictures and the debt that Sony was assuming, *Variety* reported that Sony's "ticket into the Hollywood motion-picture business" had cost about $6 billion.

Schulhof tried to put a positive spin on the outcome. "I heard two years ago, when we bought CBS Records, how much we overpaid," he said. "And I'm willing to allow people to form their own opinion."

But if Ross had been correct that Sony loathed negative press, then the company was in for a bad time. The early reviews weren't good. The *Los Angeles Times* reported that many industry veterans thought that "Sony's long-anticipated foray into American film and television production was executed with unprecedented naivete. Some analysts believe that Sony, in its haste to hire two hot producers with no experience at running a major studio, paid hundreds of millions of dollars more than necessary to get quality leadership at Columbia."

The article went on to quote an unnamed but "well-known" producer. "This is bigger even than *Indecent Exposure,*" he said, referring to David McClintick's book about Columbia's check-forging scandal. "The best-known Japanese company shot itself in the foot."

*Forbes* also weighed in with a negative appraisal. "Sony's recent deal to put producers Jon Peters and Peter Guber at the helm of Columbia Pictures makes earlier Tinseltown excesses pale," the magazine said. "[T]he Japanese corporation will be shelling out well over a half-billion dollars in cash and assets to hand an ailing movie studio to two men who have never had the top job before."

And in *Vanity Fair,* journalist Peter Boyer offered the best summary of Sony's adventure:

> Whatever movies Sony ends up making, it will be hard-pressed to match its first production: the comic epic that was the acquisition itself. It could be called "Sony Goes Hollywood," the story of a respected electronics company that, despite the Japanese style of deliberation and under-statement, arrives in Hollywood with a loud thud, which reverberates still. . . . En route, Sony woos and loses Hollywood's most powerful agent, Michael Ovitz; it is nearly seduced by the town's most convincing salesman, Kirk Kerkorian; and it stirs up a xenophobic fit over the loss of America's "soul" (the sale of its popular culture). Sony at last finds its studio but, desperate for management, it hast-ily makes zillionaires out of a former hairdresser and his ponytailed partner.

In the process, Boyer continued, Sony invited a war with Warner, "a dispute that's finally settled on terms deemed so disadvantageous to Sony that for weeks afterward they are the talk of the lunch crowd at Le Dôme, where they are referred to as 'Pearl Harbor Revenged.' "

NOT LONG AFTER the settlement was reached, Bob Daly got a call at his office at the Burbank studio. Columbia was still in its old digs but the lot was soon to be the exclusive property of Warner. The caller was Mickey Schulhof, who had come to the lot with Norio Ohga. They were taking a look at what they had given away. Now Schulhof asked: Would Daly and Semel come to meet them?

250

Daly agreed and went out to the front of the building. There by the entrance, Ohga handed a camera to his assistant, stood between Daly and Semel, and put his arms around their shoulders. After the picture was snapped, Ohga thanked them and the Sony contingent left.

"Well," Daly thought. "That was different."

# 20

## JON AND PETER
## SET UP SHOP

HOLLYWOOD WAS FLABBERGASTED by the Sony deal, which was viewed as Peters and Guber's most spectacular seduction job ever. They were the gold-dust twins: not only had they pulled off the richest deal in industry history, but Sony had paid Warner Bros. more than half a billion dollars in ransom to win their services.

Within the movie community, disbelief quickly turned into envy. Every executive in town started to feel ripped off. One major studio chairman phoned another and said, "If they're worth half a billion, I'm worth $1 billion, and you're worth $1.2 billion." His colleague responded, "If they're worth half a billion, I'm worth $1.6 billion!" It was a joke, only no one was laughing. They were dead serious about getting theirs, and they did. The Sony deal set off a round of inflation that eventually touched everyone: executives, actors, directors, agents.

Jealousy flowed through the veins of even the most successful in Hollywood. Over lunch and dinner, Hollywood's denizens swapped tales about Peters and Guber, running down the reasons why they didn't deserve the riches bestowed on them. "Those guys will fail! Not a filmmaker I know would go to work with them," said *Flashdance* producer Don Simpson when he heard about the deal. "They deserve credit for *Batman* and that's it. When I see a press release that says they did *Flashdance, The Color Purple,* and *Rain Man,* I think, 'Are these people insane? Do they think that Simpson-Bruckheimer, Steven Spielberg, and Barry Levinson let them do anything?' "

The notion that filmmakers wouldn't work with Peters and

Guber was wishful thinking, of course. Some of the very producers who were inveighing against Sony's new management —including Simpson—would end up making pictures at the studio. In Hollywood, where buyers are scarce, anyone who can write a big check can attract the brightest stars in the business.

Guber fared better than Peters in these gripe sessions. At least he had been an executive at Columbia for a time, even if it was years ago. At least he had some business background. At least he had some class. He was the one who bought *The Color Purple, The Witches of Eastwick,* and *The Bonfire of the Vanities* (though the last, a big-star package with Tom Hanks left behind at Warner, would turn out to be a terrific bomb). He even taught at UCLA. In an insecure community like Hollywood, those touches counted for something.

"I'd rather have him running Columbia than a lot of other people," observed Oliver Stone. "At least he's got a nose for literary properties, right? It could be worse."

The bitterest diatribes pivoted around Peters. Jon Peters, the barely literate hairdresser! The brawler who pulled a gun on workmen in Aspen! How could he be co-chairman of Columbia Pictures? How could he be making this kind of money?

Many predicted that Peters would incite anarchy at Columbia in record time. "If Guber can hobble Jon Peters," director George Miller said, "there's a chance. If he can't distract him, I don't think the Japanese will stand for it for long."

As Peters and Guber took charge of Columbia, keeping tabs on Jon's antics became a favorite Hollywood pastime. Jon didn't disappoint. His early moves were as colorful and intemperate as ever.

Even before he started on the job, Peters began to dream of razing the old MGM lot in Culver City, Columbia's new home, and transforming it into a sumptuously landscaped high-tech playground. Over the next year and a half, Jon would preside over a massive facelift of the lot. In the interim, the new regime took up temporary residence in Columbia Pictures' Studio Plaza Building, an eleven-floor steel-and-glass structure at 3400 Riverside Drive in Burbank.

On the very day in November 1989 that the settlement with Warner went through, Peters revealed some of his ideas for spiffing up Columbia's new digs to *Variety.* He planned to construct an Art Deco building, a twin to the venerable Irving

253

Thalberg Building. "Cost has not yet been determined, but Peters acted as if the pricetag were inconsequential," *Variety* noted, throwing fuel on the fire.

Less than two weeks later, Peters and Guber rocked the entertainment community by announcing their first "go" project. They paid a staggering $700,000 for *Radio Flyer*, a script about child abuse that touched off a bidding war among several studios. The deal for *Radio Flyer* was unusual because it guaranteed the screenwriter, a twenty-seven-year-old unknown named David Mickey Evans, an additional $300,000 to make his directing debut. Warner had been interested in the script but had refused to give Evans such a deal. That studio had wanted to hire Richard Donner, the veteran director of the *Lethal Weapon* series.

But *Radio Flyer* had won the heart of one of the new cochairmen. At a studio meeting, Jon moved his colleagues to tears talking about his own experience as an abused child and how much the script meant to him. Michael Douglas was designated to produce the film through his company Stonebridge Entertainment.

Dawn Steel was still officially running Columbia—but had not been consulted—when Peters bought *Radio Flyer*. Everyone in town was watching to see what Steel's fate would be. The scrappy head of Columbia had just made $7 million on her stock. Would she stay? Would she get fired? At first, few in Hollywood seemed likely to mourn any bad fortune that might befall Steel. But when people began hearing that she was at the mercy of Jon Peters, she was swept up in a tidal wave of sympathy.

Peters called Steel. "Look, Dawn, I want to make something really clear," he told her. "You report to me and everyone in the company reports to me. Get it?"

"Read my contract," Steel replied. "I may report to you, but everyone else reports to me."

*"Get it,"* Jon commanded. "Everyone reports to me."

He called Tom Pollock, the chairman of Universal. Pollock had been a prominent attorney in the industry and his client list had included Dawn Steel. That had ended four years ago, when he took the top job at Universal. It was Pollock's first conversation with Peters since Jon had joined the exclusive 254 fraternity of studio chiefs.

"Congratulations," Pollock said amiably. "What a great deal you've made! You've raised the price of executives."

"I want to talk about Dawn," Jon said. "You tell that girl she works for me. The marketing department works for me. Tri-Star works for me. If she doesn't like it, she can go into production."

"Okay, but why are you telling me?" Pollock asked.

"You're her lawyer, aren't you?" Jon demanded.

"Jon, I'm not her lawyer," Pollock replied. He reminded Sony's co-chairman that he was chairman of Universal. "Don't you remember? We did *Gorillas in the Mist* together."

This story quickly made the rounds, adding to the Jon Peters lore.

Another confrontation came when Peters and Guber attended one of Steel's production meetings. Her slate for the following year included Mike Nichols's *Postcards from the Edge* and the brat-packed *Flatliners,* to be followed at Christmas by Penny Marshall's *Awakenings* with Robin Williams.

The meeting got off to a bad start; Peters made negative comments about everything Steel had on the boards. Then the discussion moved on to *Skirts,* a dance movie that was to star teen pop idol Debbie Gibson, a pet project of Steel's. When Peters heard that it was to be directed by choreographer Kenny Ortega, he laid down the law: No choreographer will ever direct a picture at this studio.

"But what about Bob Fosse?" someone asked, referring to the choreographer who had directed *All That Jazz,* and who died in 1987.

"I don't want him either," Jon growled.

*Skirts* was dead, and Steel, who had been struggling with the pressures of running the studio in the first place, concluded that working for Guber and Peters was going to be intolerable. She called Guber to request a meeting, at which she planned to make a brief speech, carefully devised by her attorney, designed to get her released from her contract without damaging her financially.

The meeting was scheduled to take place at Jon's house. As Steel pulled her Jaguar up to the guard station at Beverly Park that morning, she was apprehensive. She knew all the stories about Jon Peters's volatile temper. After she was ushered into a large den, she exchanged a few pleasantries with her bosses. Then she attempted to speak her piece. She had barely begun when Jon interrupted in a rage.

"Who the fuck are you to tell me you don't want to do this

255

job?" he shouted. "What have you done in your career to tell me that?"

Steel became more alarmed when Jon began advancing toward her. She had the impression that he was going to hit her. She glanced toward Peter—who didn't make a move.

As Jon drew closer, Steel gave in to fear. She ran for the door, dashed for her car, and slid into the driver's seat, her heart pounding. As she pressed the accelerator and pulled out of Beverly Park, she frantically dialed friends on her car phone. When she arrived at her house, the phone was ringing. It was Peter Guber. "I'm sorry that happened," he said. "I'll make it up to you. I'll make it easy for you to go."

But that was not to be her last confrontation. As Steel's contract as president of Columbia was being settled in early January 1990, Jon was back, trying to take over her office. Her secretary stood in the door of the suite and said her instructions were to stay put until she was cleared to leave by Steel's attorney. Jon protested but backed down.

Guber and Peters would need to replace Steel at Columbia, but they hoped that TriStar's thirty-eight-year-old president Jeff Sagansky would stay in the job. Even though TriStar had never performed well—Sagansky had made a string of failures, including *Family Business*—he had picked one giant hit: *Look Who's Talking,* one of the most profitable films in the history of the industry. After Peters and Guber took over, Sagansky decided to leave at once, and he accepted a job running CBS. He told friends he was sick and tired of the power wielded by movie stars.

GUBER AND PETERS enacted a simple strategy for managing Columbia and TriStar that was typified by the *Radio Flyer* deal: Spend whatever it takes to attract top-of-the-line talent, material, and executives, and create a luxurious, state-of-the-art filmmaking facility. Synergy was the mantra: They imagined a felicitous if undefined marriage between Sony hardware and the software they would produce.

Film production had slowed in the final months of Coca-Cola's ownership and Steel had left behind no strong projects
256   ready to green-light. "When Jon and Peter took over the company, it was dead in the water," says a high-level Columbia executive. Schulhof authorized the co-chairmen to jump-start

the studio, filling the pipeline and boosting market share as soon as possible.

Guber set about creating the perception of a thriving, exciting film studio, on the theory profits would follow. This approach went against the trend in Hollywood, where a hardheaded austerity had set in with the dawn of the nineties. With the cost of making and marketing movies rising sharply and profit margins growing slimmer, all the other studios in town had become more bottom line oriented. Under Peters and Guber, Columbia became the land that time forgot.

Sony was certainly aware that its Hollywood adventure would be a costly undertaking. No one knew just how much red ink it was prepared to tolerate but, like most Japanese companies, it viewed this acquisition in long-range terms. It was willing to sustain short-term losses that would pay off ten or twenty years down the road.

As Peters and Guber began spending to ramp up toward a total output of twenty to thirty films a year, Sony projected a negative cash flow of around $300 million a year for two or three years. These losses would be partially offset by the studio's profitable television operations, which reliably netted around $150 million a year. Because it had no Japanese managers who understood the film business, Sony had little choice but to put its faith in Schulhof—who was also a Hollywood greenhorn. It would be Schulhof's responsibility to protect Sony's investment and determine that its expenditures were appropriate.

The ultimate success of Peters and Guber's spend-now-make-money-later plan would depend on whether they could live up to their recently acquired reputation as the Blockbuster Boys. That was why, after all, they had been hired at such a handsome price. They would need to produce the kind of mass-market hits that spawned sequels and merchandising bonanzas—as they had done for Warner Bros. with *Batman*. Just one blockbuster a year could push the studio into the black.

Peters and Guber began to install a hierarchy of executives that left outsiders who dealt with the studio baffled about the chain of command. Soon there were so many suits around that Columbia quickly got a reputation as "top-heavy." On the corporate level, Peters had wanted Terry Christensen to be named Columbia Pictures' chief operating officer. But Guber had favored Alan Levine, the television lawyer who had repre-

257

sented him since 1971. Levine was a colorless behind-the-scenes operator, an avid golfer with no real experience either in management or the film business. Peters didn't trust Levine but he gave in. Levine was named COO in December.

Guber set up an office of the chairman and began to populate it thickly with well-paid lieutenants, some of whose job descriptions were vague. He brought in his personal lawyer, Paul Schaeffer, as executive vice president for corporate affairs. Cary Woods, a young agent at William Morris, was hired at a hefty salary (rumored to be $400,000 a year) for an undefined position called vice president, office of the chairman.

On the production and marketing side, most of the executives from Coca-Cola's ownership were kept in place for the moment. In the first months of 1990, before Steel's and Sagansky's jobs were filled, it was decided that Peters would take over the day-to-day running of Columbia while Guber oversaw TriStar. Michael Nathanson eased the transition by staying on as head of production at Columbia, and TriStar was still being run by David Matalon.

With each partner responsible for one of the sister studios, Peters and Guber felt intensely competitive with each other. Their rivalry was piqued when Peters bought his second big project for Columbia in January 1990.

No one could accuse Jon Peters of not bringing premium talent to the studio: Paying back his longtime debt to Barbra Streisand, he set up *The Prince of Tides* at Columbia. Streisand had been shopping a script based on Pat Conroy's novel, hoping to star in and direct it.

"Thank God, everyone turned down her picture," Jon says. He says he had read the book but not the screenplay when he committed to it. "I felt it was a great opportunity for me to be there for Barbra, the way she was there for me in the beginning. And I felt she was such a genius that if she believed in it, I knew it would be a big hit."

Guber disagreed. He thought *The Prince of Tides* was too risky —Barbra wouldn't be singing in it, after all. He and Levine tried to talk Peters out of making it. Levine told Nathanson, "Why don't you try and convince Jon to produce the movie and let him go off to North Carolina, so he'd be away from us all?" Peters would not drop the film—or go to North Carolina.

The *Prince of Tides* budget was set at $27 million, a figure that

258

eventually would climb to $30 million. There were discussions about casting Tom Berenger opposite Streisand, but Nick Nolte got the nod. "As long as we've got a good-looking blond actor and we've got Barbra, we're doing fine," Peters said. He was all swagger on the outside but privately he was nervous about the film. He knew that if it failed, public derision would be heaped on him for indulging his ex-girlfriend.

Peters and Guber embarked on a script-buying spree, paying top dollar for material. They bought a thriller set against Kentucky coal mining called *Fire Down Below* for $750,000; *Black Box,* the story of a sportswriter who finds the cockpit tape recorder in a plane wreck, for $300,000; and *Cold As Ice,* a sexy thriller about a detective and a young widow caught up in a diamond robbery, for $400,000. Agents cheered as spec script prices shot up. None of these scripts has been made into a film.

*Cold As Ice* was purchased for the Guber-Peters Entertainment Co.—which Sony now owned, having bought it for a hefty $200 million. In an unusual arrangement, Peters and Guber had elected to keep their old company operating as a third unit of Columbia Pictures. In January 1990, Guber named his protégée, Stacey Snider, GPEC's executive vice president. He funded the company with $5 million for development costs.

Many in town were suspicious about GPEC. Why did the co-chairmen of Columbia and TriStar need a third film company? No one could understand the point of paying all that extra overhead. Some producers with deals at Columbia called it a conflict of interest and worried about bidding against their bosses for material. They wondered whether Guber and Peters stood to gain financially by making movies through the unit.

"Jon and Peter have no economic interest and will not personally produce any movies," said Alan Levine in an interview, finally answering the critics. He put forth the official explanation: "We want to make a lot of movies and there are just so many movies a single team of people can develop, produce, market and release." Then Levine backed down from the notion that GPEC would make movies, saying that it would only develop material that would be handed to Columbia or TriStar.

The real reason for GPEC's continued existence was that Guber was hedging his bets. "I think he wanted it as an escape vehicle," says Terry Christensen, who had negotiated the

259

Guber-Peters deal with Sony. "So if there was something that went wrong with this deal quickly, in the early stages, GPEC would be an entity that he could crawl back into—and jettison right off the Columbia-Sony ship."

FROM THE OUTSET, Peters and Guber could not stem the management chaos that had long been the curse of Columbia Pictures. The place needed a strong hand and they were not good administrators; they presided over a workplace in perpetual disarray. "Peter has the capacity to be inspirational, but he never stays around and he's never there for the tough decisions," explains one high-level Columbia executive. "Jon operates with a blowtorch. He makes instant decisions. You moved from one extreme to another—from instant decisions to no decisions."

The studio's production executives struggled to adapt to the ways of their new bosses. There was no clear system for pitching projects and getting them approved; Guber and Levine avoided making commitments. The co-chairmen's presence in the Burbank offices was erratic. As ever, Peters preferred to take meetings in workout clothes by his pool. While Guber was around more, he wasn't very accessible.

Stacey Snider was supposed to be running GPEC, but she attended Columbia production meetings and functioned as Guber's confidante. Although competent, she was referred to as Peter's "geisha" by other employees.

"Jon and Peter were fairly scarce," remembers another Columbia executive. "It was never clear how it was going to work. . . . It was confused. Everything was flowing to Stacey because she had Peter's ear. . . . There were long periods of silence when nothing was happening. Once in a while, you'd get Jon, Peter, and Stacey in a flurry about a script."

Michael Nathanson found himself in an especially awkward position. Nathanson was the classic clean-cut and well-groomed Hollywood "suit," and his longevity at Columbia through several administrations practically defied the laws of nature. David Begelman had been his mentor in the seventies and he had also worked for Guy McElwaine, David Puttnam, and Dawn Steel. Anyone who had lasted as long as Nathanson knew a little something about getting along with his bosses. But now, he couldn't seem to locate a boss to get along with.

When Guber and Levine were around, Nathanson would

ask whether a particular movie could be green-lit. They would demur, explaining that they didn't make those decisions. "Have you spent any time with Jon?" Peter would ask. But Nathanson's calls to Jon went unanswered.

Then one Friday morning at about eleven, the Amtel on Nathanson's desk indicated that Peters was on the phone. "What are you doing this afternoon?" Jon asked.

"I'm working," Nathanson replied.

"Come up to the house. We gotta have a meeting."

Nathanson was rattled. "Nathanson is the type of guy who changes his wardrobe depending on who he's working for," says one executive with a long track record at the studio. "He wore a lot of Armani when Dawn was around." Most days he wore a suit but Fridays were a designated casual day; he usually wore a sweater and slacks or a shirt with no tie. Now here was Jon, demanding an audience. Should he rush home and change? He had seen Jon striding around in hiking boots and a T-shirt, but maybe the casual look wouldn't do for an employee. He decided to call Mark Canton's wife, Wendy Finerman, and ask her opinion.

"Are you kidding me?" Finerman responded. "You go as you are."

Nathanson took her at her word. He drove to Jon's house and met his boss, who was sitting by the pool.

"Come on, I want to show you around," Jon said, and took him on a tour of the grounds. Then Jon looked Nathanson up and down and ordered, "From now on, you wear a suit and tie every day!"

Nathanson tried to explain. "I generally . . ."

"Don't tell me you generally," Jon interrupted. "Suit and tie, every day. You run a company."

Peters put Nathanson through a hazing that lasted for months. He dressed him down in meetings, once pouncing on him in front of a roomful of other executives and tightening his necktie until Nathanson turned red. He phoned him in the middle of the night with abusive tirades. Once he summoned Nathanson to fly with him to Aspen on such short notice that Nathanson didn't have time to go home and pack; he had to shop for cold-weather wear when they arrived. Jon berated him for not being prepared to give a detailed extemporaneous briefing on all the Columbia projects in development.

One firsthand observer concluded that Jon was acting out of

261

his own fear. "He was completely scared of what he had to do," that executive says. "He knew he was competing with Peter. Peter took TriStar and he took Columbia. And every ounce of fear that he had about that, [Jon] took out on Nathanson. About as brutally as anybody could have."

Nathanson considered leaving the company, but he liked his job. Although the stress took its toll, he concluded that he could survive this, too. Unfortunately, one of his coping mechanisms wasn't healthy. "He was a walking *Physicians' Desk Reference,*" says one colleague.

Jon followed rough treatment with affection and a reward, as he always had. The quid pro quo didn't need to be stated: Jon was testing Nathanson's mettle, his discretion, and his loyalty. If he came through the fire, Jon would become his protector. It wasn't Nathanson's nature to fight—"He was a quintessential suck-up," says a high-level Columbia insider. So he toughed it out, and the two men reached an understanding.

A KEY ASPECT of Guber and Peters's management philosophy was having attractive women working at the studio—talent magnets, so to speak—preferably blondes with curvy figures. Amy Pascal, a creative vice president who had been hired by Steel, was an executive whose taste and literacy were respected. She was also a brunette with funky, whimsical taste in clothing. She was told to spiff up her wardrobe.

Snider filled Guber's bill for a high-end blonde with smarts. Meanwhile, Peters seemed to hire a blonde a week, and Hollywood delighted in chronicling their arrivals at Columbia.

Not one to be sensitive about charges of nepotism, Peters gave his ex-wife Christine a production deal, reportedly paying her a quarter of a million dollars a year. "Christine is one of the best producers in Hollywood," he explained—although she did not have a single credit to her name. Peters assigned her to develop *Girls' Club,* a Schwarzenegger-Stallone film he described as *"Tootsie* meets *48 HRS."* She scouted locations but the film never materialized. He also raised eyebrows by hiring his son Christopher's girlfriend, Liz Spete, as a junior-level creative executive.

262    But the real rumpus occurred when he brought one of his former girlfriends, Darris Hatch, into the Columbia family. Describing her as a "lissome agent" at International Creative Man-

agement, *Variety* reported that Hatch, a blonde, was "reluctant to talk about pre-ICM experience, and refused to name writer, director and actor clients she handled at ICM. She did acknowledge that she worked with Peters and his company . . . as an agent, and that probably helped formulate the evaluation that led to her job offer at Columbia."

She must have made quite an impression. Hatch was hired for the newly created post of executive vice president of production and paid $250,000 a year with a Mercedes-Benz thrown in. Her appointment was a slap in the face to seasoned staffers such as Pascal or vice president Gareth Wigan, who had real qualifications and seniority. "If she's executive vice president, I should be emperor," groused one employee. An unflattering nickname quickly attached itself to Columbia's new executive vice president of production: "Darris Snatch."

Guber was not opposed to keeping it all in the family, either. He set up his twenty-two-year-old daughter Jodi as an assistant in the studio's physical production department. And his wife, Lynda, the most impressive entry on whose filmmaking résumé was co-producing a one-hour yoga video, was handed a production deal at TriStar. The Lynda Guber Organization would develop several projects, including an adaptation of Robert Holdstock's novel *Mythago Wood*. But the chairman's wife—like Christine Peters—would never make a film for the studio.

PETERS AND GUBER got busy upgrading their office decor. Even as the Thalberg Building in Culver City was undergoing a massive renovation for their arrival, they spared no expense refurbishing their temporary digs in Burbank. Russ Kavanaugh, a contractor who had worked privately for both Peters and Guber, was hired to renovate the penthouse floor in Columbia's Studio Plaza Building, which was occupied by Levine, Woods, and Schaeffer along with Peters and Guber.

"Peter was doing a Japanese office, all authentic," says Kavanaugh. "They flew in mudworkers from Japan to make real mud walls. We were told that it had to be done correctly because Peter could not have a meeting with Morita in his office if the Japanese design was not authentic."

Guber's walls were framed in cedar before being filled in with mud. But what worked in Tokyo was a failure in Burbank. "The humidity in the building was too high," Kavanaugh says.

263

"The mud started to melt and slump and the floors started to buckle." By the time the humidity was adjusted that summer, Guber had moved out.

Guber had Kavanaugh custom-design furniture for the offices, including an S-shaped receptionist's desk of military steel which weighed 3,000 pounds. His private office was austere, furnished with dark leather couches. Peters favored a more informal look and instructed Kavanaugh to install 20-inch-wide distressed Douglas fir paneling and wood-beamed ceilings in his office. He mixed antiques with light tan chenille upholstery.

After Kavanaugh had put the finishing touches on the finest wood detailing throughout the penthouse—the polish on the cherrywood floors shone and the wainscoting and crown molding had been buffed to perfection—the co-chairmen and their staff relocated to Culver City.

Meanwhile, their lavish compensation packages enabled Peters and Guber to pour cash into their personal construction projects. In 1989, Guber had bought a $4.5 million oceanfront house at 23440 Malibu Colony Road. Now he was having the five-bedroom, 3,661-square-foot residence transformed into a Japanese showpiece finished with shoji screens and bamboo, and with a sunken dining-room table where guests would sit on pillows. Guber would take great pride in his house and enjoy showing it off to guests, though some found it cold and sterile. "Peter's houses don't look very lived in," Kavanaugh says. "They look like houses, not homes."

In early 1990, Jon too purchased an oceanfront property in the Colony, just down the street from his partner. Formerly owned by actress Pia Zadora and her billionaire husband, Meshulam Riklis, the house cost $3.5 million. Peters quickly added the requisite koi pond with a bridge that led to the front door. He installed pegged-wood floors, a hot tub on a beachfront patio, and added a projection room to the guest cottage.

Peters also acquired a new twenty-two-acre ranch in Aspen near Snowmass Mountain, and immediately hired round-the-clock crews to build a guest house and a main lodge. In his first year at Columbia, he frequently flew by company jet to Colorado, where he oversaw the construction while conducting studio business by phone. He imported llamas and reindeer to graze the grounds and flew in huge boulders for landscaping. For the main house he chose furnishings by Ralph Lauren with touches of lace. As soon as the renovation was complete, Jon began to ferry stars, including Stallone, Streisand, and Michael Douglas, to Aspen for ranch weekends. "Everything I did, I copied Steve Ross," he says.

Guber showed off his own Aspen ranch, "Mandalay," in an April 1990 photo spread and interview in *GQ* magazine. The article opened with a full-page portrait of the owner in a cowboy hat, looking uncomfortable astride an Appaloosa horse. Guber took the writer on a tour of the main house, crammed full of trendy Mission-style furniture, Navajo rugs, and Remington sculptures. "God is in the details," he said, quoting Mies van der Rohe, "and nobody can look at the cumulative effect of the details like I can."

The *GQ* journalist noted that the screening room walls were covered with pictures of Guber with celebrities: Peter with Castro, Peter with Nixon, Peter with Jack as the Joker, Peter with Michael Jackson. Then he took his interviewer snowmobiling, speeding through the aspen groves and fields. "We're big boys and girls, with big toys," Guber said.

THE TIME HAD COME to get a couple of big cannons on deck. By early March, three months after the takeover, Peters and Guber needed to hire new chairmen for Columbia and TriStar. They planned to make TriStar a full-fledged sister studio again, reversing the previous regime's cost-cutting measure of 1989, when the TriStar banner was subsumed under Columbia and the marketing departments merged.

Jon Peters intended to install his old friend Mark Canton as head of Columbia. But he would have to bide his time: Canton was under contract to Warner, and as part of the settlement of its litigation with that studio, Sony had agreed to a no-raid clause.

Though Peters and Guber may not have been Michael Ovitz's favored candidates to run Sony, they knew enough to consult him now. Anyone who was trying to run a studio had to kiss Ovitz's ring. His goodwill was essential to their success; his antipathy could bring ruin.

And so the new co-CEOs trooped over to Beverly Hills for lunch with Ovitz and his second-in-command, Ron Meyer. At an Italian restaurant around the corner from CAA's marble fortress on Wilshire Boulevard, the four discussed candidates

265

to run Columbia and TriStar. Out of these discussions Peters and Guber would select a pair of studio heads whose only predictable attributes were that they were expensive.

With much fanfare they appointed Mike Medavoy as TriStar's boss in early March. The job was a godsend for Medavoy, who was being edged out of his position as head of production at the financially troubled Orion Pictures Corporation. Medavoy's superiors at Orion were laying some of the blame for the company's woes—probably more than he deserved—on him.

Medavoy had an unusual background. He was born to a Russian father who emigrated to China and there married the daughter of another émigré. His father worked for the phone company and his mother had a dress shop. The family lived in Shanghai until Michael was eight, when they moved to Santiago, Chile. At seventeen, Medavoy moved in with an aunt who was living in Long Beach, California, and eventually enrolled in UCLA. Though he grew up speaking Spanish and Russian, he learned to speak English with no trace of an accent.

He got the cliché job in the mailroom at Universal Studios and eventually became a rather well regarded agent, with young-and-coming clients like Steven Spielberg and Francis Ford Coppola. When he was thirty-four, he became vice president of production at United Artists. The company was based in New York and Medavoy was hired in the early seventies to enliven the Los Angeles office. At the time, says Eric Pleskow, who was one of the partners who ran UA, that office was "like Forest Lawn [cemetery]. Nobody called us."

The middle seventies were UA's golden age. In an unmatched feat, its films won best picture Academy Awards three years in a row for *One Flew Over the Cuckoo's Nest*, *Rocky*, and *Annie Hall*. These successes imbued the executives who ran the company with a lasting aura, enviable in Hollywood, of elegance and good taste. Despite the kudos, UA's owner, Transamerica, clashed with Pleskow and his partners over management issues. When the top echelon of UA executives quit and set up Orion, Medavoy joined the breakaway group.

Orion kept the UA prestige but the company struggled financially. "We were always underfinanced," Pleskow says. "We always were sailing close to the wind. It's a very cash-intensive business and it takes quite a long time for the [profit] to come back."

266

Throughout the UA and Orion years, Medavoy enjoyed a reputation for being good with talent. Barbara Boyle, who was head of production at Orion, says Medavoy's strength was his ability to mix together the key ingredients in a project like "a master chef." He did his job "in a non-bullying way, took a gentle approach to getting talent involved," she says.

But in Hollywood, gentleness can be a shortcoming. And the line between gentleness and passivity can be blurred. Gradually Medavoy was regarded as perhaps too eager to befriend talent and not aggressive enough in getting projects through the pipeline.

Boyle suggests that Orion was too reluctant to ante up for big stars. "Mike could never convince his partners that we had to go out on a limb once in a while and pay the big bucks. They didn't understand that and Mike didn't argue enough for it," she says. To be fair, Medavoy tried to get Pleskow and the others to take chances—he urged the company to pay $4 million to put Dustin Hoffman in *Gorky Park*, for example—but they resisted.

For Medavoy, life changed when he became co-chairman of Gary Hart's presidential campaign in 1984. Colleagues believed he was influenced by Arthur Krim, the eminent Orion partner who had had close ties to John Kennedy and Lyndon Johnson. Around this time, Medavoy met and fell for Patricia Duff, a beautiful blond woman who came to Los Angeles from Washington with the Hart posse. Medavoy's first marriage ended.

Between politics and romance, Medavoy's interest in the movie business seemed to wane. "He became at best ambivalent and that's not good in an industry that requires maximum enthusiasm," Boyle says. Even before, his concentration was "relatively limited," she adds. "The criticism of Mike was, we didn't have his full attention."

"Mike takes it easy," Pleskow says. "He was sidetracked by his political involvement and that was not helpful."

Years later, Medavoy conceded that some of the criticism was justified. "I got so involved in '84 and for all intents and purposes let these guys down," he said. "They were pretty angry at me and they had every right to be angry."

According to Boyle, Medavoy's partners at Orion became increasingly resentful as the company lurched toward bankruptcy. "During that terrible last year of a company he created

267

and loved and was proud of, Pleskow began to believe more and more that Mike's lack of attention was the primary cause of this terrible happening," she says. "I think it's partly true."

For Medavoy, the chairmanship at TriStar represented an end to all his financial worries, both personal and professional. He had labored in the vineyards, making some great films at a company that had perennial money problems. Now, finally, he could afford to spend on projects that would have been out of Orion's reach.

Medavoy got off to a quick start at TriStar with a sequel to *Look Who's Talking* and *Hudson Hawk*, both of which were in the pipeline before he arrived. And he was the beneficiary of a distribution deal with Carolco, a company that was known for expensive "event films," especially big action flicks. Generally, TriStar paid for Carolco's prints and advertising costs in exchange for a distribution fee of 20 to 30 percent of the box office. In April 1990, Carolco delivered an Arnold Schwarzenegger special-effects extravaganza, *Total Recall.* With his new war chest, Medavoy quickly signed deals with the Hudlin brothers (producers of the comedy *House Party*), Denzel Washington, Richard Gere, Cher, and Dennis Quaid. TriStar would pick up overhead costs for the actors to develop their own projects at the studio. Historically these kinds of housekeeping deals with stars sounded impressive to outsiders, but they were expensive, risky, and rarely yielded results.

FOR THE COLUMBIA JOB, Guber approached several players around town, including his old friend Ned Tanen, who had formerly run Universal and Paramount; CAA agent Jack Rapke; and director Ron Howard's partner, producer Brian Grazer. None of these men was interested. Given their desire to stay on the right side of Ovitz, Peters and Guber's final choice for the Columbia job was hardly surprising: Frank Price, the man who had nearly been hired for the job they now shared.

Price and Guber had been acquainted since the seventies, of course. As head of Columbia, Price had shepherded Guber's *Midnight Express* and *The Hollywood Knights.* When Price took over at Universal in 1982, one of his first moves was to put the Guber-Peters project *The Clan of the Cave Bear* in turnaround. His relationship with Guber wasn't warm but they were friendly enough to have lunch together occasionally. The offices of the

268

Price Entertainment Company occupied the floor below Peters and Guber's penthouse in the Studio Plaza Building in Burbank.

Price had a great résumé—he took justifiable pride in having green-lit *Tootsie* and *Out of Africa*. But, of course, he had been fired by Columbia and Universal. And as a producer he had not made a film in three years. He was fifty-nine years old and the town was starting to view him as washed up—until Ovitz resurrected his executive career. In an industry that constantly recycles its studio heads, Price was about to capture the crown for most times around.

Although Ovitz had not been able to get Price the top Sony job, Price had his consolations. When Coca-Cola fired him, he'd been given a substantial block of Columbia stock as part of his settlement, and he had made millions on the Sony purchase. "So that was very nice," he remembers. "I certainly welcomed the Japanese." Price believed that foreign companies acquiring American movie studios wasn't such a bad thing. The new owners, he reasoned, would have an incentive to use their muscle to alter restrictive laws affecting Hollywood product in their countries.

Peters and Guber were aware that Price was unlikely to set any land-speed records. In fact, they considered him old and stodgy. But they were confident that, with their help, Price could assemble a winning slate of projects—a notion that Price would have found ridiculous and insulting had he been aware of it.

They also figured Price would be an easy sell to their new colleagues at Sony. He was a gracious man who looked, walked, and talked like a real executive. Schulhof had approved when Price had been in the running for the chairmanship.

Having come close to the top slot occupied by Peters and Guber, Price now agreed to run just one of the motion picture units. Few can resist the allure of the power that accrues to studio chiefs. Many producers would be happy to make such a shift, to go from being a seller—with its required hustling and pitching—to a buyer, the person who has the power to say yes. The problem was, Frank Price hadn't been saying yes enough to satisfy his employers for years. And he wasn't about to start now. By the end of the summer, Price would have announced only one new Columbia movie, *Return to the Blue Lagoon;* it was a project he had already been developing at his production company. He would receive a percentage of the gross.

IF JON AND PETER worried that Price might be pokey, they had no reason to be optimistic about Medavoy's vigor either. "They picked two senior movie executives who would project a sense of stability, rather than go in hot and young," a producer associated with the studio said at the time. They figured they could use their own frenetic energy to fill in the gaps, with Jon jolting Price into action and Peter riding Medavoy. While Price and Medavoy said in interviews that they had total autonomy and authority to green-light pictures, sources in the studio maintained that both operated under tight constraints: Price could approve only five films a year on his own, for example, and neither had the authority to okay a movie costing more than $25 million.

Now Guber and Peters launched a public relations assault on a new front. Having scrupulously avoided any evaluation of the studio before their deal was made, they made it plain that they didn't like what they had found. On April 14, 1990, they made that point through their lieutenants. Frank Price, Mike Medavoy, and Alan Levine sat down in the commissary at the Culver City lot for a wide-ranging interview with the *Los Angeles Times*. When the new management arrived at Columbia and TriStar, Levine told the reporters, there were plenty of projects in development but few ready to be made. "We opened the door in the vault and it was virtually empty," he said.

Price chimed in that the paucity of pictures in the pipeline created "a real morale problem." But having just spent three years without making a single film, he was vulnerable to the obvious question about his own lack of speed at his production company. "No. No, I was moving very rapidly," Price protested.

"Doing what?" the *Times* reporters asked.

"Developing scripts," he replied. "That process is very hard to do extremely rapidly. There are probably over forty projects that we have in development there." (Those projects had been moved to Sony, and Levine refused to discuss the terms.)

Levine's complaints about the bare cupboard at Columbia and TriStar opened the door to other questions he may not have wished to answer. Did Sony's investment bankers at the Blackstone Group do proper due diligence? Did they give a full and accurate report of what Sony was buying? Was the level of surprise at the shortage of product so great that Sony now must conclude that it had overpaid for the studio?

Levine said he knew nothing about what Blackstone had done. Did Sony overpay? "Oh, no," he said.

There were more questions about whether Peters and Guber had overpaid for scripts on their spending spree.

"Look at the track record of Jon and Peter," Levine argued. "These guys know value in the marketplace. They have not been precipitous in any of their purchases of literary material in the past. . . . They know value and so I'm amused by the implication or even the direct statement that we overpaid for stuff."

The *Times* reporters asked whether Sony executives in Japan had been alarmed by the media attention that Jon and Peter had attracted in their first months at the company.

"They didn't display any emotion about that at all," Levine responded.

"The notion that Jon and Peter had been asked to cool it, to become less visible and let the publicity burn off—that's probably not correct then?"

"Probably not correct," Levine replied.

ANY ANTI-JAPANESE feeling in Hollywood triggered by the Sony deal already had begun to soften, thanks to a growing amount of bad press over the gaffes and spendthrift ways of the studio's management. Columbia's new owners were having their money spent so fast that people almost felt sorry for them. Why bash the Japanese when Guber and Peters were doing such a good job of it?

Guber and Peters won a major early victory when they talked Sony into purchasing a fleet of Falcon 900 jets for the studios. At first the Tokyo brass reportedly issued an edict that the planes were to be used only for corporate purposes: There would be no flying stars all over the globe, as Warner did. But Jon and Peter convinced the Japanese that the studio would be at a disadvantage if the jets could not be used as candy for talent. They argued that a superstar like Barbra Streisand, for instance, should not have to fly commercial when she scouted locations for *The Prince of Tides*.

From the beginning the parent company maintained a low

profile on the studio premises. Ohga and Morita occasionally came to town and were discreetly entertained by Schulhof and Guber. "Morita really liked Peter, and he never liked Jon," says a highly placed source. Guber wowed Morita with fervid discourses on technology and the future. "Peter could play a guy like Morita because he's brilliant," this source says. "He could talk to Morita in a way he could understand. It wasn't about whether Arnold Schwarzenegger took a bath today. It was about how you'll be able to grow a tree in six days in the next century."

It was commonly believed that Sony's "mole" at Columbia was Ken Munekata, a twenty-eight-year-old Japanese with an MBA from Harvard. Munekata sat quietly in Guber's office taking notes, and when Ohga and Morita were in Los Angeles he would join them for dinner at Spago. Most executives on the lot had no idea of the substance of Munekata's communications with Tokyo. By spring, however, reports were filtering back to Los Angeles that the home office was mortified by the shenanigans of Jon Peters.

What reportedly most irked the Sony brass in Japan had been a February article by Aljean Harmetz in the *New York Times* —a publication taken seriously in Tokyo. The piece portrayed Peters as a laughingstock who went around boasting, "You have no idea how much power I have."

In March, Peters may have displeased Sony for another reason: He made overtures to buy the San Ysidro ranch, a posh 540-acre resort in Montecito, an hour and a half north of Los Angeles, for $22 million.

Gene O'Hagan, Peters's broker at the Jon Douglas Company in Montecito, says Peters spent considerable time and money trying to nail down the San Ysidro deal. "I spent three months running to Los Angeles three times a week talking to hotel experts, attorneys, accountants," O'Hagan says. "Right when we were all on the line for $22 million and the baton was raised, Sony gets wind that Jon is buying a hotel."

O'Hagan was amused because the negotiations had been conducted in great secrecy—but the story leaked to the trades anyway. O'Hagan figures that his client couldn't resist bragging about his contemplated conquest. "It had to come from Jon," O'Hagan says. "He must have slipped it out there."

O'Hagan says he was told that Sony refused to allow Jon to divide his time between the studio and another business. "Had

I given a thought to the Sony feelings, I could have called it myself," O'Hagan says. "The ink had not dried on the Sony contract, and here we were buying a hotel. They wanted Jon and Peter's undivided attention. That was fair, for the money they were spending." (A Sony source denies, however, that the company vetoed the deal.)

Even after the San Ysidro scheme was scotched, Peters kept boasting about it. A top executive at another studio says Peters bragged to him that he had bought the ranch and then quickly sold it, making a killing. But O'Hagan says the deal never closed and he estimates that Jon lost as much as $300,000 on surveys and consulting fees. "A good story is much more important to Jon than facts," O'Hagan says with a smile. "He's not into detail."

In April, *Spy* magazine—whose pseudonymous columnist Celia Brady kept a relentless eye on the machinations in Hollywood—noted that Sony had "a major public-relations fiasco on its hands, and its name is Jon Peters." The magazine reported that Schulhof, nettled by the press attention Peters was receiving, had called Walter Yetnikoff to complain about what Yetnikoff's matchmaking had wrought. Yetnikoff reportedly responded that Jon was "tough" and "hip" and a bit of a bad boy, not unlike himself—all of which, he argued, would update the studio's image. "Yes, but you were smart enough to keep it out of the *New York Times*," Schulhof replied. "At least you never made us look foolish."

Yetnikoff reportedly broached the issue with Peters, who replied, with devil-may-care economy, "Fuck 'em." He assured Walter that in a year or so his string of hits would silence the critics.

Then on April 26, a *New York Post* column item appeared which instantly became the most notorious—and emblematic —entry in the Jon Peters book of lore: that he had dispatched a Sony jet laden with flowers to the East Coast to court a lady (namely Vendela, the blond Swedish supermodel). Bruce Willis, who had been promised the plane to travel to the New Jersey set of *Mortal Thoughts,* was supposedly left stranded— and fuming—at the Van Nuys airport. The *Post* reported rumors that Columbia had to rent another plane for $50,000 for Willis. The star and studio denied the incident but everyone in the entertainment community was inclined to believe it. 273

It was true that Jon had begun courting Vendela over the

course of the winter, and he hadn't been shy about using the power of the chairman's office to enhance his chances. They first met when he lured her to Los Angeles by saying that Sony might be interested in signing her to a talent contract; the fact that Vendela was a supermodel, not an actress, seemed a small point. For her arrival Jon filled every corner of her room at the Four Seasons Hotel, including the bathtub, with orchids. While Jon vehemently denied that he had ever sent a flower-filled company jet to fetch Vendela, he acknowledges that after they became romantically involved he once flew on a Sony plane from New York to Puerto Rico to rendezvous with her for a private weekend.

FOR AN APRIL budget meeting with Ohga, Guber called Yetnikoff for tips on the best way to deal with his bosses.

"Make it look terrible," Yetnikoff advised. "First of all, the Japanese like you to tell them everything. Two, you have a new corporate owner, you should tell him all the negative things. . . . Put in all the negatives, it's not your fault."

The meeting took place in the eleventh-floor conference room at Studio Plaza. Paul Schaeffer was on hand to man the slide show for Guber's presentation. Ohga was accompanied by Ken Hoshikawa, a Sony executive based in New York.

Peters had his own agenda for the meeting: to promote the construction of his dream project, a theme park called Sonyland. He had already mentioned the idea to Ohga, suggesting that it should be located in the San Fernando Valley. Ohga had seemed to like the idea but rejected the Valley as too hot. Sony already owned two thousand acres of lemon groves in Oxnard, north of Los Angeles. Wouldn't that make a perfect site?

Peters had had a Sonyland model built and gave a spirited presentation that was simultaneously translated for Ohga. He proposed building two hotels in which guests could board glass-sided submarines that would explore an underwater shark exhibit and surface inside the lobbies. Foreign governments would contribute exhibits—a miniature Eiffel Tower, for example—in the interest of promoting tourism abroad. He talked of displays of movie memorabilia and attractions based on films, such as a *Total Recall* ride to Mars.

As the pitch went on, Ohga asked to take a break. Jon, caught up in his enthusiasm over his plans to "kick the shit out of Warner," as he put it, dogged the Japanese gentleman as he left the room. "We're going to make Sonyland!" he yelped, following him into the men's room.

"Tiger-san!" Ohga chastised him. "We make peepee now! Go outside!"

Throughout the meeting, Peters and Yetnikoff both noticed that Ohga did not appear alert. In fact, he dozed through Guber's rather complex budget presentation. But according to Yetnikoff, Ohga registered one crucial piece of information: a projected half-billion-dollar negative cash flow for the coming fiscal year. "Ohga is sitting there, blanket over his head, 'cause he was cold," Yetnikoff says. "I bring him a cup of tea and I put it in front of him—and he's out. And he wakes up every once in a while, and he cannot miss *negative cash flow of half a billion dollars*. . . . And he looks up and he says, 'Huh! You bankrupt Sony!' And passes out again."

BY MAY, it was clear that first-time director David Mickey Evans wasn't up to the task of realizing his vision of *Radio Flyer*. Dailies were disappointing, and Peters, Guber, and producer Michael Douglas (whose first picture as a producer, *One Flew Over the Cuckoo's Nest*, had won an Academy Award) anxiously discussed what to do about it.

Evans's screenplay was a small, personal tale about two young boys who cope with their stepfather's abuse and alcoholism by escaping into a fantasy world. They build wings onto their Radio Flyer wagon and plan to soar away from their troubles. The script achieved a delicate tone of magical realism and was framed entirely from the boys' point of view.

But as filming began, Evans was floundering. According to a Columbia executive involved with the project, Peters was so caught up in the story of child abuse that he completely steamrolled the novice. "Jon overwhelmed this guy by trying to direct through him, and tell the kid what he really meant when he talked about abuse."

Columbia made the rare and costly decision to pull the plug on *Radio Flyer* three weeks into production. "I just didn't think it was going right," says Douglas, who drove from his home in Santa Barbara to Los Angeles to tell Evans personally that he was being taken off the project. "There were too many areas to kind of correct, so we shut down. It cost about $5 million in terms of what we lost."

The community was astounded—and frankly not that dis-

275

pleased—that Guber and Peters were experiencing such a high-profile debacle so early in their tenure. "The collapsed production marks a significant setback for studio heads Guber and Peters," noted *Variety.* Douglas recognized that the fate of the film was regarded as a comeuppance. "I guess everyone took some solace and joy in the fact that we had to do it, but I think sometimes those decisions have to be made."

Now, director Richard Donner and his wife, Lauren Shuler Donner, were approached about taking over the project. (Donner had been Warner's choice to direct when that studio had considered making the movie.) Columbia coughed up a staggering $6 million for the husband-and-wife team to direct and produce *Radio Flyer.* The *Wall Street Journal* observed that the deal "could trigger the latest round of inflation in the movie business." Donner's $5 million directing fee appeared to set a new record; the closest anyone had come was Renny Harlin, who had received a reported $3 million from Carolco Pictures to direct *Die Hard 2.* "We were trading an unknown director for a major hit director," says a Columbia executive. "It seemed like a good idea."

The original cast and crew, many of whom had to be paid in full, were dismissed as Donner reconceived the project. He hired Lorraine Bracco to replace Rosanna Arquette as the boys' mother and scouted Northern California for locations. Tom Hanks was hired to appear as one of the young boys— years later—in an epilogue that was ultimately cut. The budget ballooned from $17 million to $32.6 million. When the cameras rolled again, wags on the lot referred to the film as *Radio Flyer II.*

That same month, the studio tried to shore up its prestige by announcing an unusually wide-ranging seven-year film and television deal with James L. Brooks, the respected writer-director of *Terms of Endearment* and *Broadcast News,* and creator of the television hit *The Simpsons.* While terms weren't disclosed, the deal was a rich one, worth as much as $100 million in production funding. Columbia outbid both Fox and Universal by more than $20 million. "Sony must be opening up some kind of treasure chest," said industry analyst Paul Marsh.

Guber had been pursuing Brooks for months with sweet talk, telling him that he understood that Brooks stood for quality and that the studio wouldn't demand a high volume of product from him. "I'll be able to make movies I believe in even if I'm the only one who wants to make them," Brooks said in an interview. Guber had sealed the deal by promising him the most coveted of perks: use of the Sony jets.

For six years Brooks had made his home at 20th Century Fox, where he had produced *Big* and *The War of the Roses*. His relationship with Fox chairman Barry Diller went back even further, to the days when Diller ran Paramount and Brooks made *The Mary Tyler Moore Show* there. Diller had every desire to keep Brooks at Fox but balked at matching what he called Sony's "extraordinary deal."

A highly placed Columbia insider says the terms of the deal, which he considered "insane," were crafted by Alan Levine. "Peter's theory was that [Brooks] was our first piece of talent. If we could get him, we could get anybody we wanted in town. There may be some merit to that, I don't know. If I were Alan Levine, I would have argued, 'If we do this, we'll never be able to make a reasonable deal with anybody else.' And they weren't. Every other deal was the moon."

Other A-list filmmakers followed Brooks, wooed by Guber into bountiful arrangements to set up production companies on the Columbia lot. They included director Penny Marshall (*Big*), despite the fact that Jon Peters had annoyed her when he visited the New York set of *Awakenings*. "He talked loudly when Robin Williams was doing a dramatic scene," says a studio source. "Penny couldn't handle it." Guber bestowed the jets on Marshall, too.

Also signed up were producer Laura Ziskin (*Pretty Woman*), director Tim Burton (*Batman*), the producing-directing team the Zucker brothers (*The Naked Gun, Ghost*), Francis Ford Coppola (the *Godfather* trilogy), and actor-producer-director Danny DeVito. DeVito was enticed by Guber's promise that he could produce a few movies that he didn't star in himself—along with others in which he would appear.

"Everyone wants a big fancy deal and everyone wants the jets," observed one former Columbia executive, adding that the extravagance set the wrong tone and created an environment that actually inhibited filmmakers. "Tim, Penny, Jim Brooks shouldn't have deals like this. They are guilty and fragile by nature. The lushness of the surroundings and the buildings. . . . When you have that much, you get afraid of losing it." 277

# 21

# WHINE AND ROSES

Having reached the mountaintop, Jon Peters attacked his biggest decorating project ever: the renovation of the old MGM. He and Guber set about pouring hundreds of millions of Sony's dollars into making Columbia Pictures' new home in Culver City as grand as possible, despite its unglamorous West Washington Boulevard location.

In February 1990, a COLUMBIA STUDIOS sign in big blue letters had been mounted over the main Madison Avenue gate. The new studio chiefs made much of the dilapidated condition in which they found their new digs. "Rats! There were rats everywhere!" Jon Peters exclaimed.

The forty-four-acre lot was indeed a faded beauty. Many classic films, including *The Wizard of Oz*, had been shot there in MGM's heyday. Now, it was a collection of shabby soundstages and bungalows. Its most elegant structure was the four-story Art Deco Thalberg Building, just inside the main gate, built in 1937 to honor Louis B. Mayer's brilliant head of production, Irving Thalberg. In fact, Peters and Guber had sat together on the Thalberg Building steps one Sunday afternoon in 1988, commiserating over the dissolution of their short-lived bid to buy MGM.

In recent years the lot had changed hands several times. The Turner Broadcasting System acquired it from Kirk Kerkorian in 1986 but sold it later that year to Lorimar Pictures. Warner picked it up in 1989 when it acquired Lorimar.

Peters and Guber's tiny principality could never rival Steve Ross's 144-acre fiefdom at Warner. But if they couldn't have the biggest lot, they could try to have the best. Jon Peters vowed to "turn an empty shell into a jewel box."

278

Culver City officials were known for their restrictive attitude toward development; there were many zoning regulations on the books intended to preserve the city's historic nature. No structure could be taller than four stories. Any plans for renovation or new construction on the lot had to be approved by the Planning Commission and the City Council. Some studio buildings on the property had been earmarked for preservation. When Sony arrived, the local citizens were suspicious of any changes the Japanese company wanted to make.

Peters, impatient about getting the studio's facelift underway, put the renovation plans into high gear. Amid jokes that Columbia soon would be transformed into a land of koi ponds and mini–amusement parks, Jon recruited Anton Furst, *Batman*'s production designer, to help him redesign the lot. Furst was in New York early in 1990 working for Penny Marshall on *Awakenings*. In April he would win an Academy Award for his art direction on *Batman*.

Jon had big plans for Furst, whom he recognized as an uncommonly charismatic talent. He wanted the designer to relocate from London to Los Angeles, help him spiff up the lot—and then make his debut as a film director.

Furst moved to Los Angeles in the summer. He established the Furst Company in a decrepit freestanding Spanish bungalow on the lot called the Joan Crawford Building. With his long hair and jeans tucked into knee-high motorcycle boots, Furst didn't strike corporate types like Alan Levine as an appropriate custodian of the massive lot renovation. In fact, Jon could not get Sony to approve Furst. Gensler & Associates, a Santa Monica architectural group, was named as the official design firm of Columbia Pictures studios. But Furst became a consultant to Peters, frequently conferring with him in the fourth-floor conference room of the Thalberg Building, where Peters set up easels bearing design schemes. Ken Williams, a corporate vice president, was chosen to oversee the renovation.

On an August evening, Sony's fifteen-year master plan, called the Comprehensive Plan, was unveiled before three hundred Culver City officials and residents on Soundstage 30. The studio proposed to construct 1.1 million square feet of new offices and production facilities in nineteen new buildings. On the drawing board were two eleven-story, two nine-story, and several six-story buildings, all in Deco style. The plan also included

279

underground parking, a grand circular driveway, lots of retail shops, and fountains and park squares.

Jon Peters's imprint was all over the plan, beginning with lavish landscaping and tree planting that would turn the lot into a verdant playground. He had given the Thalberg Building a special VIP drive-up lane so that celebrities and filmmakers wouldn't have to park in the main parking lot and walk one hundred feet to their destination. And he planned to build a mini–theme park on top of an underground parking structure, its centerpiece being the pirate ship set from the upcoming Spielberg movie, *Hook*.

Peters wanted every corner of the lot to be suitable for filming. "His idea was you should be able to shoot everywhere," says Russ Kavanaugh, who was brought in to oversee all construction. Peters proposed designing the commissary as an Old West saloon, and he wanted to create a health club and spa illuminated with klieg lights.

The studio won approval from Culver City for the first phase of the plan, which essentially involved renovation of the premises, while the balance was submitted for study. Completion of Phase One would take more than three years, during which time Hollywood would make note of every tree planted and gape at the expenditures. (The later and more elaborate phases of construction, including the high-rise buildings, were shelved.)

Phase One included restoration of the Thalberg Building and of the old Lorimar Building on the western side of the lot, earmarked as TriStar's new home. Several producers' buildings and bungalows were to be refurbished in high style, starting with the Jean Harlow Building, which would house James L. Brooks and his Gracie Films. Technical facilities would also be upgraded.

During the summer months Peters was in his element as he and Kavanaugh presided over bulldozers and crews working around the clock. Over the opposition of Ken Williams, who feared labor troubles, they hired a combination of union and non-union labor. Kavanaugh says Peters saved Sony up to $10 million, and "we got two years of work done in six months."

280     Peters lavished special attention on the Thalberg Building, making it the diamond in his jewel box. He wanted to return it to an authentic opulence, and dug up period photographs for

reference. He hired Costa Chamberledes, an interior designer who had worked for him and Streisand, to furnish the lobby with Deco furniture. Six basement screening rooms were renovated with Peters approving every detail from fabrics to floor coverings. Posters from old Columbia movies were hung on the walls throughout the executive offices.

Peters and Guber moved into Louis B. Mayer's former suite of offices on the third floor, for which Peters found an antique English partners' desk. Requisitions show that Guber ordered four rugs for the office costing a total of $67,124.40. Guber also had a giant mural of Peter O'Toole as Lawrence of Arabia —a touchstone film for him—painted and placed above the mantel.

As chairman of Columbia, Guber would frequently invoke the spirit of David Lean's classic film, even appropriating Lawrence's battle cry—"Aqaba! Aqaba!"—as an inspirational slogan. But Guber would prove to be touchy about his identification with Lawrence, as filmmaker David Zucker learned. Not long after David and his brother Jerry signed their deal with Guber to make films at Columbia, David played a practical joke on his new boss. He went to some lengths to have a portrait made of Lawrence in Arab garb—substituting Guber's head for Peter O'Toole's—and switched it with the picture in Guber's office.

The chairman was conducting a meeting in his office with some Columbia executives and Ray Stark when someone noticed the Peter-of-Arabia picture and began to chuckle. David Zucker was later informed that Guber was not only not amused by his prank—he was furious. "It was a little chilling to hear how it was received," says Zucker. "I mean, the Marx Brothers were always doing things to Thalberg. He kept them waiting one day for a couple of hours and when he finally came out he found them naked in front of the fireplace roasting marshmallows. We thought we were continuing that tradition."

One of Jon Peters's first moves was to install a giant stereo system in the Thalberg Building, which blasted the occupants with rock and roll. The music was turned off after people complained that they couldn't concentrate on their work. A high-level executive grumbled: "Everything they do is too much, too loud, and too expensive."

Twice a week, oversized fresh flower arrangements and fruit

281

baskets arrived in Thalberg's suites. Columbia chairman Frank Price recoiled at the excess. He requested that his book-filled office be cut in half because he thought it was too large. Of the flowers, he says, "That's very thoughtful stuff, but when you look at the amount of money! And those giant fruit baskets. I found out what we were paying for it. My secretary said she could pick me up fruit if I wanted it for a couple of dollars. It's kind of a lavish lifestyle. When you do that on a studiowide basis, it's ridiculous."

For a man with humble origins, Jon quickly assumed an imperial air. When he arrived at the studio each day, his driver would call ahead so that a guard in the Thalberg Building could dash to the front door to hold it open. Another staffer was designated to punch the button on an elevator that had been reserved exclusively for Jon and Peter's use. Guards were stationed by the golf carts that shuttled the bosses around the lot to make sure that no one else used them.

Meanwhile, Guber and Peters wiped out two handicapped spaces in front of the building where they parked their matching green Range Rovers. Tom Hershey, an employee who walked with arm braces and had a reserved spot in front of the building, was now told to park farther away in the main lot. The departed Dawn Steel got wind of Hershey's hardship and threatened to tell the press about the change. The handicapped parking was reinstated.

On the other side of the lot, the TriStar renovation lagged a few months behind Thalberg. The old Lorimar Building was a graceless structure, which was not much improved by its costly facelift. The building was redone in a style that one producer called "Hitlerian Fascist architecture—a Leni Riefenstahl, neoclassical look with huge square-fluted pillars and parquet floors. When you walk down the halls of TriStar, you say, 'This is money that could have been used for my movies.' "

The TriStar building was soon stuffed full of fine antiques. Mike Medavoy selected an 1890 English mahogany desk from Ralf's Antiques on La Cienega Boulevard, which sent Sony a bill for $20,235. Sony also paid for a $26,000 Chippendale writing table (c. 1780) and a $26,000 Regency mahogany linen press (c. 1820) to grace Medavoy's suite.

The co-chairmen's wife and ex-wife, Lynda Guber and Christine Peters, also called TriStar home. After Lynda moved into

Room 201 and Christine was ensconced in Room 218, other executives began calling the corridor "the hall of shame." Lynda Guber enjoyed one of the most fabulously appointed offices on the lot, courtesy of Sony. Studio purchasing orders show that Lynda feathered her nest with the following antiques:

Two Art Deco antique club chairs . . . . . . . . . . . . $8,700.00
English cherrywood table, c. 1860 . . . . . . . . . . . . $3,200.00
Four English oak leather chairs, c. 1860 . . . . . . . $2,720.00
Oak refectory, c. 1840. . . . . . . . . . . . . . . . . . . . . . $8,800.00
French cherrywood bouchiere, c. 1780 . . . . . . . $12,400.00

The wives were also given parking spaces with their names on them in coveted slots close to the entrance of the TriStar building, displacing employees with seniority.

In the heady early days of Peters and Guber's reign, everyone seemed to catch decorating fever—sanctioned by Jon Peters. Producer Steve Roth filled his office in the TriStar building with sumptuous rugs, antiques, and Angelo Donghia leather chairs. After Frank Price had turned down Roth's request for his own private bathroom, Roth decided that Peters was more likely to approve the $250,000 budget he desired for office furniture. "You're head of decorating, aren't you?" Roth asked the co-chairman.

"That afternoon my budget was approved," Roth said later. "I had silk wall coverings, and couches with leather piping."

As THE SUMMER of 1990 drew to a close, there were signs of activity on the filmmaking as well as design front. Steven Spielberg was in discussions with Medavoy about making a project called *Captain Hook* for TriStar. Streisand was preparing to shoot *The Prince of Tides;* Robin Williams had signed to star in *The Fisher King. Flatliners*—part of Dawn Steel's slim legacy— had just opened. It was a hit.

Already Guber wasn't happy and he made no secret of it. "He was vocal about complaining about what his responsibilities were," says an executive who worked at TriStar in 1990. "Peter bemoaned the loss of independence and flexibility and freedom. He would tell anyone who walked in that he hated his job."

Only a few months after arriving at Sony, Guber went to

283

lunch with one of the industry's preeminent power brokers. His lunch companion heard Guber's complaints, then asked him why he had taken the job. "It was so sexy, I couldn't say no," Guber replied. "It was like an aphrodisiac." He was told, in effect, to get a grip.

Many noticed that Peter always spoke about what would benefit him, rather than what was good for Sony. He was not a company man; he had a most un-Japanese sense of himself as separate from Sony. Flying back from Herbert Allen's annual media titans' retreat in Sun Valley that first summer, he confided to another studio chairman: "They haven't bought me. They're only renting me for five years. I haven't been bought."

Guber's distaste for management meant that by August the studio still felt like a rudderless ship. Peters may have failed in his bid to install Terry Christensen instead of Levine as the number-two man at the company, but now he conspired with Frank Price to hire a seasoned entertainment industry executive who could impose some order.

"I brought in Jon Dolgen," says Price. A former president at 20th Century Fox, Dolgen was known as an abrasive but shrewd manager with the kind of business acumen that was sorely lacking. "Dolgen was one of my key business affairs financial guys," says Price. "I said, 'I've got to have someone like this.'"

Not surprisingly, Levine vigorously resisted the hiring of Dolgen, whose executive experience far surpassed his own. "Over my dead body" were Levine's words, according to one top-ranking executive. In his noncommittal way, Guber endorsed the hiring of Dolgen. He placed an ultra-confidential phone call to Frank Price. "Stick to your guns but don't tell anybody I said so," he whispered. Levine yielded.

Dolgen's title was president of Columbia, and he was also to fulfill an ill-defined strategy-making role for the entire entertainment company. Levine promptly invited him to a budget meeting. Dolgen spoke up, observing that the company's overhead was running $50 to $75 million higher than any of its competitors'. "How are we going to improve?" he asked.

His question was met with silence. Dolgen was never invited to a budget meeting again.

THAT SUMMER, GOSSIP wasn't the only thing that was tailing Jon Peters. Someone was investigating him, and he knew it. Friends were receiving phone calls from a private detective who wouldn't disclose his client's identity. Journalists who had written about Peters were being approached. Producer Don Simpson, on location in North Carolina making *Days of Thunder* with Tom Cruise, was contacted by an investigator who flew to the set to ask him questions. Perhaps Simpson, a single man well known for his own bad-boy habits, seemed like a rich vein to mine. The investigator appeared to be casting a broad net. He was interested in every detail of Jon's past.

Jon had a hunch who the client might be. So did his friend Terren Peizer, the former Drexel Burnham Lambert salesman who had set Peters and Guber up in business with Burt Sugarman at Barris. It was around this time that federal investigators were closing in on Peizer's old boss, Michael Milken. Peizer, who had sat beside Milken at his X-shaped desk, was cooperating with the feds. And he believed, as did Jon, that Milken or his allies were out to destroy his effectiveness as a potential witness. Whoever had commissioned the investigation apparently thought that Peizer might be vulnerable when it came to his relationship with Jon Peters.

Peizer knew that there had been rumors about him and Jon from the days when they had caroused together, rumors that Jon had supplied him with women and drugs in exchange for trading tips. After all, some had wondered, what bound a guy like Peizer, then in his late twenties, to a man like Peters, who was nearly twenty years older? Peizer maintained that the rumors were groundless. And Milken, through an associate, denied that he or anyone at Drexel had commissioned the investigation of Jon. But someone was looking for something.

"When we became the gold-dust twins, they wanted to show we were insider traders and Peizer was a crook," Jon remembers. Jon and Vendela were vacationing with Peter and Lynda in Hawaii when they received a call from Paul Schaeffer. Schaeffer told them to be prepared to leave the country to avoid a subpoena. "We struck a deal with the government that we would show them our tax returns, to show we didn't make money on trading tips," Jon remembers. He says that once they provided the government with returns they were never subpoenaed.

Someone shopped around some copies of Guber and Peters's trading records to journalists, hoping to plant some kind

285

of story in the press. There wasn't enough there to get anyone to bite. Whoever was behind the investigation apparently came up empty, and the crisis passed. Still, Peters suffered from what might be called subpoena skittishness, and sought to avoid confrontations with strangers. On August 30, his assistant sent a memo to the courier service that was routinely used to send material to Jon's house. The memo instructed messengers to park on the street, buzz the house from the gate, and proceed to the garage, where they were to wait for someone to come for the package. "NEVER, under any circumstances, go to the front door of the house," the memo warned. A handwritten addition further cautioned: *Never look at the house.*

But these precautions did not stop Peters from being served with a subpoena on Friday, November 2, in his third-floor office in the Thalberg Building. The staff was buzzing with speculation after word spread that the co-chairman had received legal papers. No one ever discovered the content of the subpoena, but yet another edict was issued the following Monday. Until further notice, Columbia employees were informed that no more messengers would be allowed inside the Thalberg Building.

THE ACQUISITION he had so deeply desired was accomplished but nothing was going well for Walter Yetnikoff. He was being blamed in some media reports for the strategic errors Sony had made in its entry into Hollywood. An article in *Forbes* was headlined: WALTER YETNIKOFF'S $300 MILLION MISTAKE—and that reflected an extremely conservative estimate of the cost of Sony's settlement with Warner. After recounting the debacle, the article speculated, "At this point, Sony chairman Akio Morita must be wondering whether he ought to let Walter Yetnikoff do any more negotiating for him. As one Hollywoodite put it, 'Walter didn't shoot himself in the foot in this one, he shot himself in the head.' "

Before Warner sued, Walter had told reporters that he would be chairman of a Sony entertainment committee that would oversee both CBS Records and Columbia Pictures Entertainment. Guber, Peters, and Schulhof would be on the committee, but he would be in charge. "Music and movies will report to me," he boasted.

But Yetnikoff had discovered that his power was illusory when he tried to get Ohga to define his authority.

"You're the chairman of the steering committee," Ohga told him.

"What does that mean? Does that mean the steering committee has one vote—me—and the rest is advisory?"

"No. You are the chairman, but like the chairman of a board of directors, you only have one vote," Ohga replied.

Yetnikoff had protested. What did being chairman mean if you didn't have any power? But he didn't have to worry about that for long. The committee never materialized. Yetnikoff's sphere was not to include Columbia Pictures after all.

Peter Guber had moved at once to cement his relationship with Schulhof, who proved to be a remarkably susceptible quarry. Guber soon had his boss mesmerized. "Mickey, God bless him, didn't know what hit him," says a friend of Schulhof's. "Peter Guber is a barracuda. Peter Guber died and went to heaven the day he met Mickey Schulhof."

"Guber thought through the possibilities and made a special relationship with Schulhof," says a prominent Hollywood executive. "Walter was excluded from operations within two weeks of the time Peter took over. Peter is brilliant. He started talking to Mickey and isolated Yetnikoff entirely out of the loop. It was easy to do. All of a sudden, Walter is not part of it." It was a strategy that Guber would strictly maintain: In the future, even top Columbia executives were explicitly instructed not to speak to Schulhof. He even kept Jon at arm's length. Guber told his partner, "You build the company and let me handle Schulhof."

The ordeal of the Warner suit might have been expected to drive Guber and Schulhof apart. Schulhof had relied on Guber's assurances that Warner would release him from his contract and had been humiliated. But instead of being cast asunder, the two were brought together. "When women and men are thrown into a fire together, either they meld or they kill each other," says one high-level Hollywood executive. "Mickey's not a killer. Neither is Peter."

When Walter made a maneuver to demand responsibility for Columbia's video unit, Guber and Schulhof shut him out. By spring of 1990, Yetnikoff saw signs of serious trouble. His ace in the hole, his long-standing relationship with Ohga, was showing signs of strain. Strange things were happening.

There was a troubling episode in June. Walter had authority to approve the use of one of Sony's Falcon jets. Morita had told him that the plane should never be used for trips to the Far East because it was too expensive. One day, Walter got a call from Sony aviation saying that Schulhof wanted the plane for a trip to Singapore. Perhaps he was happy to turn down a request from Schulhof, and he claims that he thought he was following Morita's instructions. The next day, he received a letter from an infuriated Ohga demanding to know how Walter had dared to turn down a request for Akio Morita himself to use the plane for a trip to Singapore.

Stunned, Walter fired off an angry response. This was an example of communications problems with Mickey Schulhof that he had been complaining about, he said. Then he sent another message: "I am absolutely hurt that you, my old friend, think so little of me to believe that I would do such a thing as to insult Mr. Morita." Ohga responded by fax: "You are my old friend and we will stay as friends forever." Yetnikoff set about collecting evidence to prove his innocence—memos from staff who had not known that the plane was being requested by Morita and accordingly had left Yetnikoff with the impression that Schulhof wanted it. But Ohga showed no interest in Walter's proof that he had been unjustly accused.

Walter thought his rift with Sony may have come about partly because he was focusing on kicking his addictions and was less a part of the team than he had been in the past. But he had other more tangible problems. Aside from the debacle of the Warner suit, his old associations with independent record promoters were becoming a hot topic. Journalist Fredric Dannen was about to publish a book about the music industry, *Hit Men,* which would raise questions about record promoters and Walter's use of them. The book painted an unflattering portrait of the music business, and examined apparent ties between independent promoters and organized crime figures. Dannen also contended that Walter was losing his edge and that CBS Records was writing too many big checks to existing acts rather than nurturing and breaking new talent.

In August 1990, Walter read in the *Wall Street Journal* that he would be phased out of day-to-day operations at the record company. The article—followed by a similar report in the *Los Angeles Times*—didn't comport with Walter's understanding of his situation. True, he had turned over domestic operations to Tommy Mottola, the former talent manager whom he had

288

hired after Sony bought CBS Records. But he wasn't yielding control of the company.

At this point, Yetnikoff was surrounded by enemies in the industry. The heads of other major record companies all had feuds with him. Irving Azoff, former head of MCA Records and now head of his own company, Giant, gave a speech in which he said CBS Records was run by a "drug addict." Al Teller, who later headed MCA Records, had been fired by Yetnikoff from CBS Records. But his most dangerous enemy appeared to be David Geffen, the man who had sold his record label to MCA for more than $500 million. Geffen had a long memory. He was a bad enemy to have.

Yetnikoff had tossed a number of insults at Geffen over the years, but one story emerged from the many. The general outlines involved Yetnikoff coming across one of Geffen's female assistants and asking her in crude terms whether Geffen, who was gay but not yet openly so, would teach Walter's girlfriend to perform oral sex. Whether that especially enraged Geffen or some other Yetnikoff behavior was to blame, there was a widespread perception that Geffen did what he could to undermine Walter.

And Geffen was a man of influence with two of CBS Records' biggest stars. He was close to Bruce Springsteen's manager, Jon Landau, and Michael Jackson, who began to complain about the way CBS Records was treating him. Walter was said to be incensed when Jackson dropped his lawyer and retained Allen Grubman. Grubman had become one of the most influential attorneys in the music business, in part with Yetnikoff's assistance. Yetnikoff had steered many clients to him, including Bruce Springsteen. Now he and Walter had split and Grubman was closer to Geffen. Yetnikoff took a hit when Grubman landed Jackson as a client.

Yetnikoff sustained another serious injury. Jon Landau issued a statement: "Walter Yetnikoff was a good friend to Bruce Springsteen and me for many many years. We enjoyed a superb professional relationship and a pleasant social one. For reasons that remain obscure to us, the relationship ended not long after CBS was purchased by Sony. Neither Bruce nor I have had a significant conversation with him in nearly two years."

"This was serious," journalist Fred Goodman reported in *Rolling Stone*. "The message to Sony was quite clear: 'We are done with Yetnikoff; if you want us, you'll have to show us that we're a priority.' . . . The maneuver was out of character for the normally low-key Jon Landau. Journalists who covered the record business knew you practically had to tie Landau down and beat him with a stick just to get the most pedestrian comment on the record."

A couple of days later, Ohga interrupted a vacation and flew to New York for a day. His purpose was to meet with Walter and issue a warning that Sony's patience was wearing thin.

Even Tommy Mottola, who had been Walter's best friend and protégé, was rumored to have decided that he could not afford to remain loyal. He reportedly supplied Sony executives with an advance copy of Dannen's book, *Hit Men*.

"I have never seen a human being put himself in a more vulnerable position than Walter did," said one of Hollywood's eminent executives. "You can't fight a war on all fronts. Walter literally allowed himself to get in a fight with everyone around him. . . . He couldn't get enough arrows in his quiver."

Yetnikoff attempted to fire Mottola, who told Sony that he would take the entire management team with him. In a reported meeting with Ohga—later dubbed the Labor Day Massacre in the industry—Mottola was assured that Walter was the one who would have to leave.

On September 4, Sony announced that Yetnikoff would take a sabbatical of unspecified length, eventually returning as a special assistant to Ohga. The fig leaf fell off a week later when one of Walter's assistants reportedly was escorted from his offices at 4:00 A.M. after being found going through files. Walter was banned from the building. He called Jon Peters and asked to use his New York office, but Peters told his old friend that he could not allow it. By early October 1990, Yetnikoff had settled his contract for a reported $25 million—just a few million less than his newly signed three-year contract was worth.

A couple of weeks later, Mottola was honored at a high-profile charity dinner on the Sony lot in Los Angeles. Harry Connick, Jr., performed; the room was packed with industry heavyweights. Mottola hadn't yet been given Yetnikoff's job, but Schulhof sat at his table. So did Michael Jackson—with three bodyguards and a turbaned Sikh chef who prepared Jackson's vegetarian dinner while standing behind him.

The perception that Mottola's ascension was imminent was

290

underscored by Jackson's presence. Michael Jackson was in the process of negotiating a new contract with Sony, a relationship that Mottola would inherit from Yetnikoff.

Jackson, whose *Thriller* album held the record as the best-selling album of all time with 40 million copies, had not put out a new disc since *Bad* in 1986. Nevertheless, he was still the biggest music entertainer in the world, and Sony was eager to tie up his talent for many years to come.

Along with his musical enterprises, Jackson wanted to be a movie star. Various studios had tried to develop film projects for him—a Peter Pan project had been talked about for years —but nothing had jelled. Many in Hollywood felt that Jackson would never have a film career. His persona was too fey and eccentric, and extensive plastic surgery had given his face an almost macabre look.

But Jon Peters was enamored of the superstar and did not believe the conventional wisdom. He courted Jackson with promises of his own movie company. "Close your eyes," Peters told him, according to a *Los Angeles Times* interview. "Now picture yourself getting out of a limo. You open your eyes and it's an Art Deco building that says Michael Jackson Entertainment Company on top. You walk in the lobby and there are guys with epaulets and hats standing there. It's your family, your home and you're the boss."

Jackson had loved *Batman*'s production design and was keen to work with Anton Furst. Peters began to develop a project about a fantasy superhero for Jackson called *MidKnight,* which Furst would direct. Caroline Thompson was hired to write the original script. She had written Tim Burton's *Edward Scissorhands*—a role that Jackson had wanted to play. Furst began planning extraordinary visual effects that would use Sony technology, including lasers for the character's eyes.

Peters and Jackson met frequently about *MidKnight* at their respective homes. "Jon was very sweet with Michael, and Michael adored Jon," Thompson says. Jackson raved about his new pal to the *Los Angeles Times*. "Jon Peters is brilliant, original, sensitive and dynamic," he said through his manager Sandy Gallin. "He is the rare combination of effortless spontaneity, ferocity and intensity . . . he gets so enthusiastic. One day at lunch while talking about a movie idea, his glasses fell into his soup. I love him."

In November came the news that Sony was about to sign

Michael Jackson to a "multifaceted entertainment arrangement" under which he would record six albums and start a record label. In another facet of the deal, Jackson was to produce and star in movie and television projects.

The deal was hyped as the industry's most lucrative ever for a single entertainer. While the terms were never spelled out publicly, industry sources estimated that the advances on albums alone would be worth at least $60 million to Jackson. It was estimated with wild optimism that projects generated by "the Jackson Entertainment Complex" would be worth at least $1 billion in sales to Sony over the life of the contract.

# 22

---

# ET TU?

Mike Medavoy was enjoying an intimate fiftieth birthday dinner with his wife, Patricia, on the evening of January 24, 1991, when he received an urgent summons. Peter Guber needed to see him right away on Soundstage 7. Norio Ohga was fuming over the spiraling cost of *Hook,* TriStar's massive Spielberg production currently filming on the lot. As Medavoy hurried to heed the call, he felt trepidation. If the Japanese were upset, what could Medavoy do? Nobody told Steven Spielberg how to make movies.

Medavoy had been feeling pretty good. He had two huge projects in the works for the following Christmas. Director Barry Levinson and Warren Beatty were collaborating on *Bugsy,* a drama in which Beatty would co-star as the mobster Bugsy Siegel with Annette Bening. And there was *Hook.* The project was expensive, but it was the jewel in Medavoy's crown. What studio wouldn't pay for a Spielberg-directed holiday extravaganza for the whole family?

In December, Medavoy had staged a splashy press conference at the Studio Plaza Building in Burbank to announce his slate of upcoming films. Surrounded by his lieutenants, he had trumpeted a fifteen-picture, $360 million production program including Paul Verhoeven's *Basic Instinct* from Carolco; *Thunderheart,* a contemporary American Indian drama; and *Mr. Jones,* a Ray Stark project starring Richard Gere. He also announced that David Lean, the eighty-two-year-old director of *Lawrence of Arabia,* would come out of retirement to film a version of Conrad's novel *Nostromo.*

Medavoy said that twelve pictures would be ready for release in the coming year. They included *Look Who's Talking Too, L.A.*

*Story, The Doors, The Fisher King, Hudson Hawk, Terminator 2, Bingo,* and *Another You.* Medavoy also unveiled new deals with Al Pacino and Robert De Niro. As he boasted about what he described as the "spectacular" number of films he had put into the pipeline in the past nine months, some observers felt Medavoy was tweaking his Columbia counterpart Frank Price for not keeping pace. After the conference, Medavoy ran into Columbia production chief Michael Nathanson in the executive offices. Puffing on his cigar, he told the younger man, "Someday you'll have a slate too, kid."

Now, as Medavoy strode purposefully through the door to Soundstage 7 to meet Guber, three hundred guests yelled, "Surprise!" Jon Peters had pulled out all the stops to throw Medavoy a lavish fiftieth birthday party; he wanted to show the town that the Sony studios were now as vibrant as any of their competitors. There was a full orchestra in dinner jackets playing in front of a glittering L.A. skyline, and Art Deco chandeliers had been hung for the occasion. A flock of celebrity guests was present to wish Mike well: Warren Beatty with his thengirlfriend, model Stephanie Seymour; Barbra Streisand; Don Johnson; Sylvester Stallone; Richard Gere; and Sally Field. Terry Semel approached Jon, shook his hand, and paid him the supreme compliment: "This is just like the old days at Warner," he said.

The event, a vintage Jon Peters production, went 60 percent over budget and cost $100,000. It was perceived as a slight to Price and another display of overspending. Ohga may not have been upset about the price of *Hook.* But he would be angry indeed when he learned the cost of Mike's birthday bash.

FRANK PRICE was in no mood to celebrate. Almost as soon as he had been hired, he started to hear rumors that he was about to get fired. The persistent word was that despite his five-year contract, he would keep his job only until Mark Canton became available. But he pressed ahead, and with the help of Michael Nathanson, he put some attractive properties into the pipeline. His first great pick was *Boyz N the Hood,* an original screenplay by John Singleton, an unknown twenty-two-year-old film student at the University of Southern California. The script, a story about a South Central L.A. youth who is struggling not to succumb to the gang culture, had been discovered by production executive Stephanie Allain, who couldn't get Nathanson interested. She had taken it to Jon, who recommended it to Price. Price green-lit *Boyz* at a modest $6 million budget with Singleton as director.

Price had given the go-ahead to a couple of projects that he had brought with him from Price Entertainment: a boxing movie called *Gladiator,* as well as the sequel to *The Blue Lagoon.* He was overseeing *The Prince of Tides* and developing *Bram Stoker's Dracula* and *A League of Their Own.* But Peters and Guber were frustrated by his deliberate style. "Frank had his own very slow pace, very hands-on," remembers one of his former executives. "Nothing could be delegated. He had disdain for everyone else's taste. So many people complained. The hallways were so still and dead. Nothing got done."

During Dawn Steel's tenure, only low-level executives went to meetings where a writer or director pitched ideas. But Price insisted on attending every such meeting. "The whole process ground to a halt," says one insider. "It was Rip Van Winkle time, and to prove it, there was the Rip Van Winkle bet—that one of the team could fall asleep in their office for the entire afternoon and not miss anything significant." At any other studio, the boss might call every twenty minutes with a question or instruction about a project in some stage of development. But Price's staff had no fear of that. The bet was on. "This person lay down, went to sleep—and the phone never rang," that executive says.

Another executive, more sympathetic to Price, viewed the situation from a different perspective. "You must understand the perspective Frank came from," he says. "He was not a hotshot agent type who, through lots of bullying and maneuvering, became what he became. He was always someone who paid attention to story and characters that people cared about. His success in television and movies in the late seventies and early eighties is largely attributable to that strength. I think Frank's own success victimized him. I think Frank became extremely exacting about his tastes."

But with Medavoy announcing a big slate of films, Price felt the pressure, and he responded with his own press conference in February in the newly lustrous Thalberg Building. Like Medavoy, he was flanked by executives as he announced that he would put thirteen pictures into production in the coming year, with a possible seventeen more waiting in the wings. He promised to release eighteen movies in 1991—six more than his rival at TriStar. He announced a deal with Harold Ramis, the bespectacled filmmaker who had co-written and directed *Caddyshack* and who had both co-written and acted as the eccentric scientist in *Ghostbusters*. And Price let it be known that he had outbid TriStar for a deal with producer-writer-director Amy Heckerling, who had made the sequel *Look Who's Talking Too*. He talked about keeping costs down and avoiding big-budget action pictures.

After Price had announced his plans, a reporter asked him whether he found his new bosses at the studio intrusive. Price protested that the question was like being asked whether he had stopped beating his wife, but replied diplomatically that Jon and Peter were helpful to him. As the briefing wound down, Price had these parting words for the press: "Maybe now you'll believe I'm not getting fired."

No one did.

WHILE PRICE CONTINUED to provide grist for the rumor mill, he wasn't the only executive in trouble. The bell had begun tolling for Jon Peters. By the beginning of 1991, he was keeping a lower profile at the studio and trying to boost his reputation by pointing out some of his good works to the news media. He gave $50,000 to a women's shelter and threw a fundraiser at his Beverly Park home for Senator Chris Dodd (D-Conn.). Hosting a political party was a novel experience for Jon and he clearly was uncomfortable. As the guests arrived, he found Mark Canton in the kitchen and begged him to take over the meeting and greeting duties.

It had come to this: Guber was becoming weary of his unhousebroken partner, his erstwhile karmic brother. The press continued to be negative. Jon's behavior was always extravagant, and he always managed to top himself. While some filmmakers and executives appreciated Peters's verve, many complained about his bullying. Reportedly he went through secretaries so fast that he had to use a temp agency.

In March 1991, a cover story by Nina Easton in the *Los Angeles Times* Sunday Calendar section delineated the excesses of Guber and Peters: the prices paid for scripts and talent, the Medavoy party, the jets, the private elevator, their lavish compensation—contrasting with the comparatively stingy 2 to 5 percent pay raises offered to employees. Peters prattled about bringing therapists to the lot while Guber defended the big spending and the bloated corporate ranks. "The railroad industry made a big mistake in the 1930s when it saw itself as being in the train business instead of the transportation business," Guber said. "It would be the same mistake to view us as being in the motion picture business rather than the communications business."

"I don't think we look expensive or out of line at all," Alan Levine chimed in. "Maybe our goals are a lot larger than other studios."

But some readers didn't buy the grand prognostication; the article brought a torrent of mail. "Guber and Peters are where they are because they are shameless self-promoters, profligate loose cannons and generally larger-than-life," wrote one angry reader. "They are showmen . . . and they speak fluent hyperbole, which translates nicely into modern Japanese."

"Finally someone has told of the obscene, vulgar waste of money by the Guber/Peters team," wrote another, who mentioned that she worked for Columbia and took home $337 per week after taxes. "I don't need Guber and Peters' analyst to tell me the 12 steps to inner happiness," she continued. "Here are two: 1—Get rid of Guber. 2—Get rid of Peters. The rest will follow."

Still, Jon may have found some words of comfort in the *Times* piece. Guber, asked whether Jon was on his way out, had replied: "We enjoy a very tight relationship. Notwithstanding the noise you hear from time to time, we are together. . . . I adore him."

GUBER MADE still more corporate appointments. In January 1991, Sid Ganis, the former chief of Paramount, was hired at $650,000 a year to perform what was described as "a strategic job" to "help develop and implement strategies that will distinguish [the company] in the global marketplace." Skeptical onlookers wondered what all the executives in the corporate offices were supposed to do and speculated that their primary function was to insulate Guber. "Peter needs power and he's not comfortable with it," says one longtime associate. "When he gets scared, he hires people."

297

Jon was still battling with Alan Levine, who was widely perceived to be a weak manager. Almost from the start, Peter and Jon had clashed over the roles that were to be played by Jon Dolgen, the president of the Columbia unit, and Alan Levine, the number-two man at the studio. Jon, whose dislike for Levine grew by the day, wanted to promote Dolgen to second-in-command. Jon thought Levine was an untalented television lawyer, while Dolgen—bad-tempered though he sometimes was—had proven experience managing the Fox studio for Barry Diller.

"Levine must go to second position behind Dolgen," Jon told Guber during one particularly angry fight. "Fire him or get him into television."

Guber ran out on the argument and jumped onto the Sony jet to New York to commiserate with Mickey Schulhof, with whom he had been cultivating an even-closer relationship. Though Schulhof rarely talked to Jon, he called now to reproach him for upsetting Guber. Then Guber came on the line. "After ten years, you run to this guy in New York?" Jon demanded. The two decided to rendezvous in Aspen to try and work out their differences.

In Colorado, Peter came to Jon's house, and the two sat out on the deck in the spring sunshine. Jon suggested that they sit down with Schulhof to discuss the company's future and the conflict over Levine and Dolgen. Peter, protective of his special access to Schulhof, refused. Nothing was resolved, but somehow Jon wound up feeling reassured about their relationship. "We talked and I think it's fine," he told his contractor and friend, Russ Kavanaugh.

Still, Jon's friends were telling him that he was in danger. "I smell a rat and it smells like Peter Guber," David Geffen said.

"Don't be silly. We were in therapy together today, holding hands," Jon replied.

In fact, the two had been to see Margaret Paul, co-author of *Healing Your Aloneness: Finding Love & Wholeness Through Your Inner Child.* Jon still wanted to believe that he had found love and wholeness in his partnership with Peter. "I love you," he remembers Guber telling him in this session. "No, I don't love you—I feel like I'm *in love* with you."

But another warning came from Jon's lawyer, Bert Fields. "They're planning something," he said. Still, Jon was loyal to Peter. It was beyond his capacity to believe that his best friend

298

and partner would transfer his allegiance to the next person who could help him achieve the goals that he wrote down on his yellow legal pads.

Some Columbia insiders believed that Ray Stark was working behind the scenes to persuade Guber to cut Peters loose. Stark still wielded enormous influence over studio affairs, and although Guber resented it, he paid proper homage to the godfather. Some said Stark had disliked Peters ever since the hairdresser had spirited away his Funny Girl, Streisand.

Those who knew Lynda Guber believed that she, too, was encouraging her husband to get rid of Jon. She had long viewed him as her rival, and now she wanted to protect the role she had come to enjoy as corporate wife. She reveled in accompanying her husband on high-style business trips on the Sony jet, often with Mickey Schulhof and his Belgian wife, Paola.

Whatever his influences, Peter had clearly concluded that the time had come to rewrite the terms of his lifetime partnership with Jon.

He told friends that it was because the Tokyo brass were fed up with Tiger-san. "Peter said Jon offended the Japanese so much," says a Columbia source. But it seemed that Guber was the one who was tired of Jon. He appealed to Mickey Schulhof. He told Schulhof that he and Jon were deadlocking over issues and that he simply couldn't continue to work under the circumstances. "I can't do this," he said. "I'm going to leave."

As Schulhof had managed to consolidate his control over Sony's U.S. operations, Guber had simultaneously perfected his mastery of Schulhof. In December 1990, Schulhof had become chairman of CBS Records—a position previously held by Ohga—and had been elevated to vice chairman of the U.S. company. A month later, Sony brought together film, music, and a new electronic publishing operation and named Schulhof president of the $5 billion–a–year enterprise. He was now in charge of all Sony software.

Some observers questioned whether Schulhof had the character and intuition—not to mention background—for show business. He addressed those questions at the end of March 1991 by asserting that he would rely heavily on Guber and Peters for creative decision making. A month later, he was ready to rely on Guber alone.

In the Shakespearean scenario that began to unfold, Levine

299

would be the vehicle for dispatching Jon Peters. Sources close to the situation say that Guber and Schulhof began nudging Levine to square off against his number-one detractor, assuring him that he would prevail. Meanwhile, Guber continued to complain to Schulhof about Jon's recalcitrant behavior. One April day, Schulhof called Peters and said that Levine was in his office—and that Jon would have to come to New York at once. Jon called Guber, and became uneasy when his partner —who always picked up the phone—didn't take his call. He drove to Peter's Brownwood Place house and confronted him. "If this is about Levine, Levine has to go," Jon said. Guber avoided his gaze and remained noncommittal.

Jon returned home and the phone rang. It was Schulhof.

"We're coming to New York," Jon said.

"Peter isn't coming," Schulhof countered, adding—ominously—that he had ordered Guber not to make the trip.

Jon flew to New York on the Sony jet. As he sat down in Schulhof's office, Mickey told him that he respected him and, in some ways, wished he could be like him. Then Schulhof moved closer to his point. "This is not the Jon Peters company," he said. He complained, among other things, about the cost of the Medavoy party. Jon argued that he wanted to show off the studio renovations, that the cost of the party was "nothing." Terry Semel had congratulated him and told him that he was "jealous," Jon told Schulhof. Wasn't that worthwhile?

"We want you to work out of your house, since you like working out of your house," Schulhof persisted.

"This isn't going to work," Jon said.

Schulhof continued toward his objective. He wanted Guber to run the company, he said. Jon would have to report to Peter. Finally, he lowered the boom: Jon was out as co-chairman. "If you don't agree and you want to fight, we're prepared to fight," Schulhof said at last.

Jon was devastated. A few years later, he still struggles to describe the moment. "Honestly, I was numb," he says. "I was catatonic."

He retreated to his room in the Regency Hotel. He threw up. He called Guber repeatedly. Guber wouldn't take his call.

300    "It was the ultimate de-manning of Jon," says one longtime associate. "To have his best friend, his brother, turn on him. Forget 'Et tu, Brute?' It goes a lot deeper than that. To have

that friend clearly have made a decision to cut him loose. Who has the emotional equipment to deal with that?"

Peters remained in New York for several days, absorbing the news. He was so hurt that, uncharacteristically, he didn't say much to most people about this traumatic episode. He did tell some friends that Peter had "put on a kimono."

"I was at his house when he came back from New York," says Russ Kavanaugh. "It was one of the only times I've seen Jon look tired. His light was a little dimmer."

On May 7, the day of Peters's return from New York, a press release went out announcing his resignation as co-chairman of Columbia Pictures. "After lengthy consideration and discussion, we have approved Jon's proposal to establish an entertainment company," Schulhof said in a statement.

"He's been my friend and partner for 12 years," Guber's statement read. "In this new endeavor, he has my unbridled support." Peters's company would be "fully staffed in its own independent headquarters and will have the highest level of autonomy in developing, producing, and marketing its product."

At the studio, the news came as a surprise to no one. Jon wasn't mourned—except, perhaps, by a few. That afternoon, a producer who shared a corridor in the TriStar building with the female executives hired during the Peters era posted a sign by the elevator: BAD DAY FOR BLONDES.

JON WASN'T SO DISTRAUGHT that he didn't hire two of the toughest lawyers in the entertainment business to represent him. His tag-team consisted of Jake Bloom, one of the ablest negotiators in the business, and Bert Fields, his personal lawyer and one of Hollywood's most ferocious litigators. Peters demanded that his contract should be paid in full—including his share of the bonus pool promised at the end of five years.

Jon and Peter were deeply estranged, but when lawyers called from Sony's offices to say that they had reached an impasse in the settlement discussions, Jon demanded that he and Peter sit down and hold a private conversation.

The two men got into their cars and returned for one final visit to therapist Margaret Paul's office in Mar Vista. For the next two hours, Jon poured out his heart and exacted his price. He later declined to elaborate on the conversation, but said an

301

understanding was reached. "We came to an agreement on the formula, which at the end of the day would take the angst out of everything because we'd made sure that nobody got fucked," Jon said.

The amount of Peters's settlement was never disclosed, but estimates put the figure at about $30 millon. He also retained his share in the bonus pool and the payment based on any increase in the studio's value over five years. One Peters associate believes that Jon ultimately received as much as $50 million from Sony to go away.

Guber paid a visit to Frank Price and told him that Jon would be producing films for the studio—and Guber's promises of autonomy for Peters were revealed as window dressing. "He said I had to be tough here and treat Jon as I would any producer," Price says. Price replied that he never had any particular difficulty with Jon and he was happy to work with him. The two met once or twice to discuss projects that Peters would develop for Sony under his new deal, including the John Gotti story and a Paul Verhoeven pirate movie, but nothing materialized. "My guess is that Jon didn't like the changed situation," Price said. "I must say, I treated him very well and was quite interested in those projects but I think he felt uncomfortable. He was no longer the co-CEO."

Jon says he wasn't really capable of holding serious discussions with Price. "I never dealt with Frank," he says. "I was so devastated, I couldn't talk. If I started to talk movies, I broke out in a cold sweat. I needed to heal."

Jon was given offices in Beverly Hills and was contractually forbidden to enter the Sony premises without Guber's consent. The arrangement suited both men. Jon's presence seemed to embarrass Guber. In his first year as a producer, Peters would pour millions of Columbia's money into developing material —so much, according to several industry sources, that there was little money left for other projects at the studio.

After ousting Jon, Peter would occasionally call and pretend that nothing had gone wrong. Once, Peter asked him to accompany him to a screening. As they drove to the theater together, Jon suddenly found that he couldn't maintain the charade. "I broke down in the car and started crying and said, 'How could you do this?' " he remembers.

According to Jon, Peter cried, too, and began to reminisce

302

about his previous partner, Neil Bogart. Jon surmised that there was a parallel between the situations in Guber's mind. "He left Neil for me and he felt guilty," Jon says. As he often did, Jon started to hope that reconciliation was possible. "He said something like, 'You know why I loved being partners with you?' And I thought he was going to talk about all the creative and emotional experiences we shared. And he looked at me and said, 'I was always jealous of you because you had the prettiest girlfriends.' "

Jon was floored by Guber's statement. "It was like a part of me died. He could not acknowledge my existence."

# 23

# MICKEY GOES HOLLYWOOD

MICKEY SCHULHOF was having a heady year. Sony continued to expand its U.S. operations, and his empire was growing. In May 1991 came a potent symbol of Sony's intentions in the American market, the announcement that it would acquire Manhattan's AT&T "Chippendale" Building, designed by Philip Johnson, at Madison and 56th Street. Desiring a corporate headquarters that would reflect its prestige, Sony eventually paid a reported $320 million for the building. That sounded like a lot, until one computed that the thirty-five-story granite tower cost a fraction of the total tab for hiring Jon Peters and Peter Guber.

Schulhof embarked on a renovation that seemed inspired by Peters and Guber in its extravagance and showmanship. The building was transformed into a dazzling public showcase for Sony products, while its offices were made equally impressive in their luxuriousness. Schulhof hired Barry Wines of the famed Manhattan restaurant the Quilted Giraffe to oversee the corporate dining room, which featured a sushi bar with a stream running through it.

In May the company also announced that it had purchased the historic Culver Studios, the place where *Gone With the Wind* was filmed, as headquarters for its television division. Just a few blocks east of the main Sony lot, Culver Studios consisted of seventeen acres and fourteen soundstages. The new soundstages were sorely needed, thanks to increased production of Sony movies; *Hook* and *Bugsy* had already filled up all of the available space on the main lot.

In early August, Columbia Pictures Entertainment was re-christened: It was now called Sony Pictures Entertainment. (The two film studios were still TriStar and Columbia.) The studio's name change caused some grumbling in Hollywood about cultural heritage—especially when the big sign at the entrance to the lot was changed. But Morita insisted that Tokyo had nothing to do with it. "Look, it wasn't our decision," he said. "That was their decision in Los Angeles." In fact, the decision was Schulhof's.

Schulhof found himself on a steep learning curve. If he could get the film studio to perform as well as Sony Music, he would be fine. Since Sony had acquired CBS Records in 1988, Schulhof had established a good rapport with its management and cultivated relationships with Sony artists. Tommy Mottola and his wife, Mariah Carey, one of the label's brightest stars, were regular guests in his home. Schulhof was friendly with Billy Joel and Barbra Streisand, and talked frequently on the phone with Michael Jackson.

Now Schulhof tried to bring himself up to speed in the film business. During the summer of 1991, he would hop aboard the Sony helicopter in Manhattan on Friday afternoons with his wife Paola and their two sons, David and Jonathan. The family would fly to their summer home in East Hampton, a two-story white contemporary adjacent to the famous Maid-stone golf course. A visitor to the East Hampton home recalls that Schulhof read a lot of scripts and was eager to talk about films and filmmakers. Prints of soon-to-be-released Sony movies were flown in for his viewing in a new screening room that had been built on the property.

"Once they had the film company, he immersed himself in the movies," says a Schulhof acquaintance. Peter Guber and his family were occasional weekend guests at the beach house. As the two families grew friendly, twenty-three-year-old David Schulhof struck up a romance with Guber's daughter, Jodi. The young couple lived together in the East Hampton house and eventually became engaged, though they split up later.

Despite his conscientiousness, Schulhof did not seem to display the aptitude for the film business that he did for music. "Mickey had very unsophisticated tastes," says one friend. "There was no way he could learn cinematic language in a minute. And he had Peter Guber tap-dancing all around him."

305

As Schulhof struggled to comprehend the ways of Hollywood, synergy was not yet anywhere in evidence. Sony's grand vision of a marriage between hardware and software had been the justification for its $6 billion investment in Columbia Pictures. But critics pointed out that Sony didn't seem to have any clear strategy for coordinating its divisions.

In fact, as some observers had predicted, tensions started to fester between Sony's electronics and entertainment divisions. The hardware side began to resent the software unit for extravagant spending and lavish executive salaries. The problem came to light when the electronics unit was pushing digital audio tape (DAT), a high-quality audio format that produced perfect copies of digital recordings.

At first, the record industry shunned DAT because it was perceived as a threat to sales. Sony's own music division would not even agree to release artists such as Michael Jackson in the format. Eventually, the music companies relented when electronics companies agreed to compensate them with royalties from DAT sales. But then Schulhof fanned the flames in July 1991 when he told a reporter that the company would make a digital tape recorder using technology developed by Sony's rival, Philips N.V. Ron Sommer, president of the Sony consumer electronics business based in Park Ridge, New Jersey, was irked enough to go public with his criticism that Schulhof had said too much too soon. As far as he was concerned, no such decision had been made. It was just one of several irritants that led to reports that Sony's hardware executives were actually rooting for the software side to fail spectacularly.

"My gut feeling is that there is a lot of disagreement and even rancor" between the hardware and the software side, David Lachenbruch, editorial director of *Television Digest,* told an interviewer. "It is very uncustomary for Sony, which has always had its act together."

David Londoner, a financial analyst with Wertheim Schroder in New York, saw the digital audio tape conflict as "a classic example of [synergy] not working." Morita tried to smooth over the differences. "Sometimes people misunderstand the culture of our company," he said. "Each division is always competing with the others."

But competition between the hardware and software divisions would not help Sony to meet the challenges that lay in store. Several opportunities for synergistic interactions simply fizzled. Among them were the Data Discman, a $400 digital reference tool providing encyclopedic and other information. The software would be provided by Sony Electronic Publishing in conjunction with publishers. It never caught on.

Sony also was disappointed by the response to its MiniDisc system, featuring a $2^1/_2$-inch recordable disc, aimed at the Walkman market. Its attempt to set the format for video disc players was stymied by its competitors. And Sony was pouring millions into developing high-definition television when many observers predicted that the format was doomed.

Although both Schulhof and Guber touted the notion of synergy, neither articulated a lucid vision for its implementation. Guber's discussion of the concept tended to consist of forecasting about technologies of the future. He had done this years earlier in *The New Ballgame,* and he did it again now. But his pronouncements about "the vitality of the home entertainment center as a laboratory for creative innovations" in the future had no practical impact. Such talk did not move Sony closer to its goals of linking its businesses. For the moment, Guber was forced to admit, Sony motion pictures could not make or break the company's hardware products.

Still, Guber spun. "It's a much overused word, but there is synergy happening in the talent pool here," Guber told a *Wall Street Journal* reporter. As evidence, Guber pointed out that Jim Brooks had taken a walk around the Sony lot with Danny DeVito, and that the two had dropped in on Francis Coppola, who was working on *Bram Stoker's Dracula.* Dealing in the present, Guber could produce only the most pedestrian examples to illustrate Sony's synergies.

There were other indications that synergy was proving to be a balky concept: Spielberg, hard at work on *Hook,* was said to be reluctant to go along with plans for a raft of promotional tie-ins between the movie and Sony products.

Schulhof told the press that the synergy concept was alive and predicted that the entertainment business, still about 20 percent of Sony's overall revenues, would eventually contribute as much operating income as electronics. That was years away, he acknowledged. Sommer agreed: Sony hardware sales in the United States were growing 15 percent to 20 percent per year; the software side would have a hard time catching up.

Some experts weren't buying Schulhof's optimism. "There is a disaster waiting to happen called Columbia Pictures," said financial analyst Emanuel Gerard at the time. "I don't know that Sony knows how to deal with this. They ought to be scared." He concluded that the Columbia acquisition was "an unmitigated debacle."

And when a reporter asked Akio Morita if he was comfortable with Sony's level of investment in its entertainment business, his response was evasive. " 'Comfortable' is a very delicate word," he said. "Once we get the return on the investment, we will be comfortable."

MORITA'S BEST HOPE for a return on Sony's investment lay in the studio's television operations. Gary Lieberthal, the head of the unit, wasn't particularly popular but he ran a successful division. During his seven years in charge of the unit, it had never thrown off an operating profit of less than $100 million —and sometimes the number was much higher. Indeed, television had been the real engine that had driven Columbia for some time. Some maintained that Lieberthal was lucky: Coca-Cola had made some valuable acquisitions when it owned the studio, including Norman Lear's production company and Merv Griffin Enterprises. Those deals brought successful sitcoms and a pair of highly profitable game shows: *Jeopardy!* and *Wheel of Fortune.* These programs and Columbia's long-running soaps—*The Young and the Restless* and *Days of Our Lives*—were reliable profit machines.

The company had cranked out so many successful sitcoms that some producers called it "Clone-numbia." Just before the Sony acquisition, Columbia had gotten a spate of new shows on network television. And it already had a couple of mega-hits on the air: *Married . . . With Children* and *Who's the Boss?*

The trick in television was to keep shows on the air for several seasons, long enough to generate a sufficient number of episodes to sell the reruns into the lucrative syndication market. That was where the studio stood to make its money. In its recent history, it had sold episodes of *Who's the Boss?* for more than $1.5 million an episode, then the second-highest amount ever paid for syndication rights (*The Cosby Show* was number one).

308

The show was generating hundreds of millions of dollars in profit. But when Sony bought the studio, the syndication market for television programming was becoming saturated. The value of television reruns was dropping—not that Sony would have to worry about that much. Most of the shows that the studio had on network television wouldn't survive long enough to sell in the syndication market anyway. Columbia's hot streak with launching new sitcoms ended just as Sony showed up. The studio soon ranked last among the six majors in new shows sold to the networks.

"We had an extremely good selling season on Victor [Kaufman]'s last go-round," says one television executive who was at the studio then. "That was a big factor in selling the company —not only the success that the company historically enjoyed, but that big burst right before [the sale]. We did eleven pilots and sold nine. Most of them didn't stay on the air. But the Japanese didn't understand the business. . . . I just don't think they looked into how television works and who was going to run the company. They were hustled and they were willing to be hustled because they had a theory that you needed software to make hardware work."

Guber had little interest in television, that executive says. "He doesn't watch television. He never made money in television. It's really not his game. He's a pirate and buccaneer. Television is much more a business than movies. You only have three big buyers and you can't bullshit 'em. . . . All that hucksterism and wheeler-dealer stuff that Peter excels in isn't that useful in television."

With Sony's money in hand, Lieberthal went shopping. The *Los Angeles Times* said Lieberthal had embarked upon "the biggest spending spree in the history of the television business, dispensing buckets of money on 'hot' writers and producers." The paper estimated that the studio had committed to spend $100 million over three years just for writers and producers, excluding the cost of actually making programming.

Lieberthal disputes that he went on a spree after Sony bought the company. "The talent was bought before Sony got there," he says. "Sony did not open the floodgates in television. That started when Coke was there and when television was making a fortune."

Certainly, Lieberthal had a reputation for spending big before the arrival of Sony. A spate of deals with talent, including an agreement with *Taxi* creator Ed Weinberger in 1988, had drawn attention because Columbia had outspent at least three other studios to get them. "The best comes dear," Lieberthal had said then.

One source who was a top Sony television executive at the time concurs that Coke initiated the spending and Sony continued it. The studio was spending about $25 million a year on writers and producers before Sony came on the scene, he estimates. With the division's success, Victor Kaufman had told television executives to come up with a wish list of every talent deal that might be feasible and desirable. The tab came to $47 million a year. The new administration rubber-stamped the requests. "Gary handed in his [wish] list and Sony said, 'Fine,' " that executive says.

"The strategy ended up being absolutely ill-timed against the market," says another former high-level Sony television executive. The focus was on selling sitcoms to the networks for prime time instead of developing shows for the lucrative first-run syndication market. "Columbia put all its eggs in one basket," he says. "The euphemisms flowed about the 'gap' or 'dip' before our next *Who's the Boss?*" But for a seven-year stretch beginning in 1988—the year before Sony purchased the studio—*Mad About You* was the only Columbia or TriStar show that stayed on the air long enough to go into syndication.

Meanwhile, Alan Levine and Gary Lieberthal weren't a match. "Alan told me on a number of occasions that he couldn't stand Gary and wanted to get rid of him," says a former Columbia executive. "Gary told me Alan was incompetent, had never run a business, and was the only entertainment lawyer in Hollywood who never got rich."

According to one high-ranking insider, "Gary wasn't shy about tooting his own horn and going directly to Guber to undermine Alan. In what continued to be a very fluid political situation, Gary felt Dolgen would emerge the victor. At any social function, Gary would sit with Jon Dolgen. It was clear he was putting himself in Jon's camp."

Lieberthal denies that he had any quarrel with Levine. "Alan had a great understanding and appreciation of television," Lieberthal says. "Alan would say, 'Jesus, I saw the deal in Cleveland and that was a hell of a deal.' He knew what it meant."

310

Nonetheless, Lieberthal's tenure at the studio came to an end in February 1992. Some say he was pushed; Lieberthal says he wanted to spend time on his farm in Middleburg, Virginia.

Lieberthal's replacement was Mel Harris, a chain-smoking executive with a Ph.D. in mass communications who had recently parted ways with Paramount. Harris had overseen Paramount's aggressive home-video division as well as its successful foray into making television shows for first-run syndication. "Alan told a number of people, 'This is your savior,' " says a former Columbia television executive. "Mel kept extremely close to Alan. He talked to him ten or fifteen times a day by phone." But according to that executive, Harris wasn't a hands-on manager. "He sees himself as a real intellectual," he says. "He's not a dealmaker. He gathers enormous amounts of information. You could talk to Mel Harris about anything pertinent to worldwide telecommunications in the last century and he could write you a term paper."

While the television division showed little improvement under Harris, Lieberthal, the former head of the television division, defends Sony's faltering performance. "We had *Who's the Boss?* and *Married . . . With Children*—the second- and third-biggest-grossing shows in the history of the business," he says. "To look at what happened after that is like saying, 'Universal fell on its ass because they didn't have another *Jurassic Park* the following year.' "

Meanwhile, other units of the company had their own problems. Within months of Sony's acquisition of Columbia, NBC had filed a suit charging that Sony was trying to wriggle out of a long-term video joint venture that had been negotiated years before. NBC was a partner in that arrangement and demanded $250 million as compensation. As proof of Sony's alleged misconduct, NBC pointed out that Sony had made an independent deal with Orion for video rights to its next fifty films. That deal had amazed observers in its own right, since Sony agreed to pay $175 million for those rights while Orion was teetering on the brink of bankruptcy. Many doubted—with reason—whether Orion would ever make fifty more movies. But a Columbia insider says it was "an ego thing" for the company to have a home-video division that bore the name Columbia-TriStar. Orion later went into bankruptcy; Sony reportedly lost over $100 million.

311

Sony ended up buying NBC out of the video joint venture in May 1991. While terms weren't disclosed, industry executives estimated that the transaction was worth $300 million. Again, it seemed, Sony may have overpaid. When Sony was still negotiating to buy Columbia, one source says, it had inquired how much it might cost to get out of the video joint venture. Columbia executives at that time had estimated that Sony could buy its way out of the deal for less than half what it eventually spent to settle the suit.

# 24

## PRICE ON ICE

THE RELEASE of Bruce Willis's vanity project, *Hudson Hawk*, loomed on May 24, 1991. The town anticipated a major bomb. Willis's film, a caper movie about a cat burglar which blended action and comedy, had been all but green-lit when Guber and Peters came to Sony. Guber had pulled the trigger despite some misgivings.

Willis had great expectations for *Hudson Hawk*. The star called all the creative shots, co-writing the script and the movie's title song, and imposing his will on director Michael Lehmann and producer Joel Silver. "He thought he was making *Wayne's World*—a hip, MTV-type movie," says a source from the set. Willis had shown little interest in financial restraint during the making of the film, which was shot in several European locations. He had been responsible in part for TriStar's biggest hit ever, having provided the baby voice for the sleeper block-buster *Look Who's Talking*. He felt the studio could afford to subsidize a project that was near to his heart.

When *Hudson Hawk* had been shooting in Rome, says one source who was there, Willis was told that the cost of the film had just passed $50 million. "I don't give a shit," he reportedly answered. The studio was nervous about the runaway budget, but neither Medavoy nor Guber issued a directive to contain it. "They saw what was going on and never said a fucking word to Willis," an insider says. "They didn't ever stop him. They let him go totally insane." Willis was so oblivious to the impending disaster that he insisted on inviting Guber and Peters to a test screening in Long Beach. "Bruce really thought he was going to be anointed," one source says.

But the audience wasn't in an anointing mood. *Hudson Hawk*

313

took in a disastrous $17 million at the U.S. box office, losing Sony more than $42 million.

In a negative review, the *Wall Street Journal*'s Julie Salamon took issue with Bruce Willis, who had been publicly complaining that journalists kept harping on the cost of the film. "The inane action takes place in splendiferous settings," wrote Salamon. "Mr. Willis may not want his audiences to think about how much those settings cost, but I think he's making a mistake. The picture's 'entertainment value' can only be enhanced by the realization that the movie's financiers are probably suffering much more than the audience."

THE REST OF THE summer of 1991 brought mixed results for Sony films.

*City Slickers* got Columbia off to a promising start. The Billy Crystal cowboy romp, released in June, grossed more than $124 million, making it the number-one comedy of 1991. The picture was produced by Castle Rock, one of the most successful independent film companies in Hollywood. Castle Rock was one of Sony's key relationships. The company, founded in 1987, was run by five partners, the most famous of whom was Rob Reiner, director of *This Is Spinal Tap* and *Stand by Me*. Columbia Pictures (then owned by Coca-Cola) had been a major investor and owned 44 percent of Castle Rock. Columbia distributed Castle Rock films in exchange for a percentage of the domestic box office. Castle Rock paid for and controlled its own marketing.

The arrangement was paying off handsomely for Columbia. Castle Rock had scored in 1989 with *When Harry Met Sally . . . ,* Reiner's hit comedy about the war between the sexes starring Billy Crystal and Meg Ryan, which grossed $93 million. Reiner followed up the next year with his thriller *Misery,* which brought in $62 million and won a best actress Oscar for Kathy Bates. The company was showing that it could crank out movies that were commercial but not crass.

Guber had acknowledged Castle Rock's importance as soon as he took the helm at the studio, driving over to the company's Maple Drive offices to pay his compliments. From then on, he would phone in periodically from the Sony jet, his voice fuzzy, to inquire, "Are you okay? Is everything all right? We love you guys! We love you!"

Columbia netted $16 million on *City Slickers*. Castle Rock was

314

Columbia's most valuable provider of product, helping to fill its pipeline with a couple of releases a year.

Guber and his top lieutenants were enjoying a retreat in Santa Barbara on Friday, July 12, when *Boyz N the Hood* opened. The executives were horrified to hear that the film's debut was marred by violence: thirty-three people were injured and two killed in fighting among gang members at theaters around the country. Other recent urban dramas which had also appealed to gangs, including *New Jack City* and *Colors,* had spawned similar violent incidents.

Columbia called a press conference on Saturday at the Four Seasons Hotel in Beverly Hills. Neither Guber nor Price attended; John Singleton, the director of *Boyz,* and Mark Gill, senior vice president of publicity, faced the press by themselves. Reporters questioned why the studio brass did not feel compelled to show up, given the fact that two people had died at the opening of a Columbia film.

The *Boyz* marketing campaign came under fire for featuring some television spots emphasizing the violent nature of the film. In truth, Columbia's advertising was well within industry norms for targeting an urban audience, and had stressed the hopeful nature of the movie. At the press conference, Gill announced that Columbia would pay to increase security at any theater that requested it. Singleton said he did not feel responsible for the violence because "I didn't create the conditions in which people just shoot each other."

The controversy didn't hurt business. *Boyz* became a sleeper hit. The picture, which cost only $6 million, grossed $55 million and netted more than $35 million—far more than Columbia had dared hope. *Boyz* became the highest-grossing black-themed movie in Hollywood history. Soon everyone was claiming credit for the picture—Jon Peters and Frank Price both congratulated themselves for recognizing Singleton's genius—despite its tragic opening weekend.

Frank Price could only briefly savor the success of *Boyz.* In August he was clobbered by audience indifference to *Return to the Blue Lagoon*—on which Columbia took a $13 million hit. He fared better in August with *Double Impact,* a career stretch for action star Jean-Claude Van Damme in which the action star hilariously attempted to act. The movie netted the studio $6 million.

Meanwhile, TriStar scored a triumph thanks to Carolco—

and a master stroke by Guber, not Medavoy. Carolco had already delivered three pictures to the studio for distribution that year. Steve Martin's *L.A. Story* was a modest success, and Terry Gilliam's *The Fisher King,* starring Robin Williams as a homeless man, netted $18 million in profit for Sony. Oliver Stone's *The Doors,* however, had lost money.

Guber's slam-dunk was made possible because Carolco was experiencing financial woes. During production of James Cameron's sequel to *The Terminator,* starring Arnold Schwarzenegger, Carolco had suffered a cash shortage.

Guber saw a rough cut of the movie and agreed to pour in a substantial sum—more than $30 million, according to one studio source—to finish it. Sony gained generous terms from Carolco and made more than $65 million on *Terminator 2,* which grossed more than $200 million in the United States and ended up being the number-one movie of the year.

Medavoy's picks didn't do nearly as well. *Another You,* a $26 million comedy starring Gene Wilder and an ailing Richard Pryor, opened in July. A resounding bomb, the film lost more than $23 million, according to studio documents. A second Medavoy pet project, *Bingo,* a comedy about a dog, barked in August. Medavoy had green-lit the movie with Matthew Robbins as director even though some TriStar executives warned him that he was making a mistake. With a budget of $10 million, Medavoy had considered the risk minimal. The studio, which had expected to net a tidy $13 million, didn't make a dime.

TriStar executives were growing frustrated, complaining that Medavoy was passive, bedazzled by stars, and uninterested in developing compelling material. And all of his time was spent on his swankest project, *Hook.*

IN SEPTEMBER 1991, Guber felt a need to rally the troops. He invited his top executives to a luxurious weekend retreat, where sessions for discussing management issues would be interspersed with recreational activities. Guber gathered Frank Price, Mike Medavoy, Jon Dolgen, and Alan Levine together with some television executives and staff members and flew them on the company jet to his Aspen ranch. Spouses were invited.

316

The retreaters were driven through Mandalay's imposing iron gates and ushered into the rustic wood-and-glass living room with its spectacular views of the mountains and Owl Creek. Almost immediately, they were showered with paraphernalia.

"Everybody got monogrammed blue-jean jackets that said 'Sony' on them," says one former television executive. "Everybody got T-shirts with the name of Peter's ranch on them: Mandalay. We got shoes—that was a new one on me—white leather tennis shoes with 'Sony' written on the tongue of the shoe. Every day was like Christmas. Nobody could believe it." (Frank Price remembers that the denim jackets said "aSPEn," a play on the location and the initials of Sony Pictures Entertainment.)

One executive's amazement grew when he explored Guber's house. "The gym must have twenty Lifecycles in it," he says. "It could take fifteen, twenty people easily at any one time. He had a storeroom with clothes—parkas, T-shirts, khaki pants, gloves, socks—in every imaginable size and color. You could arrive there basically naked and you'd be wardrobed."

Then the group got down to what the executive calls "the New Age, touchy-feely stuff." Guber used "a facilitator and a lot of est personal relationship stuff," according to another participant. "We'd all line up tablets listing personal and company goals." The facilitator was Doug Kruschke of the In Synergy Company, who led the executives in exercises to help improve interpersonal relationships and solve administrative conflicts.

Price decided to take it all in stride. "It was not a budget review or anything like that. It was on a higher plane," he says with a bemused smile. "I felt this is not a bad thing. The cynic strikes first and then you back up and say, 'What the hell? Why not?' It's 95 percent bullshit, but the 5 percent that's productive, one can look at and say, 'That wouldn't have happened had it not been for this meeting.' "

Speculation about Frank Price's fate had now become a deafening roar: The issue was discussed openly in newspaper accounts. During the retreat Price and Guber seemed to be on reasonable terms, engaging in the type of male-bonding games that Guber liked. The two men drove around the property at breakneck speed in four-wheel-drive vehicles. Price could easily have convinced himself that the rumors about his firing were groundless. Others weren't so sanguine. 317

"It was so apocalyptic to me," says one of those in attendance. "Frank Price's neck is hanging by a thread and we're up in Aspen with the facilitators. This is supposed to be a 'safe' place—everyone should feel they can ask questions. But the one big question was, 'Are you going to ice Frank Price?' "

When everyone got back to Los Angeles, Price continued to dangle in a particularly hideous and public manner. Agents and producers were reluctant to take projects to him. Price and his lieutenants had some promising films in the hopper: *A League of Their Own* and *Bram Stoker's Dracula.* "They should be lining up to give me medals instead of writing stories that I'm on the way out," he lamented bitterly at the time. But when a concerned Columbia executive visited him in his office to commiserate, Price was philosophical. "Part of the job is the public humiliation at the end," he said.

In early September, the news broke that Mark Canton was out as executive vice president of worldwide production at Warner. After doing battle to bind Guber and Peters to their contract, Warner had decided to let Canton out fifteen months before his deal expired. Clearly, Warner chiefs Bob Daly and Terry Semel didn't feel threatened by the idea that Canton might join a competitor. In announcing his departure, the normally reticent Daly mustered a few kind words about Canton, but he also commented, "From our standpoint, this was a job that was going to be eliminated."

"Mark will be the only one from the group who will never come back to the Warner lot," a Warner insider said later. "Over Terry Semel's dead body will that happen. . . . These guys are laughing that they put him there. They feel they've completely disarmed Columbia as a competitor."

The announcement of Canton's departure stunned Columbia. Jon Peters had been promising Mark a big job at the studio from the start and Guber had gone along. It had been easy for Guber to schmooze with Canton about bringing him to Sony as long as he could assume that Warner wouldn't let him go. Now Bob Daly and Terry Semel had dropped Canton into Guber's lap.

"Peter got pregnant, and he thought he had a birth-control device," says a former Columbia executive. Perhaps that explains why Sony executives had been so vehement during the preceding weeks in denying that Canton was headed to Columbia. It was presumed that Warner, in a nose-thumbing gesture, deliberately announced Canton's exit before Columbia could sew up its arrangements. Now, there was only silence from Sony. "Warner Bros. shocked the shit out of this studio by issuing a statement today," one Columbia executive said.

There was a perception that Sony was petrified at the prospect of another high-visibility buy-out of an executive's contract. Guber tried to avoid an embarrassment by pushing Canton in a different direction. "Peter tried unbelievably hard to convince Mark to become vice chairman of the [studio]," says one high-level insider. "Mark was either smart enough or silly enough to say, 'Well, that's the kind of job I'm just leaving. You know, I have no real responsibility. Why should I do that job? I want to be chairman of Columbia.' At that point, Peter was stuck—with who he is as a person."

Negotiations got under way over Price's role at the studio if Canton should come aboard. The talks included Schulhof and Levine; two lawyers representing Price; and Michael Ovitz, who hoped to broker a face-saving solution for his longtime ally. Ovitz's idea seemed to be that Price should become chairman while Canton reported to him as president. But Canton would not agree to that.

As the press picked up on the embarrassing stalemate and ran with it, Schulhof for once tried to distance himself. When pressed by the *New York Times* about the spectacle, he responded tersely, "Sony Pictures is managed by Peter Guber. I have no comment to make."

Finally, Guber appeared in Price's office and told him that he had "great respect" for him and wanted him to stay in the Sony family forever. Price didn't understand that compliments from Guber often meant bad news. Later, Price realized that Guber never said he wanted him to stay on as head of Columbia. In the end, Price's lawyer, Barry Hirsch, broke the news to him that the company wanted him out. He had held the job only eighteen months, and during that brief time, presided over the release of seven movies. The high note was *Boyz N the Hood*. The low notes were obscure losers like *Falling From Grace*, *The Inner Circle*, and his beloved *Return to the Blue Lagoon*.

On October 2, before any official announcements had been made, Price began sending faxes to the media that included his résumé and a slate of films that he planned to make as an independent producer. Blindsided again, Sony executives

319

initially assured reporters that there would be no press release regarding Price that day. Then the studio reversed itself and admitted that Columbia's chairman was out.

Price hardly walked away empty-handed. His settlement was estimated to be $20 million—a handsome payment considering that Guber and Peters had fully expected to replace him when they had hired him. Price soon started producing films for the ill-fated Savoy Pictures, a company founded by former Columbia Pictures chairman Victor Kaufman. But Price nursed a lingering resentment that he had been unfairly tarred.

Sony was mortified by the incident, too. News reports noted that Sony had previously paid off Walter Yetnikoff and Jon Peters for many millions. Some accounts were straightforward; others weren't. "The hottest sport in Hollywood is Sony Lotto —a get-rich-quick scheme in which the lucky player is fired by the studio in exchange for a fortune," joked saucy *Spy* magazine. "Mickey Schulhof seems oblivious to the fact that Hollywood snickers at him for authorizing huge severance checks to sacked executives."

A reporter in Tokyo asked Morita about these expensive sayonaras, but the Sony chairman shrugged it off. "That's always going on in Hollywood," he said. "It's no problem."

BUT MORITA'S public nonchalance sounded hollow. The truth was that on the second anniversary of its purchase of the film studios, Sony's Tokyo bosses could hardly have felt like blowing out candles. *Variety* ran a birthday assessment in September entitled "Sony's Twins Hit Terrible Twos." The piece reported that the parent company's investment in its film operations had topped $6 billion—and that its ten-year master plan for achieving synergy was thus far a very expensive fantasy.

"Sony has made it clear to the senior executives in meetings here and in Tokyo that they want results," *Variety* quoted a high-level insider as saying. "They are long-term in their outlook, but after two years they want to see something tangible." *Variety* also took Sony Pictures to task for the "imperial disdain" of its shoguns. Guber was chastised for being elusive and creating a confusing chain of command. "If Guber has a master plan, it is not clear at this point."

Sony Pictures' financial news was not good. Its overhead was now steaming along at $300 million a year. While the film unit's losses were offset by profits in television and music, the entertainment operations were struggling to break even. Meanwhile, the company needed to produce about $500 million in cash flow just to cover its debt.

"We are not debt-ridden," Schulhof told *Variety*. "We are financially prudent. And I believe it is prudent to finance future growth with debt." In a separate interview Schulhof told the *Wall Street Journal* that the company was pleased with both management and results at Sony Pictures. The article cited SPE's big market share—an argument that Sony would repeatedly raise in its own defense, even though anyone with the most basic understanding of the business knew that market share had nothing to do with profitability. Obviously, a studio that spent lavishly and released a lot of films could grab a big chunk of market share and still not make money.

Despite Schulhof's claim that the company was comfortable with a certain amount of debt, Sony was trying to lessen its load. But executives in Tokyo got more bad news when Sony's attempts to raise money were met with a sharp rebuff. The company was reportedly looking to raise as much as $3 billion in Japan and the United States to cut debt and raise capital for its growing entertainment empire.

Sony intended to raise about $800 million by selling a 25 percent stake in the Japanese unit of Sony Music. In November 1991, the new shares went on sale in Tokyo—and bombed. Sony was insulated, having already sold most of the stock to investors before it was listed. But Sony's profits were deteriorating and investors apparently were getting nervous. Sony seemed "desperate to raise money," said analyst Boris Petersik.

Michael Jeremy of Baring Securities saw "a huge vote of no-confidence going on in Sony." Peter Wolff, an analyst in Kidder Peabody's Tokyo office, said that he suspected that the money that had been raised would "be moved to the parent to help relieve its high interest payments."

Sony still had hopes of raising as much as $2 billion in the United States. But when the company sent an emissary to ask a leading entertainment industry investor about the prospects for selling 20 percent of the studio to the public in the United States, the answer wasn't encouraging. For starters, he told them, they would have to fire Peter Guber before he would invest a penny.

321

"Everything they were doing was loony," the investor explained later. "All they kept doing was hiring people. They stacked up overhead like cords of wood. They needed to have a massive purge. Then you could probably [have gotten] Wall Street excited." Sony Pictures, he concluded, was "a runaway train."

Evidently, Sony didn't find much reason to hope that it would fare better in the United States than it had at home. The idea of a public offering was shelved.

# 25

## "AQABA! AQABA!"

IN THE SUMMER OF 1991, one of the biggest attractions in Tinseltown was the pirate ship constructed for the set of *Hook*. Security guards were posted at the door to Stage 27, which sheltered the full-size *Jolly Roger*, surrounded by wharves and shanties. This was the playground of Steven Spielberg, an elfin Robin Williams in green tights, and Dustin Hoffman wearing a frilly shirt and an ominous steel hook.

The set became an E-ticket ride, the chic place for Hollywood insiders to go for an unofficial tour. Mike Medavoy hosted a steady stream of visitors, from Warren Beatty and Kevin Costner to Queen Noor and the artist who was then still known as Prince. Bruce Willis came to have a look just days after an interview in the *Los Angeles Times* had quoted him saying that it was Hollywood unions, rather than big-star salaries, that made movies so expensive. When Willis set foot on the *Hook* set, someone—presumably a card-carrying union member in the crew—threw water on him from the rafters. When the star returned to his car he found that it had been pelted with human spittle.

The high cost of *Hook* certainly could not be blamed on unions. *Hook* was an expensive, star-stuffed package, with a staggering 40 percent of the potential gross promised in advance to Spielberg, Williams, and Hoffman. In many ways, this was the quintessential Sony "event" picture in the making. It sounded great on paper but it suffered from bloat. A year before the picture was released, the *Wall Street Journal* had posed the question: "Weighted down with a huge budget, will this version of 'Peter Pan' fly?"

All film executives dread publicity about the high cost of a picture, but Medavoy described the project as "a slam dunk." Just about any studio chief would have been happy to make an early splash with a Spielberg project—and Medavoy was overjoyed. There was talk about spin-off toys and publishing projects. Jon Peters had wanted to use some of the spectacular *Hook* sets as a basis for an attraction at the Sonyland theme park.

Spielberg—the man who had kept Jon and Peter off the *Color Purple* set a few years earlier—called his own shots. As the cost of *Hook* began to mount, it became apparent that the original $50 million budget was a fantasy. Spielberg regretted the overruns, Medavoy said, but couldn't figure out how to do the movie, whose spectacular flying sequences required costly special effects, more cheaply. And Medavoy, too, was helpless. "I don't think there's anybody who's going to tell Steven Spielberg how to direct a movie," he said.

*Hook* producer Kathleen Kennedy says Medavoy handled a difficult situation gracefully. "He never became hysterical," she says. "He always tried to understand the problems of making a movie of that size. He was definitely worried and definitely concerned. But he wasn't about to go in and start screaming and yelling at Steven."

As the film's budget soared past $80 million, Medavoy seemed distracted from his TriStar duties. Other projects languished. "He couldn't and wouldn't focus on anything other than *Hook,*" a former insider says. "Everything was, 'Let's talk about it next week.' He was playing the role of showing everyone around the *Hook* set."

Guber was rarely seen around Spielberg's *Jolly Roger* during the making of the film. Jon Dolgen made a last-minute effort to demand cost containment. But even Dolgen, known as one of the great hardball players, couldn't stem the rising budget. His interference only annoyed the already-tense Spielberg team. Sony finally got a little relief from Mike Ovitz, who renegotiated the three stars' deals to reduce TriStar's exposure.

WITH MEDAVOY consumed by *Hook,* Canton was moving into his new office in the Thalberg Building. The addition of Canton to Sony's executive ranks did nothing to clear up the confusion of everyone in Hollywood, including those inside the company, about the chain of command at Sony Pictures. No one knew who could green-light a movie; no one had a clear idea of what Alan Levine, Sid Ganis, and Jon Dolgen were supposed to do. "Dolgen was supposed to oversee long-term planning and he's running business affairs," said one producer on the lot. "What is the strategy there?"

Now Canton was dismayed by press accounts that marred his triumph by emphasizing his status as Guber's tennis buddy over his achievements at Warner. "Our friendship is not based on some of these foolish indications that have been printed in the press like playing tennis together," Canton told an interviewer. "We've only played four times."

Canton evaded questions about his autonomy as the new chairman of Columbia, saying that while that was "important to a degree," he hoped his role at the studio would be "extremely collaborative."

At forty-two, Canton was twenty years younger than Price, and *Daily Variety* obligingly portrayed him as "hip, high-energy, aggressive and trend-conscious." But industry wags weren't as generous. Jokes made the rounds, including one about a guy who falls off a ten-story building only to slide down an awning and land on a truckload of featherbeds. "You must be the luckiest man in the world!" a passer-by exclaims.

"No, that would be Mark Canton," the man replies.

Others referred to him as "the Dan Quayle of the movie business."

"This guy does not name-drop, he name-*drips,*" one journalist wrote.

When a reporter asked Canton whether it bothered him that Price was viewed in some quarters as a corporate martyr, Mark replied in pure Canton-speak. "It's not important if it bothers me, because I don't know if it bothers me," he said. But Canton vowed that Price would be "dealt the respect he deserves."

Canton had reason to praise his predecessor. Overall, 1991 was shaping up as a terrible year for the movie business. Summer box office had been 25 percent lower than 1990—the lowest since 1971. Panic seized the industry. But Price had left a couple of films in the pipeline for Columbia's holiday season that would make Canton look good.

*My Girl,* an Imagine project that featured *Home Alone*'s young star Macaulay Culkin and Anna Chlumsky, opened on November 27. Culkin had been paid $1 million to appear in a small and potentially problematic role. Guber had watched a rough 325 cut and worried about a long sequence in which Culkin is stung by a bee—and dies. While producer Brian Grazer and director

Howard Zieff thought the sequence should be protracted in slow motion, Guber worried that it would upset children in the audience. He believed the scene should end quickly.

"He advised us to cut ten minutes," Grazer says. "He was right." Guber, ever the cunning promoter, also knew that Culkin's death would generate a spate of publicity about the hazards of bee stings. He elected to open the picture on as many screens as possible to capitalize on the buzz. Meanwhile, newcomer Canton contributed the film's slogan: "Mac Is Back." The picture, which cost a modest $16.5 million, earned a superb $17 million in its opening weekend and ultimately brought the studio $33 million in profit.

Columbia's Christmas release was Streisand's keenly anticipated *The Prince of Tides*. The director-star had finished the film for $32 million—about $4 million over budget and just above the industry average. She had spent many months meticulously editing and mixing her film. For much of this time, Guber had been pressing production executive Gareth Wigan to convince Streisand to record a theme song for the end credits. But Barbra had just as steadfastly resisted the studio's entreaties. "If you ended with a song, to me it was so out of whack," she says. "I said, 'I'm tired of singing for my supper.' It's like, I always have to sing. Why? You mean the movie isn't enough?"

Streisand did record "For All We Know"—a song that plays in the film while she dances with Nick Nolte at the Rainbow Room—along with another number for the soundtrack. But she didn't want her recording used in the final credits because she thought it would detract from the focus on Nolte's character. "It's his story," she says. "It could have been a nice marketing tool and it could have gotten a best song nomination. But I felt it was overkill."

Nevertheless, she came up with four different versions of the ending, with and without the song, and solicited advice from her friends about which to use. Guber came to the dubbing stage where she was working and watched the four alternatives. After all his exhortations, he abruptly agreed with Streisand. "You definitely shouldn't sing the song," he said.

Jon Peters, *The Prince of Tides*'s champion, didn't see the finished film until he attended a studio preview. When the lights came on, a Columbia executive glanced over at him. "He was completely in tears," that executive remembers. "He sat with his head down for several minutes."

The film opened on Christmas Day. Jon was hurt that Guber did not invite him to the Los Angeles premiere—but Streisand expressed her gratitude for his support by asking him to be her escort.

*The Prince of Tides* won critical acclaim and was a solid hit, making a $20 million profit for Columbia. Jon Peters's faith in Streisand had been justified. The studio began to entertain hopes of Oscars for this melodramatic literary adaptation.

While the star-turned-auteur was savoring her triumph, she remained as finicky as ever. On New Year's Day, 1992, at 7:00 A.M., a Columbia executive received a call from a livid Streisand, who was spending the holiday in Aspen. Friends had told her the night before that hedges had grown up below a huge *Prince of Tides* billboard on Sunset Boulevard. Her name was still visible in the star's billing above the title, but her director's credit at the bottom was obscured. Without any New Year's greeting, she let loose: "It's Barbra! My name is in the bushes!"

By 10:00 A.M., Sony had defused the crisis, placating Streisand by dispatching a worker with a weed whacker to the site.

CHRISTMAS 1991 was upon him and Mike Medavoy had his hands full. He had spent so much time on *Hook* that Warren Beatty and Barry Levinson were becoming increasingly irate as they toiled on *Bugsy*. Each had an outsized ego and they worried that they weren't getting enough attention from the studio. Several TriStar sources said the marketing department labored mightily on *Bugsy*—finally giving it even more time than *Hook*—but Beatty and Levinson were relentless. "Warren and Barry would complain that they weren't getting any attention, that the [marketing] material was late," says a former executive. "The marketing department was losing its mind. Warren was being abusive: 'You're late on everything and you're not as good as Disney.' " (Beatty had been lavished with attention when he made *Dick Tracy* there.)

Beatty indulged in big-star whims. Photo shoots for the *Bugsy* poster were canceled no fewer than seven times because the star didn't show up. Each time TriStar had to pay big bills for personnel who arrived expecting to work. "They spent more on canceled photo shoots than some independents spend on movies," fumed one Columbia executive. The eighth time, the studio decided to entice Beatty with a copious buffet. Notoriously fretful about food, Beatty gave particular instructions about everything, even specifying how the vegetables were to be sliced. But this was no simple platter of crudités: for a session involving about a dozen people, the tab came to $40,000. In the end, more than $1 million was spent on still photographs alone; some of the world's most famous glamour photographers, including Herb Ritts, George Hurrell, and Patrick DeMarchelier, were hired in search of the best shot. Only the Ritts shots were ultimately used in the marketing campaign.

Meanwhile, the buzz on *Bugsy* was only lukewarm. Disney had bombed big with *Billy Bathgate,* and *Bugsy,* which cost $43 million, was perceived as another gangster movie at a time when the genre seemed to be out of favor. Then there were questions about whether Beatty, at fifty-six, still had leading-man magic.

As speculation about the fates of *Hook* and *Bugsy* intensified, Guber publicly defended the studio. "This is going to be the best Christmas ever in the history of the company!" he told a reporter emphatically enough to merit an exclamation point. At that year's employee Christmas party, held on the *Hook* set, he swung into his *Lawrence of Arabia* inspirational mode. Standing on the prow of the *Jolly Roger,* he raised his fist aloft and invited the staff to join him as he called out: "Aqaba! Aqaba!"

But the news stories inevitably focused on costs. The scrutiny coincided with the Sony Corporation's floundering cash-raising efforts. There was speculation that a successful Christmas at the box office might salvage Sony's plan to raise money in the U.S. stock market. The pressure mounted. "This is a critical juncture," said Hal Vogel, an analyst with Merrill Lynch in New York.

As it happened, *Hook* would neither make nor break the studio. It opened December 11 and went on to gross $119 million domestically, a figure that the studio had certainly hoped to surpass. The film performed well overseas, and based on its star power, TriStar had sold it to network television for a generous $10 million. Eventually Sony made at least $25 million profit. While hardly a bomb, *Hook* wasn't a cash cow, either: It didn't provide a burst of revenue that would cover other flops. And a big one was about to open in a few days.

328     For Medavoy, the headaches were just beginning. He set off a frenzy when he took off for a holiday vacation with his wife, Patricia, in Egypt just days after *Bugsy*'s premiere. The film-

makers were left fretting in Los Angeles over their movie's faltering performance.

"We had a lot of high-powered people and everybody was upset when Medavoy was gone at Christmastime," says a source from the *Bugsy* camp. The TriStar executives "didn't have a bunker mentality," he continues. "They weren't watching every figure, every movie house, every piece of publicity, ready to make a change. That place was shut down. Mike was out of town at a critical, crucial period."

Matters got worse when, in Medavoy's absence, Beatty called Guber to complain. Peter, always fastidious in avoiding unpleasantness, was furious. "Medavoy was floating down the Nile incommunicado," says a TriStar source. "That was the final straw with Peter. He was berserk that that's where Mike was. Peter had to get involved when he felt he shouldn't have."

Meanwhile, the morose Medavoy wasn't exactly having the time of his life. "We wound up on the worst boat on the Nile," he complained later. "The first night they had a cross-dressing party. A bunch of German and Spanish tourists were on board. Everything that could have gone wrong did. My wife's luggage didn't arrive. It was a nightmare." But he maintained that the trip didn't harm *Bugsy* or *Hook*. "If I had to do it all over, I wouldn't have done anything differently," he said. "I got faxes and I was talking to them on the phone and there's nothing, frankly, that I couldn't do from where I was. I certainly couldn't go out and hawk tickets." *Bugsy* ultimately grossed only $45 million, losing Sony more than $30 million.

After this episode, Medavoy began to feel that he was losing Guber's confidence. Peter never actually addressed the issue with him, yet something had changed. "I just felt uneasy," he said.

Medavoy finished up the year with a mixed report card. He defended his bombs, claimed that the studio would eventually make money on *Hudson Hawk* (the film that lost $42 million), and called his year "successful." But he couldn't claim too much credit for the bright spots in the studio's performance. Faltering Carolco, the independent company that had put *Terminator 2* into TriStar's pipeline, had provided well over half of the studio's receipts in 1991.

# 26

# NUMBER ONE
# AT THE BOX OFFICE

THE NEWS AT SONY headquarters in Tokyo was very grim. The electronics giant's sales, which had more than doubled to nearly $30 billion over the previous five years, had hit a wall. The company was projecting an operating loss for the fiscal year ending in March 1992 of about $160 million. Its operating income had declined 45 percent over the previous year. Ken Iwaki, then widely (but mistakenly) viewed as the heir to Norio Ohga, was selected to address the issue in interviews with the *New York Times* and the *Wall Street Journal*—the papers with clout in the financial markets. "Until last summer, Sony was aggressively preparing for growth," he said. "Then we saw the storm clouds gathering. Now, it's raining a bit."

And the skies didn't seem likely to clear quickly. A worldwide recession was under way and Sony, which sold 62 percent of its merchandise overseas, was hit hard. The company made plans to trim capital spending by $500 million in the coming year. No more factories were to be built. Schulhof, the guardian of the software flame, made a striking turnabout and admitted that things hadn't quite gone as planned. "Quite frankly," he told a reporter for the *New York Times,* "there have not been many software-hardware synergies."

In another blow to Sony and its dreams of synergy, high-definition television was pronounced dead. It was painfully clear that Japanese companies had spent billions of yen on a system that had been outmoded before it was even perfected. Accordingly, the expensive high-definition production facility in Culver City—which Guber used to show off to visitors—

would not be used to produce must-see software that would in turn fuel demand for Sony-manufactured HDTV sets.

In Japan, Sony's large high-definition television plant was retooled for conventional television. Meanwhile, Matsushita was off to the races, selling a new model of big brilliant-screen TVs. "We had the technology but we were not first," Iwaki lamented. "Matsushita made a big hit and we were not first."

Digital audio tape also had not found acceptance in the marketplace. Sales of Sony's 8-millimeter Camcorder—a huge hit in the late eighties that had fueled the company's expansion —fell sharply just as Sony was preparing to increase production. Sony sorely needed a new hardware hit.

Sony's struggles gave rival Matsushita an opportunity to twit it in the press. Shoji Sakuma, a Matsushita executive, stated publicly that Sony had been somewhat lucky with its earlier successes. "Sony was too good," he said. To which Iwaki could only reply weakly that, indeed, Matsushita had recently "really hit Sony across the board."

Sony's candor didn't last. Just a few months after he had conceded that the hoped-for synergies had not materialized, Schulhof flip-flopped back to defending the concept. In an interview, he declared that the links between hardware and software were "tangible." Rather than acknowledging that the expensive high-definition television facilities were a fiasco, he argued, preposterously, that the studio was planning to make movies with the HDTV equipment. He offered other examples: Michael Jackson was so excited by the upcoming miniature compact disc, Schulhof pointed out, that he had asked to work on the promotional campaign. Francis Ford Coppola, working out of his famous Silver Bullet trailer on the Sony lot, was using a Sony electronic camera, the Mavica, to plot out the story line of the upcoming *Dracula*.

None of these "synergies" could begin to pay back the company's torrential outflow of money—but apparently they were the best Schulhof could muster.

AT THIS UNHAPPY JUNCTURE in Sony's corporate life, the software division almost seemed to be a consolation. At an annual reception in Tokyo, Ohga spoke for fifteen minutes, barely mentioning the hardware business. Instead, he boasted about Sony's 20 percent market share, the release of *Hook*, the reviews that praised *The Prince of Tides*. Sony executives in Japan seemed to cling to whatever good news they could get. Indeed, it looked as if Sony's much-disparaged film studio might turn into a source of pride after all. *Hook* could be claimed as a hit and the holiday season had truly been enlivened by *My Girl* and *The Prince of Tides*.

"We finished the year in first place with twenty-four films," crowed Guber. "When we came here three years ago, the combined companies had released thirty-seven films for a total market share of 9.3 percent—dead last among the majors." As he often did, he marshaled a fleet of statistics that served his purposes, including eight Golden Globe nominations for *Bugsy* and four pictures that broke the $100 million barrier in 1991. As usual, none of these measures had anything to do with profitability.

The market share boasts did little to improve Sony's image in Hollywood, and Wall Street wasn't impressed either. Industry analyst Emanuel Gerard was still skeptical. "You can buy market share. You can't buy profits," he declared with indisputable logic. "At the rate Sony is losing money, and at the rate they have fixed their costs, they can't really talk about anything but market share."

Sony's total entertainment operations projected that operating income was up 14.3 percent, to $845 million for fiscal 1992. But those results revealed little about the fiscal health of the studio, because Sony lumped in income from the profitable music division. Also, there was a one-time-only bulge in income from the sale of *Married . . . With Children* into syndication. This could mean profits of as much as $100 million, but such results wouldn't be repeated. And despite heavy spending, Sony still had no prime-time hits to fuel its television operations. The studio was still a cash drain.

In a February 1992 interview, Ohga confided that he was "a little bit afraid" about the amounts being spent in Hollywood. His anxiety undoubtedly deepened as the post-holiday movies began rolling out. After some small-scale failures at the beginning of the year (*Falling From Grace*, *The Inner Circle*, and *Under Suspicion*), Columbia faced disaster with *Radio Flyer* in February. Jon Peters's pet project about child abuse may have been an impossible challenge: It sought to blend fantasy elements such as a flying machine and a talking buffalo with the realistic portrayal of a father beating his two young sons. The movie had been test-screened more than a dozen times for high school students with poor results. The coda with Tom Hanks playing the older boy as an adult left audiences baffled. "If you're ever going to confuse an audience," director Richard Donner admitted, "we really did it then." But even after the ending had been excised, the movie left viewers cold.

All attempts to fix the movie proved futile: *Radio Flyer* was a massive, embarrassing, high-profile flop that would lose a staggering $43 million.

It was quickly followed in March by Frank Price's long-nurtured boxing movie, *Gladiator,* a black hole into which more than $20 million vanished. Everyone had expected the worst for *Radio Flyer,* but the failure of *Gladiator* was an unpleasant surprise. When the movie bombed, there was disarray and finger-pointing at the studio—amid reports that Paula Silver, head of Columbia's marketing, or Jimmy Spitz, president of domestic distribution, would be fired. The studio had tried to generate excitement about *Gladiator* by giving it 120 sneak previews in various cities and offering thousands of free copies of its soundtrack. But the ad campaign had failed to target its core action audience: one poster depicted the two leads, Cuba Gooding, Jr., and James Marshall, from the chest up, with nothing to suggest that the film was about boxing.

The picture was cut down on its opening weekend by Stephen King's *The Lawnmower Man.* Columbia executives took further heat for not being aware that rival New Line had moved up the release date of that film so that it would go head-to-head with *Gladiator.* Eventually, both Silver and Spitz lost their jobs.

"I could see the stormclouds gathering," Spitz says. Sure enough, Sid Ganis, who at the time was still serving Guber in a vaguely defined job, called him in one day and told him he was out. "The next day, Peter called me," Spitz remembers. "He was almost Solomon-like. He said, 'Sony is a large company. I don't think you should make any precipitous moves. Maybe there's a place for you.' He was very solicitous and complimentary."

Spitz went home and told his wife what had happened. Then he called a friend, a top executive at another company, and told him what Guber had said. "What kind of bullshit is that?" his friend demanded. "Peter wants you gone. He had nothing

333

in mind for you. He's non-confrontational and he wants you to leave without rancor."

The next day, Guber asked to see Spitz again, and advised him to take a legal pad, make a list of all the things he wanted to do with his life, and describe how he envisioned himself. "If there are any problems with your settlement, call me," he said.

"It was as if he was saying, 'I've done my bit, I've done all the nice things,' " Spitz says. Spitz was bought off with a consulting arrangement and an office on the lot.

AT THE BEGINNING OF 1992, Guber-Peters Entertainment Company, the company that Guber had kept intact as a possible escape vehicle, was finally dissolved. It had one film, *Single White Female*, waiting to be released. Stacey Snider, the Guber protégée who ran the unit, had acquired *Mary Reilly* for GPEC, a retelling of *Dr. Jekyll and Mr. Hyde* from the housekeeper's point of view, from Warner for $1.5 million. She had also picked up the film rights to Kazuo Ishiguro's novel *The Remains of the Day* for $850,000. These projects and dozens more were now folded into Columbia and TriStar.

Guber named Snider president of production at TriStar, where Medavoy was rapidly losing ground. Medavoy teamed her up with TriStar's new president, Marc Platt, a former executive at Orion. Now Platt and Snider, working as a team, seemed to supplant Medavoy—for whom neither had any particular regard. When Platt was working for Medavoy at Orion, he had made it clear to the brass there that he thought Medavoy was expendable.

If anyone thought the dissolution of Guber's old company meant he was prepared, at last, to commit to his job, they were wrong. In spring of 1992, Guber marshaled the facilitators for another retreat, this time in Sedona, Arizona. The event proved as disquieting to some who attended as the Aspen retreat, where the unresolved fate of Frank Price had disturbed the good vibrations. At Sedona, Peter staged another show of togetherness. First he distributed T-shirts emblazoned with his rallying cry, "Aqaba!" Then the group was transported by helicopter to a remote mesa, where lunch was served on white linens. Thirty participants, including Levine, Medavoy, Dolgen, and television head Mel Harris, were ferried to the site.

A former top executive at the studio describes the Sedona retreat as another "touchy-feely get-together." But the esprit de corps dissipated during a session in which participants were asked to tell about the forces that motivated them in life. "The first person to speak was Guber," the executive remembers. "And the first words out of his mouth were, 'Well, I'm a short-timer.' You've just brought thirty-some people together with a facilitator to have a bonding retreat—and the first thing your leader says is, 'I'm a temporary employee.' How do you think that sets the tone?"

THAT SPRING, sixty-two-year-old Norio Ohga would rise at two each morning and make his way to his study, where he studied Mendelssohn's "Scottish Symphony" and a work by Mozart. He was preparing to conduct with a Polish ensemble at a music festival in Germany in the summer. Music was still his first love. At five each morning, Ohga returned to his bed, usually to be awakened again with an early morning call from Schulhof. With the help of a computer, Schulhof was capable of remaining in touch with Ohga every minute of the day, even if Ohga was on a plane.

"I am a businessman," Ohga told an interviewer. "I make budgets, run divisions, project profits and sales. When I come back home, I make a big switch to being a musician." Ohga, who had undergone open-heart surgery the previous summer, didn't pretend that he had resolved his old ambivalence as he grew older. "Unfortunately, I am running this company," he complained. "I cannot find a successor. If I find a good successor I'll give him my title and become a conductor full time." Guber wasn't the only ambivalent Sony executive.

By now, there were rumors that Sony had ordered its free-spending studio to cut 30 percent from its 1992 budget. Earlier in the year, Guber and his lieutenants had met with the Tokyo shoguns at headquarters in New York, and while Sony denied that any formal cost-cutting orders were given, others said Ohga had laid down the law. Sony had refrained from interfering with the record company after buying it, but Sony board member Nobuyuki Idei now warned in an interview, "We will be less patient with Sony Pictures." 335

Despite that declaration, the Japanese appeared to have nothing but patience. In entertainment operations, they remained virtually invisible with the exception of Ken Hoshi-kawa, Tokyo's man in New York, and Ken Munekata in Los Angeles.

A television executive remembers just one occasion when Ohga and a covey of Japanese executives arrived for a tour of the television operation. "We took them over to see *Who's the Boss?* All they looked at were the cameras and who made the video tape and how much lead density it had," he remembers.

The same executive said his only other contact with high-level Japanese executives came at a meeting in Sony's New York offices. "They asked the most imbecilic questions," he says dismissively. "One guy said, 'What's the difference between the television business and the motion picture business?' This was after they owned the company for three and a half years. The differences are so fundamental, and the answers so long, that you wonder if they did any due diligence [before buying the studio] at all."

THE AWARDS SEASON was in full swing and Mark Canton—who arrived too late to have had a hand in nurturing any of the contenders—still yearned for accolades. Before the Golden Globe awards in January, he had implored Nick Nolte—a nominee in the best actor category for *The Prince of Tides*—to mention him in his thank-you speech if he won.

At the glittering gala in the Beverly Hilton Hotel ballroom, Nolte won—and Canton's face lit up. But when the actor delivered his acceptance speech, he didn't mention Canton. Mark appeared crestfallen, but only momentarily. He congratulated Nolte warmly, of course, and then immediately pressured Nolte's publicist and agent to get the star to mention him if he won an Academy Award.

*The Prince of Tides* was honored with seven Oscar nominations, including best actor and best picture. Yet Streisand was passed over in the best director category—a snub that many interpreted as proof of Hollywood's entrenched sexism. Others felt that Barbra was simply not warmly regarded by her peers because of her demanding personality, and that being a woman had nothing to do with it.

Nolte lost the Oscar to Anthony Hopkins for *The Silence of the Lambs,* the year's big winner. Despite an abundance of nominations, Sony took home few bronze statuettes. *Bugsy,* which desperately needed a boost at the box office, was nominated in ten categories but won only for art direction and costume design. *The Prince of Tides* was a shutout; *Hook* hadn't been nominated in any major category.

THE DISAPPOINTING showing at the Oscars was followed by alarming news. By spring, it was clear that Sony Pictures' financial difficulties were deepening. According to a high-level insider, Columbia had spent its entire development budget for the year within the first forty-five days. Jon Dolgen, who had been promoted to president of the Motion Picture Group, and was running the business sides of Columbia and TriStar, swung into action.

Giving Dolgen combined authority to run business affairs at TriStar and Columbia might have seemed like a move that would clarify the decision-making process. But the chain of command remained as confused as ever. Though Price and Medavoy now reported to Dolgen on financial matters, he wasn't supposed to exercise any power over the creative side.

When Guber gave him the promotion, he promised to renegotiate Dolgen's contract. But after the announcement, Guber said he couldn't make the new deal for another year. Dolgen decided to be patient. Despite the studio's general extravagance, Dolgen would have a long wait.

With his dark hair, bulky form, and light-colored but deepset eyes, Dolgen manifested an unsettling appearance and discomfiting gaze. It was useful to him in his work. The incisive if disrepectful *Spy* magazine described the forty-seven-year-old president of the motion picture group as "the perfect Jon Peters surrogate—loud, abrasive, opinionated and meddlesome, the kind of guy you don't want to sit near on an airplane, let alone work with."

Dolgen didn't care for this description, which he thought was based on long-forgotten episodes from his brash youth. But his reputation wasn't easy to shed. Subordinates were known to describe gut-wrenching encounters with him as being "Dolgenized." In his last job as president of Fox, he had been nicknamed "The Beast" and his office—a den fouled with cigarette smoke and junk-food wrappers—was known as "The House of Pain and Suffering." In the conference room of his office suite at Sony, he kept a five-foot-tall Louisville Slugger bat, a gift from two producers who sent it with an imploring note: "To a big hitter, just don't hit us."

Dolgen had made his name during a previous incarnation as a Columbia executive in 1984. Then he negotiated a deal to license such films as *Ghostbusters II* to HBO on such onerous terms that the fledgling cable company almost collapsed. (Frank Biondi, then running HBO, lost his job as a result.)

Despite his abrasive personality, Dolgen had a cadre of executives who remained loyal to him. "Dolgen is brilliant and a big pain in the tush," says former Columbia distribution executive Jimmy Spitz. "He's a classic bully. I loved him." Another executive appreciated Dolgen's finely tuned bullshit detector, which caused him to inveigh against the New Age mush that sometimes substituted for decision making at Sony.

Others were less affectionate. When one unwary Columbia attorney asked Dolgen to attend a 9:00 A.M. meeting, Dolgen —who disliked such morning meetings—reportedly told him to find another job. Dolgen liked to schedule staff meetings late, at 7:00 P.M., rather than during "billing hours." (His secretary at Fox used to buzz his staff when he finally left at nine to report, "Elvis has left the premises.")

When contradicted, he would warn bluntly, "You're playing in traffic." One former employee said Dolgen had thrown a thick binder notebook at him during a meeting when he couldn't provide some details in answer to a question. Another said he sought counseling after being repeatedly Dolgen-ized.

One Dolgen story that became legend held that during his first stint at Columbia, he had thrown a chair during a negotiation with HBO. Rob Fried, an executive who worked with Dolgen for many years at Columbia and Fox, says a frustrated Dolgen merely kicked the chair, which then tipped over.

When Dolgen went to Fox, he often joked that he finally got the boss he deserved. Barry Diller, then chairman of the studio, was well established as one of the toughest and most demanding executives in the industry. By Diller's standards, Dolgen wasn't that tough at all. "Jon's a very noisy and demonstrative executive and yet he has always had the loyalty of people that have worked for him," Diller says. "Jon's an impossible person but his impossibleness is somewhat lovable."

Rob Fried, after his years of working for Dolgen, is among his loyalists. "He's hard to work for because he works hard and he focuses on details," he says. "If you're unprepared or your thinking is incomplete, it can be intimidating. But I used to end every day in his office and I couldn't wait to get there. He's

338

funny and he's smart." Fried also says Dolgen took care of his staffers—once helping to find work for a down-on-his-luck former employee without even telling that person.

Now, Dolgen—who reportedly had warned facilitator-happy staffers at a corporate retreat that Sony Pictures Entertainment might actually spend itself to death—plunged into a frenzy of cost-cutting. The results were as plain to the show business community as Sony's previous profligacy had been. Funds were suddenly scarce for scripts and other purchases. Producers were told to take projects to Jon Peters, who was flush with his millions in discretionary money, thanks to his lush settlement.

The cost-cutting was imposed in other areas that had nothing to do with getting films on the screen. Dolgen now earned himself yet another nickname, "Draco," for the draconian measures he imposed as he slashed perks. Fresh flowers and fruit baskets in executive suites became a pleasant memory. So did the "design crews" that arrived to redecorate executive offices following any promotion, no matter how minor. Dolgen banned lavish premiere parties and the corporate jets were no longer to be used to indulge talent. "Sony went from being the most spending-oriented studio in the business to the tightest studio in the business," says a Columbia executive who was amused to observe that even Guber was answering to Dolgen on some financial matters.

Dolgen handed out quarterly budgets to executives at Columbia and TriStar. "It's amazing how tight those budgets were," says one who was stunned by the new fiscal constraints. "It was sort of like going from the Louvre to a pit in Bangladesh." Or to put it in terms more appropriate to the studio, he says, "It was like going from *The Age of Innocence* to *City of Joy* in one step." (The latter film depicted slums in India.)

The friction between Dolgen and Canton, who found himself all but hamstrung by Dolgenomics, was intense. Dolgen instituted a strict financial checklist for films awaiting approval. "Dolgen put together this model for [predicting] how movies would perform, including the most pessimistic possible version of what would happen," says a Columbia executive. "It was an accountant's dream and a filmmaker's nightmare." Any picture over $40 million had to be reviewed by Schulhof, who received a script, synopsis, and copy of the financial prediction. Mickey never vetoed any projects.

Getting a movie green-lit had always been a byzantine pro-

339

cess at Sony, but now it became downright tortuous. At most studios, the chairman simply exercised his ultimate authority to say yes or no—or delegated that power. But Guber was too insecure to take the reins and accept responsibility for his decisions. If a picture were to fail, he wanted to preserve his deniability. Green-lighting was now handled by a committee consisting of Guber, Levine, and Dolgen. One insider says the committee meetings were meaningless, like "kabuki theater" orchestrated in advance by Guber. And since Guber disliked making decisions, the committee still often left questions unresolved. Frustrated filmmakers found that they were left in limbo, often not knowing whether their projects were being held up for a reason or simply because of neglect.

Meanwhile, bills for script development went unpaid for months. When creative executives ran out of money early in the quarter, they were forced to stall writers and agents. "This is a guaranteed way to feel like you're out of business, to have every agent hate you," a former Columbia executive says. Indeed, several agents let it be known that Columbia had signaled that few deals would be made in the immediate future and that payments for contracts signed would be delayed. "They're on a very tight leash," one said.

Mark Canton, who had already made several expensive acquisitions, maintained that his door was still "wide open" for business at Columbia. Reports that no new films would start shooting before the end of the year were "baloney," he said. Before the money had gotten tight, he had picked up Martin Scorsese's adaptation of Edith Wharton's *The Age of Innocence* from Fox, which had balked at the $40 million cost. He intended to start production on the studio's first effort from James L. Brooks, a risky musical called *I'll Do Anything,* in September. And in October, shooting would begin on Columbia's big picture for the summer of 1993, *Last Action Hero.*

But producers say they were told there would be no outlays for developing projects in the latter half of 1992. Some asked the studio to let them know if their projects would be canceled, so they could try to sell them elsewhere. But the studio wouldn't comply, deepening filmmakers' frustration. As the year wore on and Dolgen's influence seemed to grow, some filmmakers with projects already in production even tried to ban him from their research screenings.

Dolgen also cut some fat from films that were already in the pipeline and trimmed marketing costs to an average of $15 million per movie. He clamped down wherever he could. *The Remains of the Day* was set up to be directed by Mike Nichols with Meryl Streep in the starring role; the budget would have topped $25 million. The expensive talent was excised and the film given to the thrifty Merchant-Ivory production team; it would wind up costing $15 million with Emma Thompson. In this case, the cost-cutting was wise. *The Remains of the Day* was based on a melancholy story about a repressed butler's unrequited love for his housekeeper. It was a prestige play for the studio, which didn't expect the film to have broad commercial appeal.

AUSTERITY MAY have been the watchword at the studio, but Guber's appetite for lush living seemed to escalate. By 1992 he appeared to have become more secure in his job as the chairman of Sony Pictures, and began to see that the possibilities for personal enrichment were even vaster than he once imagined. For the remainder of his tenure he would apply his ingenuity to negotiating improved perks and deal points for himself, making his job ever more lucrative.

A close friend of Guber's—who witnessed his maneuvers at Sony and refers to his m.o. as "rape and plunder"—believes Guber had every intention of building a successful company for Sony when he took the job. But the friend speculates that Guber's greed overwhelmed him once he saw the bounty that was there for the taking. "It was literally that someone opened the chicken house door, and Peter was outside waiting to get in. He'd been waiting for this his whole life."

Access to the chicken coop was controlled by Mickey Schulhof, of course. Schulhof buffered him from the Japanese bosses and acceded to his desires. Guber, ever fleet of tongue, fed Schulhof a stream of upbeat information on the studio's performance, assuring him that it would all turn out fine in the end. With so little experience in the movie business, Schulhof chose to believe what he was hearing. "Peter had Schulhof so co-opted, [Mickey] would buy into anything," says a Guber associate. "Peter was feeding Mickey weird, bizarre good news — *'We're doing great in Thailand!'*"

Guber was thoroughly enjoying the spoils of his position. He

341

and Lynda had taken on another construction project, renovating the two-bedroom house they had bought in May 1991 on Lausanne Drive in Bel Air. The location was just behind the Bel Air Hotel—a much posher address than their Brownwood home—allowing Peter to walk down a path to the hotel for a breakfast meeting. The purchase price of the house, which had previously belonged to television mogul Grant Tinker, was $7.2 million.

The Gubers did not have to deal with the hardship of putting their old house on Brownwood on the market, thanks to Sony. Schulhof had approved a highly unusual—and many felt improper—arrangement where Sony purchased the house for $5.5 million, an estimated $2 million above market value. (Schulhof would later weakly assert that Guber would have been paid the money regardless, and that he saw no reason not to buy the house if Guber preferred to be compensated that way.)

Guber was frequently absent from the Culver City lot. By now he had grown happily accustomed to traveling around the globe—often with Schulhof—on the corporate jet. He may not have loved his job, but he and Lynda had no intention of flying commercial again anytime soon. "Peter loved that jet," says a friend. "He used to say, 'I'll do anything if I can keep that jet.'" A joke made the rounds that Guber's life would be perfect if he could only figure out how to refuel in midair.

Because of his travel and the layers of executives who surrounded him, he grew increasingly isolated from the Sony Pictures staff and its resident filmmakers. Part of Jon Peters's influence had been to bring him out of his shell, but with his former partner gone Guber became more withdrawn and kept his movements mysterious.

Perhaps partly because of the hole Peters had left behind, Guber adopted two New Age gurus as friends—and began inviting them to deliver inspirational pep talks at Sony corporate functions. Both Deepak Chopra and Tony Robbins had gotten rich peddling advice on how to be spiritual and materialistic at the same time. Chopra was an Indian doctor of Ayurvedic medicine who had written several best-sellers promoting material abundance. In one of these, *The Seven Spiritual Laws of Success*, he would write "When you really understand your true nature—you will never feel guilty, fearful, or insecure about money, or affluence, or fulfilling your desires, because you will realize that the essence of all material wealth is life energy, it is pure potentiality."

Robbins was a latter-day Dale Carnegie type who wore custom-tailored suits and ran $1,000-a-weekend "Date with Destiny" seminars. Fast-talking and charismatic, he had once pushed firewalking as a way to break through psychological barriers and achieve "personal power." Suddenly Robbins seemed to be the Sony chairman's unofficial personal guru; he was frequently glimpsed at Guber's side and accompanied him on the jet to Aspen. Guber was always advising acquaintances to buy Robbins's motivational videotapes.

Robbins was Guber's guest for a Fourth of July getaway that combined adventure with luxury. Guber arranged a five-day rafting trip down the Grand Canyon section of the Colorado River for a group of sixteen, including actors Patrick Swayze and Tony Danza, and basketball coach Pat Riley.

The trip may have been intended as a wilderness excursion, but Guber wasn't one for roughing it. The Oars Company, the outfitter that organized the trip, advised participants to bring mess kits; Guber had plates and silverware flown to Arizona instead. An extra pack boat had to be added to carry tables, chairs, and eating utensils. The crew included a chef and a full-time masseuse—the latter in violation of park rules, which impose tight controls on the number of people who can raft down the river each season. Guber attempted to bring a violinist who would serenade the group during cocktail hour, but the outfitters vetoed the idea.

A couple of days before departure, Guber anxiously called Oars and told a representative that he was worried about shoes.

"Excuse me?" she replied.

"I went to the store and there were all these different kinds of shoes," he said fretfully.

"I think you'll be just fine with the packing list I gave you."

But Guber persisted. He wanted to be "totally prepared," a notion that was amusing to the Oars employee, considering how many special arrangements had already been made to pamper this group. "He just didn't want to be simple," she says. "He was insisting on having the coolest, best, most appropriate shoes."

Later that summer, Guber organized a European family holiday that culminated in a visit to the Barcelona Olympics. He chartered a 150-foot yacht that cruised the Mediterranean car- 343 rying himself and Lynda, Mickey and Paola Schulhof, and the two couples' children. Jodi Guber and David Schulhof were both present, their romance in full flower under the approving gaze of their parents.

As 1992 rolled along, Canton was gathering steam in his new job, despite Dolgenization. Shortly after arriving at Columbia, Canton had installed Sid Ganis, then wearying of his ill-defined role as Peter's lieutenant, as Columbia's president of marketing and distribution. Canton had rounded out his team by appointing the beefy, outspoken Jeff Blake as head of distribution. Canton, Ganis, and Blake aggressively marketed *A League of Their Own*, which opened over the Fourth of July weekend. The picture starred Geena Davis, Madonna, and Tom Hanks in the tale of a women's professional baseball team during World War II. Frank Price had green-lit *League* and Jon Peters had been a great fan. But Guber had opposed the project because he didn't think that a group of actresses could look like pro baseball players.

Before it opened, the picture had several discouraging test screenings. Director Penny Marshall reshot scenes and massaged the material in the editing room until the audience reaction improved. A kiss between Davis and Hanks was excised; viewers disapproved, since Davis's character was married. *League* became a feel-good movie and a warm-weather hit, grossing more than $100 million.

If the film hadn't cost a whopping $55 million and a substantial percentage of the gross had not been promised to the talent, the studio would have made some real money. In the end, Columbia only scraped out $9.3 million for its efforts, according to studio documents. But *League* went a long way to erode the perception that Sony could do no right.

It was soon followed by *Mo' Money*, a $15 million comedy with Damon Wayans that scored an $18 million opening weekend and ended up making a $15 million profit. Then came *Honeymoon in Vegas*, a Castle Rock farce by writer-director Andrew Bergman, another solid little hit that netted $6.5 million for Columbia. In August, the studio had more good news with director Barbet Schroeder's *Single White Female*, the thriller developed by Guber-Peters Entertainment Company. The picture, starring Bridget Fonda and Jennifer Jason Leigh, grossed $48 million, leading to a profit of more than $33 million.

But Columbia's bombs tended to hit hard. On October 2, the studio released *Hero*, an ambitious seriocomic film about a bum who saves lives after a plane crash; it starred Dustin Hoffman and Geena Davis. Directed by *Dangerous Liaisons*'s Stephen Frears, the film was produced by Laura Ziskin, Jon Peters's former employee who had gone on to make *Pretty Woman* and now had a deal at Columbia. *Hero* cost $42 million and lost $25.6 million—a cataclysmic disappointment.

In September, just before the opening of Castle Rock's *Mr. Saturday Night*, Guber invited Rob Reiner and his partners to his Aspen ranch to celebrate Castle Rock's recently completed refinancing deal. The relationship between Columbia and Castle Rock was mutually beneficial, but there were constant tensions over deal points. Guber always ducked out of these financial discussions, leaving Levine and Dolgen to fight the studio's battles with Castle Rock CEO Alan Horn. Guber preferred the more pleasant task of playing host at Mandalay, where the partners rode horses and drove around the property in four-wheel drives. Guber presented them with T-shirts that said, "A Few Good Men at Mandalay"—an allusion to Castle Rock's upcoming Christmas film.

*Mr. Saturday Night*, starring and directed by Billy Crystal, was a loser, though the studio squeezed out a marginal profit thanks to the favorable terms of its deal with Castle Rock. The film, the portrait of an embittered Borscht Belt comedian, did much to erase any good feelings Guber had fostered with the Castle Rock partners. Castle Rock had exercised its usual prerogative of handling marketing, and executives at Columbia, beginning to take pride in their own selling prowess, made no secret of their contempt for the campaign. They were particularly critical of a poster showing Crystal in old-man makeup with a cigar. "We could have opened it by playing up the romance and never showing Billy in 'old' makeup," says one Columbia executive.

The dispute went public when Reiner responded to these attacks in an interview. "It's the most blown-up story I've ever heard," he fumed. "It was a poster. Billy had a cigar in the poster and they didn't want him to have a cigar. They thought it would be more youthful without the cigar. [But] there is no getting around it—in 60 percent of the film, he's an old guy." 345

Canton scored a coup when he acquired *A River Runs Through It*, a film directed by Robert Redford. The adaptation of Norman Maclean's lyrical novel about fly-fishing, family, and spirituality in Montana featured no known stars—only the charismatic Brad Pitt, just starting his film career, in the lead as the doomed brother. Redford insisted on $7.5 million for domestic distribution rights to the already finished movie. Medavoy had passed, irritating Redford by being unresponsive to his request for a decision. The Columbia brass convened to view the film at a movie theater in Santa Monica. After it was over, as agent Michael Ovitz was about to usher Redford into the theater to talk business, Dolgen implored Canton, "Don't buy it. It'll make $15 million. You'll spend $8 million to market it."

"Jon, you've obviously lost your mind and you have no heart," Canton replied.

The picture opened on October 9. Ganis and Blake gradually rolled it out on an increasing number of screens, building up word of mouth. When it finally reached eight hundred theaters, it was the number-two box-office attraction behind Steven Seagal's *Under Siege*—a big action film on twice as many screens. With no stars to sell, Ganis and Blake showed that they had the patience and skill to market a small niche film. The picture was a sleeper hit, grossing more than $33 million and netting more than $16 million for the studio.

Canton had another big card to play as the 1992 holiday season got under way. He had inherited *Bram Stoker's Dracula* from Frank Price, who had worked closely developing the film with director Francis Coppola. The studio had promised an astonishing 15 percent of the gross to Coppola—a great director but one who had suffered a drought between hits. Coppola, who made his name with the *Godfather* series and *Apocalypse Now*, had earned a reputation for chaotic productions with burgeoning budgets. This one he would keep on time and on budget at $40 million.

With Gary Oldman as Count Dracula and also starring Winona Ryder and Keanu Reeves, *Dracula* was a difficult production. Coppola's vision was darkly erotic and bloody; there were reports from early test screenings that audience members vomited in disgust. Canton pushed Coppola to recut the picture to make it less gory and more palatable to audiences. Still, rumors that *Dracula* was blood-spattered were so persistent that Columbia could not make valuable deals with a fast-food chain or a

346

toy company. Columbia devised a brilliant marketing strategy, selling it as a romance instead of a horror film. The campaign was built around the tag line: "Love Never Dies."

On its opening weekend in mid-November, the picture raked in a stunning $32 million—setting a new industry record for a non-summer release. It also broke Columbia's all-time record for an opening weekend, beating *Ghostbusters II*. The studio threw an impromptu party, with Guber boasting to the staff that the Japanese owners were so naive that they asked whether that was a good opening figure. It was—and the fact that grosses fell off rapidly after the huge first weekend showed that the marketing was better than the movie. While critics praised *Dracula*'s spectacular Transylvanian sets and cinematography, the reviews were mixed. David Denby of *New York* magazine called the film "an unholy mess, a bombastic kitschfest." Nonetheless, *Dracula* was a substantial hit, which grossed $200 million worldwide and netted Sony a $30 million profit.

Canton had *A Few Good Men* for Christmas. The story of a Marine Corps court-martial, the film was directed by Rob Reiner and boasted all the star power a studio could want with Tom Cruise, Jack Nicholson, and Demi Moore. It was a Castle Rock production but it had turned out to be prohibitively expensive. Normally, Columbia didn't finance Castle Rock films. But the studio had the option to pay full freight when the budget became burdensome to Castle Rock, which was perennially strapped for cash despite its success, primarily because it was saddled with unfavorable foreign distribution deals. In this case, Columbia agreed to finance the $33 million film in full. In return, Columbia got a higher stake in the film's revenues and a say in the marketing. Guber offered his advice about the poster. "You've gotta get Tom Cruise in starched white!" he urged frenetically. "He looks great in white!"

Canton smelled a hit in *A Few Good Men,* and he couldn't resist ordering a staffer to phone Castle Rock partners Alan Horn and Rob Reiner to ask them to thank him publicly at the premiere. "Before the premieres of all our movies, their publicity people would call and say, 'Can you thank Mark?' " an annoyed Castle Rock executive remembers. The Castle Rock partners begrudgingly obliged him. *A Few Good Men* opened December 11 and grossed more than $100 million. Columbia cleared a $38 million profit—an irritant to Castle Rock, which

347

had nurtured the project and then found itself unable to keep most of the spoils.

Canton was ebullient over Columbia's string of hits and crowed over the studio's successes as if he were responsible for all of them. That naturally irritated Frank Price, who had put several of the big pictures of 1991–92 into production: *A League of Their Own, Mo' Money,* and *Dracula.* He didn't approve Castle Rock's productions but Canton had nothing to do with those either.

"I was utterly amazed, astounded," Price says. "He walked in and took credit for *My Girl.* He arrived in October, it came out in November."

The Canton-Price contention over credit erupted into the press. The *New York Times*'s Bernard Weinraub touted Price's role in championing *Dracula.* Gossip columnist Liz Smith responded that the project was "the culmination of Mark Canton's first year at Columbia," and scolded the *New York Times* for "dredging up Frank Price for comment."

Whatever the merits of Price's claim, some Columbia executives noticed that Price's pictures seemed to perform better when Price wasn't around. One pondered this phenomenon at length before concluding that Price and Canton—inadvertently paired on these films—worked well together.

"Frank Price is the guy to have when you want to pick the movies," says this high-level executive. "But Frank Price couldn't finish a movie and market it to save his life. That's all that Mark is good at. The irony is, all those movies Frank greenlit, Mark edited and marketed. That's a hell of a team."

So when Canton saw a rough cut of *A League of Their Own,* he had complained that the crucial locker-room reconciliation scene between the sisters played by Geena Davis and Lori Petty lacked emotional punch. He asked director Penny Marshall to reshoot the scene. On *Dracula,* he argued for a last-minute addition of a voice-over narration by Anthony Hopkins to make the film more coherent.

Canton also asked for changes in *Single White Female.* Initially, he thought the audience's rooting interest in the heroine, played by Bridget Fonda, wasn't satisfied by the thriller's 348 denouement. He asked director Barbet Schroeder for sequences that would provide a *Fatal Attraction* sense of catharsis when Fonda finally prevails over her crazed roommate, Jennifer Jason Leigh. "Mark has lowest-common-denominator movie-goer's taste," says a former colleague at the studio. "He wanted very simple, very clear, very straightforward emotions."

The string of hits had done much to improve Columbia's image. But despite Dolgen's efforts, the studio was still spending too much on its movies. In 1992, the studio's average film budget was $29.5 million; its average domestic box office was $31.8 million. Not surprisingly, Columbia's average cost per film was the highest in the industry that year by a margin.

By comparison, Warner—first in the race for market share with hits like *Lethal Weapon 3* and *The Bodyguard*—spent an average of $26.5 million for an average box office of $34.1 million. And the famously cheap Disney—which came in a close second to Warner that year—had reaped an average $33 million on movies that cost an average of $18.7 million. This simple comparison showed the misleading nature of market share: Warner beat Disney in the box-office race but Disney clearly was far more profitable. While Disney had plenty of flops, its costs were generally low; the company didn't give away big percentages of the gross to talent and rarely paid big-star salaries. And Disney raked in astronomical sums on animated films like *Aladdin* and *Beauty and the Beast,* which had no stars on the screen who could demand financial concessions.

DESPITE THE HITS that had enlivened Sony Pictures in 1992, the mood at the year-end Christmas party was grumpy. Inside a huge tent erected in a parking lot, Canton, Medavoy, and finally Guber all touted Sony's hits from the podium. Now many executives whose raises had been held to 4 percent by the ever-zealous Dolgen found themselves wondering why their stockings had been so poorly stuffed. It was irritating to be told about the company's robust finances when they were having to contend with budgets so tight that doing business had become an embarrassment.

Guber's speech was uncharacteristically flat. It had been written by corporate public relations men Peter Wilkes and Don DeMesquita, and it showed: Guber opened by talking about market share and proceeded to drone on accountantlike about the year's successes. He failed to thank the employees who had 349 made those successes possible, nor did he remember to wish them and their families a joyous holiday.

"It was the most leaden thing you've ever seen," says one of the partygoers. "It sounded like he was talking to a group of investors. Guber can be motivational, but he was reading, and it wasn't like Peter talks. It was like the pod people had taken over his body."

But if Guber's gratitude had failed him, his showmanship had not. In the middle of his speech, as DeMesquita was attempting to shush the restless crowd, the tent flaps were suddenly thrown open. "We have a special guest," Guber announced, switching gears. "Somebody who is very involved in a movie of ours."

With that, a Hummer quasi-military vehicle charged into the tent, its lights on and horn honking. The astonished crowd instantly recognized the car and its driver. Arnold Schwarzenegger certainly knew how to make an entrance.

"It was like a parting of the Red Sea," recalls Columbia executive Barry Josephson. Arnold drove right up to the podium and took the microphone. "I am your Christmas present for 1992," he deadpanned, and the crowd went wild. The star then proceeded to say how excited he was to be making *Last Action Hero* at Sony, that everyone present deserved credit for Columbia's success, and that he knew that they would all work hard together to make next summer's "big ticket" movie a smash hit.

"It was genuine, it was sincere—he was having a great time," says an executive. "Arnold said all the right things, hit every button."

Guber had personally made the call to Schwarzenegger to ask if he would come spread some Christmas cheer. "I'll be there," the star answered. He left the set of *Last Action Hero* early, filming that evening on location in the Hollywood Hills, to come save the day.

WHEN GUBER TOOK his family to Aspen for the holidays, he received a chilly reception from some residents. In November he had outraged town officials, environmentalists, and citizens when it was revealed that he had flouted local zoning restrictions in the construction of two guest houses on his Mandalay property.

On September 19, 1991, Guber had been granted a permit from the Pitkin County Zoning and Building Department to

350

erect "barns or storage buildings that would be used only for agricultural purposes." The structures were to stand in the middle of elk migration and calving territory on his property. "Human use of the barns, during certain times of the year, could have a serious impact on the wildlife," explained Francis Krizmanich of the County Planning and Zoning Department.

The following autumn, a tipster had informed the *Aspen Times Daily* that Guber's "barns" were actually de luxe guest houses. Photos obtained by the paper clearly showed that the structures were tricked out with skylights, stone fireplaces, custom logs, hardwood floors, plumbing, heating, and full bathrooms. "Geez, I wish I was a cow," one local mobile-home dweller exclaimed upon seeing the photographs.

The Pitkin County commissioners filed a lawsuit demanding that Guber tear down both buildings.

The *Aspen Times* sounded off in an editorial entitled "Hollywood Arrogance on Owl Creek": "We demand that our county authorities insist that Peter Guber's illegal chalets be dismantled log by log and that he be taught that ours is not the sort of community of sycophants and whores with which he is so accustomed to dealing."

Guber fought back through his attorney, Andy Hecht. "No one intended to violate any laws," insisted Hecht, who tried to make the case that the buildings were indeed intended for "agricultural purposes." Why then were they loaded with amenities? "There are good reasons for all of it," Hecht said.

On November 20, the Pitkin County commissioners ruled that Guber's "barns" had to come down or conform to agricultural use.

The barn flap was not Guber's only scuffle with the locals. A Snowmass environmentalist named Dan Kitchen raised a ruckus over the fence surrounding Guber's property, which as winter approached was thwarting herds of elk trying to migrate to lower elevations.

Guber had made assurances that he would remove portions of his fence to permit the elk to move freely to their winter range. But he had removed slats from only two sections of the fence—a concession that Kitchen maintained was inadequate to ease the elk bottleneck. "The two sections that have been opened up are not enough," Kitchen said, and condemned Guber for his "stupidity, apathy or just greed."

351

Hecht again came to his client's defense, saying that Guber had followed recommendations put out by the Division of Wildlife. "Peter said whatever he can do to help the elk, he's willing to do."

# 27

## POLITICS AS USUAL

WHILE CANTON WAS ENJOYING a great year, Medavoy was struggling to recover from the debilitating efforts of *Hook* and *Bugsy*. TriStar released only eight films in 1992, and during that time, Medavoy put only four new projects into production. The studio seemed paralyzed by inertia. Although Medavoy trumpeted new talent deals with producer Scott Rudin, Robin Williams, and others, these would bear little fruit.

The year brought feeble financial results coupled with public relations horrors. In March, TriStar distributed Carolco's titillating lesbian-themed thriller *Basic Instinct*, starring Michael Douglas and Sharon Stone. Gay activists' protests didn't discourage audiences, but TriStar's take of the $117 million gross was limited to about $18 million by the terms of its deal with the production company. But at least *Basic Instinct* produced a profit.

In April came *City of Joy*, a triumph-of-the-spirit book adaptation starring Patrick Swayze as a doctor in the slums of Calcutta. Audiences balked; the studio lost $8.4 million. The news got worse for the balance of the year: *Thunderheart*, a thriller set on a Sioux Indian reservation starring Val Kilmer, performed poorly. *Wind*, a sailing movie about the America's Cup starring Matthew Modine and directed by *The Black Stallion*'s Carroll Ballard, was a disaster despite breathtaking footage.

TriStar was stuck with Woody Allen's *Husbands and Wives* just as Allen was engulfed in scandal over his affair with Soon-Yi Previn, daughter of his ex-lover Mia Farrow. The negative press did little to pique the public's interest in the film, which grossed a meager $10.5 million. The year ended on an especially sour note with Carolco's huge bomb, *Chaplin*—which failed despite a much-admired, Oscar-nominated performance by Robert Downey, Jr., in the title role.

Medavoy had been expected to class TriStar up a bit, but so far he had failed to do so. The year he was having would not restore Guber's faith in him after the black mark he earned for *Bugsy*. And his low energy level annoyed Guber. Several insiders say Medavoy was indolent, leaving the legwork—especially script development—to Platt and Snider. "He's a pretty lazy guy when it comes to doing the homework of a studio executive," says a producer who made films for TriStar. "He loves to go to the White House for dinner and he's got a wall full of pictures and autographs. But when it comes to reading scripts and doing notes, he doesn't confuse his staff with an aggressive style."

Medavoy's conference room wall, covered with photographs of famous friends and acquaintances, symbolized his self-aggrandizement and became known as his "wall of shame." There was Medavoy with Kevin Costner: "I'm for you, man," Costner had scrawled. Medavoy with Redford, with the cryptic inscription: "I want a separate room." Medavoy with Sean Penn: "It's rare to be able to respect the 'suit.' "

"There's something wrong with people who have to build a monument to themselves while they still exist," says one former TriStar executive. The criticism stung Medavoy. "It had nothing to do with self-aggrandizement," he said angrily. "This is a thirty-year career. The people who had photos in the room were very happy to see they were there."

Then the faltering Medavoy had a video made and given out to members of the press. *Mike Medavoy: A Life in Film* consisted of nothing but old trailers for movies made at United Artists and Orion—including *The Pink Panther* and *Annie Hall*, pictures for which Medavoy could hardly claim credit. The self-promotion annoyed his former partner, Eric Pleskow, who said that many of the films included were made without Medavoy's involvement.

Like Guber and Peters, Medavoy funneled some of his Sony paycheck into real estate. He and Patricia built a massive vanilla-colored house in Coldwater Canyon, which was displayed in a full-color spread in the November 1992 issue of *W* magazine. The article described the Medavoy mansion reverently as an intellectual salon in the midst of godless Hollywood.

"Years from now, when they talk about the Medavoy house—

and they will—it's quite likely to be listed alongside those other celebrated Hollywood salons where art, commerce and style mixed," the magazine raved. The article included a photo of Patricia Medavoy's desk, her Filofax tucked beneath a photo of her snuggling beside Bill Clinton, who was about to be elected president. She made a point of noting that she would be in Little Rock on election day. Patricia complained that decorating the manse had actually given her chronic fatigue syndrome. "I wanted a little nest," she lamented.

While Medavoy assumed a regal air as head of TriStar, most observers in Hollywood had been convinced for some time that his job was not secure—particularly after Mark Canton became chairman of Columbia. Medavoy could feel Canton's hunger for advancement and knew that his one-time assistant would do everything in his power to show him up. A former Columbia executive remembers hearing Medavoy declare, "In thirty years in this business, I've never seen such naked aggression."

Canton was indeed eager to take advantage of Medavoy's weakness. When Columbia's development funds ran out, he clamored to raid TriStar's. And he waged a campaign of seduction with Guber. "Medavoy's problems began when Canton got there," one Sony producer says. "Because Canton's the kind of guy that every Sunday night, he's at Guber's, doing whatever male-bonding kinds of things they do." Canton, then forty-three, was nearly ten years younger than Medavoy and it was logical to conclude that the age difference mattered to Guber, who seemed increasingly obsessed with youth.

Medavoy, who was not impervious to male-bonding games himself, faced off against Canton in a highly charged tennis game at his Coldwater Canyon house. The line judges were Irving Azoff, the diminutive music mogul, and comedian Chevy Chase. There was $100 riding on the game—but obviously the stakes were much higher. Medavoy trounced Canton, who immediately began to complain that Medavoy had unfairly had more warm-up time before the match. Medavoy maintained that Canton never paid up.

But even as his stewardship over TriStar was threatened, Medavoy had another source of power. A longtime Democratic activist, Medavoy had been among the very first to introduce candidate Bill Clinton to Hollywood. At a time when many in the entertainment community were still infatuated with Senator Bob Kerrey of Nebraska, Medavoy had been a Clinton man.

Medavoy was selected as that year's Motion Picture Pioneer of the Year, an honor that was bestowed upon him at a black-tie dinner on December 14, 1992. The event was somewhat strained because of rampant rumors that Medavoy was about to be fired. A Columbia executive referred to the Pioneer honor as the "For Whom the Bell Tolls" award. In fact, one TriStar executive who attended the party recalls watching Guber huddle with Ovitz and *Commitments* producer Armyan Bernstein before the dinner—and presumed they were discussing whether Bernstein would be interested in Medavoy's job.

Seated at the head table with Mike and Patricia Medavoy were Dustin Hoffman, Michelle Pfeiffer, Barbra Streisand, and Peter Guber. Patricia, concerned that not enough speakers would be lauding her husband, pressed *City of Joy* director Roland Joffe into making an impromptu speech. When Guber was obliged to stand up and say some kind words about the guest of honor, he heaped Medavoy with faint praise for being "committed to a win-win situation. He doesn't need to make anyone look bad to feel good."

The speeches may have seemed insincere, but the evening ended on a high note. The sequined Hollywood crowd was impressed when they were treated to a film of President-elect Clinton sending his congratulations to his friend Mike. The joke spread through town that Medavoy was the only studio chief to be saved by an election.

ON A BRISK DAY in January 1993, fifteen buses prepared to drive from Charlottesville, Virginia, to Washington, D.C., on President Clinton's inaugural bus ride. Peter Guber stood in the cool morning air surrounded by a clutch of reporters, distributing schedules and directing them to telephones and bathrooms. Ever the promoter, he gave out special inaugural Sony compact discs as he went. "I've done a lot of outrageous things in my life, but this is the most outrageous," he told one reporter.

Hollywood had been seized by Clintonmania and Guber, a lifelong Republican, had jumped on the bandwagon with both feet. He had given money to the Democrats before volunteering to serve as a guide to reporters. The tea-leaf readers noted that Peter and Lynda Guber snubbed Medavoy during the inaugural celebrations, which should have been an unmixed triumph for Medavoy. "When they all went to the inauguration, they did not take Mike on the Sony jet," says one director then working on the lot. "This was a big moment. All of us knew the handwriting was on the wall."

The Clinton connection seemed to have limited potency, after all. Medavoy must have noticed, as Frank Price had done before him, that no one at Sony was quelling the rumors that he was about to be fired. That same January, the *New York Times* actually reported that Medavoy had been "relieved of his duties," though it quickly ran a correction.

It was an open secret in Hollywood that Guber had temporarily asserted himself by seizing the initiative in running TriStar. He had immersed himself in everything from soundtracks to film editing to ad campaigns. Guber tried (unsuccessfully) to salvage *Mr. Jones,* a drama starring Richard Gere and Lena Olin, by ordering reshoots. He offered extensive notes on *Frankenstein,* the gothic classic he believed could mimic *Dracula*'s success and was currently in development. He assured Schulhof that the picture would be a tremendous hit. And even though he hadn't been a presence during the making of Nora Ephron's *Sleepless in Seattle*—she never met him until a test screening of the film—he had insisted on a love duet of "When I Fall in Love" for the end of the movie.

Guber was now working almost exclusively through Stacey Snider and Marc Platt; Medavoy was scarcely consulted. "They started to shut him out of his own company," says one producer. "They'd have meetings without him, and when he showed up, they'd look at him like he was a Martian."

Medavoy was living a nightmare. He exuded a depleting depression. His marriage was foundering, and in the small town of Hollywood, everyone knew it. One executive ran into Patricia in Hawaii over the Christmas holidays and she said she was there with multi-millionaire financier Ron Perelman. The same person was amused when he later ran into Perelman, who said he had come to Hawaii alone.

The executive believed Patricia. She married Perelman two years later.

As Medavoy dangled, he tried to alter the perception of his situation. In February, he released a slate of upcoming projects. Many insiders were skeptical that these films would materialize; the announcement was perceived by one as "a desperation

357

move to give the appearance of activity." Some of the projects had no scripts and no talent firmly attached. For example, the list included a Steven Spielberg–directed remake of *Zorro*. Spielberg, who had agreed only to be executive producer, reportedly called Medavoy, furious over the announcement.

Medavoy followed up by giving an interview to the *Los Angeles Times* declaring how happy he was to have Guber involved in running the studio. But Medavoy insisted that Guber was simply helping him. "The big issue is not whether my authority is eroded," he said staunchly. "The perception is yes, but the reality is no . . . I invited him in and am comfortable with his presence. Those who know me know I'm a fairly strong personality. I'm not about to have someone dictate to me."

Guber offered something less than a ringing endorsement of TriStar's chairman—and he threw in an interesting etymology lesson. "I was head of Columbia in 1972 and would be the doofus of all time to go back to that job," he said when asked about reports of his fingerprints on TriStar movies. "But I'd be equally doofus—that's a combination of foolish and dumb—not to employ the talent and energy I used for 17 years for the benefit of the company." As for Medavoy, he added, "Falling down doesn't make you a failure . . . and we're supporting Mike as he picks himself up."

But Medavoy's stock continued to fall. Within weeks, the Clinton connection became a liability when it appeared that Medavoy was overplaying that hand. Stories circulated about Mike telling disbelieving callers that he had just gotten off the phone with the president. And Medavoy infuriated Dawn Steel by sending her a condolence note on White House stationery after her mother died. Medavoy denied that he was trying to impress anyone. He never even mentioned his "friendship" with Clinton, he said. Unfortunately, he pointed out, people had found out about it.

Meanwhile, Patricia Medavoy was accused of trying to convey the impression that she and Clinton were exceptionally close. At a dinner party at a producer's home, which took place after she and Mike had slept in the Lincoln Bedroom, she told the gathering that Clinton was "a full-service president." Patricia later said she meant to refer only to Clinton's hospitality, but her listeners didn't interpret the remark that way.

Many in Hollywood would have had little sympathy for Medavoy if he had been fired. But despite the battering he was

358

taking, the chances that he would lose his job seemed to be diminishing. Sony seemed unwilling to tolerate another expensive buy-out after the highly publicized dismissals of Jon Peters and Frank Price. And Medavoy did have some potential hits in the pipeline. He had *Sleepless in Seattle* coming, as well as *Cliffhanger*, a Carolco picture in which Sylvester Stallone would attempt to resurrect his career by returning to the action genre after an ill-fated attempt to replicate Schwarzenegger's success in comedy. And director Jonathan Demme, an associate from Medavoy's days at Orion, was making *Philadelphia* for Christmas. It still was not impossible that Medavoy might have a pretty good year.

AS THE SUMMER OF 1993 approached, employees on the Sony lot were whipsawed between hope and disappointment.

In February, Columbia had a sleeper hit with Harold Ramis's comedy starring Bill Murray, *Groundhog Day*. The movie grossed more than $70 million and cleared a profit of $23.5 million. Frank Price claimed credit for that film, too: He had brought Ramis to the studio and had approved the movie as long as Ramis could get a star like Murray or Tom Hanks to take the lead role. Canton reportedly had passed on the project when he was at Warner.

*Groundhog Day* was followed by a staggering bomb. Even though investment banker Herbert Allen was no longer an owner of Columbia Pictures, producer Ray Stark was still a force. Some said Peter Guber was more terrified of Stark than he was of anyone else—a reasonable reaction given Stark's long history of successfully wreaking vengeance on his enemies. Now Stark's *Lost in Yonkers,* Martha Coolidge's version of the Pulitzer Prize–winning play, starring Richard Dreyfuss and Mercedes Ruehl, opened in May and died a horrible death. Marketing man Sid Ganis's efforts to salvage the opening failed. Dolgen, still looking for ways to cut costs, was said to be angered by Ganis's expenditures in a losing cause—particularly when the marketing department suggested running ads aimed at kids on Nickelodeon. Spending big on ads seemed like throwing good money after bad.

The picture lost $20 million, but no one expected Stark to feel the heat. "Don't worry about him," a studio executive wisecracked. "When God has a bad day, he's still God."

□

359

WHEN SONY REPORTED earnings for fiscal 1993 toward the end of May, the picture for the parent company was still dreadful. Revenues were flat, but consolidated net income had dropped almost 70 percent, to $312.6 million. The company said it was still being battered by worldwide recession and the strength of the yen against the dollar. For what it was worth, Sony's rival, Matsushita, also suffered a 71 percent drop in net income.

The entertainment operations were portrayed as the silver lining. While accounting for only 20.8 percent of sales, the music and filmed entertainment divisions had contributed 47.4 percent of operating income. Together those units had a 7 percent rise in pretax earnings to $904 million. As usual, the company did not provide net earnings from filmed entertainment, but boasted that revenue from the studios was up 20 percent. Analysts estimated that Sony Pictures made about $350 million—not counting taxes, interest, depreciation, and amortization. News reports were uniformly favorable when it came to the entertainment sector.

In reality, those profits were immediately wiped out by $300 million in interest payments plus $100 million in goodwill charges. (Goodwill represented the gulf between Columbia's net worth when Sony bought it and the price that Sony had paid. It reflected intangibles that enhanced the value of the studio and would be written off over forty years.)

Once again, Schulhof and Guber glossed over the bottom line. In interviews, they delivered the message that the results showed three straight years of "financial improvement." Sony Pictures, Schulhof said, had won a "strong vote of confidence" from its parent.

Schulhof had gotten his own vote of confidence, too. Despite the ongoing speculation that the Japanese must be concerned over the spending at the studio, Schulhof's star had continued to rise. In the spring of 1993, Sony consolidated its U.S. electronics and entertainment operations under the title "Sony Corp. of America," naming Schulhof the president and chief executive. Ron Sommer, the U.S. electronics executive who had chafed at the shenanigans on the software side, was gone —transferred to Europe. Now, Schulhof pledged, the two sides would work together even more closely.

Perhaps it was reassuring for executives at Columbia and TriStar to hear that the Japanese parent was still backing them.

But they had also gotten word on their annual bonuses, and it wasn't good. At major studios, top executives might look forward to bonuses of hundreds of thousands of dollars—sometimes $1 million or more; it was a major part of their income. "People got 50 and 75 percent bonuses at Warner Bros.," said one Columbia executive. "You could get 100 percent in a good year." Employees learned that this year Sony Pictures would dole out bonuses in the meager 10–25 percent range.

Against the backdrop of big Hollywood money, executives who would have been considered well remunerated outside the entertainment world felt deprived. After all, Columbia had had a great run of hits in 1992 and was bruiting the release of its summer blockbuster-to-be, *Last Action Hero*. The disappointment was bitter. Some figured Guber was keeping most of the money for himself and a few cronies. A few considered quitting, while others returned their checks in a huff. Canton reportedly got Guber to ante up some more money, with the intercession of entertainment attorney Jake Bloom.

# 28

## HOW THEY BUILT
## THE BOMB

Mark Canton was bursting with optimism. After a year and a half at Columbia, he would soon be judged on his own handpicked slate of movies: *Poetic Justice, The Age of Innocence, Striking Distance,* and *Geronimo* would start rolling into the theaters in the summer and continue through the end of 1993.

While Canton was happy enough with these films, they couldn't inspire even a fraction of the excitement he felt about the one project that was consuming most of his time and energy. Canton had all his hopes and dreams pinned on *Last Action Hero,* a project that he said "would make me or break me."

"This movie should become a hallmark of the company—we hope," said Canton, sitting in his office on the third floor of the Thalberg Building one cool afternoon in March 1993. Columbia's chairman had hired a top designer to furnish his spacious suite in dark wood and deep shades of green. Outside his private office was a waiting room filled with English antiques. Two secretaries breathlessly directed Canton's incoming calls like air traffic controllers stacking planes. Mark Canton had become a powerful man.

Some people felt Canton had become far too convinced of his own importance. Director Mike Nichols, who was working on *Wolf* with Jack Nicholson, was kept waiting outside Canton's office for an hour and a half one afternoon. Such behavior was unheard of and Nichols was so livid that he sat muttering that he would punch a hole through the window. Doug Wick, the film's producer, tried to calm him. In the end, Nichols decided to twit Canton about his bad habits by sending him a pillow that read: "Mark will be here soon." Canton, seeming not to comprehend its ironic message, proudly displayed the pillow.

In Canton's sitting room an array of photographs of himself with celebrities was on view: Mark with Madonna, Mark with Mel, Mark with Barbra, Mark and Jon Peters with Michael Keaton in his *Batman* costume. On a photograph of Canton posing with Danny DeVito attired as the Penguin, DeVito had scrawled: "Which one is the studio executive?"

From the moment he arrived at Columbia, Canton had been determined to find the kind of "franchise" that Warner Bros. had scored with the *Batman* and *Lethal Weapon* series. Columbia hadn't owned such a lucrative property since Ivan Reitman's *Ghostbusters*. *Last Action Hero* was conceived to be just such a blockbuster: an event picture starring the world's biggest star— Arnold Schwarzenegger—that would spawn a merchandizing smorgasbord of CD-Roms and video games and action dolls and fast-food tie-ins. Getting hold of such a franchise so early in his tenure, Canton observed in an interview at the time, was not just extraordinary but "very unique."

*Last Action Hero* was Columbia's attempt to make a pan-demographic smash—a fantasy-action-adventure-comedy about a fatherless boy named Danny (Austin O'Brien) who is magically blasted into a movie that stars his favorite action hero, Jack Slater (Schwarzenegger). After several escapades in the movie world, the boy brings his hero into the real world, where Slater discovers that his gun runs out of bullets, and the bad guys sometimes win.

Toning down violence in films was a popular topic of conversation in Hollywood in 1993 and Canton proudly held up *Last Action Hero* as Sony's contribution to the greater good. Not incidentally, movie executives were starting to think that family films with less carnage might also mean better business: A recent survey had concluded that a PG-rated film was three times more likely to reach $100 million at the box office than one with an R rating.

While Schwarzenegger's brutish characters had killed some 275 people on screen, as the recent father of two girls he was looking to reinvent himself as a gentler hero. "The country is going in an anti-violence direction," he said during an outdoor 363 lunch break on a Long Beach location as he tipped his face up to catch the winter sunshine. "I think America has seen now enough of what violence has done in the cities." When Mattel was licensed to manufacture *Last Action Hero* toys, Arnold vetoed the company's plan to arm the Slater action figure with flamethrowers and missile launchers. "That was okay for the Arnold of the eighties," he said, "but not the Arnold of the nineties." That was the last thing anyone wanted to hear—as one prominent producer pointed out, an action figure without weapons "is a *doll*."

But Columbia still expected that its bow to reducing on-screen violence would be abundantly repaid. "The first smart thing we all did was decide to make this PG-13, instead of R-rated," boasted Canton. *Last Action Hero*'s violence would be cartoony and over-the-top. The trick would be to hang on to Arnold's hard-core action fans, appeal to viewers who loved his comedies such as *Twins*—and attract young kids as well. "There's no genre for this movie," admitted marketing chief Sid Ganis. "It only looks like an action movie. It's about an action movie star. I think it's more—what it is, it's, it's, uh, fantasy."

Or, as one of *Last Action Hero*'s original screenwriters, Adam Leff, put it, "It's having your cake and eating it too."

Another, less sanguine industry observer thought the situation might not turn out so well. Various sources claimed credit for coining the phrase he used to describe this attempt to create a genre-straddling film: feathered fish. A feathered fish would neither swim nor fly.

*Last Action Hero* was born in the word processors of Adam Leff and Zak Penn, two young graduates of Wesleyan University who wrote a screenplay originally entitled *Extremely Violent*. As they were writing, they envisioned Schwarzenegger in the role and would blurt out one-liners like, "Big mistake!" in Arnold's accent. Steve Roth, a producer with a deal at Sony, brought the script to the attention of production vice president Barry Josephson. Josephson took it to Canton, and the two executives agreed that it would be a perfect vehicle for Arnold—if they could get him.

Getting into business with Arnold was at the top of Canton's wish list. Studio executives all over town felt the same way. Schwarzenegger's last four films had grossed a staggering $1 billion worldwide. Among them were *Terminator 2* and *Total Recall*—both Carolco pictures distributed by TriStar.

Dreaming of a relationship with Arnold similar to the one Terry Semel and Bob Daly enjoyed with Clint Eastwood at Warner, Canton authorized Josephson and Nathanson to bid on *Extremely Violent*. There was little competition for the script and in October 1991, Columbia purchased it for $350,000.

Early in January 1992, Guber, Canton, Nathanson, and Josephson drove to Santa Monica to have lunch with Schwarzenegger at his restaurant, Schatzi. After a big Austrian meal and schnapps—more potent than the executives' usual Perrier—it was agreed that action screenwriter Shane Black (*Lethal Weapon*) would be brought in to do a $1 million rewrite. "Write me an E-ticket," were Arnold's instructions to Black and his partner, David Arnott.

At the time, Arnold was actively developing several projects around town and planned to commit to one of them over the summer. The front-runner happened to be another Columbia project, a script about a tooth fairy called *Sweet Tooth*. Finding himself in the odd position of competing against himself, Canton favored *Last Action Hero*.

Canton and Josephson wanted Arnold so badly that they were determined to do whatever it took to beat out the other contenders for Schwarzenegger's attention. The star approved John McTiernan, the director with whom he had made *Predator*, to direct. After reading a second draft of Black and Arnott's script in July 1992, Arnold wanted more emotional depth in the scenes between him and the boy. He asked for a rewrite by veteran screenwriter William Goldman (*Butch Cassidy and the Sundance Kid, All the President's Men*). "It was Bill Goldman or nothing," recalled Josephson. On July 29, Goldman agreed to do four weeks of work on what was now called *Last Action Hero* —for a cool $1 million.

With Goldman on board, Arnold was officially in—and Columbia exulted. *Last Action Hero* was a surefire winner. Schwarzenegger's instincts about his persona and the kind of material that fit into what Sid Ganis called "the Arnold groove" had never failed. And Schwarzenegger was a promotional powerhouse. "When you have Arnold, you have Arnold plus," explained Ganis. "Arnold plus his total understanding of his public. And he knows how to market himself within that awareness."

Canton had Guber's full support on *Last Action Hero*. Guber, after all, had demonstrated his confidence in Arnold by kicking in $30 million to finish *Terminator 2* when Carolco ran out of cash, sweetening TriStar's distribution deal in the process. *T2* wasn't a Sony Pictures product, but it was the most profitable film of Guber's tenure. "Arnold feels that Peter has always been a stand-up guy," Canton said.

Being the stand-up guy on *Last Action Hero* meant saying yes to the largest investment that had ever been made on a feature film. The budget was originally set at $60 million, but everyone knew it would soon soar into the $80s. Arnold would receive $15 million up front and a handsome piece of the back end. McTiernan's fee was $5 million. Because *Last Action Hero*'s budget exceeded $40 million, Canton had his staff put together a forty-page business plan for the film that was rubber-stamped by Schulhof.

Schulhof clearly hoped that *Last Action Hero* would finally provide an opportunity to realize that elusive concept, the S word. In August, Canton convened seventy executives from various Sony divisions in Los Angeles for what was termed a "synergy" meeting. Among the attendees were Olaf Olafsson, the head of Sony's games division, and Sony Music executives Michele Anthony and Donny Ienner. There were also honchos from merchandising, advertising, marketing, publicity, business affairs, physical production, and the legal department.

In Screening Room A of the Thalberg Building, Josephson warmed up the group with a reel of highlights from the star's and the director's careers. Canton, Guber, Ganis, and McTiernan spoke. "Mark talked about the synergy that was possible in one film," said Josephson. "A lot of people hadn't met before and we basically laid out our game plan. Sid Ganis spoke about marketing and how we would tie everything together."

Then Schwarzenegger took the podium, cigar in hand, and socked 'em with his Knute Rockne teamwork speech. "I want to be involved with every facet of this film from start to finish," he said. "I'm behind you, I'm accessible to each and every person in this room, anytime."

"Everyone was on a real high," said Josephson.

Shooting began in November. While most big-budget films are shepherded by a strong, experienced producer, Canton didn't want to share the glory. Action picture veteran Joel Silver (*Die Hard, Lethal Weapon*) had lobbied with both Canton and Schwarzenegger to produce the film, but he was rebuffed. In-

366

stead, Columbia would essentially produce the movie itself, hiring line producers while Canton and Josephson worked closely with the creative team. This approach duplicated Canton's strategy on *The Bonfire of the Vanities,* which he had overseen as head of production at Warner Bros. On that film, Canton's judgment was spectacularly impaired: He repeatedly declared *Bonfire* "the best movie I ever saw" upon emerging from the first screening. When the film bombed, he had walked away unscathed, his confidence still intact.

There was another producer whose name was on the film: Steve Roth, who had found the material, was officially attached to the project. Roth was a troubled man who had been a friend of Frank Price's, and Canton was less than eager to be in business with him. Roth would be paid $1 million to stay away from *Last Action Hero.* Later, after things had gone terribly wrong, Columbia would find it convenient to point to Roth as the movie's producer.

EARLY IN 1993, Canton had planted his flag in the sand: *Last Action Hero* would be released on June 18. It was a tight deadline. But no matter how punishing the schedule—both production and editing would be uncomfortably squeezed—he did not intend to budge. After Universal announced that it would open Spielberg's *Jurassic Park* just one week before *Last Action Hero,* Canton took a big gulp—and became more determined than ever to stand his ground. Why should the Columbia team be afraid of a few fake dinosaurs? They had Arnold.

In March, Canton made the keynote address at ShoWest, the annual convention of theater owners in Las Vegas. In the middle of shooting the most expensive movie of all time, Canton chose to speak out on cost-cutting. It was time for a little image adjustment. "We're still making expensive movies but only when they're very good bets," he told the crowd. "More often, today, we're making films for $15 million that would have cost $20 or $25 million three years ago. We've stopped overpaying. We're making the right film at the right price. . . . We're leaner and much more flexible. We used to say, 'We want it, no matter how much it costs.' Now we've adopted the mantra of all well-run businesses: 'We want it, but only if the price is right—or if Arnold is in it.' "

Columbia executives unveiled a plan that they perceived as

367

an incredible coup: Not content with earthly hype, the company had made a deal to advertise *Last Action Hero* in outer space. In early May, NASA would launch an unmanned Conestoga 1620 rocket into orbit. Its fuselage and booster rockets would be plastered with the movie's logo and Schwarzenegger's name in large red, yellow, and orange letters. Sony committed $500,000 for this privilege, outbidding Procter & Gamble, Eveready, and Bristol-Myers for a publicity stunt that fit perfectly with the spirit of the movie. "It's the first time in the history of advertising that a space vehicle has been used," crowed Sid Ganis. "If it were *The Age of Innocence*, you know, it wouldn't quite work."

A six-foot prototype of the rocket was on display to impress the theater owners. Arnold joked that NASA wanted him to fly in it but his and Maria's luggage wouldn't fit. At the official launch, however, Columbia said that Arnold would press the button. "It makes it look like we are dealing here with a monster movie," the star noted approvingly. "A giant monster."

The Columbia brass was ecstatic when newspapers all over the country ran stories on the *Last Action Hero* rocket. Stunt marketing, sure, but the awareness level of the movie literally was being raised into the stratosphere. Said one executive, "Ridiculous or embarrassing as it may seem, people are talking about it all over the place." Only director John McTiernan, typically laconic, voiced skepticism. "I hope it flies," he muttered.

Canton may have paused to consider that all the hype was setting up the movie—and him—for a fall. Schwarzenegger remained popular, but he was due to be knocked off his perch. And with Canton seen in Hollywood as an unconscionable credit-grabber, *Last Action Hero* made him into a big piñata waiting to get slammed. But Canton did not stanch the flow of self-congratulatory superlatives as he sat in his office with a reporter. "It's probably the greatest action movie of all time," he declared, six weeks before he saw a finished version of the film. It was as though he had imbibed the Guber and Peters lesson that hype is good, but lacked their instincts for bringing it off.

368   In fact, Canton and Guber had ceded unprecedented control over the making and marketing of the film to the star. Acting as a producer for the first time in his career, Schwarz-

enegger operated like a field marshal out of his 40-foot trailer on the Sony lot. Equipped with a special telephone that allowed him to punch directly into offices in the Thalberg Building, he would summon executives—who would immediately be seen streaking out of their offices and tearing across the lot to Camp Arnold.

One day advertising head Marc Shmuger was called to the trailer to discuss the movie's poster. The star had taken a special interest in the poster design and he didn't like the efforts commissioned by the studio so far. "My hair isn't flying," Arnold complained, pointing to one rendering of Slater bursting through the movie screen, hanging from a helicopter and holding Danny under one arm. Arnold had gone so far as to commission an artist to come up with an alternative poster, which he pulled out of the back of his trailer and showed Shmuger. The executive's face drained of color. Within minutes of Shmuger's return to the Thalberg Building, the Columbia marketing department was in an uproar. Never before had a star seized the initiative on their turf like this. Canton made a beeline for Arnold's trailer himself and assured the actor that they would work together to get the poster on track. "Do me a favor," Canton joked. "Have your distribution plan on my desk tomorrow."

Schwarzenegger couldn't resist an opportunity to smooth over a strained situation with a dose of levity. The next morning, Canton did in fact find a release plan for *Last Action Hero* on his desk. Facetiously, Arnold called on Columbia to repeat the gradual roll-out—usually reserved for high-toned material—that the studio had used successfully the previous fall for another story about a boy who seeks solace in a world of his own creation: *A River Runs Through It.*

Ultimately, the studio incorporated Schwarzenegger's poster ideas and satisfied his taste for explosive action and rippling muscles. Canton, Ganis, and Shmuger presented it for his approval: Audible sighs of relief could be heard when the star said the magic words: "It's terrific. Thank you, guys, well done."

With Arnold deeply involved in *Last Action Hero*'s marketing challenges, the director shouldered his way through the shooting schedule. John McTiernan had been hired in part because he was fast and efficient, a technically brilliant director with lots of experience on *Die Hard* and other big films. The studio

369

felt confident that he could guide this juggernaut to a June 18 release, come what may. McTiernan seemed to be the only one in a sober mood about what he called "the immutability of the release date."

Canton, meanwhile, was in his element, luring a glittering roster of stars to make cameo appearances in the film: Chevy Chase, Damon Wayans, Jean-Claude Van Damme, and Danny DeVito, who would provide the voice for an animated cat. Sharon Stone appeared briefly as the character from *Basic Instinct,* french twist and all, even though she and Arnold had not exactly bonded when they made *Total Recall.*

Throughout the shoot Guber would drop by Arnold's trailer occasionally to make sure the star was happy. Was he pleased with the way the poster was sizing up? Yes, it was getting better. Would he be willing to appear in a music video to boost the soundtrack? Love to. Schwarzenegger and Guber found that their promoters' hearts were beating in synch. "In ten minutes, Peter had more ideas than anyone could dream of," Schwarzenegger said. "That is the enthusiasm you want on a movie."

*Last Action Hero* was consuming so much time and energy that other projects languished. Agents with material to sell and Columbia executives who wanted to get their movies green-lit complained that they couldn't get Canton's attention. *Last Action Hero* would eventually cause the same problem for Canton that bedeviled Medavoy after the massive efforts on *Hook* and *Bugsy:* product deficit. But at the moment, Canton wasn't looking beyond the opening of *Last Action Hero.*

MARK CANTON WAS wearing his denim Planet Hollywood jacket as he hopped into the back of a black limousine outside his Holmby Hills home on the clear, pleasant evening of Saturday, May 1—May Day. He was on his way to Pacific's Lakewood Center, a suburban multiplex forty-five minutes south of Los Angeles with a thousand-seat theater. There, a research screening would be held for *Last Action Hero.*

The movie was midway through its truncated ten-week post-production schedule. Although still in a rough state, Canton decided it was time to get some audience reaction. Two days before, he had seen the film on the Sony lot and been sufficiently impressed to call for this test screening at what he regarded as his lucky theater. Just two weeks earlier Columbia had previewed Clint Eastwood's *In the Line of Fire* there and seen it earn a resounding 94 percent very-good-to-excellent rating on the audience's cards. That night, Canton had called friends from his limo to spread the good news.

All around L.A.'s lush west side enclaves, Canton's colleagues were being fetched: Peter Guber, Jon Dolgen, Alan Levine, Sid Ganis, Michael Nathanson, even executives Amy Pascal and Gareth Wigan, who were not directly involved with the movie. Producer Steve Roth found his limo stocked with Cristal champagne, See's chocolates, and a card which read: "Have a wonderful night—from the Sony family."

Meanwhile, Schwarzenegger and McTiernan opted to drive themselves to Lakewood, Arnold hopping onto the 405 Freeway from his Pacific Palisades home with his wife Maria Shriver. In Malibu, Josephson climbed into his Toyota truck. It was only 60 degrees outside but he had dressed lightly in denim. He thought it could be a sweaty evening.

Canton was all pumped up as he took his seat in the center section of the theater next to Guber, who would be seeing the film for the first time. How could these kids not love seeing Arnold spoofing his action-star status as Jack Slater, a cop armed with an arsenal of weapons and one-liners?

The seats were packed with a frisky young audience recruited by Joe Farrell's National Research Group (NRG), hired at Columbia's behest to organize the preview with as much secrecy as possible. The audience responses tonight would guide the studio and filmmakers in finishing the film. The audience did not know what movie would be shown until an NRG representative announced: "Tonight we will be showing you a work-in-progress, Arnold Schwarzenegger's *Last Action. . . .*" Before he could finish saying the title, the audience drowned him out with whooping and foot-stomping. As the lights went down, Schwarzenegger slipped unnoticed into the back of the theater.

This was the moment that marked the end of innocence for the *Last Action Hero* team. The night of May 1 catapulted them into a seven-week nightmare of industry rumor, bad press, and dashed hopes, derailing their carefully laid plans for a half-billion-dollar blockbuster.

The version of *Last Action Hero* shown to the Lakewood audience was little more than an editor's first assemblage. It ran two hours and eighteen minutes, with a temporary sound dub

371

which made much of the dialogue incomprehensible, as well as a very rough temporary score and an incomplete special-effects shot which showed Arnold falling off a building with no background behind him. "I would say the movie was shown in the roughest form I've ever seen a movie screened," Schwarzenegger said later. Added McTiernan, "I had great trepidation about showing the movie in that state."

By the middle of the movie, the audience's mood had changed from buoyant enthusiasm to lassitude. By Act III, when Slater and the boy have their adventures in the real world of New York, the audience was almost catatonic. "The movie lay there like a big fried egg," said one person who was present.

Throughout the screening, Canton kept jumping up out of his seat to whisper to his colleagues. Schwarzenegger watched the end of the movie from the projection booth, where the brass gathered after the lights came up. While audience members filled out their response cards, the Sony contingent congratulated one another on how well the screening had gone. But the truth was written all over their faces. "They looked like a group of people who had just gotten on a ship and saw the name *Poseidon*," said the same source.

Normally, the market research representatives would have collected the audience's cards and calculated what percentage of them scored the movie "good" or "excellent." But Canton abruptly seized the cards. The last thing he needed was for a low test score to leak out. And he figured the numbers wouldn't help McTiernan and Schwarzenegger, since there was so little time left to tinker with the movie. "I didn't want the director, who had literally been working eighteen hours a day, and our star, to come up with fourteen more ideas that would take three weeks," Canton said. "We didn't *have* three weeks." One thing was for sure: Tonight there would be no jubilant phone calls from the limo.

At Schwarzenegger's suggestion the brass adjourned to Schatzi for a strategy session about what needed to be fixed—and what *could* be fixed in the time remaining. There Guber, Canton, Nathanson, Josephson, Ganis, editor Frank Urioste, co-producer Neil Nordlinger, McTiernan, and Schwarzenegger brainstormed at a long rectangular table until 2:00 A.M. "The feeling was downbeat, but also optimistic that we could make it work," recalled one participant.

372

The comments of the focus group following the screening illuminated several weak and confusing areas in the film. Guber argued forcefully that Slater had to be smarter and more redemptive in Act III; the audience was bothered by the hero's helplessness.

"What the people want to see at that point is, stop having the kid suggest to me what to do next: Arnold should kick in gear and get aggressive," Schwarzenegger said. They decided to bring back Shane Black to rewrite a few scenes. The reshoots would be filmed the following weekend.

These changes were like Band-Aids on a terminally ill patient. Meanwhile, the studio struggled to address problems without being sure where the trouble lay. The movie had been screened in such poor condition that the filmmakers could not fairly judge how it would play when finished. The jokes hadn't gone over well but perhaps that was because the audience couldn't hear them. The feeling was that as editing progressed and the sound got better and the score was added, the laughs would be there.

There was, of course, an elephant in the room that had yet to be discussed.

Schwarzenegger and McTiernan had broached with Columbia—in November 1992 and again in January—the possibility of pushing Last Action Hero's release date back a bit. Clearly the film would have a better chance if McTiernan had more time to reshoot scenes and fine-tune his edit. And despite his public bluster, Arnold was very concerned about going up against Universal's Jurassic Park. As he puffed on a stogie at Schatzi and contemplated with his director just how much work needed to be done in the next seven weeks, the question of the release date was raised again.

But Canton remained adamant that night. Moving the date from June 18 would create a perception that the film was in trouble, he argued. Guber agreed, and for once, the star and director capitulated to the studio. "The studio folks assured us that the movie was more likely to make money this way, that the amount of money that the studio would see would decrease by about $10 million per week for each week of the summer that you cut off," McTiernan said later. "I'm not about to argue about things like that."

Before the meeting broke up that night, someone offered a

373

word of caution. "We ought to be careful," that executive warned. "If the press gets hold of this, it could make us look bad."

EVEN AS ONE of Canton's assistants was running the *Last Action Hero* research cards through the office shredder on Monday morning, the calls to the studio began. Urioste and his editors received several telephone queries in the cutting room: How did the screening go? Columbia creative executive Doug Belgrade took a call from Wendy Wanderman, one of Joel Silver's development people. What were the numbers in Lakewood? she wanted to know. There were no numbers, he told her.

No numbers? Hollywood didn't need an interpreter to figure *that* one out, and the town pounced on Columbia's bad news with barely concealed glee. The whisper campaign gathered steam all around town. "I heard it got a 71." ... "Someone told me it was a 46!" Despite its denials, the studio watched in horror as the rumor mill ground the movie to bits. The nasty word of mouth quickly spread to the press.

Snafus added to the impression that this film simply had "bad karma." The much-touted May NASA rocket launch was postponed—and then canceled. Sony was trying to use the film to launch a new digital sound system, but by now it was clear that the system wouldn't be in place. Columbia fought back by publicizing the reshoots, on the assumption that their limited nature would indicate that the rest of the film was in fine shape.

Simultaneously, there were signs that the marketing campaign was not working. Surely Ganis and his crew envied their rivals at Universal, who had only to show the public a scary dinosaur to get *Jurassic*'s message across. Columbia had to sell the fish with feathers. The TV spots and trailers were leaving some viewers confused about what type of movie *Last Action Hero* was. Arnold's pet project, the much-agonized-over poster, made it look like a kids' movie.

With disaster all around, Columbia looked for a villain to hold responsible. It found one in a freelance writer named Jeffrey Wells, who had already earned the studio's disfavor by writing unflattering pieces about Canton. Wells had written 374 about the troubled Bruce Willis project *Striking Distance* in the *Los Angeles Times*. He had also reportedly contributed to a scathing column by Celia Brady in *Spy* which asserted that Canton had snoozed through a screening of *The Age of Innocence*. The same article said that while Canton was at Warner Bros. he had been assigned to work on Franco Zeffirelli's *Hamlet*, starring Mel Gibson, and had asked for a plot summary.

But all that was merely a prelude to what Columbia would see as Wells's unforgivable transgression. On Friday, June 4, Canton opened an early edition of his weekend *Los Angeles Times* to read a story by Wells entitled, PHANTOM SCREENING: YOU HAVEN'T HEARD THE LAST ABOUT ACTION HERO. The piece speculated about a disastrous *Hero* screening that had allegedly taken place in Pasadena in late May, according to "varied sources, from actors, directors, and film industry executives to social workers, bodybuilders, and dental technicians." None of those purported sources was identified by name or quoted directly in the story, which also ran denials from Columbia that such a screening had ever taken place.

Canton's headache worsened on Monday morning when *Entertainment Weekly* arrived with a cover story billed: SCHWARZENEGGER FINISHES "LAST"!! The article emphasized "the rewrites, reshoots and rumors," reinforcing the idea that the film was troubled and out of control, with its budget soaring to $120 million. Jeffrey Wells was credited as a contributor to the story. In a rage, Canton had the offending issues of *EW* pulled from the shelves of the Columbia bookstore.

"LADIES AND GENTLEMEN, it's Anthony Quinn!"

Despite the woes of the past weeks, the knives were sheathed and the smiles firmly in place on Sunday, June 13, the evening that saw *Last Action Hero*'s $500,000 Westwood premiere for 2,300 invited guests. In keeping with the spirit of the enterprise, the event was excessive, self-congratulatory, and self-delusional.

*Daily Variety*'s Army Archerd heralded the stars' arrivals over a loudspeaker—a role he played traditionally on Oscar night. But the talent turnout was disappointing: Along with Quinn, who played a mafioso in the film, Danny DeVito, Rosanna Arquette, and John Lithgow showed up. Jack Nicholson and Sylvester Stallone stayed home, although Schwarzenegger had recently put in an appearance at Stallone's premiere of *Cliffhanger*. 375

Meanwhile, industry honchos came out in force. As Arnold

worked the paparazzi in front of the theater, a tanned Mike Ovitz swept into the lobby, while David Geffen planted himself in the VIP section with a bag of popcorn. Barry Josephson greeted a flying wedge of young agents. Peter Guber, hair moussed, came over to offer him an encouraging handshake.

The Hollywood premiere is an industry ritual in which members of the audience compliment the filmmakers even if they hate the movie. Then they huddle with their friends to discuss its real prospects. McTiernan and Schwarzenegger greeted the crowd that night. "I've turned out another great movie and everyone seems to love it and the critics have already said that it's a great summer hit," Arnold said, keeping his game face on. The audience responded well to the movie's funniest bits —gags involving a pyramid of Dobermans and Arnold playing Hamlet. But many other jokes, and especially a long sequence revolving around a character called Leo the Fart, fell flat.

After the credits rolled, the guests were guided four blocks along a red carpet to a nearby parking lot, which had been elaborately tricked up with backdrops and props from the film. Fireworks screamed from an adjacent parking structure. A 40-foot Arnold balloon had been inflated for the occasion. Looming over the festivities was a billboard for *Jurassic Park,* then in its smash opening weekend.

Schwarzenegger, McTiernan, and the Columbia team received well-wishers near Elsinore Castle—an *hommage* to Arnold's turn as Hamlet—where maids in medieval costume served up BLT pizzas and rock shrimp. Canton exchanged pleasantries with *Variety* editor Peter Bart and *The Hollywood Reporter*'s Bob Dowling, among others; he was convinced that they had enjoyed the movie. But many guests had reached a less cheery consensus.

As if in silent but deadly reproach, Leo the Fart dangled above the scene from a crane hook. Screenwriter Zak Penn, less than pleased with changes that had been inserted in the script by Shane Black, surveyed the scene with a bad feeling about what was to come. "Leo the Fart," he muttered. "Great idea, Shane."

LEAPIN' LIZARDS! 50 MILLION, yelped *Variety* the next morning, after *Jurassic Park*'s record-breaking opening weekend. The trades brought euphoria to Universal Pictures and despondency to Columbia: Both *Variety* critic Todd McCarthy and *The*

376

*Hollywood Reporter*'s Duane Byrge decimated *Last Action Hero*. "A noisy monstrosity," wrote Byrge. "A joyless, soulless machine of a movie," McCarthy called it, and then went for the kill: *"Last Action Hero* is enough to make one nostalgic for *Hudson Hawk."*

An apoplectic Canton, his hospitality to Dowling and Bart still fresh in his mind, got both editors on the phone before noon. "Don't you see how bad this is for the industry?" he told each of them. To Bart, he registered particular displeasure with the *Hudson Hawk* reference, and Canton would later say that Bart had agreed with him—and had told him that he instructed McCarthy to delete the reference, but that a computer glitch had foiled his plans. Bart disputes that he spoke to McCarthy about the review. "I would never monkey with Todd McCarthy's reviews," he says. "Why would I want to take Mark Canton's dictates?"

By now, the denizens of the Thalberg Building were gripped with panic. That Monday, *Time* printed a review called "The Dinosaur and the Dog" which noted the "doomsday rumors" swirling around the Sony film. Tuesday's *Wall Street Journal* cited the trade reviews in an article headlined: SUMMER MOVIE PUNDITS PREDICT LOSING BATTLE FOR "LAST ACTION HERO." Wednesday's *Los Angeles Times* quoted Columbia spokesman Mark Gill as saying the studio was expecting an opening of "at least $20 million." On Thursday, *USA Today* anchored its Life section with a *Hero* piece that began: "Bad buzz. Ugly reviews. Damage control." More critical devastation rolled in: *Good Morning America*'s Joel Siegel panned *Hero; Today*'s Gene Shalit quipped, "It's supposed to be a movie within a movie. Turns out it's a movie without a movie."

The studio watched helplessly as its audience-tracking polls reflected the media meltdown in the week before the film opened. Research showed that only 12 percent of those polled said *Last Action Hero* was the movie they most wanted to see. The number grew to 16 percent on Monday, compared with 38 percent for *Jurassic Park*. In the normal course of events that number could be expected to rise as opening day approached; but it dropped to 12 percent again as the week wore on.

Schwarzenegger recognized the feeble numbers as a death knell. "Arnold believes that one point represents $1 million over the opening weekend," says McTiernan. "He knew on Wednesday of that week that it was all over."

As they worked almost round the clock to open the film, Columbia executives had enough energy left to foment conspiracy theories on which of its enemies colluded with reporters to sabotage the movie. Some of the *Last Action Hero* team fingered producer Joel Silver as the likeliest culprit. Silver did have a number of apparent motives, starting with being rejected by Canton as the film's producer. And Silver carried a notorious grudge against Barry Josephson, his one-time protégé who had abandoned his post to become a Columbia executive. Silver denied that he had set out to destroy *Last Action Hero*. "It's ludicrous," he said.

Some employees were accused of leaking bad news to the press. But Columbia never grasped the disturbing truth: There was, in fact, a traitor in its midst, a high-level employee inside the Thalberg Building, who had sought out Wells and other members of the press and filled their ears with vivid accounts of the problems on *Last Action Hero*. Columbia had its very own Deep Throat whose identity is still secret.

The movie was going down and somebody had to be blamed. At 6:00 P.M. on Tuesday, June 15, a three-page letter was sent to editor John Lindsay at the *Los Angeles Times*. Signed by Mark Gill, it was a declaration of war: "Columbia Pictures will be out of business with the entire *Los Angeles Times* editorial staff as of noon on Monday, June 21 unless you guarantee that your paper will never again run a story written by Jeff Wells about (or even mentioning) this studio, its executives, or its movies." If the newspaper failed to respond, all *Times* reporters would be barred from studio screenings and their phone calls would go unreturned. Columbia was also considering pulling its reported $5 million in advertising from the paper. "In my three years as Calendar editor," Lindsay said then, "I've never seen anything like this."

Such hardball tactics left the *Times* with no choice but to stand by its story and its reporter: The paper could not be seen as caving in to Columbia. Lindsay defended the "Phantom Screening" piece on the grounds that it reported on rumors of the screening and gave adequate space to the studio's denials. Nevertheless, Calendar movie editor Claudia Eller called sources trying to verify that there had been a Pasadena screening, while Wells desperately tried to get his original sources on the phone. But the "social workers, bodybuilders, and dental technicians" had either disappeared or recanted their stories.

Guber was concerned that Canton had sought a public show-down with Los Angeles's daily newspaper of record. Ganis made a call to editor Shelby Coffey III. "Can we get beyond this?" he wanted to know. It was agreed that Ganis and Gill would meet with the Calendar editors and Coffey at the *Times* downtown offices on the following Tuesday.

While the executives wrestled with the media behind the scenes, Schwarzenegger did what he does best, charming his way through the talk shows. But McTiernan believed that for all his bravado, Schwarzenegger had to be feeling wounded by the nosedive his film was taking. McTiernan pointed out that the star had been quietly working to develop the skills of a real actor on this movie. "He could never have done that before, he never would have allowed himself to," McTiernan says. "It made him very vulnerable, and he was very proud of it . . . and to be rejected so soundly when he had allowed himself to be so naked—it sort of, like, broke his heart, but I suppose that's too flowery a phrase. It broke him up terribly."

Still, as the 800-pound gorilla on this particular show, the star saw it as his job "to keep everyone's spirits up." At the cast and crew screening in the Cary Grant Theater on the Sony lot on the night of Monday, June 14, Schwarzenegger showed up to thank everyone who had worked on the movie. Seeing that Josephson was in a state of shock over the trade reviews, Schwarzenegger took him aside for a private chat. "What-ever happens, don't blame yourself," the star said, as they strolled toward Arnold's Hummer in the parking lot. "You did a great job. You're very smart and you'll do many great pictures in the future—I want you to know that."

The studio's strategy was to preview *Last Action Hero* at 1,400 theaters on Thursday night, as Universal had done with *Jurassic,* to get a running start on the weekend grosses. That evening, Canton, Ganis, and distribution head Jeff Blake went to the AMC Century 14 Theaters in Century City; upon approaching the ticket booth, they were delighted to see a "sold out" sign next to the movie's title. But their joy would be short-lived: When they entered the theater, they saw to their horror that it was nowhere near full. When they returned to the lobby to find out why, an AMC manager explained that a computer malfunction had caused the 10:00 P.M. show to register as sold out even though 25 percent of the tickets remained. The suits hit the ceiling, with Blake loudly lambasting theater personnel.

379

"There was blood all over this place," said an AMC employee, gesturing toward the lobby.

Josephson wanted to be in his hometown, New York, on opening night. It had been the roughest week in his career: In addition to morning sessions with his exercise trainer, he squeezed a manicure into his schedule on Tuesday because he was afraid of biting his nails down to the quick. He flew to New York for *Last Action Hero*'s charity benefit premiere and Planet Hollywood party, and managed to enjoy himself. But the daytime hours monitoring the reviews in his Four Seasons hotel room were agony. Industry friends called to commiserate.

"What floor is your room on?" a producer inquired.

"Twenty-first," Josephson replied.

Pause. "High enough," mused his friend.

By Saturday evening the opening weekend projections were in. The gross would be around $15 million—an even more disappointing figure than the studio had expected. All winter, Mark Canton had imagined that his forty-fourth birthday on June 19 would be especially exultant. A small group of friends gathered to fête him at his home, but the mood was as flat as the champagne was bubbly. It soothed Canton somewhat that many of the guests had weathered their own box-office batterings. But it was Arnold who consoled Canton as no one else could. Lifting a glass, Schwarzenegger toasted the executive who had said yes to pretty much everything the star wanted on *Last Action Hero*. "I met Mark on a professional level," he said, "but over the course of shooting this movie I have gotten to know him as a family man and as a friend. Everything he promised on this picture he came through with, and he never short-changed anyone. And I would do anytime a movie with him again."

"WE ARE VERY, VERY, VERY HAPPY," Ganis was quoted as saying in the Monday trades. The studio had to put a positive spin on the $15.3 million opening, of course, but his claim sounded absurdly hollow.

In a last-ditch attempt to save the movie, Ganis had ordered Marc Shmuger to spend the weekend working up a couple of new TV commercials. The studio knew from its tracking that the young male action crowd was turned off by the ads; now they would be enticed by spots focusing on Arnold doing *Termi-*

380

*nator*-type damage to bad guys. Soon the PG-13 Arnold would be ditched in the newspaper ads, which would feature a mean-looking Slater brandishing a gun. So much for the non-violent Arnold.

On the morning of Monday the 21st, Canton rallied the troops with a pep talk in his office. He thanked everyone for their hard work, reprimanded no one, and called upon the team to stay positive and not give up. The second weekend would be the clincher. If the grosses didn't drop too sharply, all might not be lost.

Ganis and Gill made their pilgrimage on Tuesday to the *Los Angeles Times* to put to rest the Wells affair. Each side restated its position, but it was clear that Columbia had no intention of carrying out its threats to stonewall the paper. "Everyone left the room understanding that nothing was going to happen," Lindsay says.

On its second weekend, *Last Action Hero*'s grosses dropped a precipitous 47 percent, to $8 million. This turkey had no legs. Canton's humiliation was compounded by the $17.4 million debut of *Sleepless in Seattle*, TriStar's romantic comedy, which cost a fraction of *Hero*'s budget.

Distribution chief Jeff Blake had his hands full. A tough, grizzled executive who was used to dealing with demanding exhibitors, Blake had made extra-tough terms on *Hero*. Now theater owners were calling nonstop, wanting to know what the studio would do to make sure they didn't sustain big losses. Blake was forced to ease up on the exhibitors' terms.

On Saturday, June 26, President Clinton ordered a military strike against Saddam Hussein in retaliation for a plot to assassinate George Bush. "We dropped two bombs," industry jokesters said. "One on Iraq and one on Japan."

Each member of the *Last Action Hero* team dealt with crushing disappointment in his own way. Guber stayed out of sight. Canton reversed his usual press-happy policy and refused to talk on the record to reporters about the film that he had aggressively claimed as his own when it looked like a winner. Behind closed doors he raged against the media in a vengeful frenzy which one witness deemed "Nixonian."

At the same time, Canton took some measure of responsibility for the film's downfall. "I would never again want to make that date," he said at the time. "You're promising something too extraordinary and it can cause a backlash." He conceded that he had been wrong to assume that simply having Arnold meant an automatic blockbuster.

"We really got tromped on by a dinosaur, period," McTiernan said dolefully soon after his film opened. More deeply and personally stung than anyone else by the bad reviews and audience indifference, McTiernan wondered if he'd henceforth be consigned to directing straight action pictures. He was convinced that the pre-release pounding kept the movie from getting a fair shake. "In some other circumstance people might have, if not applauded, at least noticed the attempt to make an honest movie," he said. "I can't be articulate about that; I guess I'm still too hurt."

Of the creative principals, only Schwarzenegger simply acknowledged that the movie was not strong enough to overcome bad press and bad word of mouth. The truth was that *Last Action Hero,* by aiming to please both action and comedy fans, had satisfied neither. Arnold had learned that action fans don't want their carnage diluted. "In hindsight, if the kids see 'PG-13' they say, 'Well, I've heard you talk about that, Arnold, you want to tone down the violence. I'm not interested in that—I want to have limbs come off, I want to have heads come off like in *Total Recall.* I want to see bodies flying around.' "

The star wasn't foolish enough to engage in any recriminations against Columbia. "I [could] sit here and say, 'Those motherfuckers, they didn't come through with the promise, they didn't bring the trailer out, the ad campaign was shitty, John McTiernan is a low-forehead, never again—boom.' But that's not the case. Because I love those guys, they are a great team. Everyone did their best, and no one shortchanged anyone," he said.

Jeffrey Wells, meanwhile, finally gave up trying to nail down the confirmation he needed to salvage his reputation regarding that elusive Pasadena screening. His sources, like the screening, turned out to be phantoms. "My conclusion is that it didn't happen," he said, expressing "complete befuddlement" that people would fabricate such information.

After the Fourth of July holiday, Canton found himself the victim of yet another Hollywood rumor: that he had spent the entire weekend slumped in a chair in his den, like Michael Corleone in *The Godfather, Part II,* watching a print of *Jurassic*

*Park* over and over again. "Oh please," sputtered Canton when asked about the story. "What, are you kidding? Why would I be doing that?"

Schwarzenegger was in Spain over the Fourth, preparing to promote *Last Action Hero* in Madrid and Paris. But before he left town, he took care of some correspondence. Peter Bart had written a *Variety* column which gave the star some tips on how to recover from his "image whiplash." The column had sent Canton into yet another rage, but his star struck a more agreeable note.

"Dear Dr. Bart," Schwarzenegger wrote by hand, enclosing a picture of himself wearing a huge neck brace and being ministered to by a doctor in a white coat, "Took your prescription and am feeling better already. Arnold."

As THE SUMMER wore on, morale at Columbia remained low. *Last Action Hero* was supposed to replenish the studio's coffers but it had turned into a black hole. Just how hard Sony would be hit would not be calculable until revenues from international and video sales slowly trickled in over the next few years. But with a final budget approaching $87 million and another $30 million in marketing costs, the studio had projected its break-even point to be somewhere around $80 million in domestic grosses. By late July, *Hero* looked as if it might barely limp to $50 million at the box office.

Ancillary revenues would not soften the blow, either. While the soundtrack performed well, a week after the movie opened Mattel's line of *Last Action Hero* toys had already been relegated to the back shelves of a Toys 'R' Us in Los Angeles, aisles away from the *Jurassic* dinos—which were selling so fast that Kenner Products was scrambling to refill orders.

Guber and Canton grappled with both a cash shortage and a painful question: What had gone so terribly wrong? *Last Action Hero* wasn't the coveted franchise of their dreams, but was it a bad decision to make it?

Arguably, any studio head in town would have been tempted to green-light a big-budget Schwarzenegger project. But many industry observers felt that the movie was doomed by its cynical origins. *Last Action Hero* was born of studio executives' greed rather than the passion of a filmmaker wanting to tell a story.

Still, Canton had also made a number of questionable judg-

383

ment calls: approving the $2.5 million script, which many felt was weak; loudly boasting about the movie's prospects even as Universal remained low-key about *Jurassic Park;* previewing the film on May 1 in rough form to a large audience, virtually guaranteeing leaks; handling the press backlash clumsily.

Some felt that above all, *Last Action Hero* called into question the wisdom of spending more than $100 million on a film and then subjecting it to a severe production and post-production schedule. As a source close to the film said mournfully after the opening, "We shouldn't have had Siskel and Ebert telling us that the movie is ten minutes too long." In his breakneck race to meet the studio's deadline, McTiernan had scarcely had a chance to see his movie completed, much less trim and fine-tune it. Several of Columbia's successes, notably *Bram Stoker's Dracula* and *Groundhog Day,* had been honed during relatively lengthy post-productions, aided by several re-search screenings. *A League of Their Own,* which topped $100 million, was screened three times to poor audience response before it was edited into winning shape.

Now *Last Action Hero* would cause Canton difficulties for at least a year to come. With so much manpower and money poured into *Hero*'s massive effort, Columbia's other business had been relegated to the back burner. Several neglected film-makers were waiting and hoping that Canton could now focus on the future. Jerry Zucker was just one frustrated director who had been unable to get a go-ahead on any of his projects. But *Hero*'s failure meant that the studio would not be flush with cash to bankroll new projects.

While independent industry analysts called *Last Action Hero* an unqualified debacle, the film's executive producer insisted that upfront fees would preclude Sony's taking a loss. "They will make their money back, trust me," said Schwarzenegger. "What they got in advances—between selling the music, with Mattel, the monies coming in from Burger King—I guarantee you, when everything is settled they will have their money back and a profit."

In the long run, *Hero* would not top the studio's list of expen-sive failures: *I'll Do Anything, Geronimo,* even *Lost in Yonkers* would lose much more money. But *Last Action Hero*'s high-profile ride to ruin had earned it a permanent place in the pantheon of Hollywood mega-flops, alongside *Hudson Hawk, The Bonfire of the Vanities,* and *Ishtar.*

384

And what was worse, *Last Action Hero* compounded Sony's humiliation at the hands of its archrival Matsushita, the Japanese electronics giant. It was Matsushita that had bested Sony in the Betamax-VHS home-video battle. In 1990, Matsushita had bought MCA, the parent of Universal Studios, and become Sony's competitor in the entertainment business. Matsushita had kept the studio's management team, headed by Lew Wasserman, one of Hollywood's most powerful executives, and his number-two man, Sid Sheinberg.

Wasserman and Sheinberg did not get along with their new bosses very well. Sheinberg in particular may have struck the Japanese (and some Americans, for that matter) as abrasive and jarringly blunt. But while Sony was buffeted by bad press over excesses at its studio, there were no reports of profligacy, no bizarre antics from these two veterans. Now, while Sony was suffering over *Last Action Hero,* Matsushita was enjoying the Spielberg blockbuster, *Jurassic Park.* Before the year was out, MCA would release another Spielberg hit, *Schindler's List.*

As Matsushita counted its dinosaur dollars and looked forward to sweeping the Oscars, Sony weathered yet another embarrassment. Its expensive Sony Dynamic Digital Sound (SDDS) system, intended to enhance the audience's listening experience, was clobbered by Matsushita's cheaper version. Schulhof had cited the SDDS system as an example of Sony's effort to "integrate entertainment into its core businesses." But while Matsushita had its system available in theaters in time for *Jurassic Park,* Sony had managed to install one in the Village Theatre in Westwood—and it malfunctioned, blowing out the theater's speakers. Around the studio, the acronym SDDS was said to stand for "Still Doesn't Do Shit."

# 29

# HEIDI HO

$B$Y THE END OF SUMMER, Guber, Canton, and Josephson may have hoped to have recovered their equilibrium after the *Last Action Hero* bruising. But as Labor Day approached, they found themselves seized by the clammy terror of job insecurity. A brand-new scandal engulfed Columbia Pictures, and this one was not about box-office bombs. Sony's black summer of 1993 was not over yet.

For weeks after *Last Action Hero* went down in flames, Canton and Ganis continued to rage over journalist Jeff Wells, who had stung them with his unverified account of the screening in Pasadena. Convinced that Wells had deliberately spread lies, Columbia executives tried to damage Wells's reputation with prospective employers. One Columbia executive referred to him as "a cockroach in a nuclear war" that had to be destroyed.

Columbia had another reason for wanting Wells vaporized. Since early in the year the reporter had been checking into tips about a link between the studio and twenty-seven-year-old Heidi Fleiss, Hollywood's reigning madam. Fleiss had become the preferred provider of high-class, $1,500-a-night call girls to the town's players—including stars, executives, and producers. She had succeeded the legendary Madam Alex, aka Elizabeth Adams, whose activities were scaled back after she was arrested for pandering in 1988.

Wells's inquiries had alarmed at least one executive enough to seek legal assistance. A nervous Michael Nathanson, the long-surviving head of production who had made it through Jon's brutal hazing, instructed attorney Bert Fields to send two letters to Wells threatening legal action if Columbia Pictures or Nathanson's name were linked with a prostitution or drug

386

scandal. Nathanson had also retained private detective Anthony Pellicano to investigate and squelch rumors.

At the *Last Action Hero* premiere on June 18, Nathanson had seemed highly agitated, jumping out of his seat several times as the movie played. Although the film's prospects would naturally affect him as the studio's president of production, Nathanson did not have a big personal stake in its success. In fact, he had opposed green-lighting it and had let Barry Josephson, whom he viewed as a detested rival, be the front man who talked to the press during production.

But the day before the premiere, a 397-word item buried on page 3 of the *Los Angeles Times*'s Saturday Metro section reported that Heidi Fleiss had been arrested at her Benedict Canyon home and charged with five counts of pandering and one count of cocaine possession. She was picked up following a sting operation staged by the LAPD, the Beverly Hills Police, and the Justice Department. An undercover cop had hired four of Fleiss's prostitutes for a night of partying—no group sex, condoms required.

Fleiss was taking out the trash in front of her home at around 8:30 P.M. on the clear, starry night of June 9 when eight law enforcement officers with two dogs jumped out of the bushes. "LAPD!" they cried. They searched her house, a $1.6 million property with a pool and spectacular view, formerly owned by actor Michael Douglas. Fleiss was charged and released on $100,000 bail.

The Hollywood rumor mill, already in high gear over the showdown between Schwarzenegger and Spielberg, was thrown into overdrive. The Monday after Fleiss's arrest, reporters at the *Los Angeles Times, Variety,* and *The Hollywood Reporter* started to get anonymous phone calls purporting to name Heidi's clients.

Stars were mentioned—especially Charlie Sheen, allegedly a big customer who was rumored to like the hookers to dress as cheerleaders. The rumors swirled around one studio in particular, Columbia, and its president of production, Michael Nathanson. According to callers, who provided no documentation, he was a Fleiss client, and may have used Sony money to procure drugs and prostitutes. Tales also circulated that Steve Roth, the nominal producer of *Last Action Hero,* was a Heidi client, and that some of Heidi's girls had been hired to appear as extras in the film.

Jaded industry insiders were delighted to have their attention diverted from box-office bombs to bombshells, from talk of research screenings and tracking scores to speculation about what lascivious acts were paid for by which Hollywood players, with which studio's money.

Within days of Heidi's arrest, nervous clients—including several prominent players—had called her to wish her well and to exhort her to be discreet. Certain big-time producers, including Don Simpson, gave her thousands of dollars to help pay her legal bills. Heidigate had hit Hollywood.

BY THE END OF THE EIGHTIES, Hollywood's business culture was defined by legions of "suits," agents and executives who patrolled their turf in expensive German cars, cellular phones to their ears. Like the moneymen of Wall Street, they were sleek young warriors who spent twelve-hour work days doing battle. Some of them were under thirty and made $1 million a year; to them, money and power were sexier than sex. For those so inclined, the drug of choice was cocaine.

But the nineties ushered in a new asceticism. Everyone seemed to be working on recovery in a twelve-step program. There remained committed hedonists like Jack Nicholson, who lamented the new aversion to almost everything pleasurable. "My type of man is not attracted to society at this moment," he told *Vanity Fair* magazine. ". . . all this flat-belly bullshit is killing the country. . . . Reich said a long time ago that the flat-bellied male martinet is the main problem with our entire culture."

But others sought cachet by leaving the dressing off the Chinese chicken salad, passing up the Chardonnay in favor of Pellegrino, deferring relationships with women while keeping dates with exercise machines. The only permissible addiction was to *lattes* from the Starbucks coffeehouses that sprang up all over town. But this new asceticism was about as deep as the finish on an agent's Saab Turbo 900S.

Certainly it hadn't seemed to put much of a crimp into Heidi Fleiss's booming business. Some of Heidi's clients were married; others simply didn't have the time or inclination or possibly the social skills to go through the most minimal rituals associated with dating. It was easier to pay a bill than to incur some kind of obligation. Hiring hookers wasn't really about sex: It was about power and money and style. A call girl did exactly what she was told—and then left you alone. As Don Simpson put it, "You're not paying hookers to come, you're paying them to leave."

Some executives and agents who handled big stars reportedly facilitated their clients' access to hookers. This had become more common since the tabloid media, from the *Star* and the *Enquirer* to *Hard Copy* and *Inside Edition,* had become rabid in their quest for salacious stories. No longer could an actor risk picking up a girl in a bar or on a movie location; soon he might be reading about their "torrid night of love" at the supermarket checkout counter. Married actors were particularly vulnerable to such exposure, and studios wanted to protect their investments.

One of Hollywood's most visible bachelors was Columbia vice president Barry Josephson, who was frequently seen squiring beautiful women around town. When he had worked for producer Joel Silver, Josephson had been known as "the vice president of chicks and clubs." Fastidiously groomed and dressed, by day Josephson was a hardworking and ambitious professional. By night he was a playboy who caroused with models while telling friends that he was lonely and eager to settle down with a nice girl.

In the summer of 1993, the executive culture inside the Thalberg Building was like a boys' club whose members had too much money and too little supervision. The core group included Guber, Canton, Nathanson, and Josephson. Dolgen and Levine remained outside the fraternal order, while Ganis hovered on the periphery. Women were excluded from the decision making and a locker-room mentality prevailed. "When I think about Columbia," muses one former insider, "I think about all those tiny little men in tiny little jeans endlessly high-fiving each other."

In the spirit of the times Guber, Canton, and Nathanson all projected images as happily married husbands and fathers, upstanding citizens. As the oldest, Guber was the one who retained some predilections from the hot-tub days. When he entertained a visitor for lunch in his private dining room, he served low-fat cuisine but extolled the sybaritic pleasures of lolling in his new at-home flotation tank—which included a 389 television screen on which he could watch films.

Whenever possible Guber emphasized his commitment to

family, children, and education. He posed with his daughters Jodi and Elizabeth for a Father's Day spread in the *Los Angeles Weekly*. "My daughters are my best friends," he told the paper. He contined to teach at UCLA—he was now co-chair of the producers' program—and served on the board of Education First!, a non-profit organization formed by Lynda Guber to encourage educational messages in the media. While many viewed Education First! as primarily a social platform for Lynda, Guber involved Sony in many of the organization's activities, helping it raise money.

While Lynda appeared at her husband's side at corporate functions and they enjoyed time together in Aspen, Guber also engaged in many solo activities. Even as chairman of Sony, he kept up his habit of talking dirty in one-on-one professional encounters with women. During one "job interview" conducted over dinner in a Beverly Hills restaurant, one disappointed applicant found that Guber talked mostly about sex. "He has a very foul mouth," she remembered. "Every other sentence had to do with 'hard-ons' and 'wetness' and his dick and stuff."

Guber was getting older and he seemed acutely aware of it. He was dyeing his hair and he had the wrinkles around his eyes smoothed by a plastic surgeon. He spent a lot of time consorting with some of the town's young bachelors, including Josephson and CAA agent Jay Moloney. He organized retreats where the men could discuss their feelings and howl at the moon in pampered surroundings.

Mark Canton spent plenty of time hanging around with Guber and his young friends, and he was even more aggressive than his boss in promoting himself as a family man. He often mentioned his wife, producer Wendy Finerman, and their two small children in interviews. In a flattering profile in *Vanity Fair*, he referred to their home as "the *Leave It to Beaver* Hotel."

Yet it is difficult to imagine Ward Cleaver disporting himself, as Columbia's chairman did, at the very special dinner party that Jon Peters threw at his Beverly Park home in 1991. The host had invited Canton and two other male friends to dine that night and hired two young women to serve the meal. The girls were fetchingly turned out as French maids with crisp white aprons. When a guest rose from the table to go to the bathroom, one of the girls would follow and ask if he might like some, um, dessert. Peters had hired these hard workers not from a local catering outfit but from Heidi Fleiss.

390

Being serviced in almost every way imaginable was a key aspect of several Columbia executives' lifestyle. Since he had plenty of money and almost no free time, an executive relieved stress and honed his image as an important person by availing himself of an array of people who buffed, massaged, outfitted, clipped, and analyzed him. Aside from his gurus, Peter Guber had his own chef and a full-time driver who idled the boss's Range Rover at the curb outside the Thalberg Building. Barry Josephson rose at 6:00 A.M. to submit his whippet-thin frame to a workout with his trainer before showering and heading for the office. To shave minutes from his schedule, Canton was known to hold a meeting in his office and get a manicure simultaneously.

Michael Nathanson had long been a champion consumer of services. He was making $650,000 a year in salary, with bonuses up to $300,000. He emulated the extravagant lifestyles of his wealthier acquaintances in the movie world, including Jon Peters and Michael Douglas. After his wedding in 1990, Nathanson moved with his wife into the Beverly Hills Hotel while their home in Beverly Hills underwent extensive renovations. They rented a beach house in Malibu for the summer for $30,000. They paid many thousands of dollars a month to Williams-Sonoma, La Fromagerie, and the local florist and chocolatier. Nathanson had bagels and lox sent by Federal Express from the Barney Greengrass deli in New York, even though there were a number of authentic delis in L.A. When his wife gave birth to the couple's first child, Michael bought her a black-and-white pearl collar and bracelet from Frances Klein on Rodeo Drive for $10,283.75.

"CAN I TELL YOU how happy I am I never spoke to this woman?" said one relieved Columbia producer the week after Heidi's arrest.

With Heidi free on bail and due to be arraigned on August 9, it was going to be a long, hot, sweaty summer. Certain high-level residents of the Thalberg Building went about their business in a state of apprehension. What if Heidi spilled the beans about the names in her appointment books? The town's tongue-waggers were predicting the immolation of high-profile marriages and careers.

Those intimately acquainted with Ms. Fleiss had cause to fret. A thin, feral brunette, Heidi was a nice Jewish girl gone bad, a pediatrician's daughter who became an overnight success in the prostitution business. She had lured some of Madam Alex's girls away to start her own business with her former lover, a Hungarian-born film director and convicted bookmaker named Ivan Nagy.

The sex trade at the upper levels of Hollywood had traditionally been conducted discreetly. But veterans had feared for some time that Heidi would be trouble: Young and brash, she was a loose cannon. She had a history of drug abuse and erratic, vengeful behavior. One reason she was arrested, according to LAPD vice captain Glenn Ackerman, was because of "her own big mouth." Heidi had boasted in a *Los Angeles Times* interview that she had bested her former employer. "What it took Alex years to build, I built in one," she said. Although she wasn't quoted by name, authorities knew who was doing the bragging and felt compelled to act.

After her arrest, Fleiss told *Variety* that she would tell all to any publisher who offered her $1 million. That threat, combined with the cache of evidence confiscated from her home —including several red Gucci notebooks containing client appointments and phone numbers—had some of the town's most prominent men mopping their brows.

If Nathanson were innocent of improper use of Columbia money to procure girls or drugs, it didn't look that way. Ivan Nagy had been his close friend for some ten years; the two men played tennis, sailed, and partied together. One source reported having been present at an outing on Nagy's sailboat in the mid-eighties at which Nathanson, Nagy, and a young producer named Brad Wyman were joined by a bevy of topless girls in the employ of Madam Alex.

Nagy was a blustery, profane man who had directed episodes of *Starsky and Hutch* and *The Hitchhiker*, along with nine TV movies. When his Hollywood career began to fade, he had gone to work for Madam Alex, helping her manage her business. Nagy had a lot of social contacts—he was a tennis friend of former TriStar head Jeff Sagansky—and he always seemed to have lots of pretty girls and cocaine around him. He was arrested in May 1991 on six felony counts of bookmaking, possession of cocaine with intent to sell, and cultivation of marijuana. Convicted only on the bookmaking charge, he was placed on probation.

392

In the late eighties Nagy became involved in a tempestuous romance with Heidi, then in her early twenties and allegedly turning tricks for Madam Alex. The couple were regular guests at Nathanson's home for holiday parties, where Nagy and his girlfriend raised eyebrows among more clean-cut types. "Nagy is a pig—horrible," says one source. "I would see him at Michael's house for football games. Heidi and Nagy would be there amidst all these executive types, and you'd sit there and think to yourself, 'What's wrong with this picture?' "

It was commonly assumed that Nagy took care of Nathanson's needs for drugs and women. Although Nathanson has denied that Nagy supplied him with drugs or prostitutes, copies of his bank records show that he did write personal checks to Nagy: one for $750 on February 23, 1989, and one for $500 on October 24, 1990.

The rumors surrounding Nathanson were bolstered in mid-1992 when he went into rehab at the Daniel Freeman Marina Hospital in Marina del Rey for drug addiction. Nathanson claimed that he had gotten hooked on the painkiller Percodan after he broke his ankle jogging. He returned to work after a few weeks.

As a new father, Nathanson had said he was staying clean of drugs, hoping to pursue a quiet life as a family man. But his nightmare had just begun. Nagy and Heidi had broken up and were engaged in a dirty war: According to a transcript of a surreptitiously taped telephone call, Nagy had discussed setting up a new prostitution business with a former girl of Heidi's, Julie Conaster, and an enraged Fleiss was now determined to destroy her ex-lover. One sure way to hurt him, she figured, was to expose and sabotage Nagy's relationship with Columbia Pictures and its president of production.

In June of 1992, Fleiss had sat down for an interview with *Premiere* magazine's John H. Richardson. She told him that Nagy supplied Nathanson with women and drugs—Percodan, specifically. "Sometimes he was even begging Ivan, Nathanson wanted it so much," she said. She told Richardson that Nathanson had even been so foolish as to give Nagy a $25,000 development deal with Columbia Pictures.

When Richardson confronted Nathanson with Fleiss's 393 charge, Nathanson swore that he had never made a deal of any kind with Nagy. But this was only technically true. Nathanson had made a deal in early 1992 with Brad Wyman, the young producer who had spent time on the sailboat with Nathanson, Nagy, and the topless party girls. Nagy became Wyman's partner in Nagy-Wyman Productions, located in a Sony office. Nagy's name, phone number, and office address were listed in the Columbia studio directory.

Wyman was a rich kid from Bel Air whose mother had once served on the Los Angeles City Council, and he ran with brat-packers Charlie Sheen, Judd Nelson, and Rob Lowe. He became a kind of Hollywood legend at a young age when he attended the 1988 Cannes Film Festival, trying to raise financing for a feature film called *The Dark Backward.* In Cannes, Wyman lost his mind and crawled through the Hôtel du Cap bar, begged people at parties for spare change with which to fund his movie, and in a flashy finish streaked naked through the airport screaming: "Vive la France! Vive la France!" He eventually made *The Dark Backward,* which starred Judd Nelson and James Caan, both acquaintances of Heidi's.

Columbia's investment in Nagy-Wyman was not a fruitful one. Nagy directed a low-budget thriller starring ex–porn queen Traci Lords, called *Skinner,* which was not released theatrically. Columbia home video also declined to distribute it. A feature entitled *Indiscretion,* a twist on *Fatal Attraction* in which a boy gets obsessed with a girl, was developed but never made; its screenwriter Zeke Richardson, who was paid less than $200,000, had several script meetings with Columbia executive vice president Teddy Zee, Nagy, and Wyman. After Heidi's arrest, the writer received a call from Zee. "This project is in turnaround," he was told.

Brad Wyman was also listed as a co-producer—with Jon Peters—on a $50 million version of Alexandre Dumas's *The Three Musketeers,* which was shelved after a script was written by John Fasano. Nagy later told the *New York Daily News* that when he and Heidi were breaking up, she squelched *The Three Musketeers* with a phone call to someone inside Columbia threatening to leak tapes of her conversations with clients. Columbia sources deny, plausibly, that Heidi had anything to do with the death of *The Three Musketeers;* more likely it withered because Disney had a version of the classic in the works that was closer to production.

But Heidi *had* been calling Nathanson, pestering him in her effort to undermine Nagy. Nathanson had told Jon Peters about the calls and Jon phoned Heidi to tell her to lay off. After Heidi was busted, however, the din of rumors surrounding Nathanson, Heidi, and Nagy grew loud and persistent. Some sources alleged that Columbia executives compensated Nagy for procuring girls and drugs through the Nagy-Wyman deal. Nathanson reportedly threatened to sue two *Hollywood Reporter* journalists who were working on the story.

On July 29, the *New York Post*'s Richard Johnson wrote that "heads are about to roll at a certain movie studio," where the services of call girls "were paid for by the studio and written off as 'development costs.' " The *Los Angeles Times* explored the Heidi scandal in a lengthy front-page story on August 1. Still, no paper had named names. For all their efforts, the reporters had no hard evidence identifying Heidi's clients or demonstrating that anyone at Columbia Pictures had patronized her.

Then the media got an incredible break, courtesy of the very fish they wanted to fry. On August 3, Nathanson made a foolish move. No longer able to withstand the rumors, he put himself on the record with a preemptive denial of reports that might never have been published if he had kept silent. Reportedly acting on the advice of Detective Pellicano, hardly a public relations expert, Nathanson issued a statement through his lawyer, Howard Weitzman, saying that he had no business relationship of any kind with Fleiss. Nathanson "has not done anything that should cause concern on behalf of Columbia," Weitzman's statement said, adding—perhaps with an infelicitous choice of words—that "it's time he confront the rumors, put them to bed and get on with his life."

Now Nathanson got to see himself on the nightly news and read his name in practically every newspaper and magazine across the country. His denial made the Heidi-Columbia scandal legitimate news and every media outlet had an excuse to run with the hookers-in-Hollywood piece.

"Guber freaked" when he heard about Nathanson's statement, says one Columbia insider. Perhaps fearing that the studio was about to turn on him, Nathanson had not consulted his superiors before he released his denial to the press. That weekend, the agenda at a previously scheduled retreat for Columbia and TriStar executives at Santa Barbara's Biltmore Hotel was transformed into a crisis-management session. Guber addressed the group and outlined a plan for moving through the Heidi meltdown. It was decided that an executive shuffle that had been in the works for some months—the appointment of Lisa Henson, daughter of Muppeteer Jim Henson, as Columbia's production president—would be announced on August 9. At the same time Michael Nathanson would be named executive vice president—a position that didn't appear to have any clear mandate.

On Wednesday, August 4, Nagy was arrested outside a La Cienega Boulevard coffee shop as he stepped out of his white Mercedes-Benz, and booked on pandering charges, along with his alleged partner Julie Conaster. Now it was Barry Josephson's turn to suffer. In a clear attempt to turn attention from his friend Nathanson's woes, Nagy leaked a Xeroxed page from Heidi's diary to the *New York Daily News,* which reprinted it on August 6. Next to the name "Barry," scrawled in what was presumably Heidi's handwriting, was the phone number 280-5888—Josephson's direct office line. The name "Cantin" (*sic*) also appeared faintly in the upper right corner of the page. Heidi would claim the book was stolen and doctored before it was leaked to the press.

With both Nathanson and Josephson's names in the press, Columbia had to do something. Reportedly Mickey Schulhof called every top studio executive into his office one at a time. "Tell me what you know about the Heidi matter," he instructed. "If you tell the truth, we'll do everything we can to protect you. But if you lie to me you're finished."

Columbia made no official comment on the Heidi Fleiss imbroglio. Instead, as *Entertainment Weekly* reported that Columbia officials were "caught up in an ever-widening sex scandal," the studio leaked word that Guber had ordered an "internal investigation" into whether company funds had been used to procure prostitutes. The studio's relationship with Nagy was severed and his name removed from the company directory, though the charges against him and Conaster were later dropped.

With Paul Schaeffer heading up the internal investigation with the help of outside lawyers, executives were grilled about any information they might have regarding call girls at the studio. The financial statements for five Columbia movies—including *Last Action Hero*—were audited. Employees were asked such questions as "Were you aware of any Heidi Fleiss

396

girls working on this movie?" One Columbia creative executive who never expected to be investigated was surprised to be notified by Howard Weitzman that the studio had cleared that employee of any wrongdoing regarding Fleiss.

On August 9, Heidi Fleiss was arraigned in the Los Angeles downtown municipal court building at 210 West Temple Street. By dawn the courthouse was already surrounded by television vans with satellite dishes, and paparazzi hung on the fences. The courtroom was jammed with reporters who craned their necks to catch a glimpse of Fleiss, escorted by her attorney Anthony Brooklier. Dressed in a taupe Norma Kamali minidress, Fleiss fiddled with her hair as she pled not guilty to five felony charges of pandering and one count of possession of cocaine. Accompanied by her friends Victoria Sellers and Bonita Money, who said they had turned out to give her "moral support," Fleiss was ordered to appear at a preliminary hearing on September 10.

By now the media were desperate to find a smoking gun—and many reporters remained convinced that call girls had been buried somewhere in the *Last Action Hero* budget. It is not hard to comprehend how these rumors had sprung up and then caught fire: that production had been awash in pretty girls, and the testosterone level on the set was sky-high. Thousands of extras, many of them beautiful models, had been hired from the Central Casting Agency to appear in the background of the film.

Extras casting on *Last Action Hero* had been supervised by second assistant director Carl Goldstein. Barry Josephson had been openly and enthusiastically involved in the screening of attractive women—scrutinizing Polaroids, meeting candidates, and occasionally asking one for her phone number. Josephson's activities were a running joke on the set, where crew members would ask Goldstein: "Carl, are you casting gorgeous girls again? Are you off to Barry's office?"

Journalists tried in vain to confirm reports that prostitutes had appeared in a scene shot in a Malibu video store in which Schwarzenegger is surrounded by big-breasted, scantily clad babes. Although it was not impossible that any of these extras might have moonlighted as call girls, there was no evidence that sexual favors had been part of the terms of their—or any other extra's—employment on the film. 397

But as the rumors persisted, Columbia looked for a way to

distract attention from its beleaguered insiders. Steve Roth, the producer-in-name of *Last Action Hero*, represented the ideal scapegoat. The unfortunate Roth, whose deal with Columbia was in the process of being terminated by the studio, had been coping with a drug problem as well as a divorce and financial difficulties. Conveniently for Columbia, he had also patronized Heidi Fleiss. "Did I get a girl from Heidi? Yes," admits Roth. "And I'm not the first."

Although Roth had been frozen out of any real involvement on *Last Action Hero*—had scarcely even visited the set, in fact—he was now fingered by Columbia. On August 28, the *Los Angeles Times* ran a story, citing anonymous sources close to the studio, reporting that Roth was now the focus of an investigation into possible ties between Columbia and Fleiss, and that Sony auditors were poring over financial records from *Last Action Hero* and Steve Roth Productions. Roth's deal was terminated and he says he was "booted out of my office."

The *Times* story implied that Roth had exercised some measure of control over the *Last Action Hero* budget, which was untrue. "I had made certain mistakes in my life, but that was out-and-out lying," says Roth, who is bitter over his treatment by Columbia. "When sharks see that you are wounded, they'll take you apart." Roth says that today he is clean and sober, and "I've paid in excess for what I did."

Sony never did make a statement about the results of its "internal investigation," although sources say the *Last Action Hero* books came up clean. That fall, the Heidi Fleiss story finally died down when the media lit upon a new scandal, Michael Jackson's alleged child molestation.

Throughout the Heidi tempest, many expressed surprise that while Nathanson and Josephson were linked publicly with Heidi, Jon Peters's name was left out of media speculations about Fleiss's clients. Columbia sources say it was commonly assumed that Peters was at least as active a client as the younger men. But no one on the inside of the scandal came forward to implicate Peters, still a powerful presence at Columbia.

In any case, Nathanson and Josephson maintained stoic silence throughout their ordeal—and they prospered. Nathanson soon departed Columbia to work as president of producer Arnon Milchan's company at Warner Bros.—a job that Jon Peters helped arrange. Josephson became the new president of production. Some observers thought it odd that Josephson was promoted after presiding over the *Last Action Hero* debacle.

"Barry and Michael were fall guys," Fleiss told *Vanity Fair* in an article that came out once all the fuss was over.

As for Jon Peters, "He got girls for everyone," said Fleiss. "He knew Alex for years. He was a *huge* client. He was the guy everyone went to when they wanted a girl."

# 30

---

# A BAD YEAR
# ENDS BADLY

As ONE CRISIS after another rocked Columbia in 1993, Hollywood insiders noticed that Guber seemed less visible than ever. Just when the studio most desperately needed some steadying leadership, Guber resorted to his familiar vanishing act. During the Heidi Fleiss scandal, reports circulated that he was vacationing on his yacht. "He's gone completely AWOL," remarked one prominent agent.

"We all called him the Wizard of Oz," remembers a former high-level executive who found the boss more inaccessible all the time. "He was like the man behind the screen . . . but no one thought he was this sweet old wizard."

Guber still managed to enjoy the perks of his job—particularly when they took him away from the beleaguered Culver City lot. In May, as *Last Action Hero* was careering toward disaster, he and Mickey Schulhof and their wives had traveled on the Sony jet to Bangkok after a business trip to Tokyo. In Thailand they had dinner with expatriate screenwriter Sterling Silliphant, who had won an Academy Award for *In the Heat of the Night*. Silliphant, who had known Guber in the seventies, had found him "brilliant, enthusiastic, boyish" in those days. But when Silliphant joined the Gubers and Schulhofs in the Chinese restaurant of the sumptuous Oriental Hotel in Bangkok, he was disappointed by the jaded tone of the conversation. "It reminded me how vacuous Hollywood can be," he says.

That day the two couples had been granted a reception with Bhumibol Adulyadej, the king of Thailand, at the royal residence, the Grand Palace. Silliphant was offended by how casually they seemed to view this privilege, which had been arranged by Sony. "This is a very remarkable king; to us he's almost sacred. It's difficult to arrange an audience. They certainly didn't seem to appreciate the honor."

Back in Los Angeles, one area of his job that held Guber's interest was a new division he launched called Sony New Technologies, which became his favorite playground. In the middle of 1993, as part of Sony New Technologies, he announced Sony's entry into the huge-screen IMAX business. The company would both produce IMAX movies and build an IMAX theater as part of the Sony Theatres Lincoln Square complex at Sixty-eighth Street and Broadway in Manhattan. Guber bought a one-hour IMAX project called *Across the Sea of Time* and spent a dozen hours developing the script with the writer and director, delivering copious notes. One executive recalls that Guber was more attentive to the IMAX film than to most of the features the studio was producing.

Another aspect of studio business that genuinely seemed to engage Guber was the ongoing lot renovation. Since Jon Peters's departure, Guber had thrown himself into the project with almost as much zeal as his former partner had. Administering the elaborate buffer zone of landscaped flower beds and trees that was materializing in front of the Thalberg Building may have provided welcome respite from the more serious problems that weighed on him. Guber took particular interest in the trees, ordering several freshly planted ones yanked out of the ground—because they looked too young. They were replaced by more mature-looking specimens.

Over the course of the year, a giant multi-million-dollar Deco wall of stucco and ironwork was raised around the perimeter of the studio. One high-level occupant of the Thalberg Building saw it as a symbol of Guber and his team's increasing isolation from the larger world. "The wall would hide the real world of Culver City from the vaunted expanses of the Thalberg Building," that executive said.

While Jon Peters's notion in the initial plans had been to make every corner of the back lot suitable for filming, as the renovation progressed it became clear that his wish would go unfulfilled. A visitor venturing west from the plush enclave of the Thalberg Building would pass beneath a giant Lawrence of Arabia mural and through another guard gate onto Sony's

401

back lot—and enter a world that felt distinctly dislodged from reality. By this time the lot had been transformed into an ersatz version of a film studio, with a Main Street of false fronts. There was a faux bowling alley and a sporting goods store that displayed the costumes and bats from *A League of Their Own*. One's sense of disorientation was heightened by the fact that the real entrances to buildings were indistinguishable from phony ones. A joke made the rounds that only at Sony did doors open to nowhere.

Had this Disneyesque version of a back lot had a utilitarian purpose, it might not have seemed so absurd. But the streets were too narrow for filmmaking trucks. Sony's hundreds of millions had paid for a back lot that was merely a handsome facade. It was, in the final analysis, the quintessential Peter Guber production.

IN THE DARKEST days of the summer, with *Last Action Hero* imploding, Mark Canton had something he could cling to: On July 9, the studio released *In the Line of Fire*, Castle Rock's film starring Clint Eastwood as a Secret Service agent who has to prevent a presidential assassination. The studio's expectations had not been especially high, but the picture would gross more than $100 million and generate a profit of $33.6 million for the studio. Canton managed to take this windfall and turn it into a problem.

His relations with filmmaker Rob Reiner and his colleagues at Castle Rock already were strained—a state of affairs that would not be helpful to Columbia considering that Reiner's production company had provided much-needed hits: *City Slickers* and *A Few Good Men*, as well as a hit prime-time television show distributed by Sony: *Seinfeld*. TriStar collected a $50 million distribution fee for selling the show in syndication.

True, Castle Rock had slipped Columbia a few bombs like *Mr. Saturday Night*. But all things considered, Columbia benefited enormously from its relationship with Castle Rock. Meanwhile, the Castle Rock partners were perennially unhappy that the terms of their distribution deals cost them so much of the profits from their successful films. Now came word that Castle Rock was negotiating in earnest to escape from its bonds and start over with a new investor.

Sony had tried to mend its fences with Reiner and his part-

402

ners, with Guber singing their praises at a party at Spago after the *In the Line of Fire* premiere. "That only made them feel better about Peter—not about Columbia," says a former Columbia executive. The following Monday, Canton issued a press release touting the film's $15 million opening and celebrating Columbia's "partnership" with Castle Rock during its making, on everything from the acquisition of the script to "casting, production and post-production, to marketing and distribution of the film."

This was too much for the Castle Rock faction, which had wearied of hearing Columbia executives boasting about "their" movie before the film was released. "Their" movie was *Last Action Hero*, not *In the Line of Fire*. Like so many projects, *In the Line of Fire* had a long and tortured history, but unquestionably it was Castle Rock—not Columbia—that had picked up the script, developed it, hired Clint Eastwood and John Malkovich, and attached director Wolfgang Petersen. Josephson had worked with Petersen on developing the script, and Canton had courted Eastwood, with whom he was well acquainted from his days at Warner. But while Canton took particular credit for luring Eastwood, the Castle Rock side said Eastwood had independently contacted the company about the picture and had wanted to do it regardless of Canton. Columbia fairly deserved credit for paying the $40 million tab and—significantly —for marketing the film well.

In a rare exhibition of pique, Castle Rock partner Martin Shafer rebuffed Canton in a *Los Angeles Times* interview. "Columbia did not initiate or package [the film]," he said. "From a creative standpoint, it was a Castle Rock movie." He explained the steps that Castle Rock had taken in making the film, crediting Canton only with suggesting Rene Russo for the female lead.

The unvarnished truth was, the guys at Castle Rock were sick of Sony and the guys at Sony were just as sick of Castle Rock. The relationship was like a romance that had gone on too long. But Castle Rock had just signed a worldwide distribution deal with Sony, and Sony had been trying to help the partners raise $200 million in financing.

Late in the spring, Castle Rock had attracted some suitors, notably cable-TV mogul Ted Turner, who had an itch to buy himself a big hunk of Hollywood. The match made sense: 403

Turner would be acquiring one of the most prestigious production companies in the movie business, while cash-poor Castle Rock would be getting a deep-pocketed owner. Horn and his partners would at last be free of the humiliation of always having to beg for money.

The only obstacle to the Turner–Castle Rock deal was of course Sony, which owned 44 percent of Castle Rock. "Sony knew they had to either buy us or go along with the Turner deal," says Horn. "They could have brought us in-house, as a third branch of the company. But Peter Guber told me, 'You won't like that, because I can't have a third arm here that has 100% autonomy without budget constraints.' " Guber knew that the Castle Rock partners would not agree to any limitations on their green-light ability.

At the end of July, Peter Guber was a surprise no-show at Herbie Allen's annual gathering of media and Wall Street tycoons in Sun Valley. When Alan Horn was seen playing tennis and huddling with Turner Entertainment executive Scott Sassa, there was speculation that a merger announcement might be imminent. Jeffrey Katzenberg, then chairman of Disney Studios, taunted Horn as the two flew back to Los Angeles on the Warner jet. He'd lay 100 to 1 odds, he said, that Sony would never relinquish its stake in the company that had produced three of its biggest hits in the previous three years.

Katzenberg was wrong. By August, Castle Rock's marriage with Ted Turner was arranged. Alan Levine negotiated a deal to sell Sony's stake in the company for $44 million plus an extended distribution arrangement. Columbia would release Castle Rock movies through 1997—with an enhanced distribution fee. Katzenberg was licked; he paid his bet by sending a thousand-dollar check to the Natural Resources Defense Council, Horn's choice.

Many people at Columbia had long feared this day. "A lot of years, the only reason Columbia had market share was because of Castle Rock," says an executive there. Over the duration of Sony's ownership, the company had contributed approximately 40 percent of Columbia's total revenues. But although Sony's critics blamed the breakdown of the relationship with Castle Rock on bad management, the studio had pulled out at an opportune time—and at favorable terms. After its long string of successes, Castle Rock was about to hit rough waters with a string of losers. Within two years, the wisdom of Guber's decision would be evident.

GUBER AND CANTON were not going to get much of a break. Another mega-flop was in the works. On the evening of August 7, Jim Brooks was pacing nervously in the back of the Cary Grant Theater on the Sony lot. The celebrated director's musical about Hollywood, *I'll Do Anything*, was about to be previewed for the first time. Brooks had reason to be anxious: He had never directed a musical before. This one featured Nick Nolte, Tracey Ullman, Albert Brooks, and Julie Kavner, none of whom were known for their musical ability, bursting into songs written by Prince, Sinéad O'Connor, and Carole King. Nolte and Brooks were even attempting a bit of Twyla Tharp choreography.

Shortly after the lights went down, Tracey Ullman trilled the movie's first number, "Don't Talk to Strangers," when her character sends her six-year-old daughter off to Los Angeles to live with her father (Nolte). Brooks winced when he heard an ominous sound: snickers from the front of the theater. A short time later the little girl, played by Whittni Wright, sang a ballad, which occasioned a dozen walkouts. Finally, when Julie Kavner opened her mouth to sing, the audience rose in virtual insurrection. A huge group fled for the doors, while others hooted.

"It was an out-of-body experience," Brooks says, "the worst night of my life." He and producer Polly Platt and their team repaired to the lush offices of Gracie Films, Brooks's company, in the restored Jean Harlow Building. Brooks opened a bottle of bourbon. He had spent the last three years of his life devoting himself to *I'll Do Anything*. And it didn't work.

The devastated director spent the next few days in discussions with Platt about his plans to edit some of the musical numbers out of the film and retest it. Then the phone rang. It was the *Los Angeles Times*. The paper was planning to run an item saying that *I'll Do Anything* had had a disastrous preview. Brooks had hoped to preview his film quietly (Columbia brass hadn't even been invited to the screening), but it had been a blunder to show it on the Sony lot. *Times* reporters, after the *Last Action Hero* flap, had become quick to smell trouble on movies-in-progress. Brooks begged *Times* Calendar editor Claudia Eller not to run the item—and was cornered into a deal. He

405

agreed to allow a *Times* reporter to attend two of his upcoming screenings and grant an interview in exchange for the paper killing the item. Any negative press at this sensitive juncture, he figured, would mean "I was gonna be dead in the water."

*I'll Do Anything* was not part of Brooks's overall deal at Sony. Although many in the industry felt that it was a poor risk with a budget of $39.5 million—just under the $40 million that would have required Schulhof to sign off on it—Canton had been quick to embrace it. "Don't tell me that as his first movie for Columbia, he wants to make that picture that no one else wants to make," Guber reportedly said to Canton when he got wind of the project. But Guber gave Canton his head, at the same time making clear that he was washing his hands of the movie.

A week after the film's first disastrous preview, Brooks screened it for Columbia executives, including Guber, Canton, Ganis, Henson, and Pascal. The studio "suits" arrived in a somber mood. Polly Platt was grateful when, as the film unspooled, Canton repeatedly tugged on her chair and whispered, "They didn't like this? Why not? Didn't they laugh here? I love this!"

When the lights went up, Brooks told the executives that he planned to keep testing the film and that he hoped it could remain a musical. It was 1:30 A.M. by the time the group broke up. Guber, who had listened carefully but said little, turned to Brooks and offered soothing words. "Jim, I think you should make the picture that's in your heart, and not listen to the whispers in the hallway."

Over the next months, Brooks would edit and re-edit his film, screening it seven times. In a state of considerable agony —and, thanks to the *Times*, in full public view—he eventually amputated all of the musical numbers. *I'll Do Anything* became the first musical in Hollywood history to lose its tunes.

But the picture that was in Brooks's heart was still not pleasing to audiences. When the director asked the studio for money to shoot additional scenes in order to transform *I'll Do Anything* into a straight comedy, Dolgen balked. "Don't pretend that you love me and then tell me I can't make the movie as good as it can be," Brooks thundered to executives Lisa Henson and Amy Pascal when they were dispatched to his office to discuss the matter. Eventually, Columbia ponied up. As post-production costs mounted, the budget rose to $44 million.

With the fate of the film hanging in the balance, Brooks's cast staunchly defended the idea of handing a director with no track record in musicals more than $40 million to make this offbeat project. "How many billions of dollars does Sony spend a year?" wondered Albert Brooks. The actor tried to cheer his friend Jim by telling him that he was preparing for press interviews by working up a comedy routine about all the famous Hollywood movies that had started out as musicals. Exhibit A: *Twelve Angry Men.*

THE BAD NEWS kept coming. That fall, as Los Angeles baked in its usual autumn heat, one of Sony's superstars was caught up in a scandal that dwarfed the Heidi affair. Michael Jackson was enmeshed in allegations of child molestation, setting off a media frenzy of global proportions. The drumbeat of scandal may have contributed to an overall sense that Western civilization was truly on the decline, but at least Sony Pictures would barely be touched by the nightmare.

While Sony Music would be forced to postpone release of a greatest hits album, the impact at the studio was negligible. Jackson's much-vaunted deal, brokered by Jon Peters, had amounted to nothing. It had been "all window dressing" from the start, said a Columbia executive. "Everyone knew it was."

Everyone except Peters and Anton Furst, *Batman's* brilliant production designer, that is. While most people in Hollywood had long been convinced that Jackson was simply too weird to put into a feature-length film, Peters and Furst had tried to develop *MidKnight* for the star. But Jackson had lost his two collaborators in 1991. Peters had left the studio, while Furst had died tragically in November. On the day he was scheduled to admit himself into a detox program for an addiction to Valium, Furst had either fallen or jumped off the eighth floor of a Culver City parking garage.

When the Jackson scandal broke, the two projects that had been in the works at Jackson's production company, *Jack and the Beanstalk* and *MidKnight,* had been in turnaround for some time. Executives could breathe a sigh of relief that this scandal, at least, would not tar the studio.

407

MORE MISFORTUNE awaited Canton. Setting aside the troubles on *I'll Do Anything,* he was looking at a string of box-office disappointments. In August, John Singleton's new movie, *Poetic Justice,* had a dazzling $11.7 million opening weekend. But the following weekend, after poor reviews and bad word of mouth, it tumbled a precipitous 57 percent. The film had cost less than $14 million, and despite its early death it would ultimately manage to turn a modest $6 million profit. But Canton would be criticized for having left Singleton too much on his own and permitting him to start filming a project that wasn't fully developed. Singleton's debut, *Boyz N the Hood,* had been such a success for Columbia in 1991 that Canton may have felt justified in letting the filmmaker do his work.

*The Age of Innocence,* the first picture Canton had put into the pipeline, opened in September. The budget had been kept to $32 million, despite director Martin Scorsese's meticulous re-creation of nineteenth-century New York interiors and society dinners. The film was supposed to have been released for Christmas 1992, but had been postponed because of the death of Scorsese's father and problems getting it right in post-production. Canton had kept his hands off, perhaps out of respect for the stature of the director. But after early test screenings had not gone well, he pressured Scorsese to cut the picture from two hours and forty-five minutes to two hours and ten minutes.

After a great deal of editing and reshaping, *The Age of Innocence* was as ready as it would ever get—and it wasn't an easy sell. The marketing department tried to play up the subtle tension and eroticism between its stars, Michelle Pfeiffer and Daniel Day-Lewis. But a staid period piece with no explosions and no happy ending had little chance to become a blockbuster. Privately, studio insiders were expecting to gross $50 million at best domestically, which wouldn't begin to pay for making and marketing the film. In fact, the film would gross only $31 million domestically. But though *The Age of Innocence* would be overlooked at the Oscars, it brought the studio some respect. The community awarded points for a serious run at artistry even if the attempt wasn't entirely successful.

There were no such points awarded to the benighted Bruce Willis vehicle, *Striking Distance,* which opened on the same day as *The Age of Innocence.* The action film, shepherded by Barry Josephson, had been hung up in reshoots for more than six months. The studio managed, as it often did, to open the pic-

408

ture exceptionally well—but it too nose-dived. "You could justify spending a lot of time and money to break even on *Age of Innocence* as a prestige play," says a former Columbia executive. "I don't know the argument you make for spending time and money to break even on *Striking Distance,* other than, 'Ooops.' " *Striking Distance* would ultimately make a small profit.

Columbia had another prestige costume drama with *The Remains of the Day,* which opened in November to critical raves. Anthony Hopkins and Emma Thompson would get Oscar nominations for their performances. But *Remains,* which was rolled out slowly into the theaters, didn't perform especially well at the box office, grossing only $29 million. Columbia executives had never expected the Merchant-Ivory film to have broad commercial appeal—and they were convinced that those low expectations would be fulfilled the first time they viewed it. The critical moment comes when the butler (Hopkins) watches his sweetheart (Thompson) slowly disappear from his life as she rides away on a bus. This was hardly a Hollywood ending, and distribution executive Jeff Blake must have seen his grosses evaporating. "It's $20 million if he stands there, $50 million if he runs after her!" Blake yelled. Blake's prediction would prove correct.

At Christmas, Columbia released one of its biggest though least-publicized bombs—*Geronimo.* Canton's brother, Neil, a seasoned line producer, had brought him the project about the great Apache warrior, with Wes Studi in the title role. The film was no *Dances with Wolves*: It cost about $50 million, boasted no major stars, no love story, and a meandering story line. It was hard to see how the studio ever expected to make its money back—and it didn't come close.

Columbia had not shown *Geronimo* to Jason Patric, who played the lead, an American cavalry officer, before the premiere at the Academy of Motion Picture Arts and Sciences Theater in Beverly Hills. That turned out to be a mistake. Patric was so dismayed by the way the film turned out that he ran out of the theater and into his limo. He had himself driven around for a while as he raged about the sheer awfulness of the movie. Then he pulled himself together and went back to the premiere party.

409

*Geronimo* lost $40 million—far more than *Last Action Hero*—without a fraction of the fanfare.

□

As 1993 WOUND TO A hellacious close, a casual observer would have been justified in wondering whether Peter Guber was about to be thrown out of the job that he had mismanaged so thoroughly. But some in the industry also hypothesized that, in the loopy world of Sony, he might be promoted. His purchase of a $6 million co-op apartment in New York had fueled speculation that he would take some sort of place beside Mickey Schulhof in the Manhattan offices.

It seemed that Guber still had Schulhof under a spell. And no wonder: Schulhof had seen his entire life change through his association with Guber and with Hollywood. He and Paola were now dashing off to chic vacation spots with Peter and Lynda. The living room of their house in East Hampton was crammed with silver-framed photographs of Mickey with Barbra Streisand, with Michael Jackson, with Robert De Niro. The Schulhofs were beginning to attract an A-list crowd to their parties, with the assistance of Peggy Siegel, who specialized in fabulous soirees that drew stars from entertainment, Wall Street, and the media.

In Hollywood's eyes, Mickey Schulhof had been taken by Peter Guber and the allure of the entertainment world. Those who saw the two men together marveled at how thoroughly captivated Schulhof appeared. "I saw it," says a former high-ranking Sony Pictures executive. "I literally did see times when Mickey would have a question or a point of view, and Peter would just look him in the eye and he would melt. He would change. He was mesmerized."

Guber continued to keep Schulhof isolated from other Sony Pictures executives. A closed loop had been established: Guber talked to Schulhof, Schulhof talked to Ohga.

For the second quarter of its fiscal year, Sony announced more falling profits and—for the first time—falling sales. But without missing a beat, Schulhof announced in November that his friend Peter Guber was operating under a "long-term agreement." He declined to provide details. The news media were told that Guber had renewed his contract to remain as chairman of Sony Pictures Entertainment for at least five more years—though his duties might be expanded in some unspecified way. Guber was pulling down about $3 million a year, not counting bonuses and perks. He was also looking forward, of

410

course, to his share in the multi-million-dollar bonus pool that Sony had promised to provide after five years.

In announcing Guber's new deal, Schulhof appeared to want to dispel the public perception that the studio was in turmoil. But stating that he was prolonging the current regime was hardly the best way to achieve that result. Sony also leaked to the press that several other top executives in the software division had received new contracts, including Alan Levine and Jon Dolgen—though Dolgen was now perceived to be warring openly with Levine and had not yet renegotiated his contract since he had been promoted in 1991.

Mark Canton clearly felt secure—inexplicably, many felt. Despite the beating he had taken in recent months, he was still boldly boasting to friends that his star was on the rise.

In all the discussions of renewed contracts, Medavoy's name wasn't mentioned. This was puzzling to some, since TriStar had released a couple of movies, *Cliffhanger* and *Sleepless in Seattle,* that had been among Sony's few bright spots in 1993. And at year's end, while Canton was looking at *Geronimo,* Mike Medavoy had tasted triumph with Jonathan Demme's *Philadelphia,* a clear Oscar contender. The film, which starred Tom Hanks as a lawyer who loses his job because he has AIDS, was hailed as bold for tackling a difficult issue, though some in the gay community felt that the script pulled its punches.

Despite these successes, it was obvious that Medavoy's days at last were truly numbered. Since the *Hook* and *Bugsy* debacles, he had never regained Guber's confidence and had also lost any semblance of respect from his staff at TriStar. Mike tried to put the best face on it, but he no longer bothered to deny that he was on his way out.

While Medavoy had brought some talented people to the lot, he hadn't managed their deals in a way that yielded results for the studio. One young filmmaker whom he had cultivated was Quentin Tarantino, the writer-director of a much-touted low-budget heist picture called *Reservoir Dogs.* Tarantino liked Medavoy, and Medavoy had given him $150,000 to develop a script.

That script was called *Pulp Fiction,* which Tarantino planned to make at Danny DeVito's company, Jersey Films, which also had a deal with TriStar. But when Medavoy read *Pulp Fiction,* a fresh, offbeat, and bloody take on a group of low-life criminals,

411

he pronounced it "too violent." At a meeting at the studio he told executives that he was especially concerned about a scene in which a hapless criminal gets blown away in the back of a car and his brains splatter all over the upholstery. Medavoy knew that Congress was gearing up to hold hearings on violence in the media. Although with a budget of $10 million the film represented little risk to the studio, Medavoy passed on *Pulp Fiction*. Every other major studio in town would do the same—although surely no other studio head would regret the decision as much as Medavoy.

AKIO MORITA was playing tennis one Tuesday morning at the end of November when he complained of feeling dizzy. The seventy-two-year-old Sony chairman went home, and when he didn't feel better he went by ambulance to the Tokyo Medical and Dental University Hospital. Doctors found that he had suffered a hemorrhage on the right side of his brain. He was rushed into a four-hour operation, during which a blood clot the size of an egg was removed.

When the story started to leak a couple of days later, Sony tried to stall by saying that Morita had a cold. After the facts were revealed, a company spokesman acknowledged that Morita could not speak, though he could squeeze a doctor's hand in response to his name. There were reports that he hadn't regained consciousness fully. Morita's prospects for recovery were unclear, said Sony executive vice president Tsunao Hashimoto.

It was shocking news. Morita had seemed to be a young and fit seventy-two, poised to fulfill a cherished dream. He was about to become chairman of Keidanran, the large Japan business association that he had longed to lead. But Ohga now said that Morita would not be able to maintain his activities outside the company.

Morita's illness sharpened the focus on the questions about Sony's future. Any tangible synergy from the expensive acquisition of Columbia Pictures had still not materialized four years later. Schulhof had labored mightily to bring it about, holding "opportunities meetings" involving various hardware and software divisions. But Sony synergy was still more prophecy than reality.

Despite everything, Schulhof was still bullish. There was talk

412

that Sony would acquire an interest in the Los Angeles Lakers basketball team or its hockey team, the Kings. Guber had fervently pushed these explorations. There was more talk that the company might build a new sports arena in Los Angeles. Though none of these discussions bore fruit, they seemed to counter the idea that Sony was despairing.

Late in the year came a report that Sony had hired the Furman Selz investment banking firm in New York to explore the sale of a 25 percent stake in its studio for a reported $3 billion. Raising or borrowing money in troubled Japan seemed like an impossible mission, but Sony hoped to find a deep-pocketed partner in the United States.

Alternatively, Schulhof suggested, Sony might launch an initial public offering, selling stock in the studio in the United States. Here he seemed to have his signals crossed with Tokyo. "I don't think we have made any decisions yet on this subject," said Sony director Nobuyuki Idei in a newspaper interview. Schulhof should be "studying all the possibilities and reporting them to Sony management for discussion." It was an unusual public rebuff and Schulhof must have felt its sting.

A source close to Sony acknowledges that the studio was in such poor shape that the company could hardly have hoped to sell stock to the public. "An initial public offering was always a dream because there are a number of benefits but there are also precursors to being public—like having a successful company, a company where you're willing to open your kimono and let people peer in," that insider says.

Still, Sony cast its quest for an investor in upbeat terms. "We still have ambitious plans to expand our software business and continue the growth of electronics, and that's going to place big demands on us for financing," Schulhof said.

Schulhof had something on which to pin his hopes. The environment on Wall Street was heating up with information superhighway fever. There was suddenly a scramble in the communications industry to control the pipelines into the home as well as the content that would fill those pipelines. As phone companies battled the cable operators for technological advantage, both sides were looking for ways to hook themselves up with suppliers of programming. One answer was simply to buy a studio.

A recent bidding war for Paramount had pushed the price

413

of that studio to more than $10 billion, giving rise to hopes that Sony Pictures might be worth a lot more than the $3.4 billion plus $1.6 billion in debt that Sony had paid in 1989. Offering a quarter of the company for $3 billion would mean that Sony Pictures was worth $12 billion—a figure most analysts considered farfetched. But Schulhof told the financial world that he had no worry about the value of the goods he intended to sell. "I've met the chairman of every phone company," he boasted to *Forbes*. "And I didn't initiate the phone calls."

He was similarly confident in an interview with the *Wall Street Journal*. "The question is, who can give us an alliance . . . with complementary strengths?" he said. "It's like a game of musical chairs—there are only five major studios and ten people looking for a chair."

Of course, there were two sides to that coin. Sony was aware that it owned the only big studio with no entrée into the nation's living rooms. Fox had its television network; mighty Time Warner had vast cable holdings and the premier pay-television service, HBO; Paramount and Universal shared the USA network; Disney had its cable channel. (Within a couple of years, the gulf would widen. Time Warner would expand; Viacom would buy Paramount, putting the studio into a constellation with MTV and Showtime; Disney would acquire Capital Cities/ABC.)

With that in mind, Sony focused on a "strategic alliance" and "was not looking for a bailout even though they were losing money at a prodigious rate," says an inside source. Investors who simply wanted to buy into the studio were not of interest. But no deal materialized with the kind of partner that Sony wished to attract. At first, according to one observer, Sony seemed stoic about its situation. But as time went on and no suitor came calling, its representatives became more anxious, particularly when the prospective investors who looked closely at the studio placed a far lower value on it than Sony did. "They were intrigued with the opportunity," says a Sony source. "But they were turned off by the problems at the company and the magnitude of the losses." The quest for a partner proved futile.

Meanwhile, Sony Pictures was groping to redefine itself. In yet another series of exercises led by an outside facilitator, high-level executives were meeting regularly to discuss the studio's strategy. The meetings included mostly business affairs

414

executives. Paul Schaeffer was there, as well as Ken Williams, who ran the Sony lot, and Larry Ruisi, a financial executive from the New York office. Mel Harris, the head of the television operation, supervised the effort. Strangely, only one participant from the film side was invited: Jon Dolgen. He had tried to include Mark Canton, but Peter Guber and Alan Levine—who attended each meeting enthusiastically—declined to allow Canton to participate.

To some participants, the meetings seemed both pointless and endless. There were presentations with charts and graphs. The executives would break into subgroups and vote on motions—such as whether the studio should release a higher volume of movies or venture into the cable business. "People were voting and didn't know what they were talking about," one participant remembers. "It was bizarre. It was an extraordinary waste of time. . . . It was something you suffered through—you could be a grownup and doing this. Can you imagine?"

One insider who defends these exercises maintains that they represented an effort to address one of Sony's critical problems, its failure to devise a strategy for long-term growth. The meetings also were intended to get top executives at the company to focus their goals—to examine, for example, whether the company should be satisfied with market share or whether it should take a closer look at the meaning of profitability. This executive maintains that some positive results, such as a series of investments in overseas broadcasting networks, emerged.

After months of sessions and substantial expenditure, the group settled on calling Sony Pictures a "global communications company." "What the hell is a global communications company anyway?" one participant asks. In his opinion, these strategy powwows didn't help fix the ailing company. "The problem was, the company *wasn't doing anything*," he says. This insider concludes that Guber and Levine may have found some solace in the meetings. "That's a very managed environment," he observes. "You might not have known what was going on in the office, but you knew what was going on in those meetings."

IN EARLY DECEMBER 1993, Federal Express trucks pulled up at the homes of the voting members of the Academy of Motion Picture Arts and Sciences and dropped off glossy, custom-designed black boxes. Inside each was a library of nine videos

415

of Columbia releases for the year, films that Sony hoped might be nominated for Oscars. Campaigning for nominations is business as usual, but Sony Pictures had managed its usual excess. "It's so overdone, in typical Columbia fashion," sniffed a TriStar executive. "In this economy, I can't believe it."

"They might as well have included a couple of $20 bills," said one screenwriter.

Inside the box were contenders such as *The Age of Innocence* and *The Remains of the Day*, along with longshots like *Groundhog Day*. "Notice that they didn't include *Last Action Hero*," a rival executive snidely observed.

Oddly enough, considering his penchant for showmanship, Guber had warned against the black boxes, advising Canton that he was "leading with his chin" after the awful year he had just endured. But the advice was offered in Guber's usual passive way and the deed was done. And whatever the complaints, Columbia and TriStar wound up with thirty-one nominations, led by eight for *The Remains of the Day*.

After Christmas Guber roused himself to a slightly higher level of exertion, interrupting his Aspen vacation to try to sell the world on the success of Sony Pictures. Most industry analysts had given the 1993 box-office crown once again to Warner, but Guber argued that the studio that was once his home didn't deserve the title. Counting all its units—Columbia, TriStar, and the tiny Triumph and Sony Classics divisions—Guber said Sony had a bigger gross than Warner: $912 million at the end of December versus $888 million for Warner. "We admit that it's close," Guber said. "We just want it acknowledged that, as of now, we're on top."

Guber didn't win a lot of converts. The pictures weren't distributed under one banner, and experts pointed out that if Disney got to include films distributed by its Miramax unit, it would have more than $951 million worth of box office, clobbering Sony's combined number. And in any case Art Murphy, the veteran industry box-office tabulator, didn't even buy Guber's figures. He calculated that, all told, Warner had sold $911 million worth of tickets, compared with Sony's $903 million.

A slightly more illuminating point of comparison than market share was the average box-office gross per film, though that still didn't measure profitability since it factored in the number of films that each studio released but not the cost of making

416

them. By this measure, according to an industry source, Universal came in first in 1993 with $33 million per film (thanks to *Jurassic Park*); Paramount had a $30.6 million average. Columbia grossed an average of $24.8 million per film; while TriStar came in last with an average of $22 million.

IT WAS CHRISTMAS party time again, and the tent stood ready in the Thalberg parking lot. This year, as employees walked through the chill air to the $500,000 bash, many were upset to see some familiar figures—security guards who had worked on the lot for years—picketing outside the Madison Avenue gates. Just before Thanksgiving the security staff had been fired as part of the studio's cost-cutting efforts. The picketers carried signs that read, "The Executive Bonus Pool Is Only $50 Million"; "Japanese Profits Over American Workers"; and "If We Face a Recession, We Shall Not Lay Off Workers"—a quote from Akio Morita.

Sony corporate public relations man Don DeMesquita had gone all-out to make this an extra-special Christmas party. Since July, he had been planning the live entertainment. This would be no casual production, but a musical extravaganza. "He really wanted to be Busby Berkeley or Mike Todd," says a Columbia executive.

In September, DeMesquita had started asking employees if they would volunteer to star in the show. "The frightening thing is, he could not get anybody to do it," says a studio insider. "They had to call department heads and get them to coerce people." In the end, more than half the "entertainers" were ringers hired from outside. But DeMesquita pressed ahead, holding rehearsals with a full orchestra.

The staff was treated to "Sony Pictures Broadway." In a song called "The Meaning of Life," an "executive" sang that the meaning of life is "a $100 million movie with a sequel on the way." Others chimed in: "Life is a show that's been sold into syndication. . . . Life is a sell-through home-videotape sensation."

Another singer intoned, "No! You have it wrong. Life is how we feel when we work as a team. Life is how we feel when we share a dream. We are all a family—that's the bottom line. When we work together, everything is fine." The finale was the theme from *Les Misérables*.

417

The irony of the security guards picketing outside as this overblown spectacle unfolded was not lost on staffers. "It put a weird edge to be sitting there, listening to how magical the Sony family is," one onlooker said.

"It was entirely Big Brother entertainment," said another.

# 31

# THE EXECUTIVE SHUFFLE

ON JANUARY 7, 1994, a well-known director was preparing to meet with Mark Canton when he got a call canceling the appointment. The director's office buzzed with speculation. "Somebody said, 'I wonder if Canton got fired,' " the bemused filmmaker remembers. "I said, 'Either fired or promoted.' It's weird that you could think both things about the same guy."

But this was Sony.

Canton wasn't being fired. After telling friends that he'd be assuming Medavoy's duties by February 1, Canton found that his prediction had been fulfilled a few weeks early. Medavoy had returned from a trip to Hong Kong and given up. *Cliffhanger, Sleepless in Seattle,* and *Philadelphia* wouldn't be enough to save him—even though he looked like a genius for 1993 compared with Canton. "They were very generous in terms of allowing it to be both graceful and remunerative for me," Medavoy said later.

Graceful? Hardly. Medavoy's fall had been as protracted and agonizing as the death of Franco. But remunerative? This was Sony, after all. He was reportedly given an $11 million settlement, although some news accounts put the number far lower. Medavoy, smoking his cigar in his mansion's green-walled library, seemed forlorn. While denying many of the criticisms that had been leveled at him, he offered this analysis of his failure to put many films into production: "I had a year, 1992, when I didn't do enough. It was a function of not finding the material I wanted, of breaking in a new group of executives. *Hook* and *Bugsy* were preoccupations. We were ramping up. I'd rather have this year's three big hits."

By now, his wife had left him. His job was gone. And he told

419

friends that he had poured his financial resources into the house—now an outsized bachelor pad—that had become a symbol of excess to his enemies. "Life is kind of strange, isn't it?" he said. "You never have total control over it. Here I am, an immigrant born in China. My father fled the Russian pogroms and my mother was born in Manchuria. We survived. I survived. I'm a survivor."

Canton was named to the newly created post of chairman of the Columbia TriStar Motion Picture Companies. "I thought it would be an exciting opportunity," he said when the announcement was made. "I also like to work twenty-four hours a day." The news media took note, of course, of the fact that Canton was being rewarded after an abysmal year while Medavoy was being exiled after a comparatively good performance. Most concluded that the whole thing was a matter of styles and personalities and, of course, Guber's high comfort level with Canton.

But in fact, Guber had searched for someone else to take the TriStar job, approaching veteran film producers Larry Gordon and Ned Tanen, again, among others. Both had experience running studios, but neither was interested in wading into this particular morass. Meanwhile, Canton had lobbied relentlessly and Guber finally had yielded.

Sony had hedged by teaming Canton with Dolgen, the Motion Picture Group president. "If they had just made Canton king of all he sees, they would have come under such intense criticism," one agent said. Sony sources floated the notion that the arrangement was meant to free Guber and Levine to concentrate on the big picture—new technologies and global competition. Both were said to be yearning to shuffle off the burden of day-to-day studio management. Both were also said to have stipulated that they be released from those chores when they renegotiated their contracts. They were, hypothetically, out of the business of green-lighting films, although Levine was supposed to act as mediator if Canton and Dolgen had disputes.

There were many who anticipated with relish Canton's fate at Dolgen's hands, and no one was betting on Canton to come 420 out ahead. "I couldn't think of anyone I'd rather be partnered with in doing this," Dolgen said genially, if insincerely, at the time. "You view somebody based on his skills and abilities, not necessarily on whether his last three movies worked. Mark is possessed of appetite and enthusiasm. He's got a very steep learning curve."

Canton waxed philosophical: "I long ago decided this is a big canvas, not a small one, and a long journey."

As Canton was promoted, the studio released the nonmusical musical, *I'll Do Anything*. One could only pity Sid Ganis, who had the formidable job of selling the film. "This is a first —no one has ever marketed a movie that used to be a musical," he said. While Brooks's comedy was full of hilarious scenes, the director couldn't fill in the holes where the songs had been. Sony reported that the film opened at $4.7 million, but some found that number difficult to believe. The major studios often accuse each other of inflating their numbers, but Columbia seemed to be taking the practice to absurd lengths.

This wasn't the first time the question had arisen. At the end of 1993, Columbia had released Jerry Zucker's *My Life*, the story of a dying man, starring Michael Keaton, and reported gross receipts extrapolated from a sampling of locations where the film was playing. But a rival executive pointed out that the final tally was based on the improbable assumption that the picture had grossed more at smaller unsampled locations than it did in the larger theaters where the numbers had actually been taken.

Now the studio was once again generous with its estimates on *I'll Do Anything*. Industry analyst David Davis of Paul Kagan Associates explained: "Logically, you cannot have an average that's better than the sampling. . . . What town in Nebraska or Arkansas is going to outperform a Chicago run?"

The studio declined to answer questions about the surprising results. But it couldn't hide the fact that *I'll Do Anything* was a financial catastrophe. It barely earned $10 million in the theaters and became a $40 million write-off for Columbia.

MEDAVOY'S DEPARTURE kicked off a round of especially bad press, including major articles in *The New Yorker* and *Vanity Fair*. *The New Yorker*'s James B. Stewart had the good luck to find that Schulhof and his public relations man were out of town when he called Sony's New York headquarters to ask for an interview. Instead of running into the stone wall usually erected before potentially challenging interviewers, Stewart found himself ushered into the presence of Ken Yoshida, a Japanese executive just completing a tour at Sony Corp. of America. Yoshida, polite but nervous, told Stewart that he had never met with a member of the American press.

"He seemed largely unaware of the management turmoil inside Columbia and TriStar," Stewart wrote. "He said, with evident pride, that Schulhof had told him and other Japanese officials that 'in the past two years Sony has had the most stable management in Hollywood.' "

But Yoshida also acknowledged that the company would like to sell a stake in the entertainment business. "With nearly $12 billion in debt," he said, "it's natural to think about reducing it."

Meanwhile Mark Canton made a stab at mitigating his public relations problems. This was never his strong suit. He gave an interview to *Los Angeles* magazine that was the talk of the town. Naturally, he was asked to discuss his feelings about the failure of *Last Action Hero*.

"I am a leader," he said, "and when you are a leader, you feel the responsibility for failure and you give up the responsibility for success. But I felt hurt." He had shared his pain with his therapist, he continued. The interviewer asked what his therapist had said.

"First," Canton replied, "he thought it was a good movie."

JON PETERS was going home—again. In March 1994, it was announced that he would return to Warner, where his old friends Bob Daly and Terry Semel welcomed him back with a five-year production deal.

Peters had not yet made a single film as a producer at Sony. The joke on Sony was obvious: *Batman*'s impresario, whose services Sony had paid Warner Bros. hundreds of millions of dollars to get nearly five years ago, was now returning to the studio that had been so enriched by his departure. And what had Sony gotten for its investment in Peters? Several stalled, very expensive projects.

Peters had spent at least $20 million developing movies with his discretionary fund. One of these was *Mistress of the Seas,* a movie based on the life of Ann Bonny, a seventeenth-century female pirate who dressed like a man. Michael Cristofer had written a provocative script that had attracted director Paul Verhoeven, who became attached to the project.

422

*Mistress* had gotten bogged down and now seemed unlikely to be made. Verhoeven had wanted to cast big stars and make the film a massive action piece and costume drama, much of which would be shot on water. The budget for such a film would be at least $70 million. But when Harrison Ford was approached to play the male lead, he said he was interested— but only if his character could be beefed up to be the equal of the female lead. "Harrison didn't want to be introduced on page forty," says a source close to Verhoeven.

But *Mistress* was a woman's story and Verhoeven didn't want to alter that emphasis; he planned to film it with lots of raunchy female sexuality. Geena Davis wanted to play the lead, but without a major male box-office star to support her, Sony was not willing to foot the bill. "At the end of the day no one was going to make that movie for that amount of money," says a Columbia executive. Nevertheless, when Jon Peters was around everyone kept up a charade that it was a viable project. "You always had to pretend to Jon that you wanted to make it. Nobody wants to tell this guy bad news. He is a monster: He'll say, 'You'll be out of the business, you'll never work again.' "

Another of Peters's pet projects was *Gangland,* a movie about the life of New York mafioso John Gotti. Peters had spent $2 million developing a script, with little to show for it. The first screenwriter had been *Taxi Driver*'s Paul Schrader, who says he was lured by the $1 million fee. "They offered me a lot of money," says Schrader. "I figured I can work with anybody— and I found out I can't."

Peters hadn't liked Schrader's first draft and ordered the screenwriter to fly to Aspen immediately to talk about it. He became enraged when Schrader refused—a breach that abruptly ended their collaboration. Schrader says he didn't like the way Peters and his minions dealt with him and was happy to settle for a fraction of his fee to get out of the deal. "He never read the script," says Schrader. "He was an uninformed bully. He can win the argument because he's richer and he yells louder. He was abusive."

Next Peters brought in Joe Eszterhas, the contentious *Basic Instinct* writer, to start over on *Gangland.* "Joe and I are cut of the same cloth," Peters told underlings. One former Peters employee says that Peters paid Eszterhas most of his $1.6 million fee upfront—giving the writer no incentive to turn in his script on time or deliver revisions. After he wrote his first draft,

423

Eszterhas was asked to make extensive changes by executives—but delivered almost none of those revisions in his second draft. Columbia executives were incensed that Eszterhas had to be paid in full for so little effort.

The Peters-Eszterhas relationship turned sour after a contretemps erupted between the two in Eszterhas's house. Eszterhas, who lived across the street from Peters in the Malibu Colony, had invited Peters over to read a new spec script he had written called *Foreplay*. Peters, still a famously poor reader, got to the house and refused to read the script, saying that since Eszterhas was under contract to him, *Foreplay* was already rightfully his. "I don't need to read it, I own it!" he bellowed. An argument ensued during which Jon slammed his fist down on a glass coffee table and broke it. Then he stormed out of the house and leaped over Eszterhas's security wall. "I was just like Batman, I had to climb to the walls to get out!" Peters boasted later to his employees.

As CANTON expanded his reach to include TriStar, he was facing a severe product drought. In 1994 Hollywood would see more films released than it had in any year since 1988—no thanks to Sony. All together, the company's four distribution outlets—Columbia, TriStar, Sony Classics, and Triumph—planned to release thirty-eight movies, down from forty-four the previous year.

Columbia, especially, was now paying a steep price for its previous year from hell, during which *Last Action Hero* and the Heidi Fleiss scandal had sucked up everyone's energy. Having delayed the release of *Wolf*, its troubled Jack Nicholson–Michelle Pfeiffer thriller, from April to June, the studio had no product to release that spring. Meanwhile, *Wolf*'s budget had ballooned to $50 million.

Medavoy's exit and Canton's ascent had resulted in a promotion for Sid Ganis to vice chairman of Columbia. Lisa Henson was promoted to president of the studio, and Barry Josephson replaced her as president of production. Ganis vowed that he and Henson would "rebuild" after the debacles of 1993, and the absence of any films to release gave them some time to devote to the process. "It does leave a void and we're aware of it and we feel it," Ganis said. "But we have a great summer."

By now, filmmakers' frustrations over the difficulty in getting projects through the dreaded green-light committee had resulted in deep disaffection in the halls of the Capra and Lean buildings, where many of them had their offices. In fact, five years after Guber had arrived at Columbia and aggressively courted some of the most gifted talents in town with promises of creative freedom and prosperity, there were widespread feelings of bitterness on the lot—and the beginnings of a mass exodus.

Already, many had fled: *Batman* director Tim Burton had left after Canton declined to make his black-and-white pet project about transvestite movie director Ed Wood; Penny Marshall, said to find Canton intolerable (although she loved the Sony jet), had not made a picture there since *A League of Their Own*; Michael Douglas had departed after *Radio Flyer* and Francis Ford Coppola after *Dracula*; Walter Parkes and Laurie MacDonald, the husband-wife team who had produced *Awakenings*, had gone to run Amblin for Steven Spielberg.

Now producer Laura Ziskin was leaving, too, to run a new movie division at Fox. Many of her projects had been maddeningly stuck in limbo at Sony. Most recently Ziskin had cast Kevin Kline as the lead in the $14 million Mike Newell comedy *Old Friends*, rumored to be one of the best scripts in town. But when she couldn't get a green light, Kline had skipped off to star in Larry Kasdan's *French Kiss* with Meg Ryan instead. Ziskin's was a common complaint: when the green-light committee dithered, stars attached to a project would jump ship.

It was especially irritating to filmmakers who were trying to make moderately budgeted movies to be told no—or to be told yes, hallelujah, and then have their budgets nickel-and-dimed by Dolgen. After years of watching tens of millions of dollars go down the drain for golden parachutes to departing executives, after witnessing the profligacy of the Sony perks and the lot renovations, they resented being told to trim a few million from their movies—money that they felt was necessary to ensure quality.

Danny DeVito complained that his company, Jersey Films, had not once seen the light turn green. Jersey was, in fact, one of the worst examples of Sony's talent mismanagement. DeVito told friends that when he made his deal with Guber in 1990, Guber had promised him that Sony wanted to make pictures that DeVito would produce but not act in, along with ones in which he would star.

According to a source close to DeVito, Guber had grown

425

increasingly annoyed because DeVito hadn't yet appeared in a comedy for Sony. Guber had reportedly told Medavoy not to green-light any Jersey picture that didn't feature DeVito until he had satisfied the studio by starring in one. Over the course of DeVito's deal, Medavoy had passed on two projects he wanted to produce but not act in, the Generation X comedy *Reality Bites,* which did not perform particularly well for Universal, as well as *Pulp Fiction.*

In May 1994 *Pulp Fiction,* picked up by Miramax, won the Palme d'Or at Cannes; it became a huge international hit, grossing more than $300 million worldwide. Had Medavoy said yes to Tarantino's film, made memorable by a stunning comeback performance by John Travolta, he might have redeemed his legacy at TriStar.

Subsidizing unproductive filmmakers was a terrible financial burden on Sony; the overhead costs for some deals ran as high as $2–$3 million a year. While Guber had wanted to make a public splash by signing up all this big-name talent, he wasn't nurturing those relationships now. Several producers say that after Guber's initial courtship, he never spoke to them again. A source close to DeVito says, "Guber never called Danny and said, 'Let's try to work this out.' "

Sony executives took their cue from Guber—and in any case, many were too preoccupied with surviving the studio politics to concentrate on helping filmmakers craft movies. "The real problem was that nobody ever had a vision for the kind of movies they wanted to make," says an A-list filmmaker who says he was "conned" by Guber into coming to Sony. "The guy running the ship has to have a sense of direction. He can't just bring people on board who have had successes in the past and say, 'Go make us some money.' It started with Guber, and went all the way down the line."

One director says he yearned for an inspired collaboration with the studio—and ultimately felt underappreciated. "Guber could only make you believe in *him,*" he says. "He never made you feel great about yourself. Katzenberg and Ned Tanen and Michael Eisner, they all can make you feel great, they can make you feel like a genius. And creative people need this, because creative people are insecure and don't know if what they have deep inside is any good."

"The Japanese, when they give a guy a horse and a suit of

armor, they expect you to go out and die for them," says a filmmaker who regrets his indirect participation in what he considers to be the fleecing of Sony. "They expect you to go out and fight to the death. And Guber was just renegotiating his contract. For Guber, the point was to make as much money as he could. There was no sense of dying for the Japanese, there was no sense of shame."

JUST FIVE MONTHS AFTER the announcement that the top Sony executives had renewed their contracts, Jon Dolgen announced that he was leaving. The news abruptly upset the effort to project stability and did nothing to soothe prospective investors in the company—if there were any serious contenders. Sony maintained that discussions with potential partners were still under way, but Schulhof's earlier boasts about the swarms of interested customers now only seemed to underscore Sony's embarrassment.

By all accounts, Dolgen was little mourned by Alan Levine, who had finally renegotiated Dolgen's contract and included a provision that allowed him to walk away from the studio. Dolgen was named chairman of the newly formed Viacom Entertainment Group, a division created when Viacom bought Paramount.

There were various post-mortem assessments of Dolgen's role at Sony Pictures. No one could have doubted that Sony needed some financial restraint, which he had attempted to impose with limited success. The studio's overhead was still dramatically higher than others—one knowledgeable source pegged the number at $350 million, compared with numbers in the $200 million range for comparable operations.

But Levine had thwarted Dolgen's efforts to address overhead. Dolgen had driven down marketing expenditures and had cut the cost of film budgets, sometimes with great success. He slashed the budgets on several movies that would be counted among Columbia's few winners. The cost of *Little Women,* the Winona Ryder holiday hit to be released later in 1994, was cut from $27 million to $14 million. The budget of *Bad Boys,* another hit released after Dolgen's departure, was reduced from $34 million to $16 million.

Some still maintained that Dolgen's zeal for imposing budget constraints had been too great. They blamed him for the

427

shortage of product at Columbia. "Every time out was a fight," says one executive. "Insisting that movies come in for $4 million or $5 million less than requested precluded getting the star power necessary for a green light. We lost a lot of opportunities to assemble movies."

"The best description of Dolgen is the one Barry Diller gave him," says a former high-level Sony Pictures executive. "He said, 'Jon is the best person I've seen at fixing the broken edges of a company.' And he could be a killer on the edges." But Dolgen couldn't prevent turkeys like *Geronimo* from getting the green light, and he couldn't put the brakes on the truly fatal excesses, especially the spending on overhead. "In fairness," says his former colleague, "Peter wouldn't let him."

MANY IN THE INDUSTRY wondered how much longer Guber could keep his job. It was amazing to watch him survive and even thrive as others were fired, one after another. Acquaintances who saw him got an earful of his usual ambivalence about the great responsibilities that had been thrust upon him. He surfaced briefly to give an interview following Dolgen's departure, insisting that everything was fine. "We're still committed to the same management and philosophy," he said. "I don't consider this a job with training wheels."

Asked if he was happy in his job, Guber replied, "Happy is the wrong word for me. . . . There's not a minute when I'm not in wonder at the complexity of what confronts me. But as long as there's a challenge, I'll stay involved. When there's not, I'll move on." He also tried, in his idiosyncratic way, to dispel persistent speculation that Sony might sell TriStar. "We're committed to TriStar, period," he said. "After five years, that issue should be resolved. A parade of people here and in New York have offered to buy it. But I wonder what part of 'no' they don't understand. Some of these people must be dyslexic and think 'no' means 'on.' "

Guber tried to put over the kind of sales job that had worked so effectively on Schulhof. He pointed to a string of upcoming films as proof that a turnaround was imminent: *Wolf, Mary Shelley's Frankenstein, City Slickers II,* and *The Quick and the Dead.* Of the four, only *Wolf* would be a mere disappointment, grossing $64 million. The rest would be outright bombs.

When Hollywoodites talked about Guber now, they talked

428

about his toys. Many described the beauties of his 110-foot yacht, the *Sea Oz*. It had a captain and a staff of four, and was fitted out with a Jacuzzi on the rear deck and Jet Skis for recreation when anchored.

At fifty-two, Guber was still devoting leisure time to sailing and frolicking with executives who were twenty years his junior. Over the Martin Luther King, Jr., holiday, for example, he had flown Jay Moloney, one of the Young Turks at Creative Artists Agency, and Columbia executive Barry Josephson, to Puerto Vallarta, where the yacht awaited them.

Guber had another project at hand that was designed to impart meaning to his life: Against Lynda's wishes, he had taken steps to adopt two baby boys.

Meanwhile, morale had not improved in the Thalberg Building. "You felt like you were digging your way to China," one executive says. "I understood the line from *Alien*—'In space, no one can hear you scream.' Now it was, 'In the Thalberg Building, no one can hear you scream.' Nobody would give anybody an answer. . . . It was one of those weird, deadening feelings, like, 'We've been waiting for *that* to happen. What next?' "

Of course, there was yet more bad news to come. In May, Sony announced its fiscal 1994 results and acknowledged that it had faced a "big" loss on the movie business—though it declined to say how big. Takatoshi Yamamoto, an analyst with Morgan Stanley & Co. in Tokyo, estimated that the operating loss from the studio might have been as much as $200 million. Industry analysts figured the studio had spent $700 million in film production costs during the year, compared with an industry norm of $400 to $500 million. And overhead was still swollen far beyond the norm.

Sony announced an operating loss of $42 million from its U.S. operations, even though the record business was strong and the electronics side was performing reasonably well. Overall, Sony's net income fell to about $148.5 million, a sharp decline of more than 50 percent over the previous year.

Even Schulhof appeared to be getting sickened by it all. "If last year is just a one-year dip, the fact that Sony can be patient is to our credit," he said. "But if it becomes two years, then Sony will face some tough decisions." But he kept the flag aloft. Up until now, he insisted, Sony Pictures Entertainment had "a pretty good track record."

429

# 32

## THE LONG GOOD-BYE

JOHN EVAN FROOK was a bright twenty-nine-year-old reporter at *Variety*. Blond, with a cherubic face, Frook looked forward to the day when he might become features editor of some daily newspaper. For the time being, his beat included Columbia Pictures.

Frook worked for Peter Bart, the owlish editor of *Variety*. Short and stocky, Bart had been head of production at Paramount when Guber had held the same job at Columbia during the seventies and the two became tennis buddies. Later, he had produced a bomb called *Youngblood,* a 1986 action film with Patrick Swayze and Rob Lowe, for the Guber-Peters Company. He and Guber were still close despite the arm's-length relationship that journalism required.

*Variety*, like *The Hollywood Reporter,* wasn't known for aggressive reporting, but it considered itself the entertainment industry's publication of record. Frook was hoping that his job would be a stepping stone to something bigger for him. One day in March 1994, Frook got a break that seemed as though it might make his career.

A source delivered to him a cache of internal Sony documents: more than two hundred pages detailing deals, salaries, budget projections, and other statistics revealing the unhappy reality at Columbia. Included was information that *Variety* usually relished: how much Jack Nicholson got for starring in *Wolf* ($13 million) or the loss on *Last Action Hero* ($26 million). There was a lot of inside information that executives at other studios would find fascinating: salaries, the organization and structure of various departments, budget analyses, and more.

There was, for example, a January 1993 budget document in

which Canton patted himself on the back for *Bram Stoker's Dracula, A Few Good Men,* and *Groundhog Day.* According to the document, these projects were "fully produced by current management." Canton needed to boast about something: Production spending for fiscal 1993 had been budgeted at $274.7 million, but the real figure was $350 million—an increase exceeding $70 million. Much of that was attributed to spending on *Last Action Hero,* which the studio had anticipated would clear a profit of at least $25 million. In retrospect, Canton looked absurdly optimistic. He had predicted that Columbia would rack up $163.9 million in operating income for fiscal 1994, but by the end of the third quarter in November 1993, operating income was $42.1 million.

Frook figured this was quite simply the biggest pile of confidential studio documents ever to fall into a journalist's hands. He was about to leave for a trade show in Las Vegas, but first he called his boss at *Variety* to tell him the news. Bart had a strange reaction, according to Frook. "You don't know the people you're dealing with," he said urgently. "You have to protect yourself—now."

Bart instructed Frook to make five copies of the materials and secrete them in places that only he would know about. Frook did as he was told. He took one copy with him to Las Vegas. Once he got to his hotel, he studied the material and became even more convinced that this could be a coup for himself and for *Variety.*

"Initially, it was, 'That's a fine idea, my boy,' " he said. But soon, he recalls, "I started getting these really weird mixed signals." Instead of rushing into print with his scoop, Bart started fretting that publication of some of the material might mean a lawsuit from Sony. Then Bart—who often boasted of his dealmaking skills—started saying that he was negotiating with Sony Pictures, that *Variety* would use the documents to gain greater access to executives at Columbia. Frook was called to Bart's office for meetings several times a week to discuss the story, but nothing was decided. "I think he was delighted when I went on vacation for two weeks without having it resolved," Frook says.

When he returned, Frook continued to pursue his story. Medavoy had recently been forced out, so Frook paid him a visit in his looming Coldwater Canyon house. He took just one

431

of the documents with him. After keeping Frook waiting for a good half hour, Medavoy appeared. Frook showed him what he had and asked whether Medavoy might supply similar data about TriStar. It was worth a shot; Medavoy may have felt bitter and ready to tell tales. But instead, Frook says, Medavoy reacted with shock.

"What are you doing?" he demanded. "You need to be very, very careful. You're in possession of stolen goods! Do you know how much trouble you're in? Get a lawyer!"

Frook felt sure of his position. After all, he was a reporter doing his job. Leaked documents were commonplace. This was just an exceptionally good leak. Meanwhile, he tried to come up with a draft of a story that Bart would agree to print. Weeks crawled by. One Friday morning, Frook delivered a version of the story that he considered critical but scrupulously fair. He had merely laid out the facts. Bart took a copy and left for a meeting at Sony. "He just told me he was having a meeting with [Alan] Levine," Frook says. "He was out most of the day."

Bart says he took copies of some of the documents, but not a copy of Frook's story, to the meeting. He was concerned about the legality of printing the material and had been advised by counsel that the information contained in the documents had to be verified by Sony executives. He decided to attend to the matter himself, he says, because Frook seemed "so emotionally wrought up" over the story and because he wasn't sure Frook was mature enough to handle such a sensitive matter. After meeting with Levine Bart decided not to publish Frook's story. While some of the information in the documents was worth printing, he says, he thought that Frook had written a "breathless" story that wasn't interesting enough to print.

Frook was given a lot of assignments that had nothing to do with Columbia. "They were just hammering on me," he says. But he refused to give up on the story that really interested him. He kept plugging away at a draft that he still hoped might make it into print, working in the evenings at home. He kept bringing the story back to Bart.

"It came down to begging," he says. "It really did. I write news stories. I knew that I had something that could really help my career and help the paper."

432

Meanwhile, a source told Frook that Bart and Guber had met no fewer than fourteen times during one six-week period while he was trying to get the story printed. Finally, about two months after he had received the documents, Frook came up with a version of the story that he considered a "settlement," a version that he and Bart could both accept. Before the story could run, Frook was told to go to Sony to give Levine a chance to comment.

Levine came on "like a hamfisted fighter—very condescending, hard-edged," Frook says. Levine paced the room and tried intimidation. "We know you solicited Mike Medavoy for stolen property," he pronounced. Frook was astonished. Why would Medavoy tattle to Levine about their conversation? But he kept his cool. "I tried to be very casual and very Hollywood about it." Levine turned threatening again.

"We're going to sue you," he declared, according to Frook. "Are you prepared to be in depositions for ten years? What do you want, John? How'd you like it if we called you back for depositions in seven years? How would you like it if you were a features editor at a Cincinnati newspaper and seven years from now, we call you back for a deposition? How would your bosses like it?"

Frook stuck by his guns. When he left the office that Friday afternoon, he was expecting to see the story in print. He spent the weekend imagining the impact it would have when it broke on Monday, even in its diluted form.

He went to work early that May morning. But when he picked up the newspaper, he was shocked. "That story was gutted," he says. It was choppy, and in Frook's view, "incomprehensible." Gone were many of the facts that he had fought to report. A detailed comparison of the films released by Price and those released by Canton was eviscerated. The banner headline screamed: SONY CALCULATES COMEBACK.

"I read it and I went outside," Frook recalls. "I just sort of sat there by those big fountains in front of the building and I read it again."

Frook was married and he had bills to pay. "I thought I needed to keep working. We needed the money," he says. He never confronted Bart. "You don't have to do this," his wife told him. "You can leave." On June 11, a few weeks after the story appeared, Frook quit, the day before his thirtieth birthday.

Bart says none of the changes in the story were made to

433

appease Sony. "It was a by-the-numbers handling of this," he says. "I wouldn't 'sell out' *Variety*. I don't know what my motive would be."

HOPES WERE HIGH for the summer of 1994, but the season began badly. Reliable Castle Rock dropped a bomb into the Sony release schedule: *City Slickers II*. The film was not a big problem for Columbia since Castle Rock had financed it. But Castle Rock's *North*, which Columbia had financed to the tune of $40 million, also failed. Half of Columbia's line-up was coming from Castle Rock and now Reiner's company was hitting a cold streak.

After all the time and money that had been spent perfecting *Wolf*, the film barely broke even. The $64 million gross would have been fine if the picture hadn't cost so much. As usual, Sony had overspent.

Alan Levine, perhaps smelling decay, began to show signs that he was developing an appetite for more power. That summer Levine attended a special screening of *Wolf* for state legislators in Sacramento, part of a lobbying effort meant to remind lawmakers that the entertainment industry was important to the regional economy. Sony's public relations man, Don DeMesquita, went to the state capital to make arrangements. When he heard from the governor's office that Pete Wilson would arrive at the event with a police escort, he demanded a police escort for Levine as well.

Only the governor is entitled to a police escort, he was told. Levine was free to have private security if he liked. DeMesquita threatened to pull the film if the police escort were not provided. Other Columbia executives were astonished at the delusional sense of Levine's importance. Finally, DeMesquita backed off and the screening went on as planned.

As the summer wore on, Sony couldn't get a break. TriStar hadn't put a movie into production for nine months. Amy Pascal, the well-regarded Columbia executive who had been involved in several successful projects, including *Groundhog Day, Single White Female,* and the upcoming *Sense and Sensibility,* was leaving after seven years—to become president of production at Turner Pictures. The studio had refused to let her out of her contract and Pascal had quarreled bitterly with her longtime friend, Lisa Henson. Henson, whose hiring had seemed like an inspired, stabilizing move, was alienating many film-

makers with what was perceived as a chilly, contemptuous attitude.

In August, Sony Pictures decided to save some money by
merging the Columbia and TriStar marketing departments—a
move that Levine had denied the company would make only
three months earlier. This was a return to the system in place
when Sony had acquired the company. The TriStar marketing
team, Buffy Shutt and Kathy Jones, was supposed to head the
combined departments. Despite TriStar's woes, its marketing
had been strong and Shutt and Jones were respected. But now
they, too, had had enough of Sony Pictures. They decided to
move to Universal, leaving Sony Pictures scrambling for someone to replace them.

Sid Ganis, who had but five months earlier been promoted
from Columbia marketing chief to vice chairman of the studio,
was the obvious choice. But he wasn't eager to return to his
old duties. Mark Canton and Fred Bernstein, a business affairs
executive who had been hired after Dolgen's departure,
pleaded with Ganis until two in the morning to take the marketing job. Ganis resisted mightily, then finally yielded. For
Canton, another potential embarrassment had been modu-
lated, if not averted.

"Mark almost cried when he told the staff that he had gotten
Sid to agree," says one executive. "He was so terrified about
what would happen if he lost both marketing heads."

With Ganis in place, Canton let it be known that he had
extended his own contract with Sony. He declined to specify its
duration but said, "It's a long-term agreement and I'm very
pleased." Sources close to him said his deal ran through 1999.

AT THE END OF AUGUST, Schulhof stumbled into his biggest
public relations debacle to date. The industry was buzzing with
gossip that Jeffrey Katzenberg, who had just left Disney after a
bitter quarrel with chairman Michael Eisner, might take over
Sony Pictures. Katzenberg had departed because Eisner refused to promote him to the number-two job at Disney, despite
his reputation as a brilliant executive. Given the studio's desperate need for competent leadership, the idea that Sony
would want Katzenberg seemed plausible enough. The idea
that Katzenberg would take a job reporting to Schulhof, however, was absurd. He was hungry to run his own empire.

To counter the reports of Katzenberg's imminent arrival,

Sony had come forward with an announcement that Guber would not leave his current post. But days later, the *Los Angeles Times* reported that Jeff Sagansky, the former head of programming at CBS, was about to be named president of Sony Software. The paper's first report said that he would be in charge of filmed entertainment and music, responsible in part for cleaning up the mess at Sony Pictures. Guber might be on the way out or in line for a promotion into Sony's corporate hierarchy. The article had no comment from Schulhof, or from any official at Sony.

The next day there was a second wave of reports in other publications indicating that Sagansky would not, after all, be responsible for the motion picture unit. Guber, who had reportedly helped recruit Sagansky, would stay in his job, these articles said. Again, Schulhof remained unavailable to reporters. Without a formal statement from Sony, unnamed sources from inside the company were feeding the press such vague quotes as "[Sagansky's] role will be mostly as visionary." Or, "He and Mickey will look at the company's objectives in going forward with software in the 21st Century."

The whole matter seemed to reaffirm the description of Sony offered by financial analyst Jeff Logsdon of Seidler Cos. a few months earlier: "They know how to confound confusion with commotion out there." This was typical Sony confusion, but clearly change was coming. No one knew exactly what it meant, but everyone knew that the bell was tolling.

At the studio, people feared a purge. The anxiety built despite reports that Sagansky wasn't going to take a hands-on role there and that he would stay in New York in a strategic job. Many observers concluded that his mandate would be to sell the 25 percent stake in software that had been gathering dust for so many months, or to find other sources of financing. But the notion that Sagansky would also be responsible for fixing Sony Pictures would not be dispelled.

In some ways, Sagansky seemed an odd choice to save the troubled studio. Now forty-two, he hadn't shown any special aptitude or love for the movie business during his previous tenure as production president at TriStar under Victor Kaufman. He had a reputation for disliking the glitz of the film world, for refusing to coddle talent, for shunning the Hollywood party circuit.

Kaufman defended Sagansky. "Jeff's record at TriStar is actually much better than some people perceive," he said at the time. "Jeff was operating with limited budgets." Within those constraints, Kaufman said, Sagansky did well. "Also, Jeff did better as he was in the job longer, much in the way of Diller and Eisner. It took a few years for them to hit their stride."

Comparing Sagansky with former Fox chairman Barry Diller or Disney chairman Michael Eisner was greatly flattering to Sagansky. He had done exceptionally well for himself, but he had never presided over a multi-billion-dollar entertainment empire or tasted the kind of success that those two men had enjoyed. His track record at TriStar could generously be called mediocre.

At first blush, Sagansky seemed to have done wonders at CBS. The network had moved into first place, and with his compensation tied to the network's performance, he earned huge bonuses: $6.1 million in 1992 and $7.8 million in 1993. But a closer look showed that he benefited enormously from specials, including the Super Bowl, the 1994 Olympics, and the World Series. And most of the network's leading series had been developed by Sagansky's predecessor, Kim LeMasters, who was there when *Murder, She Wrote* and *Murphy Brown* were created.

Sagansky couldn't claim credit for the few new hits that emerged during his tenure. *Northern Exposure* was in development when he arrived, and *Dr. Quinn, Medicine Woman* was a project backed by other executives at the network. Meanwhile, CBS found that it didn't have much in the cupboard after he left in April 1994. It quickly fell into last place.

"I think he's very lucky but I think you make your luck," said a television executive who is fond of Sagansky. "He is a wonderful guy to work for, a guy who people want to do things for. He's self-effacing and aggressive at the same time." That executive pointed out that some of the blame lay with CBS, which had given Sagansky a contract for moving the network into first place without regard to the demographics of the audiences that he might attract to achieve that goal. Advertisers will pay more to buy time in programs that attract young audiences, so such programming is far more valuable to the network.

During Sagansky's tenure, CBS showed a lot of strength in movies of the week and programming that attracted older audi-

437

ences less favored by advertisers. In the same vein, CBS moved to dominance on Saturday nights. "Saturday happens to be the least important night and the demographics of the CBS shows are terrible," the executive conceded. "But Jeff's deal didn't give him incentives toward demographics. He got bonuses to bring up gross rating points, not to lower the age of the [viewers]. Jeff went for the available audience—older women. CBS has suffered for that."

But finding someone willing to take on Sony's staggering problems could not have been easy. One industry veteran close to the situation said that hiring Sagansky seemed to be Schulhof's last-ditch attempt to save his own job. Schulhof would be reluctant to fire Guber, that executive reasoned, because "he was part of hiring him, and that becomes an admission that everything in the last five years has been wrong." Schulhof's best hope was to save face by hiring someone who could try to make things right.

Sony was engulfed in confusion about Sagansky and his role, but still Schulhof remained silent. The slipshod handling of the announcement, meanwhile, caused problems with Tommy Mottola, the head of Sony Music. Mottola was said to be livid over the way the news leaked—and by the confusion over whether he would be reporting to Sagansky. "Do you think that after I netted this company $300 million last year I'm going to report to someone else? Fuck you!" Mottola reportedly shrieked to Schulhof in one phone call.

"The feeling is that Schulhof has completely panicked and that all the pressure over [Sony Pictures] has caused him to antagonize his one profitable division: Sony Music," said one insider.

"Why would any executive worth his salt do anything to alienate the biggest breadwinners in his company?" another asked. "It defies logic."

By LABOR DAY 1994, Columbia and TriStar had released between them thirteen films for the year to date. Combined, those grossed $255 million—barely topping the revenues raked in by one film released by Paramount, *Forrest Gump*. The statistic must have given pause to *Gump* producer Wendy Finerman's husband—Mark Canton.

In September, Schulhof flew to London to meet with Norio

438

Ohga. At long last, even Schulhof's patience had finally worn thin. "I've given it enough time," he told Ohga. "I've tried to get Peter to change. But it isn't in his psyche to change and the company can't afford to go on this way." After his discussion with Ohga, Schulhof summoned Guber to New York.

In his sumptuous Madison Avenue offices, Schulhof finally broached the long-overdue subject with Guber. "I can tell when you're not happy," he said. "It's reflected in the quality of your work."

"I don't know how to do it differently," Guber responded. "I can't work harder physically."

"I think you ought to resign," Schulhof suggested.

"Okay," Guber replied.

At ten o'clock on the morning of September 28, top Sony Pictures executives were summoned to a screening room in the Thalberg Building. There they were told the news that Hollywood had anticipated for months, even years: Peter Guber was resigning as Sony Pictures chairman only eighteen months after signing his "long-term" contract. Just weeks after Schulhof's formal announcement affirming that Guber would remain in his post, Guber was gone. Two weeks earlier, company operatives had insisted that Guber would be in his job until the year 2000, or longer.

In a spate of press interviews following Guber's ouster, Schulhof was typically disingenuous. He casually asserted that he had talked to Guber about his departure some four months earlier. "Peter came to me and said his time had come to an end," he said. "He had achieved most of the objectives I had set out for him, but he said he missed the hands-on creative process."

Schulhof heaped praise on Guber. "When he joined in 1989, it was with the agreement he would spend three to five years rebuilding Columbia Pictures for us," he said. "He has attracted an enormous number of people to the company and virtually all of them joined because they were hired by Peter over the past five years." Considering the studio's top-heavy management, the number of high-profile firings, and expensive payoffs, and the administrative gridlock at the company, this seemed an odd point on which to congratulate Guber. Perhaps Schulhof could think of little else to say.

Guber didn't waste his breath expressing gratitude to the company that had put faith in him for the last four years—and compensated him richly. He portrayed this decision to leave Sony as his own, casting it in New Age parlance. As usual, his only point of reference was himself. He wanted to "touch the cloth and hear the music," he told one interviewer. "Are my interests, my passions and concerns with this kind of job? Clearly, right now, they are no longer. That's what motivated the change. . . . This is the third act of my life."

The company announced that Guber would start a "new entertainment venture" and that Sony would be "a major investor" putting in a "substantial" amount of money.

"This is an opportunity for me to create an asset that will be mine and which I can manage to the point of having real value in my overall life," Guber enthused. "I'm going to be very hands-on in the creative activities of the new company and new technologies will be the center of it."

"When he told me what he had in mind, to create an entertainment company, I said, 'Not only will I support it, I'll invest in it,' " Schulhof added, expressing his delight in his continued association with Guber, "who has given so much to our company." He referred to Guber as "a builder and a visionary."

Sony's backing for his new venture wouldn't be Guber's only reward. Though the precise terms remained unclear, he would receive his share in the bonus pool that had been created when he and Jon Peters were hired. Initially, the amount was to be an 8.08 percent share in any increase in the asset value of the studio. Now, though there were suggestions that the terms had been renegotiated, it was apparent that Guber would walk away with yet another wad of Sony millions in his pocket. He may have left the studio a shambles, but he had come a long way toward achieving the goal that he had articulated to Warner boss Terry Semel years ago: to "make more money than anyone in the history of the motion picture industry."

Upon Guber's departure, the market share for Columbia and TriStar combined—the meaningless tally of which he had made so much—was 9.4 percent. Almost five years earlier, he had rebuked Columbia's previous management for their poor market share. Now, after Sony had poured an estimated $8 billion into its investment, market share was back down to where it had been when he arrived.

440

During Guber's tenure, Sony Pictures had never produced a genuine breakaway hit. And despite Schulhof's contention that

Guber had helped to revitalize the studio, Columbia could boast no high-profile film for the upcoming Christmas holidays. TriStar hadn't put a film into production for nearly a year.

Guber was not replaced. Alan Levine would remain as president and chief operating officer, reporting directly to Schulhof. "Nothing's going to change in the way we do business here," Levine declared. One of the many executives who had exited the studio earlier shared that conclusion, though not in the same spirit as Levine. "They'll keep what they have and declare a victory," he predicted. "You know, the Vietnam solution."

Pondering the wreckage at the studio, another former Sony executive viewed the fact that Peter Guber and Jon Peters had walked away unscathed as a profoundly unsatisfying outcome. "Any notion of justice and what's fair—it's not going to happen," he said. "Peter got rich. Jon got richer. There are no just deserts."

Guber was gone five years to the day after Sony had hired him. The following day, September 29, 1994, a time capsule was lowered into the ground near the entrance to the Sony lot, commemorating the completion of the extensive renovations to which he had devoted himself so single-mindedly. By prearrangement, the capsule included a copy of that day's *Variety*. It was an inauspicious time for such a stunt, but at least the trade paper was kind to Guber, even to the last. Giving him the benefit of the doubt for the ages, the paper did not report that Guber had been fired. The paper's banner headline declared: GUBER RESIGNS AS SONY'S CEO.

# EPILOGUE

IN NOVEMBER 1994, the bomb finally detonated. The Sony Corporation stunned Hollywood and Wall Street by announcing that it was taking a $3.2 billion loss in its second quarter because of its failures in Hollywood.

The write-off—essentially a clearing of the balance sheet, which included a $2.7 billion loss on the studio and an additional $510 million operating loss on "settlement of outstanding lawsuits and contract claims"—was one of the largest losses in Japanese corporate history. It was also one of the worst beatings ever sustained by a foreign investor in an American company. After five years putting on a happy public face, Sony was admitting that its foray into Hollywood had been a disaster.

Hollywood insiders once again cast the debacle as the ultimate revenge for the attack on Pearl Harbor. "They should have taken the write-down on December 7 and said, 'United States 1; Japan 1. Let's call it even,' " said a former Guber-Peters employee.

Coming just weeks after Guber had been fired, the write-off cemented his legacy: His tenure as chairman of Sony Pictures would forever be associated with billions of dollars in red ink.

But amazingly, Schulhof continued to heap rewards on his friend. As news reports suggested that Schulhof had been seduced into tolerating Guber's excesses, Sony gave Guber his own production company. The unprecedented deal, arranged by Schulhof and approved by Ohga, stipulated that his Mandalay company would receive a reported $275 million revolving fund to finance entertainment ventures. Guber would exercise considerable authority to green-light movies and would retain lucrative foreign rights to many films. His total annual compen-

442

sation was estimated at between $5 and $10 million. "As usual, Peter manages to win even when he loses," groused a high-level Columbia executive.

Levine and Canton, faced with the prospect of administering their old boss's new deal, were reportedly angered to discover that Schulhof had also granted Guber the right to pluck choice projects from TriStar and Columbia to produce under his Mandalay banner.

As details of the deal emerged, Guber surfaced briefly to deny that he was cherry-picking projects from Sony Pictures. "No one here is in charge of me," he said, adding that creative decisions were on hold anyway because he was about to leave on a six-week vacation. "Right now," he said, "I'm only dealing with me."

AKIO MORITA'S resignation as chairman of Sony was announced on November 25, 1994, less than two weeks after the write-off. Now seventy-three, he had undergone months of rehabilitation but was still wheelchair-bound and in poor health, recuperating first in Tokyo, then in Hawaii. His old friend, investment banker Pete Peterson, was still a Sony director and he urged that Morita be permitted to remain on the board. The suggestion was rebuffed. Morita was stripped of all formal power but given the title of founder and honorary chairman. The company denied that Morita's resignation was prompted by the disaster in Hollywood.

Norio Ohga resigned as president of Sony in March 1995, remaining as chief executive and taking the title of chairman. His surprise successor was Nobuyuki Idei, a mid-level managing director from the marketing side who spoke fluent English and leapfrogged at least eleven other senior associates for the job. According to some reports, a sexual harassment scandal eliminated a front-runner for the job and opened the door to Idei's surprise ascent.

The fifty-seven-year-old Idei was viewed as friendly to the entertainment operation, despite remarks he had made to the press in the past suggesting that his patience with Schulhof was running out. After his promotion, Idei said his comments about Schulhof had been taken out of context. But at the studio, no one wanted to risk any unnecessary provocations. Before Idei made his first visit to Culver City as Sony's new

443

boss, the plaque commemorating the completion of the lot renovation—inscribed with Guber's name—was unceremoniously dug up. It was replaced with a plain brass plate.

Amid rampant speculation about his fate, Mickey Schulhof gave an interview that ran in the May 1995 issue of *Vanity Fair*, reportedly under pressure from Tokyo. He haltingly tried to explain himself. For a moment, he departed from his glib assurances about his satisfaction with Sony Pictures. Asked why he had stood by Peter Guber while Guber ran the studio into the ground, he acknowledged that this was "a very deep psychological question that deserves an answer."

But Schulhof didn't have a satisfactory answer. He tried to explain it in cultural terms. It wasn't Sony's way to fire people; rather, the company tried to accept them for their strengths. "Part of my attitude toward Peter was reflected in my desire to have his behavior change in a way where he could stay on, and work well, and the company would turn around."

In the beginning, Schulhof believed that Guber was building the studio. "There had been clear signs of overspending," he admitted—but he was encouraged by the robust market share and was convinced that "the amounts being spent were not wildly out of line." To the bitter end, Schulhof insisted that Sony had made its decisions with its eyes open.

"It's easy to draw the conclusion that we were fleeced," he said finally. "But that was not true."

If Schulhof's position with Idei was already tenuous, it was further weakened in January. In a severe setback that recalled the Betamax nightmare, Sony was defeated in its attempt to set the industry standard for the digital video disc, a technology that was expected to be the successor to the VCR. On January 24, Time Warner and Matsushita announced that they had joined forces to endorse the Toshiba Company's digital videodisc system, effectively squashing the rival format developed by Sony and Philips Electronics.

The announcement was made at a press conference attended by Time Warner chairman Gerry Levin, Warner co-chairman Terry Semel, and MCA president Sid Sheinberg, among other industry leaders. The loss was seen as a particular blow to Sony because MCA's owner, Matsushita, had been expected to join forces with Sony this time; Schulhof was blamed for failing to get Hollywood companies to rally behind him.

In November 1995, Idei made his first U.S. public appearance, a speech to an entertainment industry group in New York. Schulhof stood by his side, looking poised and confident; observers came away with the impression that Mickey had survived the write-off and secured his position.

The fiscal health of the studio had improved slightly. Columbia's best picture for the year thus far had been *Bad Boys,* a Simpson-Bruckheimer action film that grossed $64.5 million domestically. The studio also had a winner with *The Net* and scored critical hits with *To Die For* and *Sense and Sensibility.* But the summer had been marred by a major disappointment in *First Knight* a big-budget retelling of the King Arthur legend directed by Jerry Zucker. The picture failed despite the star power of Sean Connery and Richard Gere.

Jon Peters, with his first film as a producer for the studio, had not helped his friend Mark Canton. He handed him an expensive flop, *Money Train.*

TriStar had gotten the year off to a good start with *Legends of the Fall,* starring Brad Pitt, then limped along with *Johnny Mnemonic,* which grossed only $18.9 million. *Mary Reilly,* the former Guber-Peters project starring Julia Roberts, was a mismanaged disaster whose release kept getting postponed. At Christmas, TriStar would pull the year out of the abyss with *Jumanji,* a $95 million family hit starring Robin Williams. All in all, just over a year after Guber's departure, Levine and Canton could claim some modest gains.

But they would not be enough to save Schulhof. The music division had suffered a sharp drop-off in market share and a new electronic publishing division was losing a lot of money. On December 5, after what was reported as a ferocious power struggle with Idei, Schulhof was abruptly fired—without even the fig leaf of a consulting job. Both the hardware and software units would now report directly to Tokyo; Idei himself would oversee electronics while Ohga would assume responsibility for the entertainment division. Sony had reclaimed direct control over its American operations.

There were reports that Schulhof's extravagance—both personal and professional—had irritated executives in Japan, where the economic downturn had necessitated a new austerity. There had been the highly publicized parties in East Hampton, including a hoedown and Polynesian night. There was also a front-page story in the *Wall Street Journal* about Schulhof's investment in WEHM, a small radio station in the Hamptons. The report described how Schulhof had brought in forty-two thousand dollars' worth of Sony equipment, including fifteen hundred Walkman units to be used in promotions and two four-thousand-dollar computer-operated CD players, so sophisticated that they collected dust for months while the staff figured out how to use them.

Schulhof said he was a silent partner with no involvement in the station's operation, but WEHM's manager said that he faxed weekly playlists to Schulhof and that Schulhof stopped by to help get the new CD players running. Sony advertising, including promotions for Columbia and TriStar, accounted for 9 percent of the station's advertising. The manager of a much larger competitor, WLNG, said his station didn't get "one iota" of the movie advertising that Schulhof's station received, and the WEHM station manager acknowledged that Schulhof "can open doors that other stations can't get through."

Idei and Schulhof had faced off over a number of strategic issues, such as Sony's decision to push into the personal computer market. But whatever the difficulties between New York and Tokyo, industry observers on Wall Street were convinced that Schulhof's critical—and ultimately fatal—mistake had been his blind loyalty to Guber. Guber was seen as responsible not only for the runaway spending at the studio, but also for whetting Schulhof's appetite for luxury. Some sources close to Guber surmised that Guber had coached Schulhof in negotiations over compensation with Japan, earning Schulhof's gratitude but perhaps also spoiling his relationships with his colleagues in Tokyo.

When Idei had taken over as president of Sony, he was reported to be stunned by Guber's production deal. By now, Guber had installed Mandalay in a huge suite of offices on the lot, which visitors described as a fantasyland with whirring ceiling fans, a mammoth fish tank, and the scent of gardenias everywhere.

Guber was spending Sony's millions to get his company up and running. He had a creative staff of fourteen—about the same as Columbia Pictures. He had made an extravagant deal to pay $16 million to John Travolta to star in *The Double*. He was shelling out millions for literary material. He had also exercised his power to appropriate some Sony Pictures projects, including *Seven Years in Tibet,* an epic with Brad Pitt attached, about an Austrian mountain climber who befriends the Dalai Lama.

By late 1995, details had been leaked to the press about Sony's 1993 purchase of Guber's old house on Brownwood. The company had paid Guber $5.5 million—substantially above its market value, which was estimated at $3 million or less. The transaction had been effected through a shell company called Lawrence Holdings. The house had become a white elephant and Sony ended up renting it out for $10,000 a month. The tenant, Julio Paz, said he initially thought he was getting "one hell of a deal." But he complained that the property was rat-infested and that the plumbing malfunctioned so severely that excrement oozed from the bathtub faucet. "The house is a big nightmare," he lamented.

Now Idei ordered the company to look for ways to scale back Guber's deal. At a January 1996 press conference, Idei admitted that at first he had been furious over the generous terms that Guber had been granted. "I used to be very emotional about that," Idei said. "But now I'm more stable." Asked about rumors that Sony was investigating Schulhof and Guber's spending habits, Idei replied, "I have no comment on it."

With Schulhof gone, it would now reportedly fall to Alan Levine, Guber's ex-lawyer, to curtail Guber's expenditures and rein in his broad autonomy to green-light pictures. Studio sources said that Guber would now be expected to bring in outside financing for Mandalay projects.

Although Sony once again denied that it was interested in selling all or part of the studio, industry analysts believed it was only a matter of time before Tokyo would have to throw in the towel and cut its losses. "They haven't yet crossed the Rubicon of 'Why are we in this business?'" mused a top executive at another entertainment company. "They will."

But even after his departure, Schulhof told friends he still believed that Sony's fundamental strategy of trying to marry hardware and software was correct. "With all [Sony's] troubles, Morita would be the first one to say, 'Yes, but we're still going down the right road and we'll fix the problem pieces as we go along,'" Schulhof said. "I believe that, if you could talk to him, he would say, 'Sure, we've got problems, but owning a studio 447 and owning a record company and merging them with electronics is the future of this company.' He, perhaps uniquely, understood this potential and was willing to invest and build."

SONY'S LONG-TIME RIVAL, Matsushita, announced in April 1995 that it was selling 80 percent of MCA to Seagram's for $5.7 billion. The Ovitz-brokered deal had soured. Matsushita had gotten into a bitter clash with its American managers, Lew Wasserman and Sid Sheinberg. The cultures didn't meld and the strong-willed Americans chafed at Matsushita's refusal to spend money on acquisitions that would enable MCA to compete with growing companies like Viacom.

Ironically, it seemed clear that Sony would have done far better had it bought MCA. The studio came with competent managers who cared passionately about the business that they had presided over for decades. Sony would have been rewarded for taking a hands-off approach to management and maintaining an open-handed attitude toward expenditures. While Matsushita's sale was perceived as an admission of defeat, analysts said the company had survived in far better shape than its rival. Its losses were far smaller, and in the end, Matsushita had a buyer eager to acquire its property.

WALTER YETNIKOFF struggled to regroup emotionally and professionally. In 1991 he formed Velvel Musical Industries and Velvel Film Industries. (Yetnikoff's grandmother called him "Velvel" when he was a boy.) Both companies remained dormant until 1996, when Yetnikoff focused on launching the music company. His prospective partner in the venture was Jon Peters.

ALAN LEVINE, little esteemed in the industry, outlasted all the top executives at Sony Pictures Entertainment. With Schulhof's departure, he even triumphed over Jeff Sagansky, who was relegated to less glamorous chores. "Anybody who managed to take out Jon Peters and Gary Lieberthal and Jon Dolgen when they didn't want to be taken out is not to be underestimated," says a former Columbia executive. But Hal Vogel, the financial analyst who is now at Cowen & Co. in New York, believed that the end was in sight. Predicting that Sony would decide to sell the studio, he delicately opined that the company "would require more charismatic leadership to attract buyers." Indeed, soon after Sony expressed its support for Levine, at least one executive at a rival company was approached by an investment banking firm that inquired whether he would be interested in Levine's job.

JON DOLGEN arrived at Paramount in time to enjoy the phenomenal success of *Forrest Gump,* the blockbuster produced by Mark Canton's wife, Wendy Finerman. Before leaving Sony, he had finally renegotiated his contract, four years after his promotion. It included an escape clause and also provided for a non-refundable $250,000 payment on signing. After his departure, Sony asked for the money back. Dolgen complied. No one called to thank him.

FRANK PRICE made several films, including *Circle of Friends, Shadowlands,* and *A Bronx Tale,* through his deal with Savoy Pictures. Those pictures enjoyed some critical success, though none set any fires at the box office. Price was very influential at the fledgling company and advised Savoy founder Victor Kaufman to green-light a number of bombs, including a $30 million disaster called *Heaven's Prisoners.* A Savoy insider says Price "lost a lot of money for the company." Savoy became embroiled in financial difficulties and was acquired by Barry Diller in 1995. The film division was folded.

MICHAEL MEDAVOY raised millions in financing from Onex, an airline food manufacturer, and set up his new film company, Phoenix Pictures, at Sony.

PATRICIA DUFF MEDAVOY married financier Ron Perelman and had a baby.

MICHAEL NATHANSON took a job running New Regency Pictures for producer Arnon Milchan, whose deal was at Warner.

JOHN EVAN FROOK became entertainment editor of a publication called *Interactive Age.*

449

IN DECEMBER 1994, Heidi Fleiss was convicted in Los Angeles Superior Court on three counts of pandering. Several jurors protested the severity of the punishment when she was sentenced to three years in prison. She subsequently was tried in federal court, where witnesses included actor Charlie Sheen. Sweating and fidgeting in his videotaped testimony, he admitted that he had spent at least $53,000 on services provided by Fleiss in 1992. In August 1995, Fleiss sobbed as she was convicted on eight federal counts of conspiracy, tax evasion, and money laundering. While she awaited sentencing, she sold her own line of underwear at two shops in Southern California.

JON PETERS was supposed to produce a Steven Seagal movie, *Under Siege II*, at Warner but dropped out after the two reportedly came to blows—literally. He went on to produce *Money Train*, his first film since *Batman*, for Columbia. Embroiled in production troubles, insiders at the studio dubbed the picture *Money Drain* as the budget climbed to a reported $80 million. Having secured a deal for 5 percent of first-dollar gross, Jon didn't need to fret over the cost. Before its release, Sony Pictures anticipated a hit and hailed the picture as a sign that it was recovering from its doldrums. *Money Train* faltered at the box office, grossing about $35 million.

In early 1996 Jon put two films into production for Warner, John Singleton's *Rosewood* and a comedy with Jack Lemmon and James Garner, *My Fellow Americans*. But he was most excited about a remake of *Superman, Superman Reborn*. Jon envisioned a blockbuster franchise that would eventually dock with his biggest hit. On the big screen, Superman would meet Batman —and the two superheroes would be united in the ultimate unbeatable partnership.

# AFTERWORD

AFTER MICKEY SCHULHOF was fired as head of Sony's U.S. operations in December 1995, the old guard at Sony Pictures Entertainment hung on much longer than most industry observers had expected. Alan Levine and Mark Canton stayed in place, although as president and COO Levine was never anointed with Guber's title, chairman. Levine worked hard to convey the impression that a new era had begun, although he had been around since the beginning of the Guber-Peters regime. While he established some greater degree of order, he brought no overriding vision or inspiration to his job, and the studio continued to drift. The television division grew stronger, but Sony's fortunes at the box office kept sinking.

"Make a successful summer," Idei had commanded Levine and Canton. The implicit message was that their job security depended on it. But Idei's mandate went unfulfilled: The summer of 1996 was a bleak one for Sony Pictures. The studio starved while Fox feasted on *Independence Day,* a sci-fi special-effects extravaganza by the writing-producing-directing team of Dean Devlin and Roland Emmerich that would eventually take in a staggering $700 million worldwide. (Canton had been offered *ID4* first, but despite the enthusiastic endorsement of Marc Platt and Barry Josephson, had let slip the project that would have redeemed his summer.) Meanwhile, Paramount enjoyed *Mission: Impossible,* Warner and Universal shared *Twister,* and Disney reaped huge profits from *The Rock* and *Phenomenon.*

Canton seemed unable to buy or steal a breakaway hit movie. He needed Levine's approval to green-light films, and producers and executives complained that it was as hard as ever to get straight answers about the fate of their projects. Canton continued his policy of spending big for star power while haphazardly managing the films the studio had in production.

At a time of escalating costs, when all the major studios were trying to keep a lid on the sky-high fees commanded by major stars, Canton had stunned and angered Hollywood by coughing up $20 million—a new high-water mark—for Jim Carrey to appear in *The Cable Guy*. The rest of the studios glumly waited for other stars to demand the new going rate, or at least a raise. In his eagerness to have what seemed like a surefire hit for summer 1996, Canton green-lit the Ben Stiller–directed comedy even though its sinister cable repairman was a dark departure from the off-center funnyman audiences had loved in Carrey's box-office smashes *Dumb & Dumber* and *The Mask*.

Canton had been confident that *The Cable Guy* would ring the $100 million bell, but once again his seemingly sure bet failed. *The Cable Guy* turned off critics and audiences, grossing a weak $60 million. When it opened on June 14, the *New York Times* decried "the shocking sight of a volatile comic talent in free fall." As with *Last Action Hero,* the media and the Hollywood community were gunning for Canton, so the movie was perceived as a bigger debacle than it really was; its cost had been kept in check at $47 million.

Other disappointments could be chalked up as much to bad luck as to poor judgment. *Groundhog Day* director Harold Ramis's *Multiplicity,* a comedy starring Michael Keaton, refused to catch fire at the box office even though test audiences seemed to love it. The sweet but pricey *Matilda,* which starred and was produced and directed by Danny DeVito, also failed to connect. Castle Rock's *Striptease,* in which Demi Moore danced topless for $12.5 million, was a shameless undertaking and it bombed, too.

But none of these pictures would lose Sony the buckets of money poured away on *The Fan,* a movie that revealed how fatally entwined Canton remained with Peter Guber almost two years after the latter's ouster as CEO of Sony Pictures. *The Fan* was one of the projects Guber had plucked from TriStar, demoralizing that studio's executive ranks, to produce through his company, Mandalay. Sony had cut back on Guber's funding, but later in the year Mandalay would announce the acquisition of up to $100 million in funding from a London bank. That allowed it to ramp up production on its slate of pictures, including the TriStar-developed *Donnie Brasco,* a gangster film with a dazzling performance from Al Pacino; *Seven Years in Tibet* (which would eventually star Brad Pitt); and *Desperate Measures,* a thriller from director Barbet Schroeder *(Single White Female).*

*The Fan,* a thriller about a baseball star and a deranged fan, had been developed as a low-budget film without stars by Wendy Finerman, producer of the Oscar-winning *Forrest Gump,* who was also Canton's wife. It became a bloated vulgarity once Guber and Canton got their hands on it. "How do you create any fiscal responsibility when the producer is married to the studio head?" asks an incredulous former Sony executive.

The high-testosterone Tony Scott *(Top Gun)* was hired to direct, Wesley Snipes was paid $7 million to star, and Robert De Niro was signed up to reprise his scary stalker role from *Cape Fear.* Early cuts of the film were, according to one executive, "ugly, mean, and misogynistic—all cocksmanship." But Canton didn't want to hear criticism, and when a test screening was held, he refused to allow the distribution of research cards that would have spelled out the audience's reaction.

Nevertheless, as *The Fan* neared completion everyone knew that it wasn't working. Scott huddled with Guber, Canton, and Finerman as they made desperate attempts to fix it, ordering expensive reshoots and driving the budget to nearly $70 million. Before Guber took over the project, TriStar executives had been told they couldn't spend another $2 million to juice up the soundtrack with some Rolling Stones songs; now the songs were in.

"It was the textbook Peter Guber–Mark Canton–Sony of it all," lamented one departed TriStar executive. "Excess. Pretending things are one way when they're not." Critics savaged *The Fan,* which grossed an embarrassing $20 million domestically.

As if that weren't enough to darken the already bleak summer, Guber also managed to lose another $20 million on a picture without producing a single foot of film. *The Double,* 453 based on a Dostoyevsky novella, told the tale of a timid accountant bedeviled by a mischievous look-alike. With Roman Polanski set to direct for Mandalay, star John Travolta flew his own jet to Paris, where the film was to be shot. (Polanski had not been in the United States since 1978, when he fled to avoid sentencing after pleading guilty to having sex with a thirteen-year-old girl.)

Only a week after he arrived in France, Travolta turned around and flew home. The ostensible reason: His four-year-old son, Jett, had fluid behind the eardrums that needed to be drained. Although the procedure is commonplace, Travolta told *Entertainment Weekly* that he wanted to make sure it was necessary. "He's my son, and I want to make sure he's properly taken care of," he said. It quickly became apparent that Mandalay wasn't buying Travolta's surge of fatherly concern as the real reason for his absence. Hiring Steve Martin to step in for more than $10 million, Mandalay slapped Travolta with a breach-of-contract suit. In court papers, the company said Travolta had "changed his mind . . . because his ego had been bruised by Polanski's legitimate efforts to direct Travolta's performance during the rehearsal period."

A source from the set of *The Double* says it was apparent from the first rehearsal that Polanski and Travolta differed wildly in their views of the accountant; the director reportedly offended the star by jumping up and acting out the part himself. Travolta acknowledged that he disagreed with Polanski on the interpretation of his character; his lawyer, Bert Fields, also said the script had been drastically changed without the star's approval. Repeatedly, Fields told reporters that Polanski wanted Travolta to come across "like a Borscht Belt comedian" and to give "a kind of performance that John could not possibly agree to."

The war of words escalated, with a source in the Mandalay camp referring to Travolta as "an actor for hire" who had overstepped his bounds. That description, Fields countered, "illustrates the arrogance of Mr. Guber's company." At one point, Fields said, Mandalay agreed to Travolta's proposal to replace Polanski (with Travolta offering to pay Polanski's $3.2 million fee). But when the parties scheduled a meeting on June 7 to discuss the dispute, Guber's representatives never showed up. "I've never seen such rudeness," Fields fumed. Despite the last-ditch hiring of Steve Martin, *The Double* was doomed. Having concluded that the film was too expensive without a star of Travolta's magnitude, Mandalay pulled the plug with nothing to show for its troubles but a court date.

Eager to fill the pipeline, Canton also said yes to a number of big-budget movies for 1997. He rushed *The Devil's Own,* a drama about a New York City cop who gets involved with an IRA member, into production in February 1996 after Harrison Ford and Brad Pitt signed up for $20 million and $12 million respectively. The script had been written in 1990, and the resumption of hostilities in Northern Ireland made extensive revisions necessary. Meanwhile, each of the stars inevitably jousted to have the screenplay tailored to his desires. Deciding he'd rather star in *Seven Years in Tibet,* the Himalayan adventure project with a finished script that Guber had taken with him to his Mandalay banner, Pitt threatened to walk off *The Devil's Own*—an idea that died when Canton said he'd sue for breach of contract.

*The Devil's Own* began shooting with director Alan Pakula at the helm. It quickly descended into chaos, plagued by constant rewriting. The picture went over schedule and its budget soared to $86 million. Pitt took revenge by publicly trashing the picture just weeks before it opened. "We had no script," Pitt lamented in a *Newsweek* interview. "Well, we had a great script but it got tossed for various reasons. To have to make something up as you go along—Jesus, what pressure! It was ridiculous. It was the most irresponsible bit of filmmaking—if you can even call it that—that I've ever seen." Pitt went on: "The movie was the complete victim of this drowning studio head [Canton] who said, 'I don't care. We're making it. I don't care what you have. Shoot something.' I tried to [quit] when there was a week before shooting and we had twenty pages of dogshit." The interview caused acute distress in Sony's executive suites, and Pitt was persuaded to offer a retraction of his comments, but it sounded unconvincing.

Meanwhile, Canton was mounting other costly projects at Columbia, including *Men in Black,* a sci-fi comedy starring Will Smith and Tommy Lee Jones; Luc Besson's futuristic *The Fifth Element,* with Bruce Willis; and *Air Force One,* a thriller directed by Wolfgang Petersen *(In the Line of Fire),* also starring Harrison Ford.

TriStar was active, too. Before Schulhof was fired, he had assisted his friend Barbra Streisand by pressuring Canton to approve her pet project: *The Mirror Has Two Faces.* According to one Sony executive, no one at the studio wanted to admit that the film would cost $50 million, so it was underbudgeted

455

at $37 million. "If Barbra can make it for that price, it's a really good deal," said Canton. She couldn't; as some had warned, the film went over schedule and over budget, costing just over $50 million. Phoenix Pictures, Mike Medavoy's new company, came aboard to share the risk, investing $10 million in the picture. The film made just over $40 million domestically and the studio was projected to lose about $15 million.

Canton also happily handed Tom Cruise a $20 million payday for TriStar's *Jerry Maguire,* a romantic comedy written and directed by Cameron Crowe *(Singles* and *Say Anything . . . )* and produced by James L. Brooks. And with Canton's approval, TriStar executives Marc Platt and Stacey Snider wooed Dean Devlin and Roland Emmerich to write, produce, and direct an $80 million remake of *Godzilla.*

Amid constant rumors that Sony was about to dump him, Canton went on a summer firing binge in an apparent attempt to save his own neck. He eliminated Lisa Henson as head of Columbia, Marc Platt as president of TriStar, and Sid Ganis as marketing chief. Henson and Ganis got independent-producer deals, while Platt landed at Universal as president of production, where he would soon be joined by Stacey Snider.

The week of September 9 started on a high note for Canton: That Monday he emerged from a screening of TriStar's upcoming Christmas release, *Jerry Maguire,* thinking that he might get a new lease on his job. The picture, featuring the radiantly grinning Tom Cruise as a sports agent in quest of redemption, had the feel of a major hit. But Canton's good mood was quickly dispelled as a Sony publicist handed him an article from *Fortune* magazine predicting his immediate dismissal. And on Wednesday the *Daily Variety*'s headline screamed that William Morris agent Arnold Rifkin had been offered Canton's job.

Canton wasn't the only one who had an unpleasant Wednesday morning. Rifkin, a forty-nine-year-old former furrier, was an aggressive agent who had spent the past few years rebuilding William Morris's film division (adding such clients as Bruce Willis and Sylvester Stallone, although the latter left in early 1997). Now *Variety*'s "scoop" had put him in an extremely awkward, even career-threatening position. He had told colleagues at William Morris that he would be flying to New York that evening to see Stallone on the set of the upcoming film *Cop-*

*Land.* Now he had to acknowledge that he was really meeting with Sony's Nobuyuki Idei about a job. Not only did this news shake confidence within the agency, but stars are notoriously skittish about being represented by agents who are anything less than one hundred percent devoted to them. Now that it was known that Rifkin was considering a career change, William Morris agents could safely assume that rivals at CAA and ICM were already trying to woo their most prized clients.

At a staff meeting Rifkin went into damage-repair mode, leaving associates with the impression that he had called off the meeting with Idei. But he told them he'd be in late the next day so he could drop his daughter off for her first day of school. Instead, Rifkin boarded a Sony jet for an overnight flight to New York. Early the next morning, he and Levine sat down with Idei in a suite at the St. Regis Hotel, close to Sony headquarters on Madison Avenue. The only other person present was Idei's aide, Tadasu Kawai.

The meeting was brief and unpleasant; Idei was so frosty that Rifkin could only suspect that the whole exercise had been planned to humiliate Levine. He hopped back on a plane and returned to his office by the early afternoon. He pledged loyalty to the agency and signed a new long-term agreement. "I only thought in my life that I had unconditional love from my wife and two children," he told his colleagues. "Now I know there is unconditional love for me at this agency . . . and I could never leave here."

Meanwhile, Canton hadn't the faintest idea what was going on. Levine wasn't returning his calls, nor had he hinted at the reason for his trip to New York. On Thursday evening, just hours after Rifkin's disastrous encounter with Idei, Canton and Levine both attended a celebrity-packed fund-raiser for Bill Clinton in L.A. They did not speak to each other. Finally, the next morning, Levine summoned Canton to breakfast at his home and dismissed him.

As Canton was ushered out, Sony's market share had tumbled to sixth place for the year to date. The studio had grossed $382.3 million on twenty-nine pictures; Disney, by comparison, had released thirty-one pictures and grossed $849.4 million.

In the Sony tradition, Canton did not walk away empty-handed. Before Guber was toppled, he had renewed Canton's deal on generous terms; more than two years remained on that

457

contract. Canton's settlement was estimated at $12 million or more. On the other hand, he failed to secure a lavish production deal as his mentors Guber and Peters had done after their dismissals. Canton began playing a lot of golf, boasting to friends about how much money he had pocketed. But months after his firing, he had failed to make any production deal or land a new job.

THE CANTON DEBACLE drove home the obvious: Levine was doomed. Sony had occasionally expressed confidence in him, but Idei had never seemed to endorse him with any warmth. In June, the *Los Angeles Times Magazine* published an interview in which Sony's president said Levine "thinks too much," described him as "always so nervous," and even mimicked the way he sounded on the phone.

On October 2, just a couple of weeks after Canton was sent packing, Idei fired Levine. Unfortunately for Levine, his boss had had enough of those lucrative exit agreements and declined to hand him either a platinum parachute or a lush independent-production deal.

Levine had not known that as he was trying to install Rifkin as Canton's replacement, Idei had already settled on his successor. Idei had been quietly educating himself about executive candidates through a series of discussions with such Hollywood eminences as Barry Diller, Michael Ovitz, and David Geffen. The top job went to United Artists president John Calley, a sixty-six-year-old entertainment-industry veteran.

A former Warner executive, Calley had rejected a seven-year, $21 million contract there in 1980. At that time he had pondered his situation and realized that he did not need to work. He was tired of being "defined by my phone list," he said later. Retreating to Fishers Island in New York, he was out of the movie business until 1989 when he became Mike Nichols's partner, producing Sony releases *Postcards from the Edge* and *The Remains of the Day*. In 1993 he was hired to revive MGM/UA's dormant United Artists label. There he enjoyed such solid successes as *Goldeneye* and *The Birdcage*, though he also suffered through losers including *Wild Bill* and *Tank Girl*.

When he returned to Hollywood, Calley had said he was planning to stay for only a few years. Given those comments and the extent of Sony's problems, many executives and analysts were surprised that Calley would take the Sony job and quickly concluded that he had been hired to prepare the studio for a sale. After all, Calley had helped fatten up MGM/UA, which had just been auctioned off. Nevertheless, his hiring was well received. Calley was a respected and sophisticated man whose presence as chief would, if nothing else, help burnish Sony's sadly tarnished reputation. Idei repeated the company line that Sony had no intention of selling, but would try to take the studio public in the next few years.

Calley was to report to Idei, tightening the link between Tokyo and Hollywood. Jeff Sagansky, whose own play to gain control of the studio had failed, was dispatched from New York to oversee the television division. And for the first time, a Japanese was added to the management mix at the studio: Idei brought in electronics executive Masayuki Nozoe to coordinate with Sony headquarters. The old laissez-faire days appeared to be over. "This team represents a new vision and new direction for the studio," Idei said.

On the Culver City lot, exultation broke out over news of Calley's appointment. *Wolf* producer Doug Wick noted that hiring the seasoned Calley was "like handing out Valium" to bruised and wary talent. A celebratory mood reigned at lunch in the Rita Hayworth Dining Room. "This guy is walking in on rose petals," said a marketing executive. A basket of flowers, a gift from a staffer, greeted Calley when he reported for his first day of work at the Thalberg Building's Louis B. Mayer Suite. "Help us, Obi-Wan Kenobi," the card read. "You're our only hope."

In his first days, Calley swiftly brought a sense of justice to Sony by announcing that the long-undervalued executive Gareth Wigan would be bumped up to a more senior role. And Calley also hired Sony alumna Amy Pascal, the well-regarded president of the newly defunct Turner Pictures, to return as president of Columbia Pictures.

IN NOVEMBER, Idei held a press conference with the new management team. It was extremely formal by American standards, with reporters seated around tables arranged in a square and permitted to ask one question each. In some ways, the event illustrated the cultural divide between Tokyo and Tinseltown

459

far more clearly than its organizers might have wished. Although the American press had frequently described Idei as fluent in English, reporters strained to make out his words. Idei talked of creating a "value chain," a new phrase that signified his hope that Sony would be able to extract maximum profit from its entertainment operations.

While other studios had been enjoying merchandising bonanzas driven by hit movies—Warner with the *Batman* franchise, Disney with *101 Dalmations,* Universal with *Jurassic Park* —Sony had never gotten to taste such profits. The one picture that might have earned a windfall from toys and games was *Jumanji,* but because of poor coordination among its divisions Sony had not milked that opportunity. The movie had cost $65 million and made $100 million in profit; analysts said the latter figure could have been much larger. But Idei was quick to distance himself from previous management errors: "I don't understand the name of synergy," he said. With those words, the mantra that had guided Sony's entire foray into Hollywood was brushed aside. Though Idei asserted again that he had no plans to sell, many investors believed that it was only a matter of time before Sony concluded that the cultural chasm was just too deep and that it couldn't stay in the entertainment business.

*Hit and Run* was published in Japan in December 1996, prompting Norio Ohga to make his first comments on the book. In the Japanese magazine *Keizaikai,* he expressed regret that Sony had turned down repeated requests for interviews while the book was being researched. A translation (supplied by our Japanese publisher) of Mr. Ohga's remarks follows:

> As long as [the authors] wanted to interview us, we should have complied with their request and provided the correct information. . . . The contents of the book became one-sided. For instance, Jon Peters and Peter Guber have been described as if they are scoundrels. However, if that is the fact, Warner Brothers would never have hired Jon Peters after he left Sony. Actually, Jon Peters might look like a vulgar guy but . . . I think Jon Peters and Peter Guber are both geniuses of the film industry.
> . . . That book also describes Jon and Peter as if they are extraordinary scoundrels who spent extravagantly and caused huge losses to Sony. However, the loss that we an-

nounced in the account settlement of 1994 was the redemption of goodwill and legal fees, which are just temporary reductions. The authors of this book did not [account for] the fact that Sony achieved the number one position in Hollywood for three consecutive years.

The book states that Jon and Peter caused a $3.2 billion loss to Sony with their extravagance. . . . [But,] for example, the elevator in the Sony Pictures building used by Peter Guber was a very old one that had been there since the former MGM. In fact, it suddenly stopped when I was in it. . . . Accordingly, we have never spent extravagantly at all.

When we purchased the company, the studio of Columbia Pictures was quite dilapidated. Therefore, it is a fact that Peter Guber and Jon Peters spent a certain amount of money for the renovation of the site. . . . The book discusses [heavy spending on florists] but it is common sense to decorate an actress's room in the studio with flowers. In fact, it might feel odd for an ordinary person, but as long as the actress is made more enthusiastic by those flowers, it is necessary.

In conclusion, we will never give up or dispose of Sony Pictures. Even though many people say that the management of the software industry is very difficult, unless you can manage it properly I think the company cannot survive in the twenty-first century.

AT YEAR'S END Guber was branching out into new ventures. Having dreamed about buying the Kings and the Lakers when he was chairman of Sony Pictures, he formed Mandalay Sports Enterprises in December and bought interests in two minor-league football teams, the Lake Elsinore Storm and the Las Vegas Stars, as well as a minor-league hockey team, the Las Vegas Thunder. "This is a business decision, an entrepreneurial decision," he told the *Los Angeles Times.* "It's not a vanity purchase."

On the home front, Peter and Lynda were occupied by ongoing improvements to their new house on Lausanne Drive in Bel Air. Visitors reported that the furnishings were extravagant even for the Gubers; a single table had cost more than $100,000. Legions of decorators and landscapers swarmed over the property, which Peter surveyed from a golf cart. "It's a vulgarian pleasure palace," says one acquaintance of the estate.

461

Lynda also had new projects to occupy her. Hotelier Ian Schrager had undertaken a stem-to-stern renovation of the Mondrian in Los Angeles and hired Lynda to "conceptualize" and oversee the hotel's new Yoga and Wellness Studio. This ambitious project did not come off without a hitch: When the hotel reopened on December 8, 1996, the Wellness Studio was the only unfinished facility, and it wasn't expected to be completed for several months to come. Nonetheless, the hotel literature promised great things from Lynda. "The exploration of the physical and spiritual potential of the body and mind is a continuing passion and mission in her life," said a biography released by Schrager's publicists. The bio reported that aside from producing the *Yoga Moves* video in 1982, Lynda had studied "Primordial Sound Meditation and Mind Body Healing" with Deepak Chopra. It also noted that Lynda's nonprofit organization, Education First!, had arranged a weekend workshop for inner-city youth called "Body, Mind and Beyond"—"a day of exploration, inspiration and participation in the discovery of the human body"—that had taken place in January 1994.

AT WARNER BROTHERS, Jon Peters had his own troubles. In a $700,000 lawsuit filed in Los Angeles Superior Court on January 29, 1996, the president of his company, Tracy Barone, was accused of sexual harassment. The suit was brought by Barone's former executive assistant, September Bradford, who claimed that Barone routinely "commented on the male sexual appendages of certain individuals," had asked Bradford if she wanted to join her and her boyfriend in a ménage à trois; and had once asked a male staffer, "Isn't September sexy? Wouldn't you love to fuck her?"

Bradford's lawsuit also named Peters, claiming that his company subjected her to a "hostile work environment." The suit became the subject of a *Los Angeles* magazine article in which some employees were quoted as saying that Bradford was "a playgirl type" who was also "rude." But other unnamed sources corroborated Bradford's depiction of the Peters Entertainment Company as a hotbed of abuse and unrestrained sex talk. "Like father, like protégé," read one of the captions under a photograph of Jon Peters. While Peters at first vowed to fight Bradford's allegations in court, he ultimately quietly paid a settlement to Bradford.

Peters's first picture under his new deal at Warner, a comedy called *My Fellow Americans,* didn't garner many votes. The studio hoped that Jack Lemmon and James Garner would share the same winning screen chemistry that made Lemmon and Walter Matthau so successful in *Grumpy Old Men* and its sequel. But despite heavy television advertising, the movie was lost in the crowded Christmas release schedule and grossed only $21.5 million. Next, Peter pinned his hopes on *Rosewood,* John Singleton's relentless recreation of a racially motivated massacre in a small Florida town in 1923. While the picture was well received by some critics, Peters knew even before *Rosewood* opened that it would be difficult to make any money on this unflinching film, but he was proud of its seriousness of purpose.

Meanwhile, he was still dreaming of another blockbuster franchise that would recall the glory of *Batman.* He planned to remake *Superman,* but his first choice in casting was perhaps even more audacious than the original decision to cast Michael Keaton as Batman. This time, Jon wanted mild-mannered Clark Kent to be portrayed by Nicolas Cage, the off-center antihero of *Leaving Las Vegas.* After all, Peters reasoned, Superman was an alien. Cage's past work had him portraying a vampire, a drunk, an obsessed one-armed baker. Surely he could convince audiences that he came from outer space.

SONY'S HOLIDAY SLATE for 1996 began disappointingly in November with *The Mirror Has Two Faces.* Hopes had been high for this Streisand vehicle, which during previews had twice scored higher than *Sleepless in Seattle.* But critics lambasted Barbra for her narcissism and the film's muddled message. She bathed herself in vanity lighting and underwent a beautifying makeover while ostensibly pushing the theme that looks aren't important.

But Christmas at last brought joy: Canton's instinct about *Jerry Maguire* had been on target. The picture had a smashing $17 million opening on December 13 and became the success story of the season, embraced by audiences and critics alike. Milos Forman's *The People vs. Larry Flynt* got some nice critical reception, too, but fell short at the box office. And after the new year, a backlash against the film's relatively restrained portrayal of pornographer Flynt would hurt it in the Oscar race. But *Jerry Maguire* turned out to be the only film produced by a

463

major studio to be nominated for best picture. (The other nominees—*Shine, The English Patient, Fargo,* and *Secrets and Lies* —all came from independents.) And the plaudits didn't stop there. In all, *Jerry Maguire* received five nominations in plum categories, including Cruise's best-actor nomination and Cuba Gooding, Jr.'s, for best supporting actor. (Only Gooding, Jr., won.)

For the moment, Sony had profit and prestige to savor. Most of the executives who had worked on *Jerry Maguire* were gone, but Jim Brooks and writer-director Cameron Crowe were generous enough to invite the exiles to a special screening on the lot. Mark Canton may have been the proudest person in the room that night.

As *Jerry Maguire* hurtled toward the $100 million mark and the town buzzed about Cruise's Oscar chances, the irony was not lost on anyone: Canton finally had that hit, that elusive combination of commercial and artistic success, which he had craved so desperately. But it had come too late to help him. "It goes to show," mused one executive at a company that had produced one of Sony's smaller losers, "God does have a sense of humor."

The studio would finish 1996 in fifth place among the majors, with 10.4 percent market share, but *Jerry Maguire* continued to swell the studio's coffers as the new year began. As the awards season rolled around, Canton predictably took credit for *Jerry Maguire* and *Larry Flynt* in calls to friends from his car phone on his way to the golf course. But at the Golden Globes in February, it was Barry Josephson who received the coveted on-camera hug that Canton felt he deserved from Milos Forman, when the director of *Larry Flynt* picked up the award for best director of a dramatic feature. And when Tom Cruise won for best actor in a comedy for *Jerry Maguire,* Canton was crestfallen to hear the star thank newcomer John Calley from the stage.

Sony Pictures still had to contend with a few more unpleasant reminders of the Canton era. One trouble spot was *Starship Troopers,* a sci-fi adventure featuring giant bugs and originally budgeted at $100 million. Against director Paul Verhoeven's wishes, Levine had insisted on using Sony's own special-effects facility, Sony ImageWorks, on the film. While Verhoeven completed filming on budget, Sony's fledgling effects house was

464

overwhelmed by the job. Finally, the work had to be farmed out to other facilities, pushing up the already high cost of the film. Even after Levine had departed, his decision "was coming back to bite 'em in the rear end," said one former Sony Pictures executive.

Still, Sony looked ready to hold its own even in a 1997 summer crowded with big-budget special-effects movies. Verhoeven was piqued when *Starship Troopers* was moved to an end-of-the-year release date, but the film's July 2 date was given to the Will Smith–Tommy Lee Jones comedy *Men in Black* at the request of that film's producer, Steven Spielberg. At early previews, *Men in Black* looked like a winner.

Calley faced monumental challenges. Aside from the pictures for summer 1997, Sony had almost nothing in production. The cupboard was at least as bare as it had been when Guber and Peters arrived and complained bitterly that their predecessors had left them with nothing. There was plenty of work to do—and, of course, no assurance of success. But for the first time in years, Sony executives could feel that they hadn't been left home alone.

# Source Notes

Sony did not cooperate in the reporting of this book. Despite repeated requests over four years, the company did not permit a single interview with any of its executives. Peter Guber also declined to cooperate despite numerous requests for interviews. Although Jon Peters spoke with us on the record, he in no way authorized this publication.

Nevertheless, we conducted more than two hundred interviews, including many with key individuals who were present while the various events described in the book occurred. Whenever possible, we asked our sources to speak on the record. In addition, dozens of sources, including many top executives at Sony Pictures Entertainment, talked to us on an anonymous basis. These conversations have enabled us to feel confident that we have reported events reliably.

Several books were invaluable to us, notably David McClintick's *Indecent Exposure* and Fredric Dannen's *Hit Men*. *Den of Thieves* by James Stewart, Akio Morita's *Made in Japan*, Connie Bruck's *Master of the Game*, Randall Riese's *Her Name Is Barbra*, and Edwin Reischauer's *The Japanese Today* were also especially useful. We drew heavily on interviews from contemporary newspaper and magazine accounts, as indicated either in the text or below. The following list includes our principal sources on a chapter-by-chapter basis:

CHAPTER ONE: Author's interviews (AI) with Silvio Pensanti, Marie Zampitella Augustine, Gene Shacove; also includes material from interviews published in *Women's Wear Daily*, 7/6/78, and *Newsday*, 11/7/76.

CHAPTER TWO: AI with Lesley Ann Warren, Bobbi Elliott, Lou Antonio, Paul Cantor, Allen Edwards, Sandy Gallin.

CHAPTER THREE: AI with Lesley Ann Warren, Geraldo Rivera, Peter Yates, Andrew Smith, Gary Le Mel, Lee Solters, Polly Platt; *Streisand: Her Life* by James Spada; *Los Angeles*, 5/76; *Los Angeles Herald Examiner*, 5/18/76.

CHAPTER FOUR: AI with Frank Pierson, Polly Platt, Laura Ziskin, Phil Ramone, Jane Jenkins, Paul Williams, Peter Zinner, Gary Le Mel; "My Battles with Barbra and Jon" by Frank Pierson, *New West*, 11/22/76; Joyce Haber columns, *Los Angeles Times*, 9/23/74, 4/16/75; "A Star Is Shorn" by Marie Brenner, *New Times*, 1/24/75; "Gone Hollywood" by John Gregory Dunne, *Esquire*, 9/76.

CHAPTER FIVE: AI with Andrew Smith, Geraldo Rivera, Roz Heller, Howard Rosenman, Bonnie Bruckheimer, Michael Meltzer, Harold Ramis, Rusty Lemorande; *Variety*, 1/16/77, 11/16/77, 8/1/78; *New York Times*, 1/29/78; *People*, 6/30/75; *Women's Wear Daily*, 7/6/78; *Los Angeles Times*, 1/22/78, 4/13/78, 1/5/79.

CHAPTER SIX: AI with Jerry Isenberg, Deborah Gilman, Barry Wish, Jim Lampert.

CHAPTER SEVEN: AI with Steve Tisch, Jerry Tokofsky, Robert Lovenheim, Peter Bart, Robert Littman, John Veitch, Paul Schrader; *Hollywood Reporter*, 8/29/73; *Columbia Pictures: Portrait of a Studio*, edited by Bernard F. Dick; *Moguls* by Michael Pye.

CHAPTER EIGHT: AI with Peter Yates, Sue Barton, Jim Watters; *Signature*, 3/79; *Women's Wear Daily*, 8/3/76; *Los Angeles Times*, 9/12/76; *New York Times*, 9/19/76; *Fast Fade* by Andrew Yule; *Moguls* by Michael Pye; *Inside "The Deep"* by Peter Guber.

CHAPTER NINE: AI with Rob Cohen, Jeff Wald, Oliver Stone, Alan Parker, David Puttnam, Lynda Obst, Bob Esty, Wolfgang Hix, Eckart Haas; *Out of Focus* by Charles Kipps; *Moguls* by Michael Pye; *Variety*, 2/2/77, 10/23/78; *Hollywood Reporter*, 3/17/78; *Los Angeles Times*, 5/1/78; *Los Angeles Herald Examiner*, 7/11/79, 2/13/80; *Village Voice*, 1/28/89; *Hollywood Reporter*, 3/10/80, 3/18/80; *BoxOffice*, 3/24/80; "The Uncertain Future of Casablanca FilmWorks," *New West*, 3/24/80; *Wall Street Journal*, 7/28/81.

CHAPTER TEN: AI with Gordon Stulberg, Eckart Haas, Wolfgang Hix, Hillary Ripps, Rob Cohen; *New West*, 3/24/80; *Los Angeles Herald Examiner*, 5/22/80, 6/30/83; *Hollywood Reporter*, 2/2/81, 8/4/81; *Los Angeles Times*, 7/26/81, 7/10/83; *Variety*, 1/28/82, 2/10/82, 3/23/82.

CHAPTER ELEVEN: AI with Gene O'Hagan, Stan Brooks, Roz Heller, Roger Birnbaum, Stan Rogow, John Bill, Tom Tannenbaum, Steven Spielberg; *Variety*, 5/17/78, 3/3/82, 7/6/82, 10/16/84, 10/30/84; *Nautical Quarterly*, Spring '85; *New York*, 1/6/85.

CHAPTER TWELVE: AI with Arne Glimcher, Roger Birnbaum, Rob Cohen, Don Devlin, Cher, George Miller, Michelle Pfeiffer, Polly Platt.

CHAPTER THIRTEEN: AI with Terren Peizer, Bud Granoff, Jeff Wald, Stephen Weinress, Chris Bearde, Ken Kragen, Terry Christensen; *Los Angeles Times*, 9/14/87; *Forbes*, 11/28/88; *Los Angeles Business Journal*, 6/11/90; *Wall Street Journal*, 10/1/91.

CHAPTER FOURTEEN: AI with Roger Birnbaum, Robert Lawrence, Steven Spielberg, Mark Johnson, Tim Burton, Anton Furst, Warren Skaaren, Chris Kenny, Harry Colomby; *Los Angeles Times*, 6/23/89; *20/20*, 7/89; *New York Times Magazine*, 4/9/89.

CHAPTER FIFTEEN: AI with Walter Yetnikoff; *Los Angeles Times*, 5/31/92; *Esquire*, 11/86; *New York Times Magazine*, 9/18/88, 2/18/90; *Rolling Stone*, 12/15–29/88.

CHAPTER SIXTEEN: *Fortune*, 4/15/85.

CHAPTER SEVENTEEN: AI with Walter Yetnikoff, Victor Kaufman, Fay Vincent, Frank Price; *New York Times*, 11/27/89; *Los Angeles Times*, 10/30/88; *Esquire*, 6/91; *Wall Street Journal*, 10/8/87.

CHAPTER EIGHTEEN: AI with Walter Yetnikoff, Terry Christensen; *Los Angeles Times*, 5/30/89, 10/16/89; *Vanity Fair*, 9/91, 5/95; *Business Week*, 3/25/91.

CHAPTER NINETEEN: AI with Terry Christensen, Nick Nicholas.

CHAPTER TWENTY: AI with Russ Kavanaugh, Don Simpson, Oliver Stone, Terry Christensen, Eric Pleskow, Barbara Boyle, Frank Price, Gene O'Hagan, Walter Yetnikoff, Michael Douglas; *Variety*, 11/17/89; *New York Times*, 2/1/90; *New York Post*, 4/26/90; *Chicago Tribune*, 5/17/90; *Los Angeles Times*, 3/10/91; *Entertainment Weekly*, 2/28/92.

CHAPTER TWENTY-ONE: AI with Russ Kavanaugh, Tom Hershey, Frank Price, Steve Roth, David Zucker; *Wall Street Journal*, 8/20/90; *New York Times*, 8/11/91.

CHAPTER TWENTY-TWO: AI with Russ Kavanaugh; *Los Angeles Times*, 10/30/88, 3/10/91, 3/24/91, 8/25/91, 9/6/91; *Business Week*, 3/25/91; *Vanity Fair*, 5/95; *Variety*, 9/6/91; *New York Times*, 8/11/91, 9/23/91, 10/3/91, 2/23/92, 7/9/92; *Hollywood Reporter*, 7/15/91; *Wall Street Journal*, 9/30/91.

CHAPTER TWENTY-THREE: AI with Gary Lieberthal; *Wall Street Journal*, 9/30/91; *Los Angeles Times*, 8/25/91.

CHAPTER TWENTY-FOUR: AI with Frank Price; *Variety*, 9/6/91, 9/9/91; *New York Times*, 9/23/91, 10/3/91; *Wall Street Journal*, 5/23/91, 7/16/91, 8/8/91, 9/27/91; *Los Angeles Times*, 7/6/91, 9/6/91; *Hollywood Reporter*, 7/15/91; *Business Week*, 10/9/91.

CHAPTER TWENTY-FIVE: AI with Kathleen Kennedy, Mike Medavoy, Brian Grazer; *Variety*, 10/4/91; *Vanity Fair*, 12/91; *Los Angeles Times*, 11/30/91; *New York Times*, 12/7/91; *Wall Street Journal*, 12/30/90, 11/15/91; *Premiere*, 12/91.

CHAPTER TWENTY-SIX: AI with Jimmy Spitz, Rob Fried; *New York Times,* 2/23/92, 7/9/92; *Wall Street Journal,* 1/7/92; *Los Angeles Times,* 3/17/92, 4/17/92, 5/31/92, 7/3/92, 12/6/92, 12/27/92; *Variety,* 8/3/92; *Hollywood Reporter,* 1/4/93.

CHAPTER TWENTY-SEVEN: AI with Mike Medavoy; *Los Angeles Times,* 3/15/93, 5/7/93, 5/21/93; *Variety,* 1/6/94.

CHAPTER TWENTY-EIGHT: AI with Mark Canton, Barry Josephson, John McTiernan, Arnold Schwarzenegger, Zak Penn, Adam Leff, Sid Ganis, Shane Black, Joel Silver, John Lindsay.

CHAPTER TWENTY-NINE: *Los Angeles Times,* 8/2/93, 8/3/93, 8/5/93, 8/6/93, 8/9/93, 8/10/93, 8/28/93, 12/31/93; *Variety,* 8/16/93, 8/23/93; New York *Daily News,* 8/6/93; *Details,* 10/93; *US,* 10/93; *Esquire,* 11/93; *Vanity Fair,* 2/94.

CHAPTER THIRTY: AI with James L. Brooks, Polly Platt; *Wall Street Journal,* 12/3/93; *Premiere,* 11/93; *Entertainment Weekly,* 12/17/93; *Los Angeles Times,* 10/25/93, 11/19/93; *Wall Street Journal,* 12/3/93.

CHAPTER THIRTY-ONE: *Los Angeles Times,* 12/9/93, 1/8/94, 1/12/94, 6/1/94; *New Yorker,* 2/28/94; *New York Times,* 1/17/94; *Variety,* 2/15/94; *Hollywood Reporter,* 3/4–6/94; *Business Week,* 6/20/94; *Los Angeles,* 2/94.

CHAPTER THIRTY-TWO: AI with John Frook, Peter Bart; *Variety,* 2/15/94, 5/2–8/94, 8/12/94, 9/30/94; *New York Times,* 8/30/94, 10/24/94; *Los Angeles Times,* 6/1/94, 7/8/94, 7/22/94, 9/6/94, 9/30/94; *Vanity Fair,* 5/95; *Hollywood Reporter,* 9/30/94; *Business Week,* 6/20/94.

EPILOGUE: *Vanity Fair,* 5/95; *Variety,* 11/18/94; *Wall Street Journal,* 11/18/94, 12/6/95; *Los Angeles Times,* 11/15/94; *New York Times,* 12/6/95, 12/7/95.

# Acknowledgments

This book was based on hundreds of hours of interviews conducted with people who have chosen not to be identified. They know who they are and we are deeply grateful for their time and effort. We are also especially indebted to those who were willing to speak to us on the record.

WE WOULD LIKE TO THANK the following people for their invaluable contributions to this book: At Simon & Schuster our editor, Alice Mayhew, for her sharp-eyed comments and guidance. Her associate Elizabeth Stein, who was always patient and efficient when we were neither. Susan Lyne, the first person who recognized a great story and gave us the chance to write it. George Hodgman, who believed in the story and saw its potential as a book. Our agent, Kris Dahl, for her zealous representation and hand-holding during trying times. Our copy supervisor, Steve Messina, for deciphering our cryptic notes and catching our mistakes. Eric Rayman and Felice Javit for their legal expertise.

Many colleagues were generous with both information and encouragement, especially Chris Connelly, Corie Brown, Rachel Abramowitz, Kristin O'Neill, Peter Biskind, John Richardson, Max Potter, Mickey Kaus, and Rich Turner.

In addition, Nancy Griffin wishes to thank everyone at *Premiere* magazine for their unflagging support; her family, especially her parents, George and Ruth Griffin; and inestimable friends whose support came in many forms: Francoise Kirkland, Douglas Kirkland, Jeanne MacDowall, Laura Davis, Marilyn Bethany, Edward Tivnan, Elizabeth Beautyman, Jim Steiner, Steven Fischer, Jim Stein, Margot Dougherty, Susan Gates, Scott

471

ACKNOWLEDGMENTS

Kaufer, Scott Mayers, Joy Horowitz, Jean Bernard, and all the J-Girls.

Kim Masters wishes to thank her beloved and infinitely patient husband, Gary Simson; her family, especially Peter and Alice Masters and Bert and Ofira Simson; and Sarah Connick, the world's most generous friend. Other friends whose help was invaluable include Bruce Bibby, Karen Spar, Vicky Stamas, Mary Hadar, and the girls (you know who you are). Thanks also to the *Washington Post* for the time and support, and to Graydon Carter.

# Index

INDEX

496